HERMINE HUG-HELLMUTH

HERMINE HUG-HELLMUTH

Her Life and Work

George MacLean and Ulrich Rappen

ROUTLEDGE   NEW YORK AND LONDON

Published in 1991 by

Routledge
An imprint of Routledge, Chapman and Hall, Inc.
29 West 35 Street
New York, NY 10001

Published in Great Britain by

Routledge
11 New Fetter Lane
London EC4P 4EE

The following publishers and author have generously given permission to use translated material from their copyrighted works. From the International Universities Press
for the translation of the paper "On the technique of child analysis" © 1921. From
the Psychoanalytic Quarterly and Anton Kris for the translation of "The child's concept
of death" © 1965. From the Psychiatric Journal of the University of Ottawa for George
MacLean's translation of "The analysis of a dream of a 5½-year-old boy" © 1986.

Library of Congress Cataloging in Publication Data

Maclean, George, 1939–
    Hermine Hug-Hellmuth, her life and work / by George MacLean and
Ulrich Rappen.
      p. cm.
    Includes bibliographical references and index.
    ISBN 0-415-90060-3
    1. Hug-Hellmuth, Hermine. 2. Psychoanalysts—Germany—Biography.
3. Child analysis. I. Rappen, Ulrich. II. Title.
RC339.52.H94M33 1990
150.19′52′092—dc20   90-8646

British Library cataloguing in publication also available

FOR NORMA, CALVIN AND RYAN

and

FOR DOROTHE, JOHANNES, LUKAS AND SEBASTIAN

Contents

Selected Works Dealing with Women and the Family

Preface

This book began about ten years ago when one of the authors, George MacLean, came across brief references to Hug-Hellmuth while reading in child psychiatry and psychoanalysis. Two brief papers resulted from his initial curiosity.[1] However, it soon became apparent that the life and work of Hug-Hellmuth had to be further clarified. Because an expert knowledge of German psychoanalytic terminology was necessary, Ulrich Rappen joined in the project.[2] The work of searching for primary archival material, its translation and that of the complete works of Hug-Hellmuth could now begin.

The authors are thankful for the help and support of Drs. Clifford Scott, Hans Aufreiter, Irwin Disher, E. James Anthony, Hector Warnes, J. B. Boulanger, Paul Roazen, and Kurt R. Eissler. In the early stages of research, Dr. Hans Aufreiter's and Dr. Hector Warnes's knowledge of German was invaluable.

The staffs of the archives of the Austrian military and of the University of Vienna were very helpful. Mr. David Ross, librarian of the Abraham A. Brill Library, the New York Psychoanalytic Institute, and his staff were tireless in their long-distance support. The staff of the New York Academy of Medicine filled in just when we were about to give up on some references. We are thankful to them for their timely help.

Claudia Peherstorfer did the actual research in the various archives. To us, she became known as "the Vienna Connection." Without her work, we could not have written this book. We owe a special thanks to her.

The form of this book arose from our conviction that more people needed to know about Hug-Hellmuth as a person and as a psychoanalyst. Hence both a biography and a selection of her work were necessary. In reviewing Hug-Hellmuth's life, we drew on both primary and secondary sources, but tried to avoid biographical speculation based on her psychoanalytic papers.

We decided not to include in this book some of Hug-Hellmuth's longer published works that were already available in English. One long work, however, is difficult to find and has not previously been translated: *The Hug-Hellmuth Lectures, 1924*, which she entitled *New Ways to the Understanding of*

Youth. As her last publication, it is so important that we have included a condensed version here.

Finally, we wish to thank our families, who have wondered whether Hug-Hellmuth was worth the time taken away from so many evenings and weekends. We hope that this book demonstrates to them that our time was well spent.

Prologue

Who was Hermine Hug-Hellmuth? What did she do? When we developed out initial curiosity and began our project, no one knew much about her. People were confused even about her name. Various writers referred to her as Hug, Hug-Hellmuth, Hug von Hellmuth and Hug von Hugenstein.

From our initial inquiry, it was clear that Hug-Hellmuth was a psychoanalytic pioneer. Brief references to her and her work existed throughout the old and new psychoanalytic literature.[1] When we sought more information, we felt dissatisfied. We wished to have some clear sense about her and her actual importance in the history of psychoanalysis. But little information existed about her as a person, and there was no clear description of her work. An air of mystery surrounded her: she even wrote a will a few days before her death expressing her wish that no account of her life or her work should appear.

Hug-Hellmuth was one of the first women to earn a doctorate in physics from the University of Vienna. She was the world's first practicing child psychoanalyst. She was also the first person to make use of systematic child observation from a psychoanalytic point of view. In addition, Hug-Hellmuth was among the very first of the lay adherents to practice psychoanalysis. She was the first gentile member of the Vienna Psychoanalytic Society and only the third female member.

Although Hug-Hellmuth was a pioneer in psychoanalysis, people seemingly knew little about her. Since her death on September 8, 1924, the few people who knew her well have died. For a brief period early in our research there was a chance that a few of these people who were still alive could be helpful in this project. However, they could not, or would not, help.[2]

Hug-Hellmuth wrote little about herself—only a few autobiographical hints and three pages of letters.[3] Nor did others write much about her, except in a rather dismissive manner. At first Hug-Hellmuth's injunction that nothing should ever be written about her or her work puzzled us. In 1980, Anna Freud responded to a letter of ours, suggesting that we abide by this injunction made in 1924.[4] Since Anna Freud did not give us any further reason, we wondered about the relationship between Hug-Hellmuth's work and her own. How did

Hug-Hellmuth's contributions, if any, relate to the work of Melanie Klein? We had many questions.

In this book, we have tried to present everything factual that we have been able to find about Hug-Hellmuth. We have examined every secondary source of information about her that we could locate. We have translated her published work and compared it with that of other important child psychoanalytic pioneers, specifically, Anna Freud and Melanie Klein. We wanted to find out whether or not she had any influence on either of them.

A Biography

1 Personal Development
1871–1911

Until recently information about Hermine Hug-Hellmuth was locked away in various archives; Hermine Hug von Hugenstein, alias Hermine Hug-Hellmuth, was descended from an aristocratic family in the Hapsburg Empire. Her father, Knight Hugo Hug von Hugenstein, was in the military, as was her grandfather.

Her father was born a Roman Catholic in Prague in what was then Bohemia on November 6, 1830. We know that he attended a polytechnical school for three years and that he joined the Austro-Hungarian military in 1848 at eighteen years of age,[1] entering an infantry regiment as a junior officer. The year of his enrollment saw many revolutions in Europe. When he joined the army, they noted that he spoke German, Italian, French and Bohemian (a linguistic ability that reflected the extent of the Hapsburg Empire). Given the regional wars within the empire, he was soon in battle.

Knight Hugo's military records were interesting in themselves, as well as for the rare reliable information they provided about Hermine Hug-Hellmuth's origins and early life. Knight Hugo's military career was successful, but not dramatically so. However, his personal life was tragic. This sad tale, which intimately involved Hermine Hug-Hellmuth, was one of illegitimacy, sickness, economic disaster, and death.

Knight Hugo's first extra-military adventure took place in 1861. Thirty-one years old at the time, ten years before Hermine's birth, he had contracted to marry the daughter of an artillery officer also of the aristocracy, Ernestine von Joanelli. He canceled his engagement and a military court ordered the dowry returned.[2] (A dowry at that time served the function of life insurance for the wives and families of military officers, since all were potential widows or fatherless children.) In the bloody battle of Koeniggraetz on July 3, 1866,[3] he injured his right foot. The Prussians routed the Austrian forces, disorganizing them and inflicting heavy losses. It was a decisive battle in world history.[4]

In the latter part of May, an upper military court had denied an application by Knight Hugo to legitimate a daughter, Antonia Farmer. Antonia had been born on January 17, 1864; her mother had the same name.[5] Antonia later

3

became a central person in Hermine Hug-Hellmuth's life. She was to reappear in 1904, when she presented herself as Hermine's two-year's-older sister, not her seven-year's-older illegitimate half-sister. She called herself Antoine Hug.[6]

Antonia's mother was the daughter of a poor accountant. Because of his poverty, he could not provide the obligatory dowry. The court predicted that Knight Hugo would not marry the mother in any case, since he was soon to come into an inheritance of his own. They refused to recognize Antonia as legitimate and Knight Hugo did not marry Antonia's mother. Three years later, on June 16, 1869, Knight Hugo married Ludovika Achelpohl. Born in Vienna on February 22, 1840, she was twenty-nine years of age. Her parents, Ludwig Achelpohl and Therese Danner, were able to provide Ludovika with a dowry of eight thousand gulden. Knight Hugo brought his illegitimate daughter into that marriage, changing her birth date to make her legitimate. She became in this change the older child awaiting her younger sister, Hermine.[7]

The tragedies began quickly. One year after the marriage a daughter was born, on August 1, 1870, only to die in less than two weeks. A year later, on August 31, 1871, the subject of this biography was born. Her name at birth was Hermine Wilhelmine Ludovika Hug von Hugenstein. The following years were problematic and tragic; a period of economic decline for the family. The year after her birth Knight Hugo sold the family estate that he could have only recently inherited after his mother's death. Hermine's paternal grandmother, therefore, died one year after her birth. The estate consisted of a house in Vienna, evaluated at about ten thousand gulden. Within two years Knight Hugo had lost all of this money in the stock market crash of 1873. Only his wife's dowry remained in trust. Beyond that the family had to depend on Knight Hugo's small pension. He arranged to be hired back by the military, but this time as a civilian. Reemployed by the military in 1873, he reappeared with two legitimate daughters: Antoine—the older by two years—and little Hermine. This was enough for Antoine's acceptance in the social order of the military and the world at that time. It created what became accepted as the truth, but it was a myth of legitimacy, and her age changed to conform with the myth.

Despite the achievement of social and family propriety, and some economic stability, further personal tragedies followed. The year after Knight Hugo had lost the family fortune and the year the army took him back, his wife gave birth to another girl. Emilie was born on May 21, 1874, and lived for only one month.[8] Hermine would have been almost three years old. Can we understand what she was thinking and feeling? We can try, for later we will see how themes of illegitimacy and death appear in her professional writing.

The trauma continued. One year later, her mother developed a severe chronic pulmonary disease, probably tuberculosis. Hermine was four years old when her mother became chronically ill. Between one year before her birth and her fourth birthday, her mother had experienced three pregnancies, the responsibility of caring for her stepdaughter, two infant deaths, the economic decline of her family, the onset of a chronic illness, and the birth of and need to care for her own only living child, Hermine. It would be almost impossible to provide mothering under such conditions, and Hug-Hellmuth must have suffered from its lack in her infancy and childhood. This maternal deprivation would have effects on her development and it would mold her adult character. Her personality functioning would be distorted, leading especially to a tendency toward depression. Her interpersonal relationships would be most affected.

Early in 1883, Knight Hugo applied to the military trustees for a release of six hundred gulden from the dowry. The medication and medical consultations for his wife were expensive. They approved the request. However, on May 18, 1883, Ludovika died. Hermine was twelve years old.[9] An aunt, Ludovika's sister, had joined the household when Ludovika became ill. Later, she lived with Hug-Hellmuth in Vienna between 1915 and 1920.

In April 1876 Knight Hugo wrote a will in which he stated that he wanted his two daughters to have good educations and provided money "to support them in their intended training as teachers." He also declared his wish to be buried at his mother's side. Some additional financial support did come into the family for Antonia, who received an educational grant of 150 gulden a year from a military fund. The military complimented Knight Hugo in his evaluations for his successful work in starting this fund for war orphans and children of military officers. Therefore, his interest in his illegitimate daughter's education was broadened by him into a recognizable social achievement.[10]

It is probable that Hermine lived with her father from the time of her mother's death until her late teenage years. Antoine would have been nineteen when her stepmother died. We lack any evidence as to where she lived at that time. We do know that she continued her education for a long time, probably attending school elsewhere.

Knight Hugo remained working for the war ministry as a civilian. Even considering all the family problems, he seems to have done well. In 1880, a military evaluation recorded him as being very industrious and having a strong sense of duty. They described continuous successes in his work and complimented his attempts to continue his education. He valued education highly and was described as gifted. He remained employed by the military until 1892, when he retired at the age of sixty-two. Hermine would have been twenty-one years old at that time.

The next known fact is that Hermine entered the University of Vienna as a special student in the winter term of 1897. She was among the first women allowed to do so, as the university had opened its enrollment to women for the first time that year.[11] She was then twenty-six years old.

Where had she spent the previous five years? Probably at another school, obtaining her qualifications as both a primary and a secondary schoolteacher. These qualifications are often referred to later. Teaching qualifications at that time were not university diplomas or degrees.

Immediately after the death of her father in 1898,[12] Hermine disappeared again. We have no knowledge of her whereabouts from 1898 to 1900 and can only guess where she was or what she was doing. Most probably she was teaching at a school or attending a school away from Vienna. In 1900 she reappeared in Vienna once again, as a special student at the university.[13] However, after completing that term, she again left Vienna, this time for a four-year period. During this time, she did something unusual, going to Prague to complete a formal academic high school degree, probably after private preparation. As a schoolteacher with both her elementary and secondary school teaching qualifications, she went back as a student to an academic high school. At that time in Europe there would have been only one reason for a person to do such a thing—to gain admission to university as a regular student. She would get an academic degree, something more than her qualifications as a teacher. She enrolled in the University of Vienna in 1904 as a regular student.

It is interesting that Antoine was leaving the University of Vienna as Hermine entered. Antoine graduated with her doctorate in philosophy in 1904. She wrote a dissertation entitled "Contributions to the History of the Texts of Novalis' Fragments," which was published in 1906.

In 1904 Hermine was living in Vienna with Antoine and registered as a regular student for the winter term at the university. She took a variety of subjects over the next five years but she concentrated on the physical sciences. On May 5, 1909, she passed her oral examination for her degree, a doctorate in physics. The university accepted her dissertation entitled "Some Physical and Chemical Properties of Radioactive Deposits at the Anode and Cathode."

In 1904 Antoine Hug's life becomes better known as it grew closely intertwined with Hug-Hellmuth's.[14] (Perhaps in some way it always had been so, but we know nothing of it.) Hug-Hellmuth's sister used the name Antoine Hug. Hermine Hug von Hugenstein had become variously known as Hermine von Hug-Hellmuth, Hermine Hug-Hellmuth or Hermine Hug.

In 1904, when she was forty-one, Antoine became involved in a close relationship with a man, an affair which was to have great significance. In that year, Antoine and a couple whom she had befriended tried to set up a private school in Muerzzuschlag. The man, Rudolf Rossi von Lichtenfels, the former headmaster at the school where she had taught, worked directly with Antoine. His wife worked as an administrator and in the kitchen of the school. The school failed, as did Antoine's affair with this man. However, it was neither in the failure of this business adventure nor in the failure of their brief relationship that this man gained his importance.

In investigating these failures it was discovered that Antoine did receive a legacy or inheritance of some sort. She invested everything she had in this school plus a loan, and whatever Hug-Hellmuth had left of her inheritance.[15] Where would a woman whose maternal origins were in poverty get an inheritance? Where did she find the financial support to get a doctorate? This probably confirms that Knight Hugo assumed financial responsibility for both of his daughters.

Antoine became pregnant by Rudolf Rossi von Lichtenfels. Illegitimately born, Antoine gave birth to an illegitimate son, Rudolf Otto Hug, in 1906. The birth was recorded as being out of wedlock, and the name of the father did not appear. Antoine moved often from one apartment to another in Vienna in the first year of Rolf's life. When he was two years of age, his father left for good—according to one informant, after having an affair with the family's nanny. Antoine's relationship with Rolf's father had lasted three years and the boy did have at least some contact with his father before he left.[16]

In 1907, Hug-Hellmuth was two years away from graduation from university. In that year an important event occurred: Isidor Sadger, one of the pioneers of the psychoanalytic movement, became Hug-Hellmuth's family doctor.[17] Born on October 29, 1869, Sadger was one of Freud's earliest Viennese colleagues, yet little has been written about him. He is referred to here and there, usually in a negative way. Despite his fervent devotion to Freud, or because of it, even Freud seemed to find him hard to take, once referring to a paper of Sadger's as "repellent." Ernest Jones did not like Sadger, calling him "mute," "morose," "pathetic," "uncouth."[18] Jones had become very upset in the early 1930s about a book Sadger had written about Freud, and as a result recommended Sadger should be put into a concentration camp. Sadger never published the book. He did publish a lot, but most of his work is still untranslated.[19]

It would appear that Sadger was a difficult, morose, depressed, but hardworking psychoanalyst. From the bits and pieces we can put together, he is one of the only people who had a relationship of some duration and depth with Hug-Hellmuth. He was, in fact, the only man that we could discover in Hug-Hellmuth's life. Their relationship began in 1907 and ended in 1924. Although it lasted seventeen years, we do not know the nature of this relationship. They were at least friends and colleagues, and sometime after 1907 Sadger became Hug-Hellmuth's psychoanalyst. Later he involved himself in her life in other ways. There is no evidence that they were ever lovers. However, at one point someone referred to Hug-Hellmuth to as the "widow of a physician."[20] Neither Hug-Hellmuth nor Sadger married, appearing to be people whose lives were without sexual relationships. Sadger gradually faded away and then disappeared during the Nazi occupation of Austria. He probably had the sad fate of being the only Viennese psychoanalyst to be killed by the Nazis.[21]

Between 1907 and 1911, Hug-Hellmuth discovered psychoanalysis. In addition to undertaking her personal psychoanalysis with Isidor Sadger, she read psychoanalytic papers and books. The beginnings of her own psychoanalytic thought and observations must have occurred at this time. She continued to work as a schoolteacher until 1912, then concentrated wholly on psychoanalysis. In the school setting she had ample material for the observation of children.

By 1911 Freud knew Hug-Hellmuth well. In a letter to Carl Jung in 1911, he recommended a paper written by her for publication.[22] In 1912 her first six psychoanalytic publications appeared in the journals of the day. Judging from their content, most of these papers must have required years of prior observation and preparation.

We do not know when Hug-Hellmuth passed from observing children from a psychoanalytic point of view to actually psychoanalyzing them. From her published work, we can see that all of the first group of papers published in 1912 were concerned with child observation only. Her first presentation on child psychoanalytic technique was in 1920.[23] Therefore, it must have been some time between 1912 and 1920 that she began to psychoanalyze children. After 1920, Hug-Hellmuth referred to many cases of children she had analyzed.[24]

After Rolf's birth in 1906, the evidence shows that Hug-Hellmuth's relationship with Antoine underwent a change. They appear to have become more distant. Antoine and her baby moved about Vienna but did not stay with Hug-Hellmuth.[25] Hug-Hellmuth observed Rolf from her newly gained psychoanalytic viewpoint;[26] he was around and they obviously visited. There is no real evidence that she tried to analyze Rolf, although it was later suggested as fact by Rolf himself. Many psychoanalytic observations of Rolf appeared in Hug-Hellmuth's papers; and this probably led to the opinion over the years that an actual analysis took place. This would not have been unusual. In those early experimental days, there were many examples of parents analyzing their children. The notable examples are Sigmund Freud with Anna Freud and Melanie Klein with her children.[27]

2 Psychoanalytic Beginnings
1912–1913

For pragmatic reasons Hug-Hellmuth's psychoanalytic career will be dated from the time of the appearance of her work in the psychoanalytic journals of the day, although her introduction to psychoanalysis must have happened earlier.

The importance of Hug-Hellmuth's work became apparent in her first papers, published in 1912. At that time the psychoanalytic movement was experiencing the schismatic and potentially fragmenting dissension of Alfred Alder and Carl Jung.[1] Hug-Hellmuth gave to Freud and his group important material from her observations and her work with children. This work and the published manuscripts helped provide supporting evidence for the existence of infantile sexuality. Sigmund Freud referred to Hug-Hellmuth's work in his letters and writings.[2]

There is a constant element of pathos in her writings, evident in her use of language. One is painfully aware that the object of many of her observations is Rolf; the illegitimate son of her illegitimate half-sister. The writings of 1912 uniquely concentrate on children and they focus on several themes: infantile sexuality, the unconscious, and death. All make use of the psychoanalytic observation of children, often Rolf.

The first of the papers is "The Analysis of a Dream of a 5½-Year-Old Boy".[3] This paper is a detailed study of a short dream told to Hug-Hellmuth one morning by Rolf. His report of the dream is as follows: "I am so afraid. A big bear wants to eat me. There was also a big picket fence there and lots of pointed arrows on top. The bear wanted to hug me with his front paws. In the middle of the ceiling there was a gigantic black spot, no, a big blot."

Hug-Hellmuth examined this example of a child's dream in detail. She considered all aspects of the day residue, the symbolic content, the manifest and latent meaning and finally the meaning the dream had in the life of the child. It is an interesting exposition and it reads well. Both Sigmund Freud and Helene Deutsch used dreams originally recorded by Hug-Hellmuth in their later work.[4]

In her second paper, "Contributions to the Topic of 'Lapses in Reading and Writing'," Hug-Hellmuth gave three examples of mistakes in reading and writing, and she traced with skill the unconscious determinants of these so-called errors. The first example was that of a doctor who wrote an error into a prescription, the second an interesting autobiographical exposition of a constant inability to spell the word *French* that Hug-Hellmuth experienced between the ages of seven and fourteen. The third and final example was also from her own life: at the age of ten she was unable to write the name "Karl." She suggested many unconscious determinants of this inability. In the manner of Sigmund Freud, she described the psychopathology of every-day life with all of its unconsciously determined parapraxes.

The third short paper of 1912, "A 'Lapse of Speech' in a Small Schoolboy," provides examples of lapses of speech in two young boys. Again psychoanalytic observations of children provide the basis for a description of unconscious functioning. In one example, while discussing the topic of the Garden of Eden, one little boy referred to Paradise as Paris. Hug-Hellmuth described the over-determined manner in which the boy made this error. She knew that the boy's family often used the word *Paris* for the toilet. In addition the family were aware that the boy had a habit of urinating in the large garden of their house. Finally, at that time in Vienna there was a popular type of candy called "Paris-sticks," whose form resembled feces.

In the second example, a father asked his little boy to congratulate his mother on her birthday. He was to say, "I congratulate you on your birthday and you are to eat this all by yourself." The father then wanted him to give her a package of candies. When the occasion arrived the boy approached his mother and said, "Mama, I congratulate you on your birthday and Papa says that I am to eat this all on my own." Hug-Hellmuth provided an explanation of the unconscious reasons for this lapse.

Hug-Hellmuth entitled the fourth paper of 1912 "The Child's Concept of Death." Even though this is a very important paper, it did not appear in English until 1965, when Anton Kris published a translation in the *Psychoanalytic Quarterly*. It is a lengthy paper which forcefully reflects Hug-Hellmuth's understanding of the psychological development of the child, as do all the papers published in 1912. It is uniquely important as it is the first paper ever published on the topic of the child's concept of death. This was a topic that Hug-Hellmuth referred to frequently in later papers. Our knowledge of Hug-Hellmuth's development and the way death pervaded her early life, culminating in the early and premature death of her mother, adds a dimension to our reading of her papers: "No event among the abundant phenomena of human life is insignificant for the child, in particular the beginning and the end of life, the entrance and exit of individuals are an inexhaustible source of his 'whys' and 'wherefores'." In her paper she displayed a well-developed understanding of the way the child's concepts of death vary with different developmental stages. She described how to the child death may mean "a state of sleep from which one can be readily awakened." She discussed how guilt is often associated with the death of a loved one. She observed that the developmental process culminates in the child noticing that he is "not excluded from the universal rule of life and death." From the egocentric infantile attitude of children she related the development of altruistic feelings. In addition, she described the psychodynamic aspects of infantile death wishes.

In this paper Hug-Hellmuth made extensive use of the work of non-psychoanalytic observers of children, and from their observations she identified and discussed death wishes and their displacement. She described the development of the concept of death from a reversible to an irreversible state. It is important to observe that present-day descriptions of the child's changing developmental concepts of death have not proceeded much beyond what Hug-Hellmuth described in 1912.

The fifth paper to appear in 1912 was "On Color Hearing; An Attempt to Explain this Phenomenon on the Basis of the Psychoanalytical Method". "On Color Hearing" is the longest and most complex of Hug-Hellmuth's early publications, and it differs from her other papers in its odd, eccentric quality. Other scientists of that era, however, also concerned themselves with the phenomenon of color hearing. Freud referred to this paper of Hug-Hellmuth's in a letter to Carl Jung, recommending it for publication. In addition, in contrast to most of her published work, it includes many references and footnotes referring to the work of others. One reference is to the work of the well-known Swiss psychiatrist Eugen Bleuler. This is the only psychoanalytic source referred to, the others coming primarily from neurology and academic psychiatry.

Hug-Hellmuth began her paper by reviewing the literature on the neurological aspects of the subjective perception of color with different auditory sensations. She examined the phenomenological material at length, discussing in detail the neurological explanations of the phenomenon of color hearing or what she termed the "anatomic-physiological school" of causality. She then described what she referred to initially as the "psychological-associative explanation." In the remainder of the paper, she tried at length to propose a psychoanalytic explanation for color hearing, listing many of her own perceptions as examples.

In the 1912 papers Hug-Hellmuth provided material in support of Freud and psychoanalysis; proceeding from the world of the child. She explicated the existence of infantile sexuality, psychic determinism, and the unconscious. She also presented an argument for the psychoanalytic interpretation of color hearing that was different from the viewpoint of the majority. In doing so she took a very definite step away from the neurological and biological toward the psychological and psychoanalytic approach.

In 1913 Hug-Hellmuth continued her entry into the world of psychoanalysis, publishing four papers and a major monograph.

The first paper was "On First Memories of Childhood." In this very long paper Hug-Hellmuth examined childhood memory from a psychoanalytic point of view. She began by presenting a view commonly held by psychologists of the day—that before the seventh year there was a "black hole of remembering." She proceeded to describe suppression, repression, and infantile amnesia, artfully employing the observations of non-psychoanalytic psychologists of children. She emphasized the sexual impulses behind suppression and repression. It is of interest that she included a child's fear of death as a cause of repression. On the subject of death and sexuality, she wrote: "Two constants are mixed together here—death that finishes life and the mystery that created all life—and between them a terrified childish soul trembles". We can now see the personal factors that might lead Hug-Hellmuth to write such a paper, her terrifying childhood that involved a prominence of death.

Page after page of the paper deals with early memories reported by non-psychoanalytic psychologists. Hug-Hellmuth illustrates what these observers did not seem to "see." She emphasizes how the early memories actually disguised broad areas of infantile sexuality. Once again she weaves together sexuality, love, and death. In one particularly poignant memory, a woman remembers the love of her grandmother, who was the "storyteller of her first year." After the grandmother's death, the woman says, "I remember that something had disappeared from my life. It was as if a door to a whole, beautiful, mystical world had closed. I had passed freely in and out of that door. Now, there was no one who knew how to open that door anymore".

In this paper, and in another of the same year, "The Nature of the Child's Soul (or Psyche)." Hug-Hellmuth referred to fairy tales from the viewpoint of psychoanalysis, anticipating some later psychoanalytic interpretations.[5] Hug-Hellmuth notes that unusual illnesses in childhood often play a significant role in the memory of the individual adult. She ends this paper by commenting on the importance of early memories in the development of character.

"The Nature of the Child's Soul (or Psyche)" is a small gem. The paper reveals a complex, condensed, in-depth survey of the psychological development of the child. Hug-Hellmuth emphasizes the early development of sexuality and comments at some length on how society at that time had difficulties reconciling early childhood with sexuality. Society faced the loss of what she called "the sweet breeze of virginity and innocence." She emphasizes the early development of intellect and sexuality in the infant during the first weeks of life, describing the sexual, erotic, masturbatory aspects of infantile development in some detail.

Hug-Hellmuth here reflects on the moods of childhood and the "pig-headedness" of some children. She felt that this reflected the child's inability to follow the parent's demands for suppression or repression, and she referred to these symptoms as the "rebellion of the child's soul against the work of suppression." With some amusement, she comments on the psychopathology of adulthood: "Some patients often behave like children and reproduce their own childhood by expressing infantile wishes and desires in new, age-inappropriate forms, expressing those unresolved suppressed wishes".

In this sort paper she also emphasizes the relationship between infantile sexuality and the love of the child in a true sense. She discusses unloved children, rejected children, and children who have suffered a deficit in love during childhood: "A deficit of love during childhood cannot be compensated for by a later attachment. The loneliness of the child's soul resembles a worm that destroys the fruit from inside, leaving its surface appearing immaculate." "The ability to love and the longing for love have their roots in sexuality in both children and adults." She talks about the relationship between love in infancy and the ability to love as an adult. She also includes some material on the child's concept of death, and finally she returns to a discussion of the Oedipal complex.

The next paper of 1913 Hug-Hellmuth entitled "Children's Dreams." Here she analyzes two dreams. First she presents a short dream of Rolf's, describing the manifest content in detail. The latent content showed the boy's sexual interests and she draws on the day residue, to describe the variety of ways by which he would attempt to see the naked female body. The second dream highlights the rivalry of two brothers for their attractive schoolteacher. One brother dreamed that his brother was ill and as a result could not attend school, and therefore could not benefit from the attention of the valued schoolteacher. Here she emphasizes infant sexuality, dream analysis, and sibling rivalry.

The next paper of 1913 is Hug-Hellmuth's first publication of a psychoanalytic discussion of women. Although Hug-Hellmuth's primary interest was children, psychoanalytic perspectives on women also assume a certain importance in her work. She entitled this first paper "On Female Masturbation," and she reviewed the topic in an exhaustive manner. She maintains a firm basis in Freud's early work and refers often to the *Three Essays on the Theory of Sexuality*. She agrees that masturbation causes "nervousness," yet, she appears to diminish this emphasis of Freud's. She argues against overt prudishness and the denial of female sexuality, her main thesis being that society's overzealous denial and "derogatory criticism" of female masturbation causes psychological trauma.

Hug-Hellmuth adopts a developmental perspective in this paper by dealing with masturbation in infancy through childhood and adolescence to adulthood. She questions whether psychoanalysts could expect women to be honest, yet conceal masturbation. After all, honesty is "an essential prerequisite and condition of psychoanalysis." She stresses the normality of masturbation and decries the prudery that exists about women masturbating. She makes a particular plea for freedom and satisfaction in one's sexual life. This she contrasts with what she termed "lonely love."

Hug-Hellmuth published her first monograph, *The Mental Life of the Child: A Psychoanalytic Study*, in 1913. In 1919 it was published in English under the title *A Study of the Mental Life of the Child*, and it also appeared in 1918 and 1919 as a series of articles in the *Psychoanalytic Review*. The monograph's main subject is the observation of childhood development from a psychoanalytic perspective. Hug-Hellmuth made use of contemporary non-psychoanalytic observers whose published writings recorded observations about children and their early development, interpreting their observations from a psychoanalytic point of view. Once again she showed how their material provided evidence for the existence of infantile sexuality, in this way avoiding the accusation of bias in her own observations.

As is revealed in this survey of early child development, Hug-Hellmuth was the first to stress the importance of child observation in psychoanalysis. "Facts that are well known to every nurse are systematically denied by accepted authorities," she argued. Although infantile sexuality provides a major theme, she presents her own classification of "the mental evolution of the child that takes place along a number of lines of development." In this classification she divided the development of the child into various stages:

1. the nursing period (the first year);
2. the period of play (the years of one to six);
3. the period of serious study (over six years of age).

In the monograph she discussed only the first two stages, the nursing period and the period of play. Anna Freud in her later work developed this idea of "lines of development" to a greater degree and brought it to a more complete fruition.[6]

This 1913 monograph is an important and unique contribution to the early history of psychoanalysis and the observation of child development. Hug-Hellmuth here describes the richness of the young child's life—sexuality, the development of character and intellect, emotions, volition, speech, ethics, and dreams. It is important to note her emphasis on the role that play served in the development of the child. She describes its importance in the understanding of the child's body, in the development of cognition, imagination, reasoning, speech, emotional life, and art. We know that she took the child's play into the consultation room, where she interpreted its symbolism and content to help the child understand his or her unconscious.[7]

Though she divided the mental evolution of the child into periods according to age and principal developmental trends, she regarded the different aspects of development as unfolding side by side coloring each other simultaneously and reflecting in all the child's experiences and reactions.

Hug-Hellmuth also concentrated on character development. "When love has not been manifested adequately in earliest childhood, the feeling of love often remains deficient throughout adolescence and adult life together with an enduring longing for this feeling." She wrote this comment in close conjunction to frequent references to Rolf, but may also have been referring to herself.

Hug-Hellmuth published three more papers in 1913 and continued her rapid entry into the mainstream of psychoanalysis. One paper was a short book review entitled "Claire Henrika Weber: 'Liddy'." Hug-Hellmuth here outlines the erotic relationship between the girl in the story and her parents, and once again emphasizes the developmental aspects of sexuality. She makes the point that although Claire Weber was ignorant of Freud's work, "the intuitive look of a poet into the soul of a maturing woman" was remarkable. The story describes the feelings of a twelve-year-old girl who on one particular night had to sleep in her parents' bedroom, in her mother's bed close to her father. Hug-Hellmuth illustrates how the writer exquisitely conveys the girl's feelings—her anxiety, her reluctance, her fear, her shame, the memories stimulated from the past, and her fantasies. The girl finally slips out of the bedroom to find a couch in another room where her mother finds her there the next morning "in the deep sleep of a child."

The second 1913 piece was a short introduction written for a paper of Sabina Spielrein, another early psychoanalytic pioneer. She was the second female member of the Vienna Psychoanalytic Society, Hug-Hellmuth being the third. Spielrein left the society shortly after joining with Jung and devoted herself to him as patient, disciple, and mistress. Spielrein's life is an interesting story in itself.[8]

In her short and simple introduction, Hug-Hellmuth comments on the "motherly feelings" that siblings have for each other, and she describes the existence of unconscious memories of these feelings as a part of adult sexuality. Spielrein's paper went on and described how early unconscious memories from childhood continue to exist and how this causes problems in adulthood.

In this productive year of 1913, Hug-Hellmuth also wrote a brief paper in response to an earlier paper of Otto Rank's. Rank had provided an example of infantile sexuality in a young boy. Hug-Hellmuth then wrote a paper entitled "A Female Counterpart to Rank's Contribution to Infantile Sexuality." In this paper she describes her observation of a four-year-old girl who showed an overt public sexual interest in a man who resembled her absent father. Hug-Hellmuth describes the incestuous dynamics: "The aggressivity of infantile sexuality can become quite prominent. This occurs because of the absence of the original love object. This absence increases and reveals the unconscious sexual feelings of the child."

In her final paper of 1913, "Children's Misdemeanors and Naughtiness," Hug-Hellmuth gives her observations of six children who had been naughty. Two of the case examples describe aspects of Rolf's behavior and one is an autobiographical note from her own childhood. The theme of this paper is how such behavior can be attributed to several different features, such as denial, fear, spoiling, jealousy, boastfulness, and manipulation of the parents. It is a commentary on the rich psychological life of the child.

3 A Psychoanalytic Career
1913–1929

In 1913 Hug-Hellmuth became a member of the Vienna Psychoanalytic Society and entered into the world of organizational psychoanalysis. Her name first appeared as a member in the minutes of the society on October 8, 1913. She was the third woman to be admitted, the first being Margarete Hilferding and the second Sabina Spielrein.[1] The entrances and exits from the Vienna society of these three woman are interesting to observe, in themselves reflecting some of the turmoil in the history of psychoanalysis.

Paul Federn first proposed Margarete Hilferding for membership on April 6, 1910. In a meeting of the society held the next week, they entitled the agenda of the meeting "Reorganization of the Society." In this meeting Federn again proposed Hilferding. During the debate over her nomination, Isidor Sadger presented himself as against membership of women in the society. Alfred Adler disagreed and approved of women members. This debate between Sadger and Adler probably had more to do with Hilferding being a supporter of Adler than with her being a woman. Sadger later changed his mind and supported Hug-Hellmuth's membership. At this meeting Freud commented that it would be a "gross inconsistency to exclude women on principle." In the vote that followed eight favored the admission of women, and three opposed women members "on principle." In conclusion, the minutes of that meeting stated that because three of eleven had voted against the admission of women, "this will oblige the president to proceed with extreme caution on this point." The actual vote on Hilferding's admission took place two weeks later after a review of her application by the executive committee. In the final vote Hilferding received twelve votes in favor of her membership, two voting against her (presumably Sadger and especially his nephew, Fritz Wittels, continued their opposition).

The admission of Hilferding made women acceptable for membership. However, her active membership did not last long; she resigned from the society eighteen months later, on October 11, 1911. That night Alfred Adler and three of his supporters announced their resignations at a "special plenary session" of the society held in the club room of the Cafe Arkaden. Sabina

Spielrein became the second woman member of the society during this meeting. At the end of the meeting Hilferding and five others joined with Adler and the other three and resigned. Rather soon after, Spielrein announced that she was a follower of Carl Jung and of the "Zürich School." She stopped attending meetings in 1912. Although she remained a member of the 1913/1914 list, she did not appear at meetings.[2]

Hilferding continued with Adler. After World War I, she was the president of the Vienna Society for Individual Psychology for a time. The Nazis murdered her sometime after 1942 in the death camp at Theresienstadt.[3]

Spielrein stopped attending society meetings and moved away from Vienna in 1912. She maintained an allegiance to Freud, but she also continued to like Jung, a situation that disturbed both men. She was a very active psychoanalyst in Germany and Geneva—for example, she was Jean Piaget's analyst. In 1923 she returned to Russia and continued her work as one of the early members of the Russian Psychoanalytic Society, until the Soviet government banned psychoanalysis in 1936. She lived through Stalin's purges of 1936–1938. However, on November 21, 1941, the Nazis murdered her in the synagogue of Rostov-on-Don. There is much more to be written about Spielrein's original contributions to psychoanalysis. Much of her work has remained unacknowledged or incorrectly attributed to Carl Jung, something he never clarified in his long lifetime.[4]

Hermine Hug von Hellmuth became the third female member of the Vienna Psychoanalytic Society on October 8, 1913. From the available minutes, it appears that at no time did any two of the three attend a meeting of the society at the same time. It was at Hug-Hellmuth's first meeting that Freud reported on the Munich congress where the break with Jung had taken place. After her acceptance, Hug-Hellmuth regularly attended the meetings of the society for the rest of her life, and she remained a strong supporter of Freud and his group. She gave her first talk on October 29, 1913, entitled "On Some Essays by Stanley Hall and his School; Seen from the Viewpoint of Psychoanalysis." Although there was a suggestion of future publication, it never occurred. A good discussion was recorded.[5]

There is a sense that Hug-Hellmuth had found a family and a father in the Vienna Psychoanalytic Society and Sigmund Freud. Sadger introduced her to Freud, and he remained in all probability her only friend.

Antoine and Rolf were not living in Vienna at that time, yet the half-sisters continued to see each other. Antoine had published her doctoral dissertation in 1906, the year of Rolf's birth. In 1907 she moved from Vienna to Hacking, where she taught in a high school. At five years of age, in about 1911, a babysitter described Rolf as being precocious, able to read and write and to use numbers. The years from 1907 to 1913 seem at least on superficial evidence to have been stable for Antoine and Rolf. They lived in one place and Antoine had steady employment.

However, tragedy was never far away from Hug-Hellmuth or her family. The stability achieved by Antoine ended in 1913 and in February of that year she became so severely ill that she was forced to quit work. She moved briefly with Rolf to Graz, then to Brixen, and later in the year to Bozen. Rolf had already changed schools once, in 1912, and his mother's illness and her frequent moves disrupted his life more and more.[6] The element of repetition is striking. Rolf was experiencing all the elements of his mother's early life and, in most points, Hug-Hellmuth's life as well. Their lives marred and distorted by illegitimacy, illness, and death.

Between 1914 and 1918 Hug-Hellmuth's publications decreased in number, and perhaps in importance. The psychoanalytic movement remained her home and provided her with some stability. Antoine and Rolf returned to Vienna to live with her in 1914. Antoine had developed tuberculosis, like her stepmother. After a brief stay with Hug-Hellmuth, Antoine and Rolf returned to Bozen, and on February 2, 1915, Antoine Hug died, leaving Rolf an orphan at nine years of age.[7]

Strangely, Hug-Hellmuth did not go to Bozen. In a letter that sounds odd and inappropriate, she apparently told Rolf to sell everything in Antoine's estate and to come to Vienna on his own to live with her.[8]

Death had pervaded Hug-Hellmuth's early life, and prematurely it made an appearance once again. In her will Antoine named a Dr. Schlesinger as Rolf's guardian. This again calls into question the relationships between Hug-Hellmuth, Antoine, and Rolf. How can we account for Hug-Hellmuth not becoming Rolf's guardian? We found an ominous clue in a statement made about Rolf shortly after his mother's death. Bluntly, his guardian Dr. Schlesinger stated, "Rolf will never become a useful member of society!"[9]

We found something more than a clue, however. Open and clear reports show that Antoine did not want Hug-Hellmuth to be Rolf's guardian. He went immediately to live with a friend of Antoine's, a Mrs. von Horvath. He began to attend school in Vienna, but that summer they sent him away to a boarding school in Krems, where he remained for the next two years. Then, he went to live with a family in Krems named Pesendorfer.[10]

Hug-Hellmuth published only two papers in 1914. Her attendance at meetings of the Vienna society faltered. She had to contend not only with the dreariness of the war years, but with the tragedies and hardships of her personal life.

The first paper of 1914, entitled "Children's Letters," was lengthy. In it, Hug-Hellmuth provided a psychoanalytic understanding of letters or notes derived from childhood experience. She stated that in adults strong resentment against writing letters is common, and she concluded that we should not accept the commonly offered explanations such as lack of time or the need to do other chores, as society always offers excuses. Specifically, she stated, "This resentment is anchored in most people's souls." She traced the resentment back to the school years where notes were passed back and forth in the classroom. She suggested that if educators could think of their own childhoods, they might remember the particular content of these notes, and they should understand that the sexual content caused their enthusiastic censorship. Remembering this might help adults to understand their reluctance to write letters.

Hug-Hellmuth also described certain children to whom letter writing had become important. She gave one particularly poignant example of this in a description of a young boy called Beppo. Beppo's mother died suddenly and his father had to have the eight-year-old Beppo and his brother placed in two separate institutions. Hug-Hellmuth quoted liberally from a collection of letters that Beppo had written to his father from his eighth to his tenth year. She identified the consciously and unconsciously expressed wishes to see his father and for reunion both with the father and mother. Again Hug-Hellmuth was treading on the familiar ground of loss and grief.

She also included other case examples. Following the divorce of her parents, a little girl wrote letters that showed her neverending wish for the return of her father. Hug-Hellmuth gave many other examples of children and their need to write, using the examples to clarify the child's unconscious. The manifest content of the letters, in the manner of dreams, led to their unconscious meanings.

It is intriguing to see in this paper how Hug-Hellmuth took the children's letters and clarified them with psychoanalytic understanding. For example, in his loneliness the boy Beppo wrote many letters to his father. Hug-Hellmuth emphasized in this 1914 paper "how deeply children feel when they are separated from one of their parents . . . and how much their longing becomes the focal point for their unconscious mental life." Lacking parents, the children used the letters not only as a vehicle for the expression of grief, but also as a means "to solve several sexual developmental problems." She referred to examples that were implicit or explicit in the letters themselves.

The letters of the children were used to highlight a number of different psychoanalytic ideas. Throughout the paper she showed how the letters carried the expression of wishes. In one example she described how a young boy wrote to his sick mother itemizing a long list of toys and books that he wanted for Christmas. It was only at the end that the truth appeared when he wrote, ". . . and it is too bad that you can't be here for Christmas."

Hug-Hellmuth devoted her second paper of 1914 to a topic comprising her older interests and her newer field of work. Entitled "Child Psychology and

Pedagogy," this paper emphasized her view of psychoanalysis as consisting of both "educating" and "curing." The paper is a review of some basic psychoanalytic principles. Hug-Hellmuth thought that psychoanalysis with children would necessarily contain both an educational and a therapeutic element. She noted that "with this deeper understanding we want to prepare for an era in which the psychoanalytic method executed with knowledge becomes a tool for education." We must note that Hug-Hellmuth did not state the opposite. That is, she did not state that psychoanalysis was a form of education. What we find expressed is a description of child psychoanalysis as consisting of two aspects, one of education and the other of therapeutics. Thus in 1914 we find Hug-Hellmuth espousing a specific approach to the psychoanalysis of children. She would later elaborate this approach in her 1920 presentation on technique, foreseeing important elements of Anna Freud's later writings.[11]

Hug-Hellmuth approached the connections between psychoanalysis and education directly, outlining several areas where they meet. The first important point of mutual confluence was "love": "It is necessary to start with the most important and obvious factor of infantile life, love. Psychoanalysis has emphasized the importance of this most powerful feeling in all its positive and negative aspects." She recognized that the psychic development of the child was dependent mainly on the extent and manner of affection shown to him from the beginning of life. To clarify, she added, "The amount of love first received becomes a measurement for the mature years," and she went on to discuss the vicissitudes of love, sexuality, and ambivalence as experienced throughout the school years.

In discussing the variety and details of infantile sexuality, she added a statement that emphasizes the noncognitive element. "The mental processes of a child are much more influenced by his feelings then by his intellect." She commented on how the excesses of punishment and threat help neither in an educational nor a psychoanalytic sense.

Hug-Hellmuth established the beginnings of a child psychoanalytic technique in this 1914 paper. The technique held that children and parents must be educated as part of their psychoanalysis.

Despite the problems mentioned earlier, or as a result of them, Hug-Hellmuth published five papers and monographs in 1915. These included: "A Dream That Interprets Itself"; "War Neurosis in Children"; "War Neurosis in Women"; "Some Relations between Eroticism and Mathematics"; and "A Case of Female Foot Fetishism, or rather, Shoe Fetishism."

In "A Dream That Interprets Itself," Hug-Hellmuth reported a dream described to her by a fifty-year-old woman. This paper is important in Hug-Hellmuth's work as a whole as it represents her move in the direction of the psychoanalysis of women. The paper was an essay which described a classical psychoanalytic interpretation of a dream. Hug-Hellmuth helped the woman understand her libidinal attachments to her son. At first, this led to her wish for his safety in the war that was devastating Europe at the time. Her main point was that the stress of war was objectively real, yet it brought out many of the original subjective fantasies and desires that were part of this woman's inner life, of her unconscious.

As far as we know, what Hug-Hellmuth described in her next paper, "A Case of Female Foot Fetishism, or rather, Shoe Fetishism," is the first case of fetishism in a female in the psychoanalytic literature. The woman's problem was a topic of discussion between her and her friends. The description of the case was a clear exposition of the growth and development of a thirty-year-old woman and the unfolding of her problem. This woman was the youngest of three daughters of a cavalry officer, and his favorite. Hug-Hellmuth described how as a child, "the woman would walk with him along the streets of the garrison, first when he was a colonel until he was the highest and most distinguished general. From early in her life she had a special love for his high leather boots." Hug-Hellmuth proceeded to describe this "love of high leather boots," a love that permeated the woman's life and interfered with her psychosexual development. This particular perversion remained present throughout her life. Although, at one point she did marry, she married a colonel who was thirty years older and particularly ugly. However, the sight of him riding his horse with his high boots was the decisive element in the beginnings of their relationship. " 'I fell deeply in love with the most exciting boots that I had ever seen', she reported to her friend with enthusiasm."

"Feet were enclosed in the boots! A man is his foot! A man who has beautiful feet is reliable . . . Imagine a civilian wearing worn, low shoes! Is that a real man?" She could not tolerate "wrinkled toes." Referring specifically to a cavalry officer who once approached her physically, she exclaimed, "That fool! He really believed that I would love him instead of his feet. Such stupidity is unbelievable." In this woman's marriage, her relationship with the naked foot was particular important. She continued to abhor wrinkled toes and to love the smell of tall leather boots. Hug-Hellmuth traced the early origin of this perversion to this woman's identification with her father. She had a strong wish to be a boy. The foot, or booted foot, to Hug-Hellmuth symbolically represented the penis that she wished to have.

"War Neurosis in Children" was in some ways a remarkable paper. It appeared in German in a morning newspaper published in Budapest. The newspaper was full of news of the war. Hug-Hellmuth's article followed the paper's lead article, which described the Austrian army's camp at the Dardenelles. She commented on the traumatic effects of war on children, the first time this subject had been dealt with in print. She reviewed the variety of traumas that war inflicts on children and provided a classification of these traumas.

Hug-Hellmuth adhered rigidly to the psychosexual etiology of all neuroses, describing war neuroses as secondary to primary sexual pathology. She wrote, "When we use the term *war neurosis* we do not forget there is no such thing in the narrow sense of the word; that is, a neurosis caused by war. We know that the roots for this suffering have to have been laid much earlier. The most common forms of war neuroses, such as hysterias, phobias, and obsessive-compulsive neuroses, are caused by sexual distortions in early childhood. War only serves as a fertile ground to bring about the manifestation of illness. The hysterical symptoms, the obsessive thoughts and concerns, are closely linked to current events. Laymen get the impression that the war actually is the cause and not its trigger, as for other neuroses and psychoses, including epilepsy, alcoholism, dementia praecox, and progressive paralysis. The public links only too quickly the disease with the incredible effects to which the soldier is helplessly exposed in the field. This happens especially if one sees that a returning soldier repeats and suffers in his fantasies the hardships, the horror of thousand's of deaths and the terrible and deeply upsetting cruelties of war. In particular, if the soldier shows in addition a total blandness towards his environment or an affective fixation to certain thoughts or feelings, one will erroneously assume that the war created that which had been already prepared and ready to appear in the unfortunate's soul."

In "War Neurosis in Women," Hug-Hellmuth described a variety of traumatic effects. She added a patriotic call to women to support the war effort, describing women as being discriminated against by not being allowed to go to the front. Even though she did concentrate more on the place of women in society and the general discrimination against women, she maintained the primary role of sexual pathology.

The lengthy paper "Some Relations between Eroticism and Mathematics" had a peculiar topic, similar to that of her paper on color hearing. For Hug-Hellmuth, there was a negative relationship between sexual drive and mathematical work. She offered as proof the example of the lack of sexual activity of the mathematical genius Sir Isaac Newton. Hug-Hellmuth stated that she derived this particular paper from another on pure mathematics, which is not surprising when we remember that her doctorate was in physics and that she spent years studying mathematics.

However, the paper is idiosyncratic, difficult in German, and difficult in the English translation. Hug-Hellmuth clearly presents the hypothesis that there is a strong connection between the cognitive and the emotional aspects of mental functioning. However, when she reviews the history of numerology in an exhaustive manner, that clarity is lost. She begins with references to the writings of ancient Egyptians, then proceeds to consider similar material through the Middle Ages until the time of her paper. She lists many connections and associations between sex, aggression, and mathematics. It is an unusual paper and out of step with Hug-Hellmuth's other publications. It reminded us of Freud's early fascination with numerology, which probably explains why she wrote it.

In 1916, Hug-Hellmuth published nothing. It was the first year that she had not published since the rush of papers that introduced her to the psycho-analytic world in 1912. Such a silence would occur only once again, 1918.

The year 1915 was another troubled time in Hug-Hellmuth's life. It brought the death of Antoine and the beginnings of an increased involvement with her nephew Rolf. Even though this involvement was at some distance, some trouble within the relationship and within Hug-Hellmuth herself were the most likely cause of the decrease in her usual productivity.

For 1916 and most of 1917, Rolf remained in Krems. He attended high school and lived with the Pesendorfer family. Mrs. Pesendorfer reported that Rolf had arrived at her home "starved and without clothes." The Pesendorfers tried hard to help Rolf, but Hug-Hellmuth was not of much help. Rolf continued to attend the high school in Krems until 1917, when he left to live with Hug-Hellmuth in Vienna. He said that the Pesendorfers didn't want him, which was probably true, as Mrs. Pesendorfer had asked for an increase in her monthly fee from Hug-Hellmuth. Rolf left the household shortly after Hug-Hellmuth refused to pay more. His school report from Krems stated tersely, "Rolf lies and is sexually premature." Hug-Hellmuth had prohibited Rolf from visiting her during holidays. Further, Mrs. Pesendorfer reported that Hug-Hellmuth "never spent any money on him." Mrs. Pesendorfer complained that she always had to pay his expenses when she took him along on a trip. However, Rolf bought flowers and sent them to Vienna for his Aunt Hermine.[12] The ambivalence in their relationship must have been present before Antoine's death. It probably accounted for her instruction that Hug-Hellmuth was not to be Rolf's guardian.[13]

Although Hug-Hellmuth did not publish anything in 1916, she was not totally inactive. She again began to attend the psychoanalytic meetings with greater regularity. At society meetings that year, she gave four presentations of papers or lectures. Three were untitled in the minutes of the meetings. Those that were recorded by name were "A Report of Some Dreams," "A Child's Anatomical Fantasy about Sunset," and "About the Fate of Three Lesbians."[14] To our knowledge, Hug-Hellmuth never published these pre-sentations.

The year 1917 appears to have been relatively unproductive, although Hug-Hellmuth seemed to show some increase in activity. She attended the society's meetings and she presented one paper consisting of two parts, "Observation of Children" and "A Parapraxis." She contributed to the discussion at two meetings. Later that year, however, she published two brief papers. In the first, "On Early Loving and Hating," Hug-Hellmuth presented four examples of different children who had held ambivalent feelings for their parents. The examples dramatized in a poignant, expository style the Oedipal striving and the consequent love and hate of the children.

The second paper, "Mother-Son, Father-Daughter," dealt with some aspects of the "subtle eroticism" in the relationship between a mother and her little boy. Noting the "feelings of a father toward a maturing girl that could not escape a sexual meaning," Hug-Hellmuth described the dialogue between a mother and her little boy that highlighted infantile sexuality.

Throughout the war years and certainly before that time, Hug-Hellmuth changed her name several times. Around 1907, Hug von Hugenstein became Hug, or Hug-Hellmuth, or more commonly Hug von Hellmuth. We do not know why she adopted the alias Hug-Hellmuth. Since Helmut was one of Rolf's names, this probably represented an attempt to dismiss her past and to accept her future with psychoanalysis. Coincidentally, in 1907 she signed her handwritten doctoral thesis von Hugenstein, a name she never used again in her later involvement with psychoanalysis. At the end of World War I, with the collapse of the Hapsburg Empire, Hug von Hellmuth changed her name as was officially requested of all nobility. She gave up the title "von" and became simply Hug-Hellmuth or Hug.

Although Hug-Hellmuth attended society meetings in 1918, she was mute and presented nothing.[15] However, her life changed in that year. As noted above, Rolf left Krems and returned to Vienna to live with Hug-Hellmuth.[16] Perhaps because of his move and the change in his residence, Rolf received a new guardian, Dr. Victor Tausk. It is not known why he was chosen. However, we suspect the influence of both Isidor Sadger and Hug-Hellmuth.[17]

Tausk was another member of the Vienna Psychoanalytic Society. A well-known psychoanalyst close to Freud, he had had careers in law and journalism before finding his way to psychoanalysis. After the war, at the time he became Rolf's guardian, he was described as a troubled man.[18]

Life with Rolf was difficult. In January 1919, Hug-Hellmuth caught him stealing from her.[19] This would later become a pattern. For the next two years, Rolf attended high school in Vienna. Troubles plagued him in this period and escalated in severity.[20]

In June 1919 Tausk committed suicide. It is curious that in all that has been written about Tausk, his guardianship of Rolf is nowhere mentioned. The most likely interpretation is that Tausk and Rolf never had a relationship. They might have met each other. Isidor Sadger was probably the real guardian. In July, Sadger stepped in as the new official guardian, Rolf's third within four years, and destined to be his last.[21]

Hug-Hellmuth published two works in 1919. Her major paper of 1913, "Aus dem Seelenleben des Kindes," was translated into English as *The Mental Life of the Child*. The second publication brought her a mixture of fame and notoriety. Subsequently translated as *A Young Girl's Diary*, it was published anonymously as a "journal written by a young girl belonging to the upper middle class." Hug-Hellmuth's name did not appear in the book until the third edition of 1922. However, people must have known from the first publication that she was at least the editor, if not the author. Certainly this fact was public knowledge by 1922. German editions of the diary appeared in 1919, 1920, and 1922, English editions in 1921 and 1936. Freud finally withdrew the book from circulation in Germany about 1928, following a prolonged public debate.[22]

The "editor" of this book, Hug-Hellmuth, included in the preface a laudatory quotation from a letter written by Freud in 1915, four years before its first publication. It reads grandly:

> This diary is a gem. Never, I believe, has anything been written enabling us to see so clearly into the soul of a young girl, belonging to our social and cultural stratum, during the years of puberal development. We are shown how the sentiments pass from the simple egoism of childhood to attain maturity; how the relationships to parents and other members of the family first shape themselves, and how they gradually become more serious and more intimate; how friendships are formed and broken. We are shown the dawn of love, feeling out toward its first objects. Above all, we are shown how the mystery of the sexual life first presses itself vaguely on the attention, and then takes entire possession of the growing intelligence, so that the child's suffers under the load of secret knowledge but gradually becomes enabled to shoulder the burden. Of all these things we have a description at once so charming, so serious, and so artless that it cannot fail to be of supreme interest to educators and psychologists.
>
> It is certainly incumbent on you to publish the diary. All students of my own writings will be grateful to you.

The diary consisted of entries reportedly made by an anonymous girl between the ages of eleven and fourteen and a half. It was organized carefully into entries made during the first year, the second year, the third year, and the first half of the fourth year. The entries were made daily or every few days and varied in length from short notes to long essays.

The diary recorded the life of "Rita," who detailed the lives of her girl-friends. All the characters were introduced in the first paragraph of the first entry. Rita described her life and her relationships with her friends. She described their interest in boys, their developing sexuality, and their own sexual interests, thoughts, and fantasies. In addition, she discussed death in the context of Rita's reaction to her mother's death when she was fourteen.

The references to the development of sexuality and its development were revealing of the inner world of a normal prepubescent and pubescent girl. The details expressed in the diary were fascinating. Whether or not we accept that the book is an actual diary of an eleven-to-fourteen-year-old girl, the diary is well written. In the debate that followed its publication, everyone acknowledged that it was a good exposition of the developing sexuality of a girl.

The diary caused a debate, a scandal. Some declared it to be fraudulent. Since Hug-Hellmuth was the only practicing child psychoanalyst, we can only assume that everyone knew she was the editor. Diaries interested the world of academic psychology at that time; their study was quite fashionable.[23] The publication of the diary in 1919 preceded her lectures on child psychoanalysis in Berlin by only a few months, and it came just before she presented the world's first paper on child psychoanalytic technique at the Hague congress.

The chief critic of *A Young Girl's Diary* was the famous English psychologist Cyril Burt. In a lengthy review of the book in 1921, he attacked with skill and guarded diplomacy,[24] stating, "The publishers are, I think, to be congratulated upon their boldness in issuing this volume. . . . It tells, in colloquial phrases, how an Austrian girl acquired, during the years of her puberty, a knowledge, more or less exact, of the chief biological facts of sex and family life." However, the publishers of the diary had made two assertions that concerned Burt. They had stated that the diary was "not a work of fiction" but "a genuine and unedited diary of a young girl." Burt responded, "Those who have made scientific study of the mental processes and literary expression of school children will feel immediately that either one of these statements must be untrue." According to Burt, the diary was a work of fiction written in the form of a diary. Further, he stated that it was written by an older person recalling her thoughts on sexuality.

Burt's opinion was important and well defended. He presented an argument of five points. (1) He did not believe that a young girl from eleven to fourteen and a half years of age could write over one-hundred-thousand words in the complete secrecy described in the book. (2) He did not believe that a young girl could write up to five pages of print, or two-thousand words in one entry. This would be four hundred words an hour for five hours. (3) Burt did not believe that the level of adult cognitive functioning that he discerned in the text was possible in a young girl. (4) He also did not believe that a young girl could write a literary work so coherent and intelligible." The text was too self-explanatory. (5) "The internal coherence and the dramatic unity of the narrative" he found to be amazing.[25]

In a somewhat sarcastic manner, Burt did allow that his observations and conclusions permitted an alternative hypothesis—that the supposed young girl who wrote the diary was an exceptional child. She "rose well above other children, other average children who lived under average conditions." Such an exceptional child, according to Burt, would be a genius. But since he had no external evidence to support this alternative hypothesis, Burt believed the internal evidence supported his preferred hypothesis of fraud.

Burt carefully emphasized that the picture provided by the book of the young girl's attitudes towards sex was quite trustworthy. He felt that the substance of the text was "as genuine as the form is disputable." Hug-Hellmuth rose somewhat feebly but promptly to the occasion. In a brief letter published in the next issue of the same journal, she gave her assurance that the diary was a "genuine record," describing its composition as "entries made at the time of the experiences noted." Finally, she promised to write more in rebuttal in a preface to the third edition that was about to appear. She ended her letter by assuming complete responsibility for the authenticity of the record.

Hug-Hellmuth's response to Burt's scholarly and polished attack was weak. She made matters even worse by writing directly to Burt, saying that she was the editor of the diary, that she had met the diarist when she (the diarist) was seventeen and that she obtained the diary when the girl was nineteen. Moreover, she claimed that the diary had not been kept. It was gone. Hug-Hellmuth also recorded the history of the girl for Burt. He alluded to this history in his report, but did not supply any further details.

Burt remained polite and diplomatic in his reply to Hug-Hellmuth. He welcomed her assurance that she was the actual editor of the diary. However, he felt that her further explanations about the unavailability of both the diary and the diarist did not call for any modification of his views. He continued to value the general substance of the book while implying that the diary form was Hug-Hellmuth's invention. The diary contained valuable basic psychoanalytic knowledge, and Burt felt that Hug-Hellmuth had created it for that purpose.

Hug-Hellmuth published a defense of the diary in a special introduction to the third German edition of 1923. As English editions of the diary appear to have been translations of the first or second German edition, her defense never appeared in English.[26] In this special introduction, Hug-Hellmuth replied indirectly and directly to her critics in a mild and brief manner. She stated that interest in the diary had resulted in curiosity about the name of the editor. She explained that she was the editor of the diary and claimed that the anonymity had been necessary for important personal reasons. She wondered why people would question the authenticity of a piece of work when it bore Sigmund Freud's introduction.

Hug-Hellmuth provided more information about the supposed author of the diary. Her description reads well and makes sense, whether or not you accept it as the truth. Hug-Hellmuth wrote that the girl had become an adult, married, and now she had died. She barely mentioned the fate of the original manuscript of the diary, although she noted in passing that she did not keep it. Hug-Hellmuth believed that those who would not want to be convinced of the authenticity of the diary would never be convinced.

In Germany, representatives of the school of developmental psychology of Karl and Charlotte Bühler questioned the diary's authenticity.[27] Bühler mentioned the diary in the foreward of a book that she wrote about the diaries of young people, a popular topic at that time. She described it as "fitting well into [Freud's] ideas but not into my knowledge of the development of a normal girl." Two of Bühler's students provided a more detailed discussion of the diary a few years after Hug-Hellmuth's death. Josef Krug demonstrated that the dates in the diary were inconsistent and incompatible with the calendar. Furthermore, the diarist mentioned some technological developments, like the telegraph, that came into use much later than stated in the diary.[28] Hedwig Fuchs, in a linguistic analysis of the diary, concluded, "The diary . . . is a fraud. Even if it contains genuine parts, the dates are false or abnormal, compared with normal development."[29]

What is the truth? Was *A Young Girl's Diary* truly a diary? We could accept the assumption of Burt and others that the diary was a fraud. However, there are several facts that are more compelling than either Burt's circumstantial argument or the intellectual arguments of the German psychologists of Bühler's school.

Burt contended that the diary was a work of pure fiction and that Hug-Hellmuth wrote it as an adult, making use of her memories, fantasies, and psychoanalytic knowledge. From our review of the topic, we have concluded that nothing has been proven. However, we suspect that Hug-Hellmuth did write the diary herself, and that she did so as an adult. She could never admit either that she was the subject of the diary or that she was the adult author, just as she could never admit that she had an illegitimate half-sister.

We suspect that the diary is not a true diary, but, we reserve the right to accept Burt's alternative hypothesis that it was the work of an exceptional person who did not live under average conditions—somebody like Hug-Hellmuth herself.

Two major reasons lead us to believe that the diary is not an actual diary. First, Hug-Hellmuth had a compelling motive for writing it. Anna Freud had appeared on the psychoanalytic scene untrained but had already established herself as a powerful rival. A psychoanalytic view of the popular interest in diaries would enhance Hug-Hellmuth's stature in Sigmund Freud's eyes. Second, a reasonable knowledge of Hug-Hellmuth as a person supports Burt's alternate hypothesis—Hug-Hellmuth *was* exceptional.

In sum, Hug-Hellmuth had a motive and she had access to a diary that was most likely her own or of her own manufacture. Its publication helped her career when she felt under threat. From the time the Diary appeared, and certainly by the time the third German edition was published in 1922, she came to the peak of her psychoanalytic career. Within months of its initial publication, in the summer of 1920, she gave a series of lectures on child psychoanalysis and education at the invitation of the Berlin Psychoanalytic Clinic, the clinical arm of the newly founded Berlin Psychoanalytic Institute.[30] The lectures went well and Hug-Hellmuth gained acceptance. She stayed with Karen Horney at her house and went on a holiday with her.[31] Horney was a central figure in the Institute. Her acceptance of and friendliness toward Hug-Hellmuth indicates the high regard the psychoanalytic community held for Hug-Hellmuth at that time.

The diary fits well with her other psychoanalytic work at that time. Every reviewer spoke highly of the diary, praising its excellent description of the psychology of a girl in puberty.

We have concluded that in the diary Hug-Hellmuth described her own development from a psychoanalytic viewpoint. The tendency to disguise autobiographical material in psychoanalytic writing was quite common at that time. That Hug-Hellmuth did so cannot be considered unusual. That she did so with such determination, considering the nature of the material, is only reasonable and understandable. That she presented the book as a diary from her own memory we consider to be an example of poor judgment rather than fraud.

We have referred to the important fact that Anna Freud began to attend the meetings of the Vienna Psychoanalytic Society in 1919 as a guest. She was twenty-four years old, and a nursery school teacher. Hug-Hellmuth was forty-seven years old and already a respected member of the society. Hug-Hellmuth did not react well to the appearance of Anna Freud on the scene.[32] We have suggested that Anna Freud's ascendence prompted Hug-Hellmuth's publication of the diary. What were Hug-Hellmuth's feelings about Anna Freud? She never wrote of Anna Freud, nor did she say anything about her. There was no reason for her to have done so. Anna Freud was equally silent about Hug-Hellmuth, although she had ample reason to express her feelings.

From September 8 to 12, 1920, Hug-Hellmuth attended the Sixth Congress of the International Psychoanalytic Association in The Hague.[33] This was the first meeting of significance after the war. Many psychoanalysts renewed friendships and made new ones. It was here that Hug-Hellmuth presented the first paper on the technique of child psychoanalysis. It was also the second congress that Anna Freud attended.[34] In 1920 Hug-Hellmuth quickly abstracted her presentation into English and published it in both English and German.[35] The English abstract occupied an honored position in the first volume of the *International Journal of Psychoanalysis*.

In this historic presentation and the published papers, Hug-Hellmuth reflected on her years of psychoanalysis with children. She described her technique as "curative and educative," emphasizing how she established rapport with the child and how she instructed the child about psychoanalysis.

Noting that she did not analyze children younger than seven or eight years of age, she recommended three to four sessions a week. She made use of talk and play in the child's home and stressed the importance of recognizing and interpreting positive and negative transference. She commented on the interpretation of dreams and on the necessity of combining instruction with patience. She carefully described the delicate relationship between the child's analyst and the child's parents. Hug-Hellmuth recommended as much involvement between the psychoanalyst and the parents as was desirable in the interests of the child.

All this should sound familiar to anyone acquainted with the form of child psychoanalytic technique that Anna Freud described in 1927.[36] Hug-Hellmuth's 1920 presentation and the later paper on technique were more important in the history of child psychoanalysis, although this has only recently been recognized.

Hug-Hellmuth published only one other paper in 1920, "Child Psychology and Education." It was translated by Barbara Low. She published another paper in 1921 as "Child Psychology and Pedagogy." Both marked a return to her original interest in education.

Anny Katan, younger contemporary and friend of Anna Freud's, observed that Hug-Hellmuth had children come to her office. There, she would help them play and talk. Apparently, she had a way of forming good relationships with children.[37] She used play in her work with children at an early stage. In her early papers, she carefully described play and its importance in fantasy and communication.[38] However, she did not at the time describe play within therapeutic sessions. She was not a "play therapist."

In her 1920 presentation and her 1921 papers on the technique of child analysis, Hug-Hellmuth emphasized these important points: an active therapeutic stance, the use of play in symbolic communications, the extensive education of the parents, and treatment in the home.

In addition to her writings related to child psychoanalysis and education, Hug-Hellmuth published several papers on the psychology of women and the family. One key paper on this theme, "Psychoanalytic Findings about Women," appeared in 1921. An exceptional work, it represented Hug-Hellmuth's beginning consideration of the psychology of family life and her emphasis on the psychology of women. Undoubtedly, Hug-Hellmuth's technique of doing analyses of children in their own homes had some influence on this. Yet we have seen that the family was always an important aspect of Hug-Hellmuth's life, in its presence, its absence, its joys, or its tragedies.

In the 1921 paper about women, she stated, "There are two kinds of mental laws, one for men and a totally different one for women. They do not understand one another and women are judged in everyday life according to the laws of men, as if they should not be women but rather men. This difference between men and women can be looked at from three different points of view, social, biological, and psychological." Even today, biological psychiatrists continue to question whether there is a psychological aspect to mental functioning. This early view of Hug-Hellmuth's was refreshing as it is a contrast to the theories and writing of many psychoanalysts who have appeared to deny the existence of a biology.

She wrote in a particularly poignant manner about the prejudice shown to women in their development. She commented on "the first pair of trousers" received by the little boy "meaning a special promotion to him." She wrote that "the girl reacts to this favoritism normally with feelings of discrimination, humiliation. . . . It is quite appropriate considering the strong reaction of the girl's soul toward the real and assumed injustice and the envy and the feeling of disadvantage that she feels when boys are the favored." This represented a mildly expressed departure from Freud's emphasis on penis envy and the Oedipal conflict.

According to Hug-Hellmuth, "The envy of women toward men is strongly suppressed whenever and for as long as they are happily in love." Of course, along with her other comments, she remained loyal to Freud. She did refer to the Oedipal complex. She stated, "We know that Freud has understood the bitterness of some daughters toward their mothers as a basic grievance that their mothers gave them birth as girls and not as boys." Hug-Hellmuth emphasized, "These factors influence the fate of women, and they explain phenomena that house the most troublesome experience in intimate relationships with men, that of frigidity." She ended her paper on a particular educative note that was prevalent early in the psychoanalytic movement. "Once our sexual customs have changed so that sexuality for the child is considered something natural and beautiful, and once we have replaced suppression of sex by a graceful, cultured acceptance of sex, men and women will go into marriage with more knowledge, cleanliness, and enjoyment." Hug-Hellmuth ended this paper with a quotation from Nietzsche: "The unresolved differences in the relationships, the character and the mentality of the parents, are continued in the character of the child and cause his internal story of suffering."

Besides the paper on technique, one other paper appeared in 1921. "The Middle Child" was lengthy and well written. The brief title was misleading, since the paper actually dealt with the large topic of the psychodynamic aspects and characterological effects of sibling relationships. Hug-Hellmuth discussed not only the middle child, but also the only child and the favored child. She described sibling rivalry and the ambivalence of sibling relationships in detail. One point in this paper is of special note: Hug-Hellmuth reported case examples of children that she had psychoanalyzed herself! This preceded the analytic work of Anna Freud and Melanie Klein, and provided a clinical followup of sorts to her unique presentations on technique of 1920 and 1921. Hug-Hellmuth described the dynamics, rivalry, and vicissitudes of sibling relationships and the effects of different orders of birth. She supplemented these observations with clinical material from her own cases.

To illustrate one of the dynamic situations in a family of three, Hug-Hellmuth quoted from a fairy tale that went as follows: There were three sisters. The oldest had three eyes. Her name was "Three Eye." The middle sister, "Two Eye," had two eyes. The youngest sister, "One Eye," had one eye. "One Eye" and "Three Eye" were proud to be different from other human beings, but they hated "Two Eye." She had two eyes like all other humans! "Two Eye" received wealth, love, and happiness. She was like all other human beings. However, the oldest and the youngest, "Three Eye" and "Two Eye," lived apart from other human beings because of their abnormalities. To Hug-Hellmuth, "Two Eye" was the symbol for the middle child. The middle child, because of a less privileged position, learned early to accommodate and to support others. This attitude helped the middle child to find a place in life.

During the autumn term of 1922 and 1923, Hug-Hellmuth lectured in Vienna at a center for adult education. These lectures were entitled "Educational Questions and Psychoanalysis."[39] In 1922, at the "Ambulatorium" of the Vienna Psychoanalytic Society, Hug-Hellmuth took charge of the teaching program. This program grew to include eighteen different courses. Later she was appointed director of the Educational Counseling Center attached to the Ambulatorium.[40] (Anna Freud would follow her in the same position a few years later.) In this capacity, she gave many lectures that were later summarized in her important publication of 1924 *New Ways to the Understanding of Youth*. All of this work added to Hug-Hellmuth's contribution to child psychoanalysis.

Things were not well at home in 1922, however. Hug-Hellmuth caught Rolf stealing again; she walked into her room as he was breaking into her desk. After this incident Rolf, then sixteen years old, attempted suicide by overdosing on alcohol.[41] (Rolf did not know that his father had died that year in Graz.) Sadger, as his guardian, acted immediately and removed Rolf from Hug-Hellmuth's home. He placed him in a group home for delinquent adolescents in St. Veith, but the local school quickly expelled him.

Rolf continued in an escalating series of problems. He enrolled in a technical school where he studied to be a laboratory assistant or a chemical technician's helper. He lasted six months at this school before they asked him to leave "because of personal difficulties." He lived in a communal home for about eight months from 1923 into 1924, where he subsisted on unemployment benefits and food and money from Hug-Hellmuth.[42]

Perhaps there was personal significance in the next paper Hug-Hellmuth published in 1923, "The Importance of the Family for the Fate of the Individual." The paper reviewed many complexities of family life. It showed the importance of the family in the development of the child. It emphasized the family's importance in character formation. Hug-Hellmuth stressed what she termed "the masculine complex," which resulted in a woman's over-attachment to her father. In such cases the woman remained single. Perhaps Hug-Hellmuth was writing about herself; but, of course, the same description applied to Anna Freud. Hug-Hellmuth went on to describe at length the effect of illegitimacy on the child. The development of such an illegitimate male corresponded closely with the life of Rolf.

Hug-Hellmuth made several hypotheses about the different experiences children can have with different family structures and their effect on adult character structure. She noted that ambivalence, characteristic of infantile sexuality, was important in the affective life of the child. She stressed the importance of realizing that the child is an affective being who develops a personality in the context of family structure. She reviewed the varieties of child development within the vicissitudes of family life and different family experiences.

She discussed in detail the "spoiled single children" with their "incredible overestimation of their selves." She commented that as adults "these people are alienated to reality and still look for the situation of their original home where they were the unquestioned center of attention." She used two German expressions to convey two possibilities for these children as they develop their adult personalities. One expression was "hooked up into the nest"; the other was "mother's little boy." As a third possibility, Hug-Hellmuth suggested that this spoiled "single child" with a close attachment to his mother may become homosexual. She referred to the work of Sadger to defend this hypothesis.

Hug-Hellmuth described the development of the child from primary narcissism to object relations within the context of the family. She described the roles of the mother, the father, the siblings, and strangers. Within this context she outlined the complexity of the different routes followed by boys and girls in their development. Hug-Hellmuth wrote about children who experience a lack of love within the family and described the effect of this experience on their development. Similarly, she described the effect on a child of an excess of love within a family. This is where her paper becomes particularly poignant. In characterizing the development of an illegitimate child who received an excess of love, she was clearly thinking of the illegitimacy of Antoine and Rolf.

In addition, Hug-Hellmuth focused on the effects on a child's development of being "unwanted." She described how this feeling of being unwanted led to a constant wish to run away. She described the effects of fostering and of being an orphan on the development of the child. She hypothesized the effects on a child of conflicts within a marriage and of divorce. Hug-Hellmuth was quite pessimistic about the effects of divorce on a child, noting that "these are the cases which are most hopeless for psychoanalysis." However, it is important to note that she saw the major problems to be in the reconstitution of a family. Modern family theory terms this the "remarried family." She described the complex relationships that exist in such a remarried situation.

Hug-Hellmuth commented at length on "sibling" rivalry between step-siblings, half-siblings, and full siblings. This was her own life's experience. It is sad that the family therapy movement is only now making strides in the understanding and treatment of remarried families. Hug-Hellmuth discussed the effects of divorce at length, concluding that it deprived the child of a firm basis for personality development.

Hug-Hellmuth considered the effect of being an only child. This had some similarity to Rolf's position. She stressed the importance of siblings or the lack of siblings for the psychic development of the child. "It is impossible to acknowledge the importance of the parents for the psychic development of the child without paying attention to the influences of the siblings or the lack of siblings." Hug-Hellmuth reviewed the effect of ordinal position within a family and the sex of the siblings.

Finally, from a true developmental perspective, Hug-Hellmuth ended the paper by reviewing the importance of aunts and grandparents in the development of children. She saw grandparents as important contributors to the child's normal narcissism, as advocates for the child, and as mother substitutes. She stressed the significance of the deaths of grandparents. "The death of a grandfather and grandmother often confronts the child for the first time with the secret of dying. Accordingly, the familiar figure of those loved ones becomes the symbol of death for the child."

The turmoil with Rolf continued throughout 1923 and into 1924. Hug-Hellmuth sounded a sad note in a 1924 paper entitled "The Libidinal Structure of Family Life." In this paper, Hug-Hellmuth described early infantile sexuality and the Oedipal complex. She went on to describe the family romance in exquisite detail. After a comprehensive and basic exposition of these ideas, she extended this knowledge to a special consideration of the illegitimate child. At that time Rolf's illegitimacy played a special role in her life. She wrote, "Children who experience a normal and healthy family life will emerge undamaged from their childhood dreams and fantasy world. Life will be much more difficult for those who grow up in a family with conflicts. The illegitimate child soon feels the special position into which a cruel society has cast him and his mother. As school begins he realizes what it means not to know his father's name when the other children assure him of the humiliating truth that his embarrassed mother could not tell him. His becoming delinquent is an unconscious protest against the unfairness and unkindness of society."

In addition, Hug-Hellmuth extended a psychoanalytic understanding to orphans. Rolf lost his mother when he was nine years old, and Hug-Hellmuth lost her mother when she was twelve. In a manner that predicted and predated a close consideration of family psychodynamics, she described the family by the ordinal position of the children. She made special reference to sibling rivalry. She ended the paper with a discussion of one's ultimate choice of a person to love.

This detailed paper is a fund of information on the early application of psychoanalytic theory and family group dynamics. Hug-Hellmuth's perspective and her technique of seeing children within their home may have benefited family theory and therapy.

Hug-Hellmuth's final work was among her most important. *New Ways to the Understanding of Youth: Psychoanalytic Lectures for Parents, Teachers, Educators, School Physicians, Kindergarten Teachers, and Social Workers* was a book of lectures. Reviewers received it well. Karen Horney stated in a review in 1925, "The book makes known what analysis has discovered about the child's development and the difficulties which this encounters and indicates the possible line of attack for the educational worker. She gives numerous clear examples that provide a vivid picture of the instinctual life of the child. . . . The book has great value, not only for educators interested in analysis, but for analysts themselves."[43] Despite this praise, no one had ever translated this book into English.[44] In our condensed translation, we have renamed it *The Hug-Hellmuth Lectures*. There are twelve lectures, all on important psychoanalytic topics and containing clinical examples from Hug-Hellmuth's own psychoanalysis of children.

As we have described, Hug-Hellmuth wished to bring psychoanalytic methodology into the mainstream of education. For this reason, and because of her long history as an elementary and secondary schoolteacher, she sought to educate schoolteachers in psychoanalytic principles. Again, others followed Hug-Hellmuth in this pursuit of a psychoanalytically influenced education system. Anna Freud lectured to child-care workers and teachers as well. These lectures were among her first published writings.[45]

One case that Hug-Hellmuth described in the lectures was that of a fourteen-year-old girl who experienced the symptom of excessive laughing. Hug-Hellmuth described her analytic sessions with the girl. These sessions included interpretation of the transference within the analysis. In the transference the girl perceived Hug-Hellmuth to be like one of her teachers. Further, in the genetic origin of the transference, the girl saw Hug-Hellmuth as her mother. Thus, the basic conflict became clear to the psychoanalyst and to her patient. The girl's conflict centered on her ambivalence toward her mother's pregnancy. This had led to the symptom. This analysis, like many analyses of that time, lasted three months.

In another clinical example, Hug-Hellmuth described the psychoanalysis of a seven-year-old boy who presented the symptom of bedwetting. Again, she described transference—the boy saw her as a parent. She described the transference as the emotional vehicle for the analysis. She clarified how it led to the correction of the symptomatology exhibited by the boy, stressing the importance of the cognitive abilities of the child for the acquisition of insight.

In another example, Hug-Hellmuth described the psychoanalysis of a nine-year-old boy who had the problem of grimacing in an inappropriate manner. Here, she emphasized the need for a good working relationship in an accepting atmosphere. She felt that this working relationship would allow the patient to explore the roots of his symptoms without having any fears. This was a very important concept. Later psychoanalysts would elaborate and describe this concept further as the working alliance or the therapeutic alliance. In this particular case, she described displacement as a defense that she interpreted before she interpreted the transference.

Another case Hug-Hellmuth described was that of a seventeen-year-old girl. She had obsessive-compulsive symptoms. In this girl's analysis, Hug-Hellmuth made use of the technique of free association in the classical manner, using the couch. Similarly, dealing with an incapacitating phobia of a sixteen-year-old girl, she described the technique of free association and the interpretation of unconscious fantasies. Again with this adolescent she used the classical technique and she used the couch.

Throughout these many clinical examples Hug-Hellmuth made a clear distinction between psychoanalytically oriented counseling and educational methods that a therapist used in a very active manner—and psychoanalytic treatment, where she employed interpretation of defense and transference. She described psychoanalysis as occurring in the manner of daily sessions and over a relatively longer duration.

4 The End—1924

The escalation of Rolf's problems continued ominously. In February 1924 he held a job for a brief period. Thereafter he began again to try to get money from Hug-Hellmuth in a variety of ways. He became increasingly intruding and persistent. In one incident he forged an invoice or bill for a considerable amount of money and tried to have it collected from Hug-Hellmuth. However, she caught him again.

In the midst of all this, Rolf went to Graz to search for his father. He discovered that his father had died two years before. Rolf returned to Vienna and immediately began to hound Hug-Hellmuth for money. On one occasion he approached her six times in one day. He was not completely unsuccessful in his demands. In early August 1924, she did give him some money. Two weeks later he received more money after a visit with Hug-Hellmuth and Sadger. Sometime just before the end of August 1924, Hug-Hellmuth gave Sadger a copy of a will in which she named Rolf as her only heir.[1]

Hug-Hellmuth lived and worked at number 10, Lustkandlgasse, in the comfortable Ninth District of Vienna. She had occupied the same apartment since 1913. It was one of four apartments on the ground floor of a small five-story building. Her apartment was small but functional. The entryway led into a small foyer from which one entered either a small kitchen, a small washroom, or a large living room. Hug-Hellmuth had a bedroom of a reasonable size that adjoined the livingroom. Both the living room and the bedroom had windows facing a garden. She was in the habit of sleeping in the livingroom during the summer months and in her bedroom during the winter.[2]

This building on Lustkandlgasse was close to the intersection with Sechsschimmelgasse. It was divided from the neighboring building by a garden of ivy. A green fence ran along the street on which she lived and along the parallel street to the back, Fuchsthalergasse. At night, the garden was dark.[3]

Magdalena Kittner had been Hug-Hellmuth's servant for three years. On September 9, 1924, she came to Hug-Hellmuth's apartment as usual at nine a.m. When she opened the door with her key, she discovered that the door was still locked from inside by the security chain. This was very unusual. Hug-Hellmuth was always up early and had regularly opened the chain for Mrs. Kittner to let herself into the apartment.

Worried, Mrs. Kittner called a locksmith and they entered the apartment along with some curious neighbors. They found Hug-Hellmuth lying on her couch in the center of the room next to a large table. Her head was resting on two pillows and she faced her office wall. A red blanket covered her body. She was dead.

When the police arrived, they found Hug-Hellmuth pale and cold with a handkerchief gagging her mouth. She had a swelling on the left side of her forehead and her neck was bruised. She had been strangled. Her head rested on a clean pillow, but blood covered the one underneath. Only one drop of blood remained at one nostril.

She had undressed in her bedroom, where her clothes were found. She had changed from a slip into a nightgown, leaving the slip hanging from the handle of an open window. From the position she was lying in, and the condition of the pillows, the police concluded that someone had murdered her and moved her to the couch. The only photograph of Hug-Hellmuth that we managed to find is one of poor quality from a newspaper showing her lying dead on her couch.

The postmortem showed that someone had hit her on the head with a blunt object. Her larynx and three ribs were broken. Outside the apartment, the police found a chair under one window. The fence and the wall by the window showed scrapes. Someone had climbed in and moved some flower pots. He or she broke the glass door of a bookcase. No one had touched the safe. When the police forced the safe open, they found Hug-Hellmuth's document of nobility, the silver cutlery, and other documents. The documents revealed that Hug-Hellmuth had received her pension of 2,082,200 kronen on September 1. She recorded spending 127,600 kronen, but the police could find only 40,000 in her purse. She dated her last entry in her records September 9, 1924, suggesting that she had been up late.

Mrs. Kittner had been at Hug-Hellmuth's apartment the day before. On that day, Monday, September 8, she arrived at about 8:30 a.m. She last saw Hug-Hellmuth when she left two hours later. No one saw Hug-Hellmuth after that. Some neighbors had heard screaming and yelling at 12:45 a.m. on Tuesday but everyone ignored it. One of the neighbors used to beat his wife, and the noise was the same. Another neighbor did hear a woman screaming, "What do you want, you pig!" and "Help!" One neighbor saw a man sneaking toward the back street.[4]

The next day, the police arrested Rolf in the railway station at Muerzzusch-lag for questioning about the murder of his aunt. Rolf knew Muerzzuschlag well. In May, he had gone there to live with a farmer. He had worked for a few weeks for an oil company just before this retreat. The past significance of this town was that it was where his mother and father had tried to set up their private school. The present significance of the town was due to the farmer's daughter to whom he had become engaged while living there.[5]

With Rolf's arrest and statement to the police, more information became available to fill in the story of Hug-Hellmuth's final days. Rolf had gone to Vienna on September 8 because of his usual financial problems. When he arrived, he went to a movie and afterwards to Hug-Hellmuth's apartment. Shortly after midnight he climbed over the fence into the adjoining garden. He climbed and entered through her open window. He made a loud noise when he landed in her apartment and Hug-Hellmuth awoke. She began to scream. She was in the room where he entered and she had begun to get up from her couch. Rolf rushed at her and in the brief fight that followed they fell to the floor. He tried to smother her with a pillow, but she kept on screaming, so he strangled her. Although she was silent, she was still moving, so he gagged her as well.

When she appeared finally quiet, he took her body and put it on her couch. He arranged the pillows, carefully placing a clean one under her head. Then he searched for the money in her underwear. He took 2,600,000 kronen and a gold watch. He climbed out of the window and put on the shoes that he had left outside. For the rest of the night he hung around the railway station. He reported that he had then taken a train to Graz. There he read a newspaper report of Hug-Hellmuth's murder. He then took another train back to Vienna to appear less suspicious. However, on the way back he stopped in Muerzzuschlag to visit his fiancée. The police found him in the railway station.

The newspapers gave detailed accounts of the murder. Although the reports do not reveal a deep scandal that reflected badly on psychoanalysis, they do add a few more bits of information about Hug-Hellmuth as a person, her ways and habits. For example, the newspapers reported that she recorded her earnings and expenses every day. Amid references to her accomplishments and fame, they described a person who always kept other people at a distance. Her only regular visitor was Dr. Isidor Sadger. She was a closed person who never talked more than was absolutely necessary, and even then reluctantly. One neighbor reported that Hug-Hellmuth talked to his cat more than she talked to him.

Hug-Hellmuth's servant, Magdalena Kittner, stated that Hug-Hellmuth never started a conversation. She was always working. Mrs. Kittner described how on one occasion Hug-Hellmuth reprimanded her for addressing her nephew as Rolf. She was plainly instructed to call him, Mister Rolf. Mrs. Kittner described Hug-Hellmuth as "pedantic and fastidious." She reported that Hug-Hellmuth was afraid that she would be murdered by Rolf. The description of Rolf in the newspapers was inaccurate in some details and differed from the more reliable testimony at his trial. The newspapers accepted the myth of Rolf's mother's legitimacy and wrongly reported Hug-Hellmuth to be Rolf's guardian.

Rolf described himself as being a competent, well-tempered, dedicated, and hopeful boy before the death of his mother. He stated that after his mother's death his Aunt Hug-Hellmuth tried various educational methods on him. At one moment he would be her spoiled little darling, only to find himself the next moment treated with rigidity and without mercy. He claimed that by giving him very little money, Hug-Hellmuth forced him to become a liar and a thief. Significantly, he did not mention psychoanalysis.

The neighbors talked to the police. What came out of these statements were a few facts, some observations, and even opinion. An aunt of Hug-Hellmuth's lived with her and Rolf for some time. This was the same aunt, Hug-Hellmuth's mother's sister, who had joined the Hugenstein family in 1874 when Hug-Hellmuth's mother became ill. Reportedly, Hug-Hellmuth and this aunt fought all the time. Many people commented on the difficult relations among Rolf, Hug-Hellmuth, and her aunt. Another neighbor reported that both Hug-Hellmuth and Sadger, his guardian, were hard on Rolf. They acknowledged Rolf's thefts from Hug-Hellmuth, but they felt that she had not properly provided for him. They described how hard he had to work around the apartment.[6]

One person who commented on Hug-Hellmuth had been a neighbor of Antoine's in 1913 and 1914. She had looked after Rolf while his mother worked. She told the police:

> Antoine was very intelligent and she had a honorable style and philosophy of life. Rolf was very precocious. At five years of age he could read and write. He was better able to read than a student in grade three or four. He looked like a ten-year-old, but pale. He never looked healthy. Because Rolf was stealing, the neighbors were warned that they should keep their eyes on their purses. Antoine might have partly caused this behavior as her tolerance for Rolf was limitless. She was a model of simplicity and modesty herself. However, she never avoided a sacrifice for Rolf.[7]

Isidor Sadger made an important statement to the police immediately after the murder. Not only was he the person closest to Hug-Hellmuth, he had known Rolf and his late mother over many years. Further, he had been Rolf's guardian since 1919. Sadger told the police the following:

> Initially, Rolf's behavior was tolerable. However, he started to steal. They were small thefts, but they were continuous. He stole jewelry and finally, in November 1922, he stole 800,000 kronen. He was banned from the house and taken out of school. He was taken to the detention home at St. Veith, where he stayed for about one year. There were some problems there as

well. After that he worked for a chemical company but he was fired. He would often come to Hug-Hellmuth for money. Previously, when he was living with her, he had enough to eat and to dress himself. He was even offered the opportunity to attend the theater and concerts. He never took advantage of that. On August 17, 1924, he came to Vienna and he demanded 3,500,000 kronen for his engagement. Hug-Hellmuth bought him a suit, three shirts and six handkerchiefs, one pair of shoes and six pairs of socks. In addition, she probably paid off some of his debts. He also wanted money from me. On August 28, he asked me for more money. I told him to go away and let Hug-Hellmuth know that he was in town. I then spent that evening with her as she was afraid of him. In one of her letters she expressed her fear of being beaten by Rolf. On another occasion, she stated that she was afraid that he would strangle her. She reported an incident where he had threatened her in Maria Trost to me in a letter. However, my letter did not reach her as she had already left. Eight days later she sent me her will. In another of her letters, she stated, "I will be killed anyway." I can attest to the fact that Hug-Hellmuth was in a severe state of anxiety ever since the incident at Maria Trost. In her will she gave everything to Rolf except some smaller legacies to me and other friends.

Rolf's mother had an affair with a private teacher. She spent her inheritance with this man in the establishment of a school. She even went into debt. Hug-Hellmuth used the remainder of her inheritance to pay off her sister's debts. After the unhappy experience with Rolf's father, his mother focused all her love on Rolf. Yet, he was put at a disadvantage, for to my knowledge they moved nineteen times. His mother and Hug-Hellmuth differed profoundly in their political views. Therefore, Rolf was not supposed to live with Hug-Hellmuth after his mother died. Dr. Guenter Schlesinger had already said that Rolf was hopeless and that he should be placed in an orphanage. However, Hug-Hellmuth had disagreed because she was of the opinion that such a move would be detrimental to Rolf's intellectual development. Neither Rolf's mother or Hug-Hellmuth ever used corporal punishment.[8]

In early 1925, Rolf appeared in court charged with the murder. The court found him guilty and sentenced him to twelve years in prison. They stipulated strict conditions in his sentencing. Every three months he would have to use a hard mattress, and every year on the anniversary of the murder he would have to spend the day in a dark cell.[9]

A terse notice appeared in the *International Journal of Psychoanalysis* in 1925. Written by Siegfried Bernfeld it reads: "On September 9, 1924, in her fifty-third year, Frau Dr. Hermine Hug-Hellmuth, a member of the Vienna society, of whose services, especially in the field of her child psychology, our readers need no reminder, was murdered by her eighteen-year-old nephew, Rudolf Hug. In a will made a few days before her death, she expressed a desire that no account of her life and work should appear, even in psychoanalytic publications.[10] In view of her loyalty to the psychoanalytic movement, it is easy to accept that she would try to contain or diminish any scandal by invoking whatever censorship she could. In effect, this is what she did with this will.

We wonder if Hug-Hellmuth felt guilty. Rolf lost many important things in his early development. He was without a father and an intact family. His mother doted on him, spoiled him, and catered to him. Hug-Hellmuth did not help. She observed him as a child. In that observation, he was more of an object than a loving-loved subject. In his early years, Hug-Hellmuth fought with his mother. Importantly, there is no evidence that she loved Rolf either. Rolf can be considered a victim of psychoanalytic study that lacked a true loving relationship.[11] There is little evidence that Hug-Hellmuth had experienced love. Her mother was either ill and unavailable or dead. Hug-Hellmuth's early life was one of deprivation. She lacked loving relationships as an adult. As Rolf became older, Hug-Hellmuth treated him unlovingly. She could observe Rolf and others and treated them with psychoanalysis. However, she was incapable of loving or being loved. This is recorded repeatedly. Yet family myths, secrecy, and mythology continued to be part of Hug-Hellmuth's reclusive personality.

In addition to this terse obituary by Bernfeld, we discovered a longer one that had appeared in 1924 in the *Zentralblatt für Psychoanalyse und Psychothera-pie*.[12] It has never been translated into English, although it is much more explicit about Hug-Hellmuth and her work. Entitled "The Psychoanalytic Movement: Dr. Hug-Hellmuth" and written by Dr. Joseph K. Friedjung, it reads as follows:

> The working and productive life of this quiet and far too modest scientist has ended with a shrill finale. Dark fate had bound her to the boy, who so often appeared in her first works, her nephew, for whom she became a second mother. He has become her murderer. Fearing him for a long time, she became depressed and lost a good deal of interest in life. So fate took its tragic course, that leaves us to regret strongly the all-too-early loss of this brave psychoanalytic pioneer.
>
> She was the first who could confirm through immediate observation, Freud's daring theories about the true character of the child; she was also able to enlarge them with many important observations. Untiring in the collection of observations, furnished with an excellent literary gift, she has for many years enriched psychoanalysts' and others' journals, sometimes with good review reports, or sometimes with original works of larger or smaller size. The best-known work is her monograph "The Mental Life of the Child," published originally eleven ago, and then especially *A Young Girl's Diary*, edited anonymously by her, that had three editions within a few years. It was repeatedly translated and was met by the greatest of

interest. For the psychoanalytic school it was a valuable, human document. For her enemies, it was the subject of malicious assault and nasty suspicions.

Her last years were overshadowed by the bitter understanding that if we are to apply our deepest pedagogic insights without being prepared ourselves, they are known to be unproductive. She acknowledged in a moving manner the deplorable opposition to the growing importance of psychoanalytic insights for education. Our scientific movement has much to thank her for. Her work will be a valuable source of psychoanalytic literature for the future.

Little is known abut Hug-Hellmuth's appearance. She was a small woman with black hair, always neatly and tastefully dressed.[13] Less is known about Rolf. He went to prison and was released after a few years. Shortly after his release he was referred by a senior colleague to Helene Deutsch for analysis. With wisdom she refused this referral. He followed her around for a while, until Felix Deutsch chased him off.[14] Rolf disappeared and we could find no trace of him.

Selected Works on
Child Analysis

Introduction

We have attempted to choose the most important works of Hug-Hellmuth for inclusion and, in most cases, translation. The translation of historical psychoanalytic texts from German into English is difficult. Its complexity has been previously described, probably most emphatically by Bruno Bettelheim.[1] The problem is also touched upon briefly, and in a scholarly fashion, by Peter Gay.[2] The need for a new translation of all of Freud's works has been addressed and the work is in progress. Yet every new text and author confront the translator with specific challenges that have to be carefully and painfully met.

Hug-Hellmuth came to psychoanalysis with quite an uncommon background and experience. Unlike today, in the early years of psychoanalysis this was not rare. Her specific background and the changes that occurred in her life are important to the translation of her work. Although she trained in the natural sciences, she maintained in her writing style an element of the bourgeois romanticism of the late nineteenth century. As a lay analyst in the true sense, her language also reflected a naiveté toward both her scientific and her human subjects. Her failure to differentiate between her private life and scientific observation and her lack of recognition of her countertransference imposed a certain quality on her language.

She was not alone, as we recognize the same in other early psychoanalytic writings. But it posed a fundamental question as to whether our translation should reflect this naivete. Hug-Hellmuth's language, at least as demonstrated in her early writings, is not precisely scientific. This could probably be attributed to a number of causes, such as an initial unfamiliarity with the "proper" terminology, the fact that psychoanalysis was struggling to find its own scientific language, and an attempt on her part to distance herself from the language used by contemporary academic psychology.

Her simultaneous appeal to the "common sense" of her audience and their willingness to follow her onto a new avenue of sophistication probably contributed to a rather clumsy approach to writing. Her writing is difficult to read even in German, especially in the early publications. This difficulty

47

seems to be due both to her style and to the content of her work. It appears as if she used the very act of writing as a process of clarification for herself. This resulted in papers that we would call today "unedited"—at best. In our opinion, the translation should reflect this difficulty in order to allow some empathy for Hug-Hellmuth. She did develop from a clumsy writer into quite a versatile one, and by the end of her life she had acquired a sophisticated style. In her later works she used the appropriate contemporary concepts with ease and precision.

Certain words and their translation warrant specific comment. Hug-Hellmuth's use of the word *Seele* is an example. Today, this word would undoubtedly be translated as "psyche." However, this translation does not reflect the many connotations of this quite overdetermined German word. We know that the psychoanalytic use of German words, with all of their multidimensional implications, was a deliberate attempt to achieve some distance from academic psychology whose language was at the time dominated by Latin and Greek terminology. With an understanding of these factors, we have chosen to translate *Seele* as "soul."

The early use of the word *ego* in psychoanalytic terminology appears to be an exception to what we described. We know from other contemporary publications in literary criticism and philosophy that the word had invaded German rather extensively and that it was even understood by laymen in its different facets and connotations. We maintained this word as it was.

On the other hand, the word *Weltanschauung* had to be handled differently. Like the word *gemuetlich*, it eludes a translation that comes anywhere close to its original meaning in German. It is simply impossible to find an English word that carries the same meaning, with its integration of religious, political, social, and furiously egotistic aspects of how man looks at his world. Therefore, we left it untranslated as well.

When Hug-Hellmuth wrote about the child, she was thinking about a male being, unless her clinical example clearly indicated the opposite. At a time when the psychoanalytic view of female psychology as represented by Hug-Hellmuth comes under renewed scrutiny, this use of the ubiquitous masculine grates on the present-day reader. Again, for the most part, we have decided to follow Hug-Hellmuth's text literally and not present a "modern" edition.

Hug-Hellmuth's papers on color-hearing and mathematics have not been included in this volume even though we have translated them. Or it may be because we did translate them that we clearly see them to be situational attempts on her part to aid her entrance into the world of organized psychoanalysis—that is, Freud's Wednesday Society. "Color Hearing" had been frequently discussed in the scientific literature of the time, and it was a fashionable topic that almost guaranteed some attention for the author. The paper on mathematics or numerology might have been motivated by Freud's particular interest in that subject. Finally, admitting our subjective opinion of these two papers, we did not find that either paper enhanced our knowledge of Hug-Hellmuth's contributions to child psychoanalysis.

Except for the few publications indicated, none of the following papers has been translated into English before.

The Analysis of a Dream of a 5½-Year-Old Boy (1912)

This paper was among Hug-Hellmuth's first and published in German as "Analyse eines Traumes eines Fünfeinhalbjährigen" (*Zentralblatt für Psychoanalyse und Psychotherapie* 2/3;122–27, 1922 [English translation by George MacLean, *Psychiatric Journal of the University of Ottawa* 11/1:1–5, 1986]).

Hug Hellmuth published a total of three papers that were exclusively concerned with dreams and dream interpretation. The other two appeared in 1913 ("Kinderträume" [Children's dreams], *Internationale Zeitschrift für Ärztliche Psychoanalyse* 5/1:470–75, 1913, this volume) and in 1915, when she reported the dream of a 50-year-old woman, whose son had gone to war ("Ein Traum der sich selbst deutel" [A dream that interprets itself], *Internationale Zeitschrift für Ärztliche Psychoanalyse* 3:33–35, 1915). Sigmund Freud also wrote in 1913 about children's dreams in the same journal ("Kindheitsträume mit spezieller Bedeutung" [Childhood dreams with a particular meaning], *Internationale Zeitschrift für Ärztliche Psychoanalyse* 1:79, 1913).

The two earlier papers deal with dreams of her nephew Rolf and were published at a time when she was not yet a member of the Psychoanalytic Society. They follow her generally liberal use of material that she obtained from Rolf without making any attempt to disguise its origin. The paper from 1915 is not included in this volume for two reasons: It does not deal with the psychoanalysis of children or women, and it is a mere reference of a dream without interpretation, as stated in the title of the paper.

The Dream

For the week before the dream, the 5½-year-old boy had been sleeping in the same room with his two aunts and his great-aunt. In the mornings he had been getting great fun out of waking up one aunt by calling and talking to her. In fact, he had concluded two years before that "she should not sleep when I am awake." Despite his great-aunt having forbidden such disturbances, the little rascal usually found a way around her. He would be quiet while she was in the room; however, as soon as she had closed the door behind her he would call out softly: "Aunt Hermine, are you awake?" Alternatively, he would talk to himself or rustle his clothes, only to become immediately silent once his great-aunt reentered the room. On the day before the dream he said to his Aunt Hermine: "You know, if I am going to sleep at my mother's again, I am going to jump on her in the middle of the night so that she cannot sleep." I said, "Oh come on, you are a horrible boy if you don't let your mother sleep. She is so good to you." He then replied with the old statement: "She should not sleep when I am awake."

Then, early one morning, at 3:30, he called very softly, as he had been doing previously later in the morning, "Aunt Hermine, Aunt Hermine, I am so afraid!" I sat up and asked him: "What is the matter?" He said: "A big bear wants to eat me." I calmed him and told him that nothing was going to happen to him, that it had only been a dream. We both lay down to sleep again. After a quarter of an hour of lying quietly, he said "I have a terrible fear." I got up again and gave him a candy left over from the evening before. He ate it, commenting, "You know that tastes good," and at the same time he held on to my hand very tightly, clutching one finger. Finally he calmed down and said spontaneously, "I am going to ask the Baby Jesus to watch over me."

In the morning the first thing he did was to retell the dream, adding: "There was also a big picket fence there and lots of pointed arrows on top. The bear wanted to hug me with his front paws. In the middle of the ceiling there was a gigantic black spot, no, a big blot."

Preceding Events

The day before he had been at the zoo at Schönbrunn where he had fed the animals and had expressed all kinds of fantasies about them. His strong auto-erotism led him to believe that the animals looked only at him and took food only from him. The bears were his "special favorites."

The following interpretations of the dream have not been told to the boy himself. In addition, I avoided pressing him with questions, so as not to make the dream too important in his consciousness. However, I tried, on the basis of the exact knowledge of his little experiences, of his home environment and his repeated longer visits in my house, to demonstrate the probable deeper meaning of the dream.

Dream Analysis

At first, through the dream he achieves permission to wake up his aunt, because nobody can really blame him when he is frightened and seeks comfort from her. In doing so, he also anticipates the pleasure of planned similar approaches to his mother. The fact that he does select his Aunt Hermine, whom he is forbidden to wake, instead of his great-aunt who had helped him with his nightly needs during a longer stay two years before, leads to the fulfillment of his wish: "If I do not sleep she should not sleep either." He practices his daily wish-fulfilling morning tactic and pauses between his calls with the fear of being reprimanded by his great-aunt.

(1) "I AM SO AFRAID" connects with a funny yet serious event of two years before. Whenever he was too restless during lunch, suddenly "a policeman is knocking on the door," even though he knew well that it was someone from the family. He clung to his mother and with exaggerated affect said, "I am afraid, protect me." He was forcing affection for himself through the pretended fear: he would not otherwise have received it at that moment because of his previous bad behavior.

(2) "A BIG BEAR WANTS TO EAT ME." The boy is a strong exhibitionist. On his visit two years previously, he lifted his blanket and stood up with his nightgown lifted high in his crib in the morning. In order to distract him without continually scolding and punishing him, I let my hand circle above the bed and swoop down like a swooping bird on his naked foot or hand, or on his toys. The bird took toy animals as it swooped, but would fly away disgusted if it saw too much nakedness. Thereafter, the exhibitionistic pleasure was transferred onto neutral parts of the body, and the attention of the boy diverted from his genitals. His question, "Aunt Hermine, does the bird also come to N . . . street?" On the first morning of his present stay (as we had changed apartments since his last visit), he showed that he had not forgotten this game. The bear that wanted to hug him primarily represents his mother, to whom he likes to run to be caught up by her in her arms: this game can be traced back to his tenth or eleventh month of life. His mother also was a climbing tree for him and he will be the bear and climb up, holding on to her hands, from the knee to the height of her breasts. The feared bear finally relates to an episode that happened in his thirteenth month. After being absent for several months, his father, a large, imposing man with a black beard, entered a room unannounced. The little boy did not recognize him at once and screamed with all his might: he identified him with the doctor, who also had a black beard, and who had vaccinated him. As his parents separated later, he had no further opportunity to see his father from his fourth year of age on. Nevertheless, he maintained the most tender feelings for him, despite the fact that his father did not care about him. The fear of the bear that wants to hug and eat (kiss) him therefore might actually represent a wish to see his father.

(3) "THERE ALSO WAS A BIG PICKET FENCE AND LOTS OF POINTED ARROWS ON TOP." There are Venetian blinds in the bedroom and the light of the street lamp creates alternating light and shadow stripes like an actual fence drawn on the ceiling; this forms the last visual impression of the day for the child as he lies open-eyed for up to half an hour sucking himself to sleep. In the dream the picket fence primarily refers to the railing of his little bed in which he slept till he was four and a half years old, and through which he exhibited

his penis. Also every evening his loved "mama" would sit at the side of this crib. He became fully aware of the status of this hour at three years of age when he said: "I always become so tender in the evening!" In connection with his lust to exhibit himself in bed he also had a habit of urinating during walks at every fence, with all conceivable and possible tricks, for example, on a certain board or exactly through two slats into a crack. The habit of urinating onto a certain board also refers back to early in his second year of life, when he repeatedly made the arm or the hand of his nurse or his mother the target of his stream, laughing as he did so and this in spite of the following punishment. The aiming at a crack between two slats could mean his own legs and his penis, but it could also refer to a vagina. He had claimed that when he was three years old, a nine-year-old girl had locked herself into the bathroom with him and stripped in front of him. He has told us repeatedly about this same girl that, while swinging with her, he had seen her "front popo" which did not have as much of a "tip" as his but a "long furrow where the peepee comes out."

(4) "THE POINTED ARROWS" refer at first to his own penis but also to the penises of several boys who lived in the neighboring house during his second year of life. They were repeatedly seen urinating through the fence into the neighboring garden. Therefore, the dream produces not one but "lots of pointed arrows." They also might refer to female breasts, specifically the teats of dogs, which also interested him. As he lived in the country, he became aware of their purpose early. He also knew that these grew during pregnancy. When he once saw his aunt by accident in her corset, he said: "You know, I definitely think that you are going to have a child soon."

(5) "I HAVE A TERRIBLE FEAR." This seemingly self-addressed statement contrasts to different attention-seeking statements in his repertoire. He again managed to trap me into dealing with him. During the day he understood how to get his mother or his aunt, or preferably both, to deal with him continually. It is interesting how he now extended his love from the mother to Aunt Hermine, whereas previously he did not want to have anything to do with anyone else when his mother came around. The little tyrant hated times when his mother and his aunt would chat with each other and he, the "principal person," was left out. Aged hardly three years, with his precocious intelligence, he verbally expressed an understanding of cause and effect. Not surprising, then, that with this phrase "a terrible fear" he was strongly imitating his mother and aunt. His first remark, "I always have such a fear at night," dated from the previous year when he stayed with friends of the family for two months, where unfortunately he slept in the couple's bedroom. The couple had the habit of retiring after lunch for two hours and the children were strictly prohibited from disturbing them during this siesta. In addition, the father routinely came home late. We can assume, therefore, that the little boy was not given any opportunity, mornings or evenings, to observe sexual

intercourse. However, he might have witnessed the nightly urination of the man or of the woman. He would repeatedly state, after his stay with this couple, that "a light flashed in the middle of the night in the east. Yes, a real flash," and he would point. The man's bed stood near the window and he knew well that sunrise occurs in the east. The flash would represent the light that lit up beside the bed of the man. As the boy had never slept in the bedroom of his parents, he missed such experiences from his earlier childhood.

(6) "THE BLACK SPOT IN THE MIDDLE OF THE CEILING, NO, A BIG BLOT." A large street lamp actually projected its shadow onto the ceiling in the dimly lit bedroom. From his first months on, the boy was an "excrement smearer": though punishment made him give up this gross coprophilic activity, he kept an active interest in his and others' defecation. Some days before the dream, he began running obsessively around and around the room, squatting here and there, and calling, "Aunt Hermine, I will sit down and make you a blot." An argument finally ended this amusement quite unpleasantly. The dream granted him the fulfillment of his wish, and, further, it was on the ceiling in a very exposed spot where everybody who entered the room could see it. In his defecation games he repeatedly selected to "blot" in the "middle" of the desk. In his dream the middle of the ceiling represented the middle of the lavatory. The black, dark spot also seemed to represent his naval, for which he has shown an intensive interest. The evidently visible black spot was certainly also a dream distortion representing his secret masturbation, which nobody was supposed to see.

At my soothing words he held my hand by holding one of my fingers, which probably represented his own penis. I frequently also saw him sit up in bed while asleep during the night, and I suspect that his raising of his body was symbolic of his erected penis after his nightly masturbation. Also, at two years of age, I noticed that he would stand up on his bed at night with an erect penis and only then would he state what he wanted. In addition, while half asleep, he would want to masturbate while he urinated.

It is remarkable that the little boy, who was brought up free of religious influence, only learned the word and gestures of prayer the year before while staying with the married couple mentioned above. Their five-year-old girl's praying was also restricted to a single pious sentence. His fear showed its infantile root in the prayer, as he said spontaneously after his dream: "I am going to ask the 'Baby Jesus' to watch over me." On the next day, when questioned by me about the "Baby Jesus," he explained, "He is golden like the sun, little, with a long dress and no pants." This he emphasized explicitly. I concluded that in the night "Baby Jesus" projects his sun-like rays into the room; the fence, which he has seen in his dream, was his shadow. On the Christmas tree that had been decorated for him the year before, there was a wax angel with blond curls, a little short red skirt, and a little golden crown in his hair. During that Christmas period the boy also stopped daily at a toy store, where there was the head of an angel in the window with the obligatory frame of lace that indeed reminded one of the delicate latticework of a fence. As an addition to the interpretation of the picket fence, an experience in the boy's second year of life should be mentioned. His parents operated an educational establishment in the country and the boy was living with a nurse in an immediately neighboring villa. After the end of every day's morning lessons his mother would come to her darling boy through the gate in the fence that connected the two adjacent gardens. He was always peeping longingly through the gaps in the picket fence, expecting her. The tall figure of the mother may often have been obscured from his view before he had recognized her, so that the Christ child, whose shadow transfers into a picket fence in his dream, refers ultimately to the longed-for mother, who is also supposed to protect him from the policeman, as now the "Baby Jesus" has to ward off the bear.

A further addition to "PICKET FENCE WITH THE POINTED ARROWS" results from a scene at an outing two months before the dream. The boy defecated and, with clear deliberation, he directed himself at a fence, removed it with a twig, and rinsed it with urine. A reference to this type of dream is mentioned in Freud's *Interpretation of Dreams* as a "dream into reality." He would not be persuaded to stop by persuasion or by anger, before the last remains were rinsed off. The rays that the "Baby Jesus" casts into the room might also represent his own urination as he is also acquainted with the saying "horses stream" [stream and ray having the same derivation in German].

An addition to the understanding of the "BIG BEAR" came during the day after the night of the dream, when the little dreamer emphasized the large size of the animal with the words: "You know, Aunt Hermine, he was very big, really very big. Naturally, since I am strong too, he would have to be big, otherwise he could not defeat me." So he fulfilled his fantasy that he is stronger than all other people and also stronger than the beasts of prey at the Schönbrunn zoo. His preference for bears might be based upon an identification of his small person in sexual matters with these animals. His glory at two years was to urinate, not sitting, but "standing up," as he would loudly announce. At approximately three and a half years of age he visited Schönbrunn for the first time. He saw the bears standing up clinging to the lattice fence or to the trunk of a tree. Excited, he cried out at that time: "Look mama, the bears are eating 'standing up,' " using unconsciously the old expression using years before while urinating "standing up." His delight knew no end as he even saw the "standing up" bears' erect penises. He could hardly be persuaded to leave.

Looking closely again at the psychological basis of the dream, it appears that, besides the fulfillment of various small wishes of the previous few days, there is the strong unfulfilled longing of the boy for his big, strong father. In his dream fantasy the father has been changed into the figure of the bear. The bear is the leitmotif of his nightly experience.

I would like to make some more remarks to add to the understanding of children's dreams in general. During the analysis of the dream of my five-and-a-half-year old nephew, it struck me that the boy, even though he had known for about two years that dreams are not "real" happenings, nevertheless attributed reality to his dream experience. For example, at night with a simple announcement, "A big bear wants to eat me," he will seek my attention. My calming word that he was only dreaming contributes little to the immediate recognition of his needless fear. That became evident from the request to the "Baby Jesus" to watch over him. He clings to the reality of his dreams; the fear only signifies the wish, whose fulfillment can be granted only by his dream. During the next day, as a thousand other little wishes direct themselves to his surrounding external world, the dream wish gets pushed aside and the child himself labels the experience as a dream. The clinging of the child's thoughts of the reality to his experience brings to my mind his first dream:

On December 12, 1909, when he was three and one-half years of age, waking up in the morning he asked his mother, with a searching glance around the room: "Where is the Christmas tree with the many pastries?" For a long time he did not want to believe that only a beautiful dream had shown him the Christmas tree. He objected continually, "I saw it! It stood there in the corner!" Only after many explanations and counterarguments, through which he wanted to hold onto the fulfillment of the wish, and with great disappointment, he came to understand the dream and its unreality. He recalls this first dream until today, and tells the story often. However, always with the addition: "My, I was still so dumb then, I believed it was a real Christmas tree but it was only a dream."

Lapses in Writing and Reading (1912)

The following two papers (see A *"Lapse of Speech" in a Small Schoolboy*) deal with anecdotal reports of parapraxis from Hug-Hellmuth's own experience or the literature of the day. Again the biographical material is not disguised and exact reference is made to the persons involved.

Both papers precede her membership in the Vienna Psychoanalytic Society and were published in the same year. This paper was published as "Beiträge zum Kapitel 'Verschreiben' und 'Verlesen' "[Lapses in writing and reading], in *Zentralblatt für Psychoanalyse and Psychotherapie* 2/5:227–80, 1912.

After her initial paper on the dream of a 5½-year-old, she covers here the second important area of manifestation of the unconscious, parapraxis in its different forms. It is of particular interest that Isidore Sadger, Hug-Hellmuth's psychoanalytical mentor in these days, presented a paper entitled "Sexualität und Erotik im Kindesalter" (Sexuality and eroticism in childhood) at the Vienna Psychoanalytic Society meeting on February 5, 1913, using an approach to childhood sexuality similar to hers.

1

Once a doctor prescribed his patient "LeVITIco" instead of "Levico-water." This error, which caused a critical remark by the pharmacist, can be better understood once one has searched for the possible reasons. Unconscious reasons cannot be denied a certain probability. Although this doctor often bawled out his patients because of their unreasonable eating behaviors, he was very popular. This was shown by his crowded waiting room before and during his consultation hours. As a result of his popularity, he was able to hurry his patients as they dressed and undressed. When he did so, he used the words *"Vite, vite"*—faster, faster! If I remember correctly, his wife was French, which accounted for his choice of French when he wanted to rush his patients. Many people love to use foreign languages when they have requests. For example, my father would try to hurry us up when we went for a walk and said, *"Avanti, gioventù"* or *"Marchez au pas!"* Also I can recall a visit to an older doctor when I was a young girl when I had a sore throat. He thought I was moving too fast and tried to slow me down by saying, *"Piano, piano."* In conclusion, I quite understand this particular doctor who followed that pattern and prescribed Levitico instead of Levico-water.

2

Another example of an error in writing was encountered when *French* became *fresh*. From the age of seven to fourteen, every time I had to label a French workbook, or during any other use of the French language, especially when I had to label my French vocabulary workbook, I would misspell the word *French* as *fresh*. The explanation is as follows: During my studies of French from the age of seven to eleven, I studied at home. During that time I would play practical jokes, e.g., disturb my sister by catching her legs under the table with mine, or untie my shoes and kick them up against the wall. If my sister sat next to me, I would poke my finger up through the cane-webbing of her chair. This was often connected to our game "Being Ill." In short, I behaved just like a "Fratz," a cheeky, naughty child. Often I was called "Fratz" by my mother when I managed to escape her punishment by hiding underneath the table with astonishing speed. Quite often this name would be used as a pet name, especially when I had done some harmless pranks, a "Fratzerei," as Papa called it. His expression "Der kleine Fratz has ideas" made me proud in spite of the critical undertone in his choice of words. I understood that the "idea," the prank, was really accepted as funny.

Later I was enrolled in a French language school which was not particularly disciplined. Once more I was mischievous and in writing letters to my colleagues under the table, I made scratchy noises with a pen point. . . . I also picked up soaked pieces of paper from the inkwell. This is a widespread game children love which is based on juvenile coprophilia according to observations during the first years of life. In short, I was again a real "Fratz," and totally emerged in my element of doing nonsense they took place always as "heroic deeds." When I was in public school, I had always admired those popular children in my class who were naughty. I dared not be one of them because of my father's firmness.

The "error" of fresh instead of French occurred so constantly that the idea that this could have a sexual motive was not presumptuous. As a fact, the French language is rich in sexual and erotic expressions taught by children of a lesser kind of upbringing, while at home their parents carefully avoid such a vocabulary. This "apparent" error in writing or in speaking shows how the children manage to find their way on "slippery" ground in spite of their parent's disapproval. When I was twelve years of age, my mother died. She had been responsible for my French instruction. So it was not until I entered the French language school thereafter that I began to be able to enjoy seeing in the French vocabulary possibilities of sexual meanings to be translated into German. Up until then I was inhibited by my fear that my classmates would consider me to be ordinary, whereas I was so proud to be the noble. I used to mispronounce or change the vowels. Errors in reading or writing used to give me great pleasure. I would make up sentences with misspelled words just like the seven-year-old hero of Bartsch's "German song" and his list of "ersten Schmutz dieses Lebens" [first smut of life, really meaning first *schutz*—protection of life]. However, after I entered the French school, I became more concerned to keep up a show of being special, which limited my naughty behaviors.

3

Another example of an error in writing that I encountered was an "inability" I experienced to spell the word *Karl*. I remember clearly the time when I was ten years old and we had to write a dictation of the subject of Karl der Grosse, i.e., Charlemagne. I tried very hard to correctly spell the word *Karl*, but only managed to write *Karel, Kardel, Kradl, Kral*. After having wasted a lot of ink, secretly I had to laugh so much that I dropped the pen. Often this also happened to me during my French lessons at home. I used to belong to the top of the class, so this unseeing lack of knowledge was regarded as surprising. There were two reasons why I did not want to write the name Karl. At one time the squealing of a little boy named Karl had gotten me into trouble at home. Secondly, my uncle Karl, a cavalry officer who led a very disreputable life, had caused my parents a lot of anguish and my father didn't like him, and I myself couldn't appreciate anybody whom my father didn't like. Once I overheard my father say, "That is it! I have had enough of Karl! I do not want to hear about him anymore!" I only saw Uncle Karl again after my father's death.

Also I remember that a little boy of one of our servants, aged 1–2 years, was called Karl. As they came originally from Czechoslovakia, in the Czech language his name is spelled Karel. Once when this child developed whooping cough, we were not permitted even to walk by his house or stop anywhere near there. I often disobeyed this rule. From Karel I associated to Kardel (which is a pet name for Karl in the Viennese dialect), and then to Kradl. *Gradl* is a fabric for underwear. My clothing was made from gradl and I had a pair of pants that I loved to lift over my knees to show off my "thick or fat thigh." Thigh is *Wade(r)ln*, which is similar to gradl. Also I used to be sexually excited by the tight pants. I nearly fainted in these moments when I derived enjoyment in misspelling my chosen words. I could not stop my embarrassed laughing—something one finds often in teenagers, and my pen would fly out of my hand. Finally, I have to explain the misplacing of the *a* and the *r* in Kral. As I was smaller and weaker than my two-year-older sister, I tried, when it came to rough fights between us, to scratch her—in Viennese *Krallen* or I would say, "I will scratch you"—"Ich kralle dich." Perhaps I would have liked to do that to my teacher as well who tortured us with lengthy dictations, especially when I was in love with a younger female teacher from another class.

A "Lapse of Speech" in a
Small Schoolboy (1912)

This paper was first published as " 'Versprechen' eines kleinen Schuljungen" [A "lapse of speech" in a small schoolboy], in *Zentralblatt für Psychoanalyse und Psychother-apie, 2/10–11:603–04, 1912.*

A woman I know has a six-and-a-half-year-old son who repeats at home the story of Adam and Eve and their fall that he has heard in school. Aided by questions of his mother, he reports that this first couple has lived in Paris. Being told of his error, he corrects himself and says, "Paradise," quickly adding, "Yes, yes, in a big garden, as big as the one in S." This was the place of his summer holidays.

The lapse of only one syllable has a deep meaning. The mother of little Ernst used to call the toilet "Paris" in her own childhood and continued to use this expression during her marriage. Further, she had used of course this expression in talking to the child. Without fail he had been quite interested in this place and he would have liked to accompany his mother there. Despite all prohibitions he stood by the door, watching and listening. His naivety associates the prohibited with Adam and Eve, and he "lets" them live in Paris, i.e., paradise.

In addition, the large garden had helped him find the right word which has meaning in his memories. The villa where he lived with his parents during the last summers stood on a wide lot with gardens and meadows that he frequently used not only as his own "Paris," but in which he also passionately searched for the droppings of the ducks, geese and the dog. He would scream, "There was a duck or a goose or a dog in Paris." He called the pigsty "Pig Paris." Finally, a remark by his father had become a frequent joke of his childhood. The father had called the boy's feces "Paris-sticks," the name of a famous Viennese candy.

In this example we see that the apparent verbal lapse of the child does not lack an unconscious intention. Therefore, it cannot be considered to be the result of hasty speech.

Another "lapse of speech" of a child was reported by E. and G. Scupin in their book *Bubi in His Fourth to Sixth Years of Life.* The four-and-a-half-year-old son Ernst Wolfgang is ordered by the father to congratulate his mother on her birthday and to give her a box of candies and to say the words: "I congratulate you on your birthday and you are to eat this all by yourself." Bubi approaches his mother with a big smile saying: "Mama, I congratulate you on your birthday and Papa says that I am to eat this all on my own." They added and explained this lapse of the little egotist, since it had been difficult to convince him that the candy was really meant for his mother and not for himself.

Certainly the lapse was not intentional, i.e., conscious. However, the result of the real misunderstanding was not. Bubi had certainly intended to repeat his words correctly before his mother. The insertion of the sentence "And Papa says I am to eat . . ." shows the work of the unconscious that changes the father to support the child and his wishes.

The Child's Concept
of Death (1912)

The third issue of the first volume of *Imago* in March 1912 contained two contributions by Hug-Hellmuth. Her lengthy article on color-hearing ("Über Farbenhören. Ein Versuch, das Phänomen auf Grund der psychoanalytischen Methode zu erklären" [On Color-hearing: An attempt to clarify the phenomenon on the basis of the psychoanalytical method], in *Imago* 3/1:228–64, 1912) as well as a new column on child psychology ("Vom wahren Wesen der Kinderseele" [The true nature of the child's soul] edited by Hug-Hellmuth. She wrote both the introduction to the new column (*Imago* 3/1:285–86, 1912) and the first contribution to this column dealing with the child's understanding of death ("Das Kind und seine Vorstellung vom Tode" [The child's concept of death], *Imago* 3/1:286–98, 1912). The introduction is clearly separate from the paper on the death concept, but not listed as such in either Grinstein's Index of Psychoanalytic Writings nor Graf-Nold's biography.

Hug-Hellmuth continued to write for this column until 1921, when it was discontinued (Über erste Kindheitserinnerungen [On first memories of childhood], *Imago* 2:78–88, 1913; "Kinderbriefe" [Children's letters], 5/3:462–76, 1914; Von frühem Lieben und Hassen [On early loving and hating], 1/5:121–22, 1917; "Vom 'mittleren' Kinde" [The "middle" child], 1/7:84–94, 1921). All her contributions are contained in this volume except for a review of Lou Andreas-Salomé's book *Im Zwischenland* (Stuttgart and Berlin, 1911) that appeared in 1914 (*Imago*, 1/3:85–90).

The paper on the concept of death is to our knowledge the first ever to address this particular aspect of child development and anticipates some of the later concepts developed in accordance with the understanding of the child's cognitive development. The English text contained in this volume is the unaltered reproduction of a translation by Anton Kris in *Psychoanalytic Quarterly* 34:499–516, 1965.

No event among the abundant phenomena of human life is insignificant for the child. In particular, the beginning and end of life, the entrance and exit of individuals, are inexhaustible sources of his "whys" and "wherefores." Once he is aware of the eternal riddle of life, he pursues it as the goal of all investigation, playful and serious. For in life and death, he sees love and hate, cruelty and pity joined to each other. The little child that laughingly crushed a worm underfoot picks it up with careful fingers to reunite the quivering parts, and he is genuinely sad that his attempts are unsuccessful. The child senses so strongly the mental superiority of human beings over every other creature that he describes to himself, without further thought, power over life and death. Sometimes, being dead may mean a state of sleep from which one can easily be awakened; at other times, it may mean being far away but able to return at will. This friendly view of death comes largely from fairy tales, which regularly make up for horrors and cruelty with a happy ending. As soon as the hero or heroine is wakened from death by the kiss of a good fairy or a sword-bearing knight, sadness and mourning are converted to wedding celebrations and happiness. And when some fairy-tale figure does not arise from his bloody death, the child's fantasy sees in this the deserved punishment for serious crimes. For this reason some children with a nervous tendency are afraid of death when they feel guilty for some misdeed. Such brooding fantasies of one's own death, which do not seem to occur very often in the tender years of childhood, indicate the germs of a psychoneurosis. But no child's life is spared the moment when he gets an inkling that he is not excluded from the universal rule of life and death. However, along with this awareness, for a long time death signifies no tragic end but simply a temporary separation. It seems, therefore, neither strange nor unusual to a child to wish dead someone whose presence means restrictions on his freedom or who may threaten him with loss of love. When my five-year-old nephew, Max, learned of the death of the man who served as caretaker and gardener for friends of ours, he came home calling happily: "Yoo-hoo, the grumbling old bear is dead. Now I can ride my wagon all over the garden as much as I want to!" Freud in his *Interpretation of Dreams* (4)* has shown in several examples how jealousy of a newborn sibling and fear of being cut off from the parents' love are expressed in rejection of the baby and death wishes towards him.

A child of this age does not know altruistic feelings; he knows and loves only himself; and this egocentric approach to life cannot hurt our feelings, lacking as it does the conscious intent of adult egocentricity. We are much more pained when a fourteen-year-old, hearing of her teacher's death and of the students' attendance at the funeral, remarks: "Bravo, that's clever; I'll drive out there too!" We tend to expect that the roots of good upbringing will have a firmer hold. Such expressions, however, are to be taken as youthful thoughtlessness rather than moral crudity, yet at the least they indicate ingratitude. An unexpected afternoon off from school is always a delight, even if the occasion is sad. Grownups all too willingly measure the wishes and actions of youth with the same yardstick they use for those of mature

*The reader should refer to Hug-Hellmuth's Appendix to this paper.

adults. This biased judgment disturbs understanding of infantile spiritual and emotional life and makes all remembrance of one's own childhood impossible. Hence, in healthy and sick alike it also pushes out of mind the infantile death wishes against the parents and other persons close to the child, with defense more acrid than in any other problem considered in Freudian theory, except for infantile incestuous thoughts. Despite the fact that Freud (4) has clearly shown how far the child's appreciation of being dead differs from its true significance, neither layman nor specialist wants to acknowledge it. The thought of even an imprudent child nurturing death wishes against a beloved person is so painful to most people that their resistance to such a chain of thoughts prevents any insight.

It is, therefore, all the more gratifying to gain from an author, whose book is not based on Freudian theories, a beautiful confirmation of that which the majority shuns. E. and G. Scupin (8) record valuable notes on the child's relationship with death in a diary in which they write about the psychological development of their little son. They neither conceal nor suppress anything; but they portray the child with all his charming idiosyncrasies and all the peculiar ideas which are produced in such remarkable abundance in the first years of life. Little Ernst Wolfgang first encountered the idea of death when he was three and a half years old and his parents took him along on a visit to a cemetery. In the diary they note:

> Nov. 2, 1907. Taken to the churchyard, Ernie pointed to the graves: "What sort of heaps are those?" He was told briefly that sick people sometimes die, that is, do not wake up again, and that they are put to bed here under grass and flower hills so that they can sleep quietly. That interested the boy. He stopped at every grave and asked: "Who sleeps there, and who sleeps there?" Furthermore, he refused to be satisfied with what we told him. Ernie doesn't believe willingly; he wants to see. And so he pleaded urgently, pointing to a grave: "Mummy, you can dig one up, huh?"

One month later, on December fifth, the little boy, who was scolded for nibbling at a loaf of bread like a "little mouse," wanted nothing to do with this designation because "the mouse is locked in the trap and dead."

> March 22, 1980. Quite suddenly the child thinks about death and dying. He says: "And when we are dead, can we only speak softly?" Here he whispered very quietly to himself. Then followed the even more singular question: "When one does, is one's hair torn out?" This question is explained by the fact that the child was often in the kitchen watching feathers being plucked from fowl, so that he applied the treatment of dead animals to dead people.

I cannot agree with the Scupins in the assumption that the child suddenly thought of death and dying. Apparently that first visit to the cemetery made a lasting impression on his receptive mind and was interwoven with all the earlier experiences in the kitchen and the daily sight of the stuffed birds in his father's study until, at last, the child gave words to his thoughts. (Scupin works at the Zoologisches Institut in Breslau.)

> April 4. The boy always has a great deal of sympathy for suffering animals, even for those used as food. For instance, he saw a plate of smoked sprats from Kiel on the supper table. In answer to questions he was told, in outline, something of how fish are caught. He took the destiny of the fish so much to heart that in greatest excitement he berated the bad men who caught such nice little fishes. Along with this he developed a rather horrible fantasy. "They're naughty men if they kill poor little fishes—I'll hit 'em and saw'm up and cut off their head and breast a(r)ms and stick needles in their eyes, and I'll throw the pieces in the water, and the swans'll come and eat 'em up . . ." Finally he asked us, with voice nearly failing, not to eat any more of the sprats, so the little fishes would come alive again. He believed that put in water they would swim again, for the concept of death is still incomprehensible to him. That came out also in the following event. He ran around the house with his gun and shot everything and everyone dead, but to his mother he said lovingly: "I'll only shoot you a little dead, mummy, just a little—then you can only run slowly." Being dead means for Ernie a decrease in life functions; for instance, no longer running and eating, and being able to speak only very quietly.

By the remark that then mummy "can only run slowly," the child expresses a wish to obtain more freedom for mischief through the lessened hindrance of his mother as soon as she is "shot a little dead" (cf. March 22, 1908).

> May 4. Ernie crushed a fly at the window and is greatly amused over it. Mother tells him of the poor mama-fly that will find her child dead and will cry about it. Ernie then said with choked voice: "If another fly-child comes, I'll leave it" . . . When later he felt a sticking pain in his finger, the little fly-killer with his guilty conscience believed that the mama-fly came secretly and wanted to hurt him because she found her child dead.

Breaking the chronological sequence, I bring here an analogous experience from Ernie's sixth year of life.

> June 28, 1909. Ernie saw a dead fly on the window ledge and pointed it out to us. In contrast to his usual behavior, this sight incited him to catch a fly that was buzzing around and to squeeze it with his fingers till it lay just as still as the other. Looking embarrassed and blushing with a guilty conscience, he told us what he had done. He was scolded and reminded never again to kill an animal that had not hurt him. After a while he pulled secretly at his mother's sleeve, pointed at the dead fly, on which by chance a little was

now crawling, and asked with voice nearly failing because of excitement: "Is this perhaps the baby-fly, and is it crying because it thinks its mother is dead?" His mother agreed seriously, embraced Ernie vigorously, pressed his face against her own in a sudden welling up of tenderness, and tried to control his tears. The destiny of the orphaned fly-child kept him busy for a long time. As the little fly went to the neighboring ledge, he asked if it was now going to look for the daddy-fly or whether he, too, was perhaps already dead. About this we gave him comforting news.

These two experiences show how the occasional death wishes against the mother become the unconscious source of pity and regret.

July 26, 1908. The child's continuing ignorance of the manifestations of death can also be seen in the following. Once again, Ernie was shooting everything dead with his wooden pistol. At the word "dead," the dead occurred to him, for he said: "When we go to the churchyard again, I'm going to shoot dead all the people who are in the graves and have died. They'll hear that, when I shoot them dead and it makes such a noise." On this occasion it was also mentioned that the dead were so fast asleep in their bed, the coffin, that they could never again wake up. Ernie asked if children who are dead also lie in such a "box" and are fast asleep, and, as we agreed: "Can they also make a rumpus there?" When Ernie doesn't want to go on sleeping in the morning, he is in the habit of making a rumpus in bed, so he thought that when the dead children happened not to be sleeping at some time they, too, would make mischief in their beds. Very seriously we told him that it is very bad. When a child dies he never wakes up, and his mother cries a great deal because she no longer has a child. Ernie listened, sighing; this conclusion did not please him. Finally he found a happy solution and called out: "So, the men can shovel the sand away and pull the flowers away from the grave and can sell the little boy to his mother again—so she can have her child again." Of the whole idea of death, visibly by far the most unbearable idea to him was the thought of a child's being separated from his mother and that she would cry.

For the first time, here, there is a clear identification of the dead with the self where the lad spontaneously spoke of the 'little boy' lying in the grave. While the train of thought in the death of the fly-child is actually the same, it does not reach expression in words.

How closely the child's death fantasies are connected with a strong sadistic tendency is shown by the sketches of April fourth and September eighteenth.

September 18. As much as Ernie fears blood on his own body, he loves to think up bloody dramas. Most of the battles that he fights, now with danger-ous animals, now with men, end with his wounding the enemy, from whom much blood flows. Today he became furious with the mailmen who, as he was once jokingly told, would on some night collect all his toys that were lying around and take them to a child who liked to keep things neat. Instead of cleaning up, Ernie rolled his eyes, stabbed wildly at the air with his arms, and threatened: "But I will shoot them dead with my shooting pistol and throw them against the door. And then I'll close the door quickly, and then they'll be completely crushed, and lots of blood will come out."

September 27. On seeing a funeral procession, the boy became upset about the gravedigger who was going to shovel earth over the coffin. He apparently blamed this man for the death, and only with the matter of burying-in-the-earth did he connect the idea of being dead, for now he can already imagine that deep under the earth a person can no longer breathe and live. Very agitatedly he called out: "The old gravers (gravediggers) shouldn't always dig such a grave and put people in it. But I'll get rid of the sand and the flowers and let the people out again. And I'll take the old graver and throw him into the water. And then I'll crawl up to the sky on a ladder and shovel a lot of ice into my bucket—there's a lot of ice up there, you know; the other time lots of ice came from the sky [memory of a recent hailstorm]— and then I'll pour the ice on the bad man's head, and then he'll get a cold, and his nose will be bloody, all bloody, and then the graver will be completely dead, and I'll pour out more and more ice, and he'll be deader and deader."

For the child, being dead continues as a graduated concept that can be interrupted at any time, like sleep. At the same time, killing seems to him a means of punishment, an act of revenge.

November 25. The lad's interest in the mystery of death increases daily. The idea that a person cannot feel and think after death is something completely incomprehensible. The questions recurs again and again: "But what does a man (or animal) say while he is dead?" Because Ernie does not yet comprehend the often cruel and painful part of death, he uses the words "die" and "be dead" quite unconsciously. The same was noticed with Lottie, his cousin, who is a few months older. For instance, she was furious when her father punished her for stubbornness by not taking her along for a walk. Watching him go she said angrily: "Now daddy should die," naturally without having any idea of the significance of these words. Ernie perpetrated a similar breach of sensitivity today when he was in a bad mood because we were going to the theatre. His mother asked jokingly: "What if I never come back?" Fighting back the tears, he replied: "Then I'll tell daddy he should marry a good mother for me who doesn't always run out." His mother asked sadly if this meant she was a bad mother. Here Ernie already regretted his words, and in order to comfort his mother and to put everything right again he corrected himself: "No, mummy, you know, only when you're dead and I'm not yet dead and daddy isn't yet, then daddy should marry another mummy for me." Ernie had also spoken of "other daddies" as something to be taken for granted. One must certainly not see in this any heartlessness on the child's part. On the contrary, he is most tenderly attached to his parents, and, for example, once when his father went away for three days, he cried. When his mother goes out for a few hours, the caresses are endless. The child embraces her and presses her vigorously to himself many times, without a word.

In what follows the Scupins suggest that the parents are themselves responsible for this apparent crudeness, since occasionally when their son misbehaved they spoke of wanting to send him away and fetch another Ernie. Even though that may play a part, the decisive factor for the infantile death wishes against the parents is the thought of getting away from routine regulations or the hope of showing the parents: "If you leave me so often, then I won't care much about you either." It is striking that little Ernst Wolfgang, in contrast to other children, cherishes death wishes against his father much less frequently than against his mother. When one considers that it is in fact she who has many more occasions to interfere when the child is engaging in inappropriate games, then it is no wonder that the wish to remain undisturbed is directed against her.

Again, on December eighth, the child is intensely concerned with death on looking at a picture in which the family does not appear complete to him (based on his observation of his own family). All absent persons are dead for him. He repeatedly names the members of his own family, grandmother, Aunt Olga, etc. Finally the people in the picture and those in reality become so fused for him that he suddenly declares his grandmother dead. A few days later (December eighteenth) he transfers his death fantasies to inanimate objects. Thus, he says to the Christmas tree: "Oh yes, Christmas tree, you're sawed through, so you're dead."

> December 23. The boy was much moved today looking at a picture of a war scene in which one soldier had just shot another. He immediately fetched his gun, placed the opening of the barrel directly on the head of the bad soldier, and pulled the trigger. Breathing easier, he gave vent to his sense of justice: "So now I've shot him dead, too, because he killed the other soldier." He asked: "When one dies, does one just fall down on the spot?" When a bit about the war and war customs was explained to him, he understood that we Germans must defend our land. He fetched his building blocks, some of which are painted red, others blue, and played war. He suggested with the suggestion that first that the reds should kill the blues and then the blues should conquer the reds: "If the reds have already killed the blues, then the blues can't kill the reds anymore," he said quite logically.

In this way, fantasy and reality are fused in the child's mind, where first one and then the other gets the upper hand. In spite of that, the child's concept of death is still unclear.

January 15, 1909. The rubber parrot that was put away for a long time greatly interests the little boy again. He asks if it is really a dead bird. He had thought that the rubber bird had once been alive and was then stuffed like his father's birds. Ernie had often seen the skull on his father's desk, but today for the he asked about it. "Is this a head?" (Yes.) "What is it a head of?" (A person.) "Is the person dead?" (Yes.) "Are these the eyes? They're so big!" (They are the eye holes.) "What was the head's name?" (We don't know that. The person has been dead a very long time.) "Why did the man die?" (Maybe because he was already old.) "Does one die when one is old?" (Yes, all people must die some day.) "Is one in the grave, then?" (Yes.) "But who took the man out of the grave?" (One may have found the head while digging in the earth to build a house.) "Why didn't the poor man become an angel? For here is his head?" Ernie stated a perfectly natural problem. How can a person be in heaven and at the same time part of his body be on earth? Nevertheless, we gave the following explanation (instead of the one generally held to be correct) because he might otherwise get into conflict with the opinion he would soon be given in school. So we said that the man whose head was lying here naturally got to heaven where the good Lord made everything new for him, clothes, a healthy body, and wings. "And a new head?" he asked eagerly. We agreed. "But is the head completely the same?" He meant by this, was the person's face exactly the way it had been on earth so that he could immediately find all his friends and relatives? And in the interest of simplicity, we agreed to this too.

The thoughts of death and dying often lead children to their first doubts of the truthfulness of assertions made by grownups and then lead them to meditate on religious conceptions as they come up incidentally in the environment.

The description of February nineteenth shows how thoughts of death are used in games.

February 19. Ever since Ernie was taken to the cemetery he has let his toy animals die a good deal, in order to be able to wrap them in newspapers and bury them under building blocks. Then he builds an oblong housing in the form of a grave and puts a monument in the form of a cross on it.

Pity for dead animals, whether real or in pictures, increases continually. In the movie theater (June third), Ernie sheds tears as a horse falls dead. His feelings are specially aroused when he can make a transference to his own person, as in the previously described scene of the "fly-child" (June 28, 1909).

The problem of death becomes particularly interesting to the child as he begins to deal with thoughts of whether he himself must die.

June 19. Ernie wants to be an architect. Very often when given a task, he asks if adult architects also perform it. If one says yes, he obeys willingly, because he uses as a model everything that architects do. The lad heard someone say that all people have to die one day. He replied that he didn't want to die. After a while he asked if architects also die. When we agreed, he said: "Well, then I want to, too."

August 21. "When all people are dead, will the earth be removed, and will the architects tear down the houses till there is just grass again, and then will the architects die too?"

On the other hand, "burying" is only a source of purest pleasure (3,9). Here is a report of this.

August 19. We had found five dead newborn rabbits in the woods. The child asked sadly: "Does good animal-lord take the little rabbits into animal heaven, and do they go on living there?" Eventually he was given permission to bury the animals in a cigar box. He shoveled on earth and scattered flowers over it, on his own initiative, and was so delighted that he danced about the grave, jumping for joy.

September 5. A dung-beetle was crawling with difficulty on the floor. Ernie was delighted and wanted to give the "dear beetle" to his cousin, Lottie. But he didn't get far before he put the beetle on the path and stepped on it lightly. Then he picked the squashed beetle up again. "But Ernie, the poor beetle!" "Well, he was crawling on my hand too much, and he made it wet. So I crushed him a little bit dead, so he would lie quietly. When Lottie comes he'll wake up again." Ernie stumbled over stones and roots of trees, but carefully, with love, he carried the dung-beetle along. It surprised him that Lottie didn't share his pleasure in the beetle. For him it was still the "dear dung-beetle," even if he was a "little dead," that is, only a form of being asleep. Ernie was firmly convinced that the beetle would soon crawl vigorously.

So the child who has been thinking about the problem of death for two years still lacks proper understanding. To him "being dead" still means to lie quietly for a while, to sleep, to be away; but always it is in man's power to change it. In this concept, the boy's unconscious finds license to action for his sadism. Cruelty to animals and death wishes against persons close to him appear, in overcompensation, as exaggerated pity for dead creatures and the belief in man's power over life and death.

Innumerable quotations of children's sayings speak for the fact that most children are satisfied with the same solution to the problem of death as the Scupins' little son. I shall give only a few of these quotations. For instance, a "grandma" (11) reports: "Rude is out walking with his governess and his brother, Fritz. They come to a fountain, and Rudi wants to splash around in it all too much. But that is forbidden. 'Well,' he says, 'Fraulein, when you, papa, and mama, and Fritz, as soon as you are all dead, I'll really splash.' "

Perhaps we can see the precursors of such wishes when father or mother is kept out of the child's room by the child's holding the door shut with force. For the proverbial child has only imitation and gesture at his disposal.

The child's egocentric Weltanschauung corresponds to his sense of importance of his own little person. It disguises the tragic when death, even of his parents, occurs in his environment. In spite of the opposition which he cannot completely dispel, he discovers a welcome cause for general attention and sympathy; in short, an abundant and unusual show of love. Hence, the new mourning clothes are of greatest importance for children. Even the funeral loses some of its gloomy character and stamps itself on the mind as both a sad and pleasurable event. Children's sayings document such thinking, as in the following example: "In the Schwarzswald, in the region of B, little boys wear a costume with a red vest. Shortly after Casper received his first red vest, his grandmother died. His father explained that Casper could not go to the funeral in his red vest. "Oh," said Casper, "if I can't put on my red vest, then I won't enjoy the funeral at all" (11, p. 31). As the child gets more experience and is taught certain conventional forms, he believes that he must force himself to express emotions on specific occasions, although they are still foreign to his simple feelings. Here is another nice example from "grandma's" collection: "You know, granny," Toni said one day, "when you die, I'll cry." "Why?" "Oh, that's what one does" (11, p. 56).

Not infrequently children expect that the pain must set in along with certain formalities. Marie von Ebner-Eschenbach (2), in *My Childhood*, tells how the death of her deeply beloved mother and particularly the numb pain of her grandmother at the deathbed had shaken her that morning. She continues: "In the evening we were playing happily in the children's rooms. Suddenly, I understood what had happened and said to my sister: 'Now the best mother is dead. We'll never see her again. Why aren't we sad?' 'Wait a bit,' she replied, 'as soon as the black dresses come, we'll be sad.' "

From a certain age level on, the little ones take it for granted that old people die. They do not hesitate on occasion to ask their grandparents when they are going to die, and they ask the question in such an unbiased way that one cannot be angry. In a recent conversation, my nephew, Max, was boasting to his great aunt that as a machine engineer he was going to earn so much money that we would live in our own house with a huge garden and that we would drive about in a car built by him. When his great-aunt replied: "Bubi, not me any more; by then I will have been dead for a long time," he answered patiently: "Well, then mummy and Aunt Hermine; naturally by then you'll be dead." And another time when Max pushed in close to me as I was reading on the chaise lounge, I called to his mother: "Look, a nice picture, mother and child." "Well, why not? You're two years younger than mummy, so you'll die two years later, and I'll have you two years longer," he said.

Also, "little Anna," whose early mental conflicts are reported by Jung (7), finished off her grandmother's explanation that she was getting older and older and then must die, with a quiet, "And then?" For that child the grandmother's answer, "And then I'll become an angel," developed into a guide in the puzzling subject of the origin of babies. The child replied: "And then you become a little child again?" With the fine logic of childhood she feared, after she was told of the birth of a brother, that the arrival of the newcomer might cause the death of her mother. She put her arms about her mother's neck and whispered hastily: "Well, don't you die now?" (7, p. 4). Here the comforting thought that one person's death is canceled by a new life shows its unfriendly reverse. The childhood fantasy that old people return as little children by way of the intermediate station of being an angel briefly gives a satisfying answer to the question: Where do babies come from? For that reason the child often conceives of the dead as shrunken to the size of infants (7, p. 102). This thought comes from the child's observations in the world around him. Countless times he sees plants, particularly buds, wilting. Just as rarely does his fine faculty for observation miss the fact that bodies of dead flies and worms, etc., dry out, that is, grow smaller.

Beyond that, occasional remarks of adults on religious views support the child's opinion. The dead body's size and weight must fit the strength of the angels that are to take it to heaven.

Outer influences and inner processing of these experiences bring a time in the life of every child when he transfers from the death and dying of others to his own ego. That this awareness is followed by lively rejection is almost the rule. It is explained by the pleasure in being and the life-force of the child. So, according to Sully (10), a three-and-a-half-year-old girl asks her mother to put a big stone on her head as she does not want to die. Asked how the stone can prevent that, she answered: "Because I won't grow up if you put a stone on my head. And the people who grow become old and die." Anxious people already see in the child's concern with death and dying a serious sign of his mental and physical health. They forget that it is precisely the healthy child that can find in every occurrence in his environment a source of joy. So long as health and the joy of life rule in his immediate environment, death is a puzzle whose solution is withheld without becoming too horrible.

As a rule, only older children regard the passing of a beloved person as a horrifying mystery: those who have been constantly reminded of an impending death through a long illness of mother and father, most often where the grownups repeatedly expressed their own fears; those who are frightened by unexpected death; and perhaps also those who have observed particularly deep psychic devastation of their own parents after the death of a beloved person. But even then it is only a vague fear of something unknown that disturbs the mood of the house and prohibits lively play and loud cheerfulness. That this fear—as every other—does not lack libidinal roots is shown by the unyielding adherence of such children to the death complex, which sometimes is maintained into maturity as a special predilection for cemeteries. Bongumil Goltz (5) reports from his tenth year of life:

> With regard to remembering the dead and my feeling in cemeteries, I have changed little if at all since the days of my childhood. At the time of unfortunate war with France, the Haberg and Rosegarten cemeteries looked very much like village churchyards. Except for a few old trees and some massive gravestones or simple fenced burial mounds and crosses, there was no sign of pomp, and therefore also no profane strolling about. Here and there an old person wandered aimlessly or stood, lost in memory. When I saw that, I trembled with feeling, as if I were to dissolve into the atoms of my existence. It was the human pain of earth and death [*Erd- und Todes-schmerz*] that already touched my soul, though still a child. At those graves I developed with pleasure-pains [*Wollustschmerzen*] for my whole life the feeling, the conception of death and the transience of all that is earthly, the destruction and worldly annulment, the consumption of life and the death which is in all life, the nonexistence in all existence and being. And I made it an integral part of myself.

Similar "pleasure plans" are reported by J. C. Heer in his autobiographical novel *Joggeli* (6), where the little hero suffers them in the following way.

> In nature he always had a sanctuary. For a time it was the grave of a Frenchman, found by cousin Diethelm and other peasants on a forest road. As they pushed the skeleton back in, Joggeli put a smooth piece of wood on the grave. Pleased with himself, he looked at the "Rest in Peace" he had written with a red pencil. Convinced that he had benefited the forgotten foreign soldier, he did not fear him, despite his superstitions, but instead considered him as his silent friend. At his resting place in the green forest he spun tales and saw woven there, half from his imagination, half out of the twilight, sentinels of distant wars moving through the forests of their native land. Therewith, something swept through his soul that was as lovely as the waves of green hair in the water, and it was resolved into a game that could occur only to a strange person. He composed epitaphs for dead and living, in which he gave vigorous expression to his affection or dislike for the people of his acquaintance and which, after new impressions, he would improve upon or set a tone lower. When it concerned someone he cared for, then he himself was astonished at the warmth of the words he found for them. He surprised himself with the wish that they might really have died, so that his epitaph might be valid for them. Then he was frightened about himself, with pangs of conscience for something abysmal within himself. But he was not always able to overcome the wishes that emerged like compulsive ideas.

The abysmal source of his pangs of conscience was, in spite of the thoughtful dreaminess of little Joggeli, not very different from the hate-rages of the

"Wlass boy" of Ossip Dymow (1) who says: "As I lowered my head over this notebook, hate for my teacher flared up from time to time, and—as was my wont at that age—I secretly wished his death."

Only on leaving childhood, in the years of ripening and fermentation, does the mind feel the horrifying in death without bowing before its majesty. The rebellion of puberty against that horror remains specially strong in the female sex where, fed by its origin in infantile death wishes against the near and beloved, it builds an unconquerable reservoir of superstition. On the other hand, death will often awaken in the young man thoughts such as the "Wlass boy" had in his fifteenth year: "It always seemed to me that in the matter of death there was something shameful, petty, and blighted, that one had to keep secret from women and particularly from girls. Death seemed a secret of life, like nakedness or some illnesses" (1, p. 126).

When a person has long since found the correct solution to the riddle of life, dying remains shrouded in enterable veils—the unexplorable secret of nirvana.

Appendix

1. Dymow, Ossip: *Der Knabe Wlass* (The wlass boy), p. 61.
2. Ebner-Eschenbach, M. von: *Meine Kinderjahre* (My childhood), pp. 82–85.
3. Ernst, Otto: *Aus Appelschnuts Leben und Taten* (The life and deeds of appelschnuts).
4. Freud: *The Interpretation of Dreams, Standard Edition*, vol. 4, pp. 248–49.
5. Goltz, Bogumil: *Buch der Kindheit* (Book of childhood), pp. 334–35.
6. Heer, J. C.: *Joggeli, Die Geschichte einer Jugend* (Joggeli, the story of a boyhood), pp. 129–30.
7. Jung, C. G.: "Uber Konflikte der kindlichen Seele" (On psychic conflict in childhood), *Jahrbuch f. Psychoan. und Psychopath. Forschgn.* 11 (1910):33–58.
8. Scupin, E. and G.: *Bubi im vierten bis sechsten Lebensjahre* (Bubi from the fourth to the sixth year), 1910. This is the second of two volumes by Ernst and Gertrud Scupin. The first, published in 1907 (second edition, 1933), is *Bubi's erste Kindheit, Tagebuch über die Entwicklung eines Knaben, die ersten drei Lebensjahre* (Bubi's infancy: diary of the development of a boy: the first three years). A third volume by Gertrud Scupin, published in 1931, ten years after her husband's death, is *Lebensbild eines deutschen Schuljungen, Tagebuch einer Mutter* (Picture of the life of a german schoolboy: Diary of a mother). It may be of interest to note that Ernst Scupin was born in 1879, Gertrud Scupin in 1880, and Ernst Wolfgang Scupin in 1904.
9. Storm, Th.: *Von Kindern und Katzen, und wie sie den Nine begruben* (Of children and cats, and how they buried nine), *Collected Works*, vol. 111.
10. Sully, James: *Untersuchungen über die Kindheit* (Studies of childhood), p. 104. (The original is in English, 1896.)
11. *Was Kinder sagen und fragen, mit 26 Zeichnungen von ihnen selbst, gesammelt von einer Grossmama* (What children say and ask, with 26 drawings of their own, collected by a grandmama), Munich: R. Piper.

On First Memories of Childhood (1913)

This paper was first published in *Imago* 2/1:78–88, in the section "Vom Wesen der Kinderseele," that is, "On the True Nature Of the Child's Soul." It was entitled "Über erste Kindheitserinnerungen," or "On First Memories of Childhood." This is the paper's second publication, and the first in English.

It is a curious thing that when grown-ups look back to their youth, they discover in their seventh year the great "black hole of remembering." Otto Ernst called the loopholes and the memory of little Asmus Semper "the black hole of remembering." Behind this dark "nothing of their mind remains but a few clear, sharply outlined pictures remembered within the fog-like chaos of their earliest childhood." These are pieces of curious clarity. The grown-up does not know what to do with this because every connection of these memories with other events has disappeared. As a result he displaces these memories into later years, and he believes they might have had great importance for him. Although the memories do not seem to fit into the later years, these conscious and unconscious errors of memory are not able to rob these "visions" of the clarity of these pieces of cognitive affective infantile life. For some people these "poetic pieces," or memories of childhood, stay into old age and often even replace more recent impressions. However, there are other people, probably the majority, who have preserved very few or no memories of the earliest times of their soul. There are researchers "who appreciate meeting someone who confesses to being unable to remember them and who pursues the revival of earliest memories which have become fashionable." In proving this statement psychoanalytically, we would discover that these people have not really forgotten what was important to them in their childhood, but have only repressed it well into their unconscious. If Compayre says, "It would seem natural for the memory of the beginning of our life to be dark; but truly it is often nonexistent," one can agree from a psychological point of view only with the first part of this scientific opinion. Psychoanalysis gives us the tool to trace back mental happenings into the first years of life. Dreams and uninhibited daydreams lead us back to the time when the soul opened its gates for the first experience of joy and pain. It then became self-conscious by the excitation of the first feelings.

According to Freud's ingenious theory, non-remembrance in adulthood is one of the main reasons for the amnesia of the children. It is caused partly by the great flexibility of the elements of the child's soul. Education and tradition are partly to blame for the deliberate suppression of some thoughts.

The memory of events which should become a lasting treasure of the soul is lost because of their specific character. The judgment of these events by the child, and more so by the adult, occurs under the influence of sexual and erotic feelings. The child lacks any ethical or aesthetic criteria. As soon as the memory of the first infantile cognitive and affective life becomes important, it is expelled from consciousness. It is returned to the unconscious. Such violent suppression frequently affects the memory of sexual feelings. Therefore, an event remains in the memory but the disapproved sexual content becomes forgotten, and instead harmless events appear in the conscious. This creates those pieces of memory which remain unclear and seem to be pure nonsense. They remain like nonsense as long as we do not use psychoanalytic research to correct them.

In his autobiographical novel *Asmus Semper's Youthland*, Otto Ernst reports the earliest memory of his little hero. He sees himself sitting in a white dress on a stair, while his mother is chatting with a neighbor over the upstairs banister. We do not know whether it was satisfied self-love that enjoyed the white dress, or the conversation that was picked up by the little boy with special interest, and hidden in his young soul as a mysterious treasure. It was certainly the affective aspect that made this insignificant event so valuable that he always remembered it. This is followed by another memory in which the erotic connection with the figure of his adored father becomes quite clear. "The next big event that stuck in his memory forever was a haircutter's sink." It hung outside the door to the street. It sparkled miraculously and was the most beautiful thing in the world. One Sunday his father, Ludwig Semper, went to the house with the beautiful sink, carrying his son Asmus on his arm. An extremely talkative man put his hand on Asmus's head, and then spread white foam onto father's face. Whenever this man talked, his father looked at him quietly with his great eyes and said, "Hmmm." The man grabbed his father's nose and scraped off some foam. After leaving the shop, Asmus and his father came onto a square with a very spacious feeling. There were several clean, nice, and well-dressed men there to whom the father spoke. The whole world seemed very nice on this day, because it was Sunday everywhere. Sunday was in the soul of the child because it was his father who "came just after God," and this was the first real love of his young life. To be alone with his father and to have his total and undivided attention was a rare occurrence. In this family which had so many children, it was a special Sunday pleasure for the little Asmus to be alone with his father. Asmus's unconscious jealousy of his siblings was displaced from the disapproved impulse toward the harmless sink, and toward the procedure of shaving. Contributing considerably to this part of the recollection was the childish astonishment that a stranger dared to "wipe foam on his father's face" and to even grab the nose of his God-like father. Things were interrupted by Asmus's mother whenever the siblings treated one another in this fashion. But here this marvelous father underwent the same procedure without complaint! While these memories only hint at the sexual erotic aspect, it is clearer in the earliest memories of Asmus.

He has a memory from his second year of life: "There was a terrible noise and then a great darkness in which I had to cry because I was so anxious. These are my first memories of my childhood in Kaufbeuren. Years later, when I told my mother about this memory, she had to think about it for a long time before she was able to solve the mystery." Once on a winter evening, the little boy had climbed on top of a table and smashed a lamp to the ground while mother was out of the kitchen. In his terror he did what any child would do to get out of a threat—he screamed sharply as remembered by his mother. She saved him from the sudden darkness. In the eyes of a child, a mother always knows how to help.

He has a second memory: "I am freezing but the sun is shining. There are many people around me, I am running fast and my feet hurt. Many people are following me and they are laughing." One March morning when I was three years old, my mother had put me into a bathtub. After being called out of the room, she came back and found the bathtub empty. She could not find me in our apartment. She ran down the stairs, looked out of the door, and a neighbor laughingly shouted: "Mrs. Aktewar, your Ludwig is running naked all over the marketplace." My mother chased me and the people helped her find me. Finally, she caught me outside of town in the Forestry Department where my father worked under Master Thoma." Who knows what endless lust the small child experienced because of his nakedness and its demonstration. He considers how he escaped mother's force while bathing him and how he strove to share such intimacy at an unusual hour with his adored father, who would understand this deed of a little hero. This has remained firmly entrenched in his memory.

Next to the memory of his third birthday party which had taken place with nice music and a merry-go-round and had ended with pain and unconsciousness, Asmus had another memory which he understood because of his profound poetic nature. He wrote, "There is another memory that goes back to my fourth year of life. I do not think I can simply skip it. It helps to answer the question of when the unconscious ideas of sexual relationships arise—or when the child's soul is touched for the first time by the eternal mystery that invisibly but strongly connects mankind.

"My parents were friends with a family who had two daughters, eighteen and nineteen years of age. These daughters filled the house with joy and laughter, and were my two other 'little mothers.' The younger of the two, Theresle, spoiled me. I spent a great deal of time with them. Once I stayed overnight. I don't remember why, perhaps because something happened at home between my parents. At that time they didn't mind the curious eyes of my two-year-old sister, but a four-year-old who was always curious was different. I assume this because I remember a saying from that time about my curiosity: 'The little rascal has eyes in the back of his head.' Around that time another brother, Fritzele, was born, but after a few months forever closed the eyes with which he never had a chance to see the world."

Here two contrasts are mixed together—the mystery that creates life, and death that finishes life. A terrified child's soul trembles between them.

"Theresle kept me overnight and shared her bed with me. I was put to bed in the early evening. When Theresle came later, I awoke and jumped around. I was naughty and made the bed so untidy that my eighteen-year-old friend had to straighten it out again. She put me with the pillows on the floor and made the bed while I lay down there. Then she wanted to pick up something from the lamp table, and stepped over me in her nightgown. An 'innocent' sleeper lying on my back, I was suddenly surprised by a terrifying shock so deep that I remembered it for all my lifetime. When the girl brought me to the freshly prepared bed, I was quiet and trembling. Never again did I let her kiss or caress me. I began to cry whenever she took me in her arms. From this time on for a dozen years, a strong disgust against anything called a girl stayed with me.

"Why do I remember this so clearly while many other things that I should have remembered disappeared from my memory?"

The sensitive soul of a poet gives the correct answer to the critical intellect that wishes to deny the suspicious terror of a child's soul. Children listen to and never discover the mystery of the sexes. Their connections to each other deeply shake the infantile soul and remain hidden in its corners. This feeling of mystery is directed towards the parents, for the little boy toward his mother, the woman. The burning desire of all little boys to solve the mystery using his mother is covered by maliciousness and by pretended clumsiness. Both are tools of the unconscious to discover about the "disapproved." All of a sudden a child sees a woman who is so much more distant than the mother and what he wanted to see from mother. Because of the "clean education the boy received," he had already suppressed such desire. In this situation he experienced only a trembling fear and disgust. Feelings of defense against women cover his soul for years. The only exception is the five-year-old Elsbethle who becomes his companion two years later. He explains: "I didn't see in her anything like in Theresle in the dark." He tells about Elsbethle:

"Initially she had to suffer because of my strong disgust for girls which had remained since my adventure with Theresle. All of a sudden that changed. On a hot summer day we played on a bank of a little river, and I had the idea to cool down by taking a bath. Of course Elsbethle joined me and to my great surprise I recognized that there was not the slightest similarity to the inexplicable darkness of Theresle. It might either be my inherited nature, or a result of my clean childhood education that I always had a strong disgust for anything that was connected with the dirty necessities of the human body.

I realized how much I preferred and enjoyed Elsbethle to the average boy when I discovered that she not only lacked any similarity to the horrible Theresle, but was even made by God more nicely than myself and the other boys. At that time I started to believe that Elsbethle was some sort of ideal creature who had no reason to deal with the inferior functions of life.

"I remember quite clearly that I then experienced something inexplicably beautiful and joyful in my six-year-old brain."

If we admit the role that sexuality plays in the child's life, then we do not need to wonder about the intensity of memories with a sexual character. Among all human drives, no other is so strong and no other is so suppressed in childhood as this one which later provides man with his greatest happiness. It is only natural that these two factors strongly support the memory of everything with a sexual source. Perez reports he remembers well a very rough and dumb nanny he had in his second year of life. She held him out the window and pretended to throw him. We can understand that the little boy experienced a terrible fright. Fear frequently evokes sexual feelings and even erections in boys. One can assume that these are the true causes of the memory. They were suppressed later with disapproval. The woman's roughness was the only thing that was remembered.

Compayre reported about Pierre Loti. He remembers clearly his first attempt at jumping and walking at the beginning of his second year of life. One doesn't have to mention specifically that muscle activity during these efforts is extremely exciting for the child. Ambition and the addiction to be admired are connected with the lustful feeling that is triggered by the stimulation of the muscles used. This double satisfaction of erotic impulses fixate the event in the soul of the child. If a thirty-five-year-old person, as the same author reports, remembers a baptism in her third year of life and a noisy market in Paris, we can assume that the lasting effect of these events was based on specific impressions of a sexual nature. It might have easily happened that the eyes and ears of the child had picked up more from this noisy market than would have been anticipated at this age. In addition, during baptism, a child might perceive rough jokes even if they were barely understood.

A series of loose memories from the earliest childhood is reported by Bogumil Goltz. These memories are quite expressive despite their simplicity. He called these loose memories the "souls of childish memories," according to the poetry of his soul. "They are disappearing memories and reflections in dreams. In such an aesthetic, supernatural way I perceive many pictures and feelings from my earliest consciousness." One of these is to be reported here.

"On a summer night in a mystical and diffused light, I am on my way in an open wagon. I do not know if I am alone or with company. For the first time I have the deeply moral experience of quietness and sleep. The whole world is silent and quiet. Nature dreams. I seem to hear the earth breathing and the little sandhills arise with morning, like the bosom of the night. Its beauty and poetry overcome my senses. Its holy mysteries tremble in my being." The poet identifies the quiet earth as a sleeping woman. This is the identification of the all-mother as an earthbound being, as found in the fairy tales and sagas of every nation. At night whenever he experiences terrifying dreams, the child clings to the bosom of the mother. He realizes the true meaning of the nightly mystery between the parents much earlier than adults believe. These thoughts are recognized as being prohibited. Therefore they are repressed from consciousness and they are linked to unusual events with which they share harmless characteristics. Using this mask they maintain a place in our memories.

At this point I would like to introduce two of my own earliest memories: a big woman with an open shirt, obviously a washwoman, fills my little pots at the well. I like this woman very much. She was a servant in the house of my parents, and she permitted me to play with water. This was strictly forbidden by my parents. It is well known that water play is connected to other necessary functions of a child. Therefore it is one of the preferred activities. It might be that the imposing body of the woman has lastingly impressed me. I cannot imagine a washwoman or servant without these attributes.

The second picture is of my mother sitting with us children in a dark garden hut, waiting for something. This stems, like the previous memory, from my fourth year of life and is linked to the move from the apartment where I was born and where I had been raised up to that point. The walls of the hut were covered with pictures from journals and from this I concluded that my interest in decorating rooms arose in later years. In addition, the earlier picture had some sort of sexual impact on me. Perhaps this is because of the very low neckline of the woman, which is linked again to the above-mentioned memory. However, another affect must play a role. A move, especially the first one, into a new apartment is for all children an exciting experience. Some little deviations from the usual schedule, less strict observation, the discovery of toys and things that have been forgotten, a visit to the attic—all are such new impressions for the child that they give rise to lustful tension and the expectation of something special. Indeed, the expectant waiting in the hut remained solidly in my memory.

It is only natural for the happiness of a child that he remembers unusually joyful events more easily than unhappy ones. However, even those unhappy events quite frequently have lustful characteristics. This is why children and adults have a surprisingly accurate picture of their earliest memories. I speak now of the memories of illness and death of a relative which does not have a lasting influence on the child, or perhaps the death of the father or mother, the day of the funeral will always be remembered. This is because he was conscious of the fact that the family or his small ego was the focus of general attention, and this pleased his child's self-love. An eight-year-old girl vividly remembers the "many cakes" that were given five and a half years ago at the funeral of her grandmother. Two sons of a military officer who lost their father at the age of three or four, preserved until late in their school life a picture of "the many generals in their uniforms who were at the funeral."

As one of her first memories, Selma Lagerlöf remembers the death of her grandmother, who was the storyteller of her first year. "When I was five years old I had a great sorrow. I do not know if I ever had a greater one. This was when my grandmother died. Up to then she had sat on this couch in the corner of the living room every day and told me fairy tales. I did not know life other than grandmother sitting there and telling stories from the morning to the evening and we children sitting beside her and listening to her. This was a happy life. There were no other children who were so well off as we were. I have only a very weak and diffuse memory, so of all the stories she told me, I only remember one clearly enough so I can tell it. It was a little story about the birth of Jesus Christ. My great sorrow when she left is almost everything that I remember of my grandmother. I remember the morning when the couch was empty and I could not understand how I would spend the hours of the day. That I will always remember; that I will never forget. I remember we were led to our dead grandmother to kiss her hand. We were anxious to do this because somebody had told us that this was the only way to thank her for all the joy that she had brought us. I remember how the old fairy tales and songs left our house and were enclosed in a long black coffin, and never came back. I remember that something had disappeared from my life. It was as if the door to a whole beautiful mystical world had been closed. We had been allowed to pass freely in and out of that door. Now there was nobody anymore who knew how to open that door."

Again we find the lustful minor details that are most important for the child and that cause the fixation in memory. The longing for the mystical fairy tales that disappeared with the grandmother and never came back will guarantee the everlasting memory. Equally important factors are candies and gifts, the importance of the family, or the devotion to the father. They even make the dark picture disappear because the child lacks an understanding of death. The child only preserves the happy moments of this overall sad event. Even if he can totally escape the memory of the death as he experienced it, a child cannot be called heartless.

Lagerlöf's memory does not lack the truly sexual and erotic aspects. After forty years she still clearly remembers the little story about the birth of Jesus Christ. One does not have to emphasize that this aspect of birth especially was quite stimulating to childhood fantasies. It contains the mystery of birth and reveals that the newborn of God is a son. This is even more than is normally heard by children. Perhaps this was the first time that the child realized that the woman is the one who gives birth, having concluded this from the words of a man: "My wife has given birth to a child." Such words are engraved on the soul of a child who longs for the truth, because they reveal a little bit of the mystery of creation.

The usual illnesses of childhood play a significant role in the memories of the individual. The statement that the event must have a lustful aspect for fixation does not apply to these examples. To a child, illnesses not only mean suffering but normally they are accompanied by an expanse of love and an increase in intimate care by the parents and other family members. The complete satisfaction of a child's need for love fixates the picture of illness and recovery to the innermost soul. Characteristically, somebody who remembers such events rarely fails to emphasize how the care of the whole family was focused on him, or how mother's bed stayed empty all night long, or how everyone treated him so kindly and nicely during the time of recovery. The lasting importance of serious childhood illnesses is reported by Goltz from his own youth: "Our first memories are normally linked to illnesses from which we have recovered. Therefore I have a dark memory from my second or third year of life where I sat crying on my father's lap while he put a piece of turkey into my mouth whenever I opened it. I lay down by the river Ruhr and longed day and night, sleeping or awake, for a drink of cold water. One day my father came to my bedside and asked in a sad voice 'Do you really want to die?' In those words I heard his love speaking to me, and I will remember them until my death."

Over the years of a lifetime, thoughts and experiences are sometimes mixed into a chaos which can hardly be managed by the aging brain. Events of later years are dated back earlier than those which come later, but the characteristics of our memory of the first events remain unchanged. They even become brighter and clearer with the background of the half-forgotten pictures of our life. It proves that the ability to feel never again reaches the intensity that we experienced in our first years. It seems that the intensity of our feelings is decisive for remembering and forgetting. Childhood memories resemble a glance of a setting sun. They make the past shine brightly in a diffuse light before it is covered by the dark shadows of death.

The memories that remind us later of our disappeared childhood are not always the same ones that were our first memories as children. They appear suddenly and become our reliable companions, or they disappear like comets in the sky. The memories that have been reported from our childhood are mainly lost in the colorful variety of our other memories. They characterize an important step in the development of the child's soul. Intellect and affect begin to work together to create associations and estimate experiences according to the lust or lack of it that was experienced. Fantasy crowns both efforts with its ornaments. Associations which are considered by adults at times as part of a hidden genius and at other times as illustrations of childhood ignorance, occur in this manner. Since most of the innermost functioning of the child's soul is hidden from the realistic eye of the adult, the working of the infantile mind is normally difficult for us to understand. We have forgotten how to orient ourselves in the directions taken by a child's soul. The child lacks the ability to share the secrets of his heart with us. He hides his secrets like treasures in the bottom of his soul as soon as he has become self-conscious because of the pressure of education. Only in very special cases such as increased pleasure, astonishment, or fear will the child allow adults to look into the inner recesses of his mind.

C. and W. Stern report about their first son Gunther: "At age five years, five months, Gunther slept in his parents' bedroom on the night following a tonsillectomy. When he awoke he was in an excellent mood because of the unusual comfort. He remembered spontaneously events of the last three of his mother's birthdays." Children like family celebrations so much that the memories are evoked with very little initiation. The increased joyfulness is always an integrating characteristic of these holidays. Besides candies and trips, children are often allowed minor deviations from normal rules without fear of consequences. The child views this as one of the main stimuli of holidays. In addition, the hearts of adults are more accessible for intimacy and respect at these times. Because of this unusual extension of love, celebrations are vividly engraved in the child's soul. Of these, Christmas memories clearly predominate, even if the young child's impression of his first Christmas is temporary astonishment. Christmas remains important although the memories of the recurring festivities may become mixed and sometimes stay unclear. The feeling of loneliness adults experience whenever they happen to be far away from their home and family during Christmastime, proves how deeply these evenings full of love and brightness have influenced the child's soul.

Besides experiences characterized by increased love and attention, events of a clearly sexual nature, in the widest sense of the word, play a leading role in the first memories in childhood as well as in adulthood.

With regard to love, we find a very interesting example in Stern's notes. At age three years and one month, Hilde remembers an event that happened five months previously. After watching mother wash the upper part of her body, Hilde asked, "Is this where the milk comes from?" It was four and a half months since her little brother had been breastfed, and Hilde had no occasion to witness breastfeeding in the meantime. The jealous behavior of breastfed children towards an assumed rival clearly illustrates that the child instinctively understands breastfeeding as a loving act of his mother. Even after infancy the child unconsciously remembers a true memory of the lust given to him by a motherly breast, not only as a source of food but also as a sexual experience. This is why the appearance of a female breast remains stimulating for years without a child being conscious of the reason.

Sexual feelings cause a memorable and astonishing effect. Tiedmamn reports on his son, at the age of one year and eleven months: "On July 20th he came to a place into our home where he had been punished four weeks earlier because he had made a mess. Immediately he said that whoever messes up this room would be spanked. This idea was not clearly expressed but clear enough to be understandable. Obviously he had memories of that earlier time." A child knows how to signal certain bodily needs. By delaying defecation, he acquires a lustful gain from the comfortable tension in his erogenous anal and urethral area. Even the punishment of a weak spank on the neighboring place of the body causes new lust in a masochistic disposition. This could be sufficient to fixate this material in the memory.

Even if they are not verbally explicit, clear memories of experiences are shown in some of the children's games, for example, the widely popular "doctor game." One cannot deny its anal-erotic character. The other example is the "father and mother" that the child uses to express his perception of his parent's relationship.

It is remarkable that children often immediately forget people and animals to whom they had been very attached, but spontaneously remember them later. We are not wrong to assume a deliberate unconscious suppression in this case, which is later allowed into consciousness for external or internal reasons. In the diary-like notes of G. and E. Scupin about the development of their son, they report that in his second year the little one was very attached to a white rabbit but had completely forgotten about it after he was separated from it in his twenty-eighth month. Therefore he could not remember anything about it when he was asked by his parents at the end of his third year. As late as the tenth month of his fourth year he remembered spontaneously. What are the reasons for this remarkable behavior? During the time that the rabbit lived with the family, little Ernst Wolfgang reported all of the animal's mishaps with pretended indignation, especially after spoiling or damage to furniture and wallpaper. Because at that time the little boy himself experienced the occasional mishap, one might have expressed some misgivings about their origin and some either serious or joking remark might have been made. This would have been enough for the child's sensitive soul to suppress everything from his unconsciousness which might have reminded him of the embarrassing events. When he had developed far enough to overcome this practice, the suppressed memories were freed. Thus the apparent forgetfulness of the child exactly parallels that of the adult, and has its origin in a need for self-defence. The child does not want to remember an event because of the intense embarrassment it would cause.

The human's ability to remember is an absolute prerequisite for education. An intense study of memory stemming from early childhood days would give us a valuable tool by which to understand the origin of children's mistakes and oddities. These are curious and sometimes cannot be explained either in children or in adults. Unconsciously connected to the earliest memories of those close to the child are acquired habits which he stubbornly refuses to give up. As long as he himself does not know about the internal connection, this remains in effect. This is why I cannot agree with researchers such as Preyer, who think that attention to the first memories is a useless experiment. Supported by the recall of these memories, one could prevent some deviations in character development. The conversation of earliest childhood impressions would also facilitate the treatment of the mentally ill by the psychoanalytic physician. He would find himself already well prepared for what he is presently searching endlessly.

The Nature of the
Child's Soul (or Psyche) (1913)

This paper was a brief overview that appeared in the journal *Sexual probleme* in 1913 (9:433–43). It appeared under the same title that was to become the title of Hug-Hellmuth's section on child psychology in the journal *Imago* that same year.

Everyone agrees that to study the child's soul is to deal with the most pleasant of subject matter. The material for study presents in ever-changing forms a full variety of pictures, appearing like a kaleidoscope to the observer. If the child has any interest in the environment, then all stimuli leave an impact on the developing soul. His interest is reflected in his face. We see astonishment, fear, joy, and pain. The entire small ego of the child takes part in this vivid kaleidoscope of colors. The child's body and soul are busy coping with all the new stimuli that come from the environment. These environmental stimuli, these sensations themselves, may become a source of lustful experience. As stated by Compayre, "The progressive and moderate exercise of perception is as lustful as the satisfaction of organic needs." To waste this "exercise of perception" is as uncomfortable for the child as it is for the adults.

Soon, from this chaos those sensations which are suitable are separated. They are suitable because of their quality, their strength, or their frequency. If they are separated out because of their similarity, they become decisively important for the affective life of the child. Community and family celebrations have a special dominating influence on a child's soul. Living far away from family and friends, an adult suffers most from his loneliness at Christmas. Such a person feels a strong need to join a similar person for company. All of this has its roots in the memory of those hours just preceding the celebration, with their secrets and joyful expectations. Naturally, no child likes sad experiences. Such shadows of sadness are usually temporary and rarely influence his soul; a prevailing joyfulness is protective. However, they might leave memory traces that become important in the further development of the child. Those happy and sad experiences form the cornerstones of the individual's memory and are joined by other recollections. These recollections seem to be separated from the whole without any connection. The adult does not remember very clear. Psychoanalytic research, the brilliant creation of Professor Freud, recognizes in such memories the valuable cornerstones from which one is able to reconstruct the past of an individual.

Although the construction of memory in different individuals develops in different ways, and it is expressed in different styles, the elements themselves are similar. This was discovered in people who undergo psychoanalysis. First this was discovered during the psychoanalytic treatment of the mentally ill. Then it was seen that the mental life of healthy persons is composed according to the same rules. Their fantasies are very similar to those seen in "nervous" and other mental disorders. However, they differentiate the ill by certain characteristics and separate the ill from the normal individual. Such memories lead back in different ways and along different paths to the area of sexuality and to the early years of childhood. This causes many concerns and many people anxiously avoid such knowledge. Some people believe that their own inner life and the inner life of others are spoiled by this understanding. How could two terms like *early childhood* and *sexuality* be connected without losing the "sweet breeze of innocence and virginity?" Those who identify sexuality simply with the drive for reproduction will not understand. We are forced to broaden that narrow border with our knowledge of psychoanalytic theory. Then we understand the child's almost unbelievable need for love in its positive and negative aspects. We understand both the intimate embrace and the temporary explosion of passionate hatred as expressions of infantile sexuality. In addition, sexuality explains a child's burning curiosity and thirst for knowledge. It is a strong drive to discover the mystery of the life of the adult. Further, when one has understood modern psychoanalytic research which does not deny the realities, a great deal about nature is disclosed. When one sees the numerous embarrassments that are tolerated by every child, and when one sees the things that are suppressed by adults with words and gestures of disgust, the sexuality is obvious to the observant individual. The nonprofessional would not be so disgusted if he did not unconsciously assume a sexual connection! Nevertheless, a child is still considered to be asexual. As the drive develops, one can lose his sexuality without psychological sequelae, yet people resist the sight of its development.

Everyone realizes that the child's intellectual and affective development begin immediately in the first few weeks of life. Parents report with incredible pride on the intellect and affect of their own children, and express jealousy about other children. However, the sexual aspect that already plays an important role in the life of the little one in various ways is only touched upon with embarrassed or anxious concern.

Psychology overlooks the expression of infantile sexuality and restricts itself even today to detailed observations of the development of the intellectual and affective forces in early or late childhood. The numerous learned papers in the field of children's language do not give us any insight into the growing vocabulary as it is influenced by the child's interest in his own body functions. The little one does not know shame nor disgust. He does not stop his thoughts and fantasies whenever he expects to experience something lustful. Defecation and food intake are equally lustful, and this is why the child's first words are linked with both of them. Memory and imagination are

formed first on the basis of erotic and sexual f
infantile speculation, Where do babies come f
early on. In the beginning it is expressed qu
later into a general curiosity under the pressu~ ~. ~.. ,
turn into a drive for discovery that tries to understand the internal life of
everything. In the end it might culminate in a well-known need for destructive anger.

Children's games have an obviously sexual, erotic aspect. The boy's pleasure in fighting for no apparent reason has this as a cause. In addition, playing
with dolls takes place when children show the first signs of being like a caring
mother. Even the smallest child does not lack these signs. Their activities
show an unconscious longing for sexual satisfaction. It has been well known
for a long time that the child experiences a strong sexual pleasure when
sucking his own body. This is seen in their face with the accompanying facial
expression of pleasure. In his first year the infant succeeds instinctively at
experiencing his lust out of all the manipulations that are necessary for his
body care.

Mothers and nannies know that masturbatory activity, especially in boys,
occurs early. Sometimes it occurs during the first months. It is frequently
triggered by the mother's cleaning activities. The child discovers these very
sensitive areas while playing experimentally with his own body. Frequently
infantile masturbation disappears during earliest childhood, due to the pressure of education as it tries to establish the borders that are the basis of later
cultural demands. These are shame, integration into the family, and the
toleration and acceptance of others' rights and wishes. During this time the
child works very hard, devoting his intellectual efforts to suppression. He is
also rebellious against suppression. He develops hatred and jealousy whenever he cannot discharge his feelings through open anger. The only difference
between children and adults is that these feelings are more obvious in children. Whenever the child rebels against suppression, one often finds a strong
stubbornness. This is difficult to understand for somebody who is not knowledgeable about the secrets of mental activity. A child will deliberately stop
playing a game that he has enjoyed earlier. He will neglect a toy that he has
longed for as soon as he gets it.

Parents are astonished by these "moods" and do not understand them.
They do not realize the real reasons for these decisions. The child experiences
a greater gratification from the spontaneous renunciation than from acceptance. This is because of two reasons: consciously he upsets the parents and
hurts them; and, secondly, he forces himself into the pain of deprivation.
Thus the mental states of sadism and masochism are satisfied at the same
moment. This is not only the sophistication of the adult, but it is a daily
exercise in the child. The child understands from early on how to proclaim
himself as a judge and educator of his parents. Refusal to eat, as well as

refusals associated with the other bodily needs, are frequently assumed to be "purely nervous." However, all of this has a meaning and according to psychoanalytic theory stems from the unconscious. Such so-called bad habits are a superb tool for the child to achieve increased love and care from his environment as soon as he feels neglected and rejected, such as the feeling stimulated by the birth of a sibling. Simulation of illness, loss of appetite, and sleep disturbance demand increased attention from the parents. This is linked closely to numerous signs of affection.

The environment suffers and those who produce these moods suffer. These are signs of hysterics and of neurotics. Therefore it is remarkable that laymen call them "childish." Indeed, these adult parents behave like children, reproducing their own youth by expressing infantile wishes and desires in a new, age-inappropriate form. Wishes which have not been fulfilled earlier and thus had to be suppressed, reappear. This is the very reason the neurotics express their present wishes so strongly and are so upset whenever they are not satisfied. Their wishes from infancy have survived in their unconscious. They continue to long for satisfaction in various forms.

Manners and tradition do not limit the freedom of this small ego despite the passage of years. Traces of the affective life of the child are left. The more they hurt a sensitive soul early on, the more serious are the consequences and the less they are compensated for later by the love and grace of the parents. This is why people who reject others with their cold and cynical character, suffer most themselves from their hidden, unsuccessful longing for love. This is a consequence of a childhood lacking in love. Those who have been betrayed in this manner will never find full compensation during their lives. The spoiled single child or the favorite child might measure love differently. They might suffer more from the harshness of life, but they will never live with an empty heart like the neglected and rarely loved child. A deficit in love during childhood cannot be compensated for by later attachment. The loneliness of the child's soul resembles a fruit that a worm has destroyed from inside, while leaving its surface looking immaculate.

The ability to love and the longing to be loved have their roots in sexuality in children. "Common sense," which normally calls things by their right name, says that the little boy is "in love" with his mother whenever he behaves accordingly. Similarly, the girl "marries" her father. These are the same expressions that are used for the erotic relationships of mature adults. No one will deny the parallel once he has seen the thousand tricks a child uses to get attention or cling to a loved person. A child learns to love in his first years. To be his teacher in this most sophisticated period of life is the sacred duty of his parents. By succeeding in this period of life they have done more for their child than by accumulating money and property, or by collecting lifeless knowledge. These activities lead the children only to external achievement and honors, but never to internal happiness.

The more the child experiences love in his childhood, the more likely good will develop later. It will be easier to avoid bad manners. Nearly all childhood disorders have at least one of their roots in false relationship between a child and his parents. The thoughts and desires disapproved of in childhood appear transformed in the adult. They sometimes cannot be discovered easily. Only the dreams of the child reveal the infantile wishes in all their clarity—to those who understand the language of dreams. These dream wishes might be a prohibited curiosity or exhibitionism. They might disclose angry and hostile impulses against parents and siblings because of rejection and jealousy. The poets who never lose the genius of childhood assume this connection. Naive people often do the same with their simple feelings. Bogumil Goltz said in his *Book of Childhood,* "The dreams of children can provide you with the most interesting material to understand the symbolic meaning of dreams. If only the philosophers would not forget their own childhood dreams while sleeping and being awake!"

Many questions move and disturb a child's soul. The mystery of life with its miraculous beginning and ending can become vivid in the day and night dreams of the child. They are vivid in the curious figures that we meet again and again in the dream symbols, and the sagas and fairy tales of all nations. These observations might even help discover a new relationship between child development and common sense. Fairy tales for a child, as well as sagas and myths for the more mature mind, contain an unexplorable magic due to the directness and primitive form of thinking. This is the basis of all true characters in fairy tales. They resemble so closely the child's perception of God and the world. No horror or terror is too great to disgust the child's soul. Their inherited sadism is the source of all conquest and victory. This is fully reflected in the individual as long as he has not learned to control his natural cruelty. It is still vivid once the sadistic component has found its compensation of justice and pity.

The child and whole nations interpret impregnation and birth similarly. In his first consideration of the origin of being, the child's mind assumes that men as well as women are able to give birth. He becomes disturbed about the contribution of the father as soon as it is explained. He becomes disturbed that the mother has exclusively acquired the role of giving birth. This thinking is also seen in the original stories and the oldest sagas about the origin of mankind. They resemble childish beliefs about impregnation and birth: the humming of the wind, the eating of a fruit, or the drinking of a miraculous drink. These are the assumed sources of new life, with birth following by the natural act of excretion.

The parallels between individual and mass beliefs are also evident in the child's understanding of death and dying. It is neither unnatural nor miraculous to a child that the fairy-tale hero starts out for a new triumph as soon as the gracious fairy has kissed him, or that the princess awakes under the kiss of an adventuresome knight from her hundred years of sleep, or that the little girl and her grandmother escape undamaged from the belly of the bad wolf. For the child, "being dead" means only lying down like during sleep, or being distant. These states are dependent on the will of man. Because of the absence of a person, the child feels allowed to perform some prohibited things undisturbed. That is why "death wishes" against relatives occur so often in little children. With the slowly growing understanding of the true meaning of death, these wishes are banished into the deepest recesses of the soul. Of all the children's stories that prove this fact, I am only going to refer to one from E. and G. Scupin. They were the sensitive authors of a diary about the mental development of their boy, called Bubi, in his fourth to sixth years of life. They report freely and openly how little Ernst Wolfgang in his fifth year didn't care to use the words *dying* and *being dead* and how he played occasionally with thoughts about the death of his parents. He spoke very naturally about "other papas and mamas." They reported further, "We observe the same with Lottchen, Bubi's cousin who is two months older than Bubi, who observed her father. He had not taken her out for a walk as a punishment for her stubbornness. Quite naturally, she said, 'Now Papa is to die,' without any understanding of the true meaning of her words."

During childhood the world seems to be filled with miraculous gracious and angry gods who represent father and mother, and have great power and strength, helpfulness and tenderness. Religious beliefs and habits have their origins in these imaginations. The nation sacrifices the best of its "flocks" to the Gods and it brings this harvest as a sacrifice for reconciliation, praise, and gratitude. The child tries to calm his parents by deliberate submission. He asks for the promise of fulfillment of his wishes. He knows that his love and affection are the best compensation that mother can get for her commitment. Prayers for the individual, as well as for the primitive tribe, are because of the fear of the power of the more potent on earth and in heaven—combined with the feeling of one's own helplessness.

In the early fantasy life of all of humans, the idea that a child might marry father or mother, brother or sister, plays a very important role. If the existing marriage has ended by the death of one of the parents, the wish of the little boy or girl to marry mother or father seems to be especially natural and lustful. Countless childhood wishes are only variations of this, and are not considered to be something monstrous. We find in the sagas of all nations the fear of incestuous and libidinal wishes for near-relatives. In addition, we find a desire that the hero will be punished for his sin by dishonorable death or insanity. In this way tradition and education protect children from their incestuous wishes by repressing them into the unconscious. This occurs at first during childhood. It occurs again during puberty when these wishes reappear. During puberty these wishes are sublimated and displaced to another love object. If this does not happen successfully, during puberty we are left with individuals who lack the strength of will to free themselves from their parents. They feel an inextinguishable guilt because of their strong childhood desire to discover the mystery of their parents. This is similar to the desecration of holy places or habits. These are the "unforgivable" sins.

Therefore, the individual in his sexual development and in his sublimation has to go the same way that has been followed by generations in thousands of different variations. This applies to the unfolding and maturation of his other gifts. The very observation of the development of the child's soul teaches us to understand humanity. It also enables us to better understand an individual's deviations from the accepted laws of thinking and feeling.

Children's Dreams (1913)

The following paper (*Internationale Zeitschrift für Ärztliche Psychoanalyse*, 5/1:470–75, 1913) continues Hug-Hellmuth's earlier paper on a dream of her 5½-year-old nephew, and she explicitly refers to this paper in the beginning of the article. This was her second article during the first year of publication of this journal. Again she opens this paper interpreting a dream by her nephew and then continues with the interpretation of a dream that has been supposedly given to her by a "lady," which is not described any further.

I have already written about two dreams of my little nephew Max in the *Zentralblatt für Psychoanalyse*. Recently, upon awakening one morning, he told his mother a dream of four parts. Then he repeated an unchanged description of the dream to me a few hours later.

1. "There are two round tables and on the top of one stood the 'magic lantern' and other apparatuses that you have."

2. "There were a number of cigarettes that were like a whole bunch of men. They were dressed in white. You know, that was the white paper. Everyone had eyes, a mouth, a nose, and hair. There was a lot of tobacco that was hanging out, and that was the hair. I knocked them over with my sleeve and they fell down the steps. A few broke in the middle, and a few rolled themselves up into balls."

3. "A very long train drove by with many people in it. Aunt Bertha was also inside it. It is the train to Wörishofen, and I even saw the train station and the sign 'Wörishofen'."

4. "Again I saw many cigarettes. However, there were also lots of women with red-checkered housecoats. They were tangled up with one another and they couldn't move. I tried to pull them apart but it wouldn't work because they were all tangled up. Then they fell over the steps and their housecoats tore so that they were half naked; (then, after a little while,) . . . I could see the shoulders of some of them, the arms and breasts of others, as well as the whole body," he said, making a wide gesture.

What is the interpretation of the dream? Without any urging, the little boy himself led in the understanding of the dream. In his understanding he said spontaneously that the white paper of the cigarettes was like the clothing of the men and that the tobacco that was hanging out was the hair. As he paused while reporting on the fourth part of the dream, his great-aunt said at that time, "Well, now he is making it up a bit." He answered to this, "Oh no, it really was like that. It often happens that you forget the most important thing, and then one must say it afterwards." The significance of little Max's contributions to the different parts of the dream points to the focal point of the dream. It seems that the first three parts are only an introduction to the main part, namely, the fourth. Since this boy's third year of life, naked female bodies have been the focus of his greatest interest. He was hardly two years old when he would lie down on the floor and try to look under the skirts of his nannies. He would be terribly happy when he got his way and he would say "hout," meaning skin that was not of the hands and the face. At the same age it was a great pleasure for him to watch little girls on swings, under which he would lie down flat on his back. At the age of three he had the chance to see a nine-year-old girl who locked the two of them into a bathroom. On this occasion he saw her naked and this impressed him greatly. At the same time his mother heard him as he propositioned a girl of the same age: "Erna, show me your behind and then I'll show you mine." This was a proposal for them to expose their genitalia to each other. This desire still continued when he was six years old, but by then he wanted to see a greater number of people. The maid was sick with influenza for a few weeks and complained especially of stomach and bowel pains. She was examined by a doctor. Max asked her in kind tones, promising her everything she wanted, to tell him where the doctor had examined her, where he had needed to expose her, etc. Finally Max suggested to his aunt, who was also sick with influenza, that she needed cold-water treatment, and then gleefully remarked: "Yes, yes, let us put you to bed. The doctor and I will do it." Lastly, a game of tag he played should be mentioned. He changed the rules of this game according to his own purposes. As a little boy he would slide and jump on all fours in the room and his aunt would have to catch him and he would try very hard to get between her legs and throw her skirts up in the air. This apparently harmless trickery was a way for him to satisfy his desire to see things. This was quickly discovered because he could not yet be devious. When he was told that he was no longer to do this, he excused himself by saying, "Oh, but I don't really look." His temporary love for dolls also comes from this desire to see something of the female body. At the age of three years he took great interest in two dolls he received, and his interest focused on the female doll. He asked his great-aunt to give him new doll clothes. He was very disappointed when he was told that any new clothes had to be put over the other ones since these dolls could not be undressed. Two years later he asked for a doll for Christmas that could be undressed completely. He said, "Otherwise I wouldn't get any enjoyment from it." This little boy's wish was obviously caused by something other than a drive for activity.

The reference to the "magic lantern," which was a Christmas gift from his continually absent father, represented a return of experiences from the day before. He likes this gift not only because of its cute pictures but specifically because of the proof of his father's love it provides. He begs us often to show it to him. All other apparatuses "on the table" are the belongings of his aunt with whom he plays occasionally. They are activated sometimes to his great pleasure. He loves to make sparks with the electric broom. Most importantly, his aunt devotes all her time to him so that he really feels like a "special" person. His desire for love is insatiable. The "two round tables" are related to a small joke. A few days before the dream, he slid on the wooden floor in the room and was close to crying because he had crushed some cardboard houses. To calm him, I built him a village out of the leftover homes, which were then destroyed by "an earthquake." In this way his grief was quickly forgotten. Probably the two round tables signify nipples. In addition, this also represents the memory of the primitive double-seated country toilet that he saw often when he stayed in N.

The "cigarettes" find their origin in a type of chocolate cigarette whose wrappings were decorated often with the heads and figures of men. That is why they also appeared to him as men. Whether the white suits bring back the memories of his father's white underwear is only an assumption. It is also possible that the little one is impressed by his own image in his white underwear, as this makes him appear like a real man. This is in contrast to the grey underwear he usually wears. When in his white underwear, he likes to present himself to the family with the remark, "Now I look like a man." At the same time this opinion is in accordance with the above-mentioned statements.

"There was a lot of tobacco that was hanging out and that was the hair." Besides this meaning which the boy has found himself, there is probably also a displacement from below to above. The tobacco might represent his own penis which, especially earlier, he liked to show very much. It is also possible that when he went to bed with his nanny he touched her pubic hair. This would be an explanation for his disgust of actual hair. It this supposition is true, this would mean that the second part of the dream is a preparation by the unconscious for a realization of a daytime wish which becomes true in the last part of the dream. "I knocked them over with my sleeve" shows that the cigarettes may represent a penis that can stand up, yet through the sleeve, i.e., the underwear, it can be squashed. Also he allows himself in his dream to put his sleeves on the table, which is normally forbidden. He often knocks over drinking glasses and this is a great disappointment to his aunt. "They rolled over the steps. A few are broken in the middle and a few have curled themselves up into balls." This shows anal eroticism. The "rolling off" refers to toilets which one can flush to "roll off" feces. The breaking of cigarettes as well as the rolling together of balls shows his intense interest in defecation.

The train plays as important a role for him as for other children. He still hopes to get more cars for his train so that the train will look more like a snake. Unconsciously, this is understood to be a symbol of the phallus. I am certain of this because during a game he will not leave this train alone but pulls it everywhere with his hand—a transfer of masturbatory activity. "There was a train to Wörishofen and Bertha was also in it." With this statement the dream comes one step closer to the desired wish. Little Max has heard from his Aunt Bertha about the spa where she went yearly in Wörishofen which we also saw in the dream. He has heard about the spa and has seen photographs of people, especially women, walking in the water and he was excited especially by their naked legs. In this dream his desire to see a naked female is clearly expressed. The strong need for suppression in his waking state can be seen by the degree of masking in the dream. He clearly recognizes the station and the sign "Wörishofen" because the fulfillment of his desires is more likely in the relaxed atmosphere of a spa rather than in a big town. Also the "many people in the train to Wörishofen" have their own meaning in the dream. In Wörishofen where there are so many people who are not properly dressed, there would be greater chance to finally see something, and it wouldn't be prohibited as something horrible.

"Again I saw so many cigarettes, however, there were also lots of women with red-checkered housecoats." The dream points even more closely to his wishes. He changes the men in the second part of his dream into women whom he dresses in these housecoats. I often played with Max as a young boy while wearing a red housecoat. In addition, his favorite coat was checkered. The "checkered" points to a bolero-jacket which he was always very eager to pull tight on me so that he could feel my body. Whenever I was dressing and I would have trouble or fumble trying to get into the sleeves of the dress, Max would come running to help me out, again with the hidden desire to see or touch something. In the dream, this tangle of clothing gives him the opportunity to see something tangled together. Obviously he remembers in the dream, that he saw two dogs "playing" the previous day in the street. Even though he did not understand the remarks and laughter of the people going by on the street when it was impossible to separate the dogs, he still must have had an idea that something sexual was going on, and that it was not quite proper for a child. Hence the statement in his dream "I tried to pull them apart but it didn't work because they were so tight together." At this point his facial expression shows a streak of sleeping sadism in him. "Then they fell also over the steps and rolled down and the housecoats tore so that they were half naked." The word *also* provides a bridge to the apparently asexual part of the second dream. That he would see the falling over the steps as a symbol of coitus does not seem likely to me because he never slept in the bedroom of his parents. Because of what some other authors have written about the mental development of children, I feel much more that this rolling down the steps is a show of muscle development at that age. The unceasing climbing up and down, as Shinny describes in her paper, remains psychologically unexplained if one doesn't recognize that muscle activity is a source of sexual excitement for every child who is physically normal. Of course the expression "rolling down the steps" is to be understood as "jumping down the steps," and he uses the meaning literally in the second part of the dream. "The housecoats were torn so I saw them half naked" shows both desire and fulfillment in the dream. Step by step this dream reveals that which was disapproved of during the daytime. Starting with only harmless pieces of body, the shoulders and arms, finally the whole body is discovered. The boy's knowledgeable smile tell us: "See, it doesn't matter anyhow, I saw you naked."

A lady told me once about a dream that her seven-year-old son reported. Two brothers, Fritz and Hans, were going into grade one in a private school. Both liked a particular young teacher very much, especially Hans. He was jealous of all his co-students but especially of his brother. Many times during this year, Hans dreamed a particular dream: "Franz is sick and he must stay at home. I must go alone to school."

From this dream his mother believed that he wanted simply to stay away from school. In fact, the meaning was completely different. This dream happened regularly on Wednesday nights. It was the next day that they had gymnastics in which this special young teacher would provide some physical help. Hans wanted his brother to be excluded from this proof of affection because he knew that if his brother wasn't there he would get his turn more often. That is to say, the more students who are absent, the greater his chances are of his beloved teacher's touch. Every time that happened it would send a wave of good feelings over him. At the same time in the dream he wished that something bad would happen to his brother because his brother stole some of this love from him.

This is a common dream that appears in many varied forms. It is very typical for schoolchildren who have strong feelings for a teacher to exhibit all the happiness and the sadness that adults also show. The dream gives the child the freedom to get rid of his dangerous rivals through fantasy. They might be the real or assumed favorites of his teacher. Fantasy lets them get sick, stay away, be late, or make mistakes that are disapproved by the teacher. The majority of the children are absent from the lesson because in this way the decreased number of students give those present a greater chance to be closer to the teacher. This interpretation has been supported by active teachers who say that the children who are present are in very good spirits and are very eager to earn whenever another student is really missing. I have noticed too that even at university there is an excitement which seems to be unexplainable like just before Christmas or at the end of a semester, when there is an occasion where a minimum of students is present, resembling the famous "tre faciunt collegium" . . . The great excitement that is experienced when the professor walks in exists because it is a souvenir of the desire that arises out of our childhood.

Mother Love (1913)

This small paper served as an introduction to an article
by Spielrein about unconscious dreaming in a novel by
A. Kuprin (*Imago* 2:524–25, 1913) and deals with the
unconscious motives of an openly expressed wish of a six-
year-old girl. It follows a review by Hug-Hellmuth (*Imago*
2:521–23, 1913) of the story of "Liddy" by Claire Henrika
Weber in *Zeitschrift für Jugenderziehung und Jugendfürsorge*
3 September 1912, Zürich), which has not been included
in this volume.

The mixture of independent contribution, anticipatory
commentary and formal introduction resembles her introduction of the column on child psychology "Vom wahren
Wesen der Kinderseele" when it was introduced in 1912.

This paper is listed in Grinstein's index but not in
Graf-Nold's biography.

A six-year-old girl asked to have her little brother in her bed. "Mother,"
she begs, "I want to enjoy his beautiful little body." The girl was very strictly
raised and she did not have any idea of sexual matters. This is an example
of the "motherly feeling" of a big sister toward the "body." We might assume
that the little brother also feels very comfortable being stroked by his sister.
Obviously a memory of such an event would leave a trace in our unconscious.
It is not unlikely that the first "bodily love" of the adult makes use of these
infantile memories. The tender touch of a loved woman is compared with
the original, the former touch by her sister. Finally, this compares with the
original touch of the mother. Again, we have to acknowledge a use of infantile
experiences. Neurotic phenomena do not seem to be strange anymore. Being
strongly fixated to the mother would cause great resistance against any object
of sexual love. The fact that any woman would evoke the former picture of
the mother would be consciously or unconsciously avoided. Even if the
picture of the mother doesn't become conscious without analysis, this is an
effective reaction to the continued existence of fantasies of incest. These are
feelings of disgust, shame, and fear.

The following report of S. Spielrein exists among others to prove that early
memories which are repressed from consciousness continue to exist to evoke
uncomfortable feelings.

Children's Misdemeanors and Naughtiness (1913)

The *Internationale Zeitschrift für Ärztliche Psychoanalyse* was founded in 1913, and Hug-Hellmuth was a regular contributor until 1921. She published some of her important papers here; she answered here (*Internationale Zeitschrift für Ärztliche Psychoanalyse* 1/3:52–56, 1915) Bleuler's devastating review of her paper on color-hearing (*Zeitschrift für Psychologie und Physiologie der Sinnesorgane* 65:1–39, 1913) and wrote a total of eighteen book reviews between 1913 and 1920 that are listed in Grinstein's *Index of Psychoanalytic Writings*. Together with *Imago*, the *Internationale Zeitschrift* had therefore become the most important journal for Hug-Hellmuth's publications.

Like her papers on children's dreams before this article ("Kindervergehen und Kinderunarten" [Children's misdemeanors and naughtiness], *Internationale Zeitschrift für Ärztliche Psychoanalyse* 4/1:372–75, 1913) follows the pattern of loose anecdotal reports of children's behaviors that are then interpreted using the psychoanalytic theory of those days. As with the dream papers, there is no inherent organizing principle to this paper that would help to identify the particular message of this publication.

Shortly after his fourth birthday my nephew rushed to his nanny with a happy smile while she was setting up the table for breakfast in the garden. He told her, "I have cut up mother's new dress." The girl thought he wanted to tease her and would only follow him when he insisted. She found it was true. Three or four long cuts had destroyed the front of the dress. When he was questioned he gave this answer: "I just did it." He received a few spanks on his hands from his mother, but this did not cause him too much grief.

During a walk in the afternoon, the question was answered in an unexpected way, especially for a nonprofessional. "Aunt," the little one said, "I thought that my mother would really spank me, but," he added in a manner half triumph and half resentment, "she did not do it." I said, "But yes, you got your spanking." He replied, "Yes, but only on my hands, not on my buttocks."

When he was five years old he spent the summer alone with his mother in the countryside. To make it easy for him to play with peers, she had chosen to go to a place where there was a camp for four-year-old children. He spent the day at the camp.

Both mother and child got sick one day with a serious infection. His mother suffered severe pain. One evening after his mother had a bad day, she asked him on the way home what he wanted to eat. She remarked that she was going to buy food right away because she did not feel well. "Oh no," he objected, "I already had ham at the camp. I cannot eat any more."

After he had been put to bed, his mother was going to bed. However, before she was able to undress she heard him mumbling. "I did not get any more food to eat today." Mother got up again and made a meal for him with a glass of milk. She told him, "I asked you if you wanted something to eat! If you do not eat right now, you will really get a spanking for the first time." He ate everything, even if he did not like his meals with milk. Weeks later he told his aunt, "I have never seen mother that angry before. I ate everything because I was so scared of her!"

A seven-year-old girl had been spoiled during her first years of life by the excessive attention she enjoyed from relatives as well as strangers. During her first grade at school she pointed out repeatedly at home that her teacher preferred her to all other children. Her teacher had asked her not to bring any lunch from home because she wanted to share her own lunch with her. The teacher was reported to share sweets and treats with her. She would help her when she had to read.

One time when the child suffered from serious vomiting, her mother mentioned when she brought the girl to school that their physician did not want the girl to eat anything other than the milk she brought with her. The teacher recognized the special quality of the mother's talk and discovered the truth. The girl belonged to that group of children who are admired by their families during their first years. They get excessively spoiled at that time. Later they have to give up this preferred role. Therefore she invented in her fantasy a role to replace the former reality. From the very moment this was discovered, the child hated the teacher whom she had loved before.

An older twelve-year-old sister received a watch as a present. The parents admonished her to pay careful attention to it. They forbade her to open the glass face. During a serious illness of the older girl, the younger sister, who was ten years old, was not looked after. Out of boredom and loneliness she got the idea to clean her sister's watch. She started at the outside, and then the inner part of the cover. Finally she was irritated by some dust under the glass. She hesitated, but finally she was tempted and opened the glass and carefully cleaned the face. However, she struck a hand and broke it. Immediately, she closed the glass and put the watch back into its case.

After the older sister recovered, she discovered the unexplainable damage. Her father asked for the watch to have it fixed. When questioned about the damage, the older girl didn't know how what to say. The little one watched the scene silently, listening to the strong words of the father directed at her older sister. The watchmaker confirmed, when examining the watch, that the glass had been opened. Repeated expressions of anger, accusations of lying, and a temporary confiscation of the watch followed. The little girl remained silent. However, she could not escape accusing herself. Any treatment of her sister that appeared to be preferential was seen to be punishment for her crime. It was only much later, after her older sister had hurt her badly, that she confessed.

An eleven-year-old girl accused a schoolmate who was often her family's guest of not putting back a book that she had borrowed from the school library. The girl's father used to invite friends home whom he had chosen against his daughter's wishes. She would react with poor behavior toward the unwelcome guests. One of those guests was the schoolmate mentioned, who was hated by her peers for her obedient behavior in school. The little girl was aware of her father's character, so she invented a plan that would help her to get rid of this forced friendship. She reported at home that this "friend" had not returned a book to the library despite repeated criticisms by the teacher. In fact, she reported that "the friend" even denied having taken it from the library. The truth was that the girl had only forgotten the book at home on this unfortunate day. The father understood the situation and immediately prohibited any further contact between the girls. The little girl had succeeded. However, she did not know that the mother of the accused girl had learned of her accusations. Her father, who liked to interfere with other children's education, admonished this mother and advised her to go and to consult a teacher.

The girl found herself in a difficult position. She was fearful of being discovered at school with her false accusations and of being punished at home. This would be a serious blow to her father's pride in his "well-behaved" daughter. Knowing this only increased her fright.

The next morning she managed to meet her "friend" on the way to school, and she explained the whole affair as a misunderstanding. She claimed to have forgotten something at home, and turned around, only to wait for her teacher with whom she walked to school frequently. She told the teacher about the affair but only to the degree that she portrayed herself as not guilty. Therefore, she did not have to expect any punishment. At home finally, she finished her system of lies by telling her family that the girl had actually brought back the book without her knowing about it. However, she still left her friend in a somewhat guilty position, and succeeded in having her father discontinue inviting the girl to their home. Thus she not only escaped guilt about her behaviors, but she was successful in not meeting this "friend" anymore.

This impressive series of "character weaknesses" had its roots in the relationship of the child to her father. The continuous praise that he paid to the disapproved schoolmate because of her quiet but modest behaviors, and the enforced friendship were an uncomfortable experience for the girl. She loved her father deeply. She did not dare to oppose his orders with his overwhelming authority because she realized this would lead nowhere. She had to invent devious ways to alienate this schoolmate from her father.

I remember the following event from my own childhood. In my tenth and eleventh years, we had the daughter of a formerly well-off but later bankrupt entrepreneur in my class. She had alienated her schoolmates because of her boasting about the lifestyle at home. After the holidays she claimed that she had brought cookies from a special bakery in Paris. The children tried to prove that she was lying by stating that she had bought the cookies at the local bakery with money that she had stolen.

Once, after Christmas, she was boasting again about her precious gifts and mentioned especially a broach with numerous diamonds. Being teased by the other children, she promised to bring the jewelry to school the next day. When we saw the jewelry, we had to give in. We found the broach somewhat old-fashioned and not quite appropriate for a child. We passed it around and we looked at it until the teacher entered the classroom.

The same afternoon the girl was not at school. Her neighbor in class, who had been the one who had insisted that she bring the jewelry to school, found the broach without its case under the desk. Instead of giving it to the teacher, she kept it and told the others. None of the children wanted to keep the broach, and pretending that it was not real, they threw it into the canal. Weeks later the girl reappeared at school, but she never mentioned the jewelry again.

The child had to repeat her grade. About one year later we were attending a higher class, we heard that in the lower class there was a great upset because of a lost precious broach. The same girl, its owner, had asked her parents to bring the jewelry to school, responding to the wish of the teacher for some examples of diamonds. We heard that then she pretended that the jewelry had been stolen from its case when she was out of the classroom for a few moments. We, the children who had caused the cruel disappearance one year before, became really frightened, but nobody dared to tell the truth. All investigations and threats of punishment were without success, and cruel as children are, they thought this girl deserved the spanking she got at home. It was discovered that the teacher had not asked her to bring the jewelry to school, but the girl had only wanted to boast.

The school, as well as the parents, never learned anything about the truth, and nobody acknowledged the pain the poor child had experienced for more than a year until she succeeded in covering up the consequences of her boasting. We did not know for sure that there had not been a second piece of jewelry. This was because probably none of us could have lived with the secret for too long.

Children's Letters (1914)

The following paper ("Kinderbriefe" [Children's letters], *Imago* 5/3-462-76, 1914) is Hug-Hellmuth's only contribution to her column on child psychology 'Vom wahren Wesen der Kinderseele' in 1914.

She combines a general consideration of children's attitudes toward letter writing with a number of examples of letters that are then interpreted by Hug-Hellmuth. She seems to follow the argumentative line of Freud's *Psychopathologie des Alltagslebens* (Psychopathology of everyday life) of 1901 (published in Berlin in 1904), providing rather superficial explanatory models that seem to be out of date at the time of publication of this particular paper.

The strong resentment of many adults against writing letters is so common in all social classes that we are righteously entitled to look for deeper, general reasons for which the professional stress of men, the lack of time of women with their chores at home, where society and work are only comfortable excuses. This resentment is anchored deeply in most people's souls but disappears all of a sudden as soon as eroticism comes into play and again gains power as soon as love in its broadest sense is not involved. Its motives go far back to childhood in those years when preferences and dislikes are developed as hardly recognized reactions to education and the milieu that later nearly unexplainably rule the individual's life.

Resentment against writing letters can be traced back to the school years. No other subject makes a child feel so uncomfortable in early as well as later years. No other subject is so honestly hated as essay writing when a teacher, normally without much success, tries to make the child's mind familiar with the secrets of style in letters that express good wishes, thanks, requests or other issues. These might be letters in which the student is supposed to report a real or invented journey to a friend according to a given plan. In these letters he is supposed to report things accurately that do not interest him at all. Yet he is not allowed to speak about eating and drinking, perhaps the most delightful experiences because of their unusual flavors, or about fellow travellers whom he really found to be ridiculous. The child feels the obligatory element of such letters and he has to swallow in these hours the disgusting and not very helpful pill of negation. Perhaps he resents it even more than on other occasions of necessary accommodation to school and learning. This could occur especially if "a letter" has meant to him a privilege of freedom of expression. At the time when the child has strenuously and without any joy composed his first obligatory letters, he also enjoys normally another stimulating experience. That results from the secret writing of those "little notes" that the grown-up Viennese remember with sensual horror and refer tersely to as "little letters." These are written under the desk in constant fear of being caught and they contain everything from touching innocence to prohibited desire and lechery. Because parents and educators look back to their own childhood and well remember the particular content of those letters, they censor frequently and strictly those letters that their children deliberately write at home to their absent peers. The habit is that in many families the correspondence of the growing children with their friends is observed, inspected, and suspected by their father and mother. This causes the young to soon give up their friendly correspondence with their absent peers. As far as the written word is concerned, either written by himself or addressed to him, the child asks for even more freedom of content and time than he does for the spoken word.

It is a brutal habit in many educational institutions that the weekly schedule allocates an hour on one or two days for writing letters. Even worse, this time is not to be used for anything else! This demands from the child more self-discipline than the adult himself is usually able to exercise. One of the strongest reasons for the resentment against writing letters is certainly opposition. A direct command and the constant surveillance spoils forever for the child what might be a source of pleasure later.

However, there are also children who haven't been directed in that respect because they were considered too young for an educational compulsory letter ritual, or they simply grew up under exceptionally reasonable educational principles. Yet, all of a sudden these children consider writing letters as a tiresome activity after a short period of passionate writing. This is caused of course by the child's desire to be "big" and normally occurs most insensitively where the child imitates his father or mother. What brings about this change that can not be traced back to influences of the environment? I think it is caused by a phenomenon that is partially typical of a very intelligent child. Intellect far precedes the clumsy hand that directs the pen. My eight-year-old nephew was a passionate writer before he went to school. With his automatic pencil he learned to write capital letters and he wrote postcards and letters with great effort as a five-year-old. When his little fingers became tired, his mental flexibility had already found another aim and thus he wasn't inhibited by his physical clumsiness. What is different is that his fantasy and curiosity, his wishes and desires leave his ability to write far behind. Now he writes epistles of many pages, but the written result is of poorer quality. We meet this "writing in thoughts" again in many grown-ups whose fantasy covers wide areas while the art of style has remained strange to them. Thus, the second less important reason of the child's resentment against writing letters is represented by the unequal development of mental capacities and manual abilities. This is slowly overcome by the child's increasing skills to direct the pen and his versatility to express his thoughts through words.

Two aspects draw our attention to children's letters: the content and the time when they start to write. In addition, the specific circumstances that urge the child to write are important.

We cannot make any general statement regarding the time when the child deliberately and with joy takes up his pen. Only one thing is seen regularly. The first letter is always the result of imitation. It might be because of love or jealousy but in itself it never lacks love in the imitation. A child might be closely attached to an absent member of the family. He might also have many wishes, but if he grows up in a family that is lazy about writing, he will never possess the wish to write a letter by himself. He will restrict himself to the question of when the loved person will return, or he might look for another person as a replacement most suitable for the fulfillment of his wishes. He might show less interest in his home, but even the most intelligent children do not spontaneously express the idea to write a letter to the absent person to express their wishes in written form. Very many small children ask to "write" and for "real" paper and pen when they frequently see father and mother involved in this activity. They identify with them because of their love. However, this identification may as well express a more or less conscious pigheadedness. Their independence from their environment is important, and they know it because they have learned that the parents must not be disturbed while writing letters. As soon as the little child succeeds in achieving his goal of imitation, he often loses his new interest. Children eight to nine years of age pursue their ambitions by other forms of adult imitation. Some children have a strong desire to write for all their school years. At first they produce only short pieces that are stimulating, not because of their content but because of their inappropriate time of writing during school hours. Later they write those languished expressions of affection that are often the predecessors of true love letters. As they are often the only documents of a deep psychic isolation, educators and psychologists should pay the greatest attention to them.

Three very early letters of children that I have at hand were written by my nephew; he wrote them at the beginning of his sixth year in printing at a time when he couldn't write in script. He was already able to read fluently:

DEAR AUNT HERMINE,
I WISH YOU ALL THE BEST FOR YOUR BIRTHDAY.
MAXI THE STARVATION ARTIST.

Some weeks later I got the following two letters:

DEAR HERMINE
THIS MORNING FINALLY I LOST MY LOOSE TOOTH. DURING THE MORNING
I SPLASHED IN THE RIVER WITH CLOTHES ON IN THE AFTERNOON NAKED.

THAT IS GREAT.
YOURS MAX.

DEAR AUNT
I DRILLED WITH A STICK IN A WASP NEST. I KILLED FIVE OF THEM. THEN
ONE OF THEM CAME ACROSS AND STUNG EVEN THROUGH MY SHIRT—I AL-
READY EAT MUCH MORE BECAUSE I HAVE A VERY GOOD COOK. THAT'S MY
MOTHER. MANY KISSES. YOUR MAX.

Enclosed in this letter is an illustration of a wasp sting so that the aunt can
see how the wasp stung him. The sting is drawn nearly as big as the wasp
itself.

There are certainly single attempts at early writing, and only intelligent
children show them quite often. However, they do not receive the psychological attention they deserve.

Even more interesting than when writing begins is the content of the
letters. At the beginning these letters originate from the first years of learning,
that is, normally from the eighth to the eleventh or twelfth year. During this
time the written notes deal strictly with the real experiences of the child, the
little events of everyday life that touch the young soul, his gains, his adventures, and sometimes his misdoings. All of these provide the material for the
content. The child's egotism is expressed with every line. It is most natural
in its charming openness. On the birthday card he was asked by his mother
to write, Little Max knows how to present his personality by describing his
eating through his signature "Maxi the starvation artist." The two remaining
letters do not show anything else but his personal interests. He reveals to us
a good deal of his sexual curiosity and his sadism. These are both expressed
by the drilling in the wasp's nest. He expresses his joy of nudity, his love
affair with his mother, and his cleverness that forces her to cook for him. The
purely concrete thinking of early childhood leads the writing towards the
illustration of his experience at the wasp's nest. The prominence and emphasis which he gives the sting in his drawing reminds us a little bit of little
Hans, who himself added the "waddler" to the drawing of a giraffe. The
sting of an insect appears to children, especially boys, like a penis. This
interest has contributed to the drawing of this picture.

The purely unvarnished letter of child, which nicely fits Schiller's word
"the letter has hands and feet" (*Wallenstein's Death* 1-5), is composed by
purely personal interests. The child does not know phrases. Also he does not
know how to change words around. He writes simply what he thinks, feels,
and wishes. To describe the correspondence of children, I wish tell you of
Beppo. Even if he has the latest phrases and the letters of a nine-year-old,
Beppo is quite familiar with conventional expectations. He starts nearly every
letter to his father with the somewhat stereotyped question: "What are you

doing? Are you healthy?" The long letter of several pages still reveals that even to him who already knows the laws of courtesy, his own experiences, gains, and wishes are the most important. Perhaps he is embarrassed sometimes by the delightful priority of his own personality. He tries to destroy the believed unfavorable impression by repeatedly asking at the end of his letter as to the well being of his father, the aunts and the grandparents.

Out of the rich correspondence of little Beppo that covers two years and was kindly given to me by his father, I will only present those that provide us with the deepest insight into the thoughts and feelings of the boy. Beppo's father, the owner of the chemical plant, was forced by the sudden death of his wife, as well as by other serious events, to have his two children put in an institution.

In one of the first two letters after his arrival at a rural educational institution near V., the then eight-year-old wrote:

> Dear Papa:
> How are you? Be healthy. I'll draw the castle K. (In the original a delightful little picture was at that point). Are you sick or healthy? I would like to be with you and I am really longing so that I am not with you anymore. There is a mountain called N. There we build our own houses and every boy has his own little garden at Mount N. But not me, and instead I have built my own house near the house with the tree boys and the garden as well. All boys have seen the house. I would like to be with my grandparents. Greetings and 100000000000000 kisses.
> > Your dear
> > Beppo

> Dear Papa:
> How are you? Are you healthy? Who owns the plant right now? Are you very busy? Aren't you missing something? Are the other servants and Marie still there or have they already left? When does Papa go to R. and then to S. to see Leo and then to Z. to see me. (Leo is Beppo's brother five years his senior who at that time lived in an institution at S.) How is the gardener and his son? The day before yesterday we had bad weather and it rained a lot. I have written a nice postcard to grandmother and grandfather. How is Papa in L. doing? Is he very busy? I don't think so because Papa doesn't own anything anymore and the beautiful big garden is not his garden anymore as well? Why did Papa sell the plant? The nice pond is also sold.
> Greeting and kissing you 100000000000000 times.
> Beppo.

Another letter Beppo sent home shortly before Christmas:

> Dear Papa:
> How are you? Are you healthy? How are the two aunts doing? I learned to play the piano here. The fraülein who teaches me is Fraülein

M. Fraülein M. has been here yesterday. I am supposed to practice at
5:00 o'clock. Yesterday we had a lot of ice. The ice looked like a
window. Near the castle there is a fountain with a lot of ice in the
fountain. Ernice Walter and myself have taken out a lot of ice yesterday.
When do the grandparents come to B.? Can I come home for Christmas?
Please come soon to Leo and to me.

Greeting and Kissing you 100000000000000 times. Beppo

I have to restrain myself from presenting all the letters in which Beppo
expressed his desire for father and brother, and for the familiar atmosphere
of his home that was destroyed by the sudden death of his mother. I will
restrict myself to citing only a few more passages:

In one of his Christmas letters to his grandparents, he writes: "Unfortunately I can't come to you because it is too far away. But perhaps I will go
to S. to Leo. I would like to come to you but I can't come. It is also very nice
in S."

In February he writes his father:

Leo wrote me that he is going to visit me every or every second Sunday. I
am looking forward to Leo visiting me. Are you also coming sometime?

And some weeks later:

Leo visited me the Sunday before last. I showed him everything. Is it
true that Leo can come in April? Please visit me. Can I come home
sometime? Today is my piano lesson. Many other children also play
piano. Wednesday we had Gleaner cake. Starting the twentieth of March
we have our Easter break and on the fourteenth of April we have to go
V. Can I come home for the Easter break? Today Mr. B. (the owner of
the institute) said March 20 is the beginning of holidays and April the
fourteenth is the start of V.

Greeting you and kissing you 100000000000000 times. Beppo.

Even in his second year of stay in the same institution, the desire to come
home to father had not decreased. It remains the burning question in all his
letters, but now he uses in a more mature way expressions that have a
delightful symbolism. He adds to his letters the drawing of a train that carries
the letters to V. (where his father stays)—Vette. In a whole series of letters,
the sparkling face of the sun plays an important role. It appeared first as a
simple disc with a few beams, then with a mouth, nose, and ears, and finally,
because father still didn't understand, the sun became like the father with a
beard. It is hardly necessary that he sometimes adds: "Now we soon have
springtime," or "now it will get really hot soon and then we have our break,"
i.e., "Then I will come home to my beloved and painfully missed father."

Beppo's opinion that his father also missed him is expressed quite clearly in the passage: "Are you missing something?"

How deeply children feel when they are separated from one of their parents! How much their longing becomes a focal point of their unconscious mental life is shown by the child whose parents got a divorce. For example, the most tender love of his mother can not replace the missed love of his father to my nephew. He has written the most loving letters to his father for years and asks him to visit. Some weeks ago he wrote:

> Dear Father
> On the twelfth we go to M . . . Perhaps you will meet us. If you still know mother, we can go out for a walk together. I am really looking forward. Is it nice in M.? I was born there. Mother keeps the photo of the house I was born in. There are also mountains in M. When I was three years old I was with mother and S's mother on the high hills. I was carried by S's mother downhill.
> So perhaps you will see us. Your Max.

A little girl whose parents are also separated writes to her father at the age of eight to nine:

> Dear Papa: Please come to us. Why don't you come? All children have a papa who lives with them. Only I don't. We have enough space and there is nobody sleeping on the sofa. Please visit us soon. You will certainly meet us in the evening.
> Best wishes. Your Emma.
> Our address is Vienna XIII District . . . Lane 12."

The whole tragedy of the devastating influence of a divorce on the sensitive heart of a child is revealed in such letters. Even if little Max holds secret hopes to see his father again, the seemingly naive note "I was born in M . . ." and the slight doubt: "If you still know mother" represent the most serious accusations against father. Also little Emma bursts out in the complaint: "All children have a father who lives with them. Only I don't." She adds cautiously the time and address so that the father won't miss them when he comes eventually.

This futile longing for his father is not only caused by his love for him. This is hardly justified because the parents only lived together for somewhat more than a year, or even because of a wish to enjoy the love of both a father and the mother. It far more represented the expression of a quiet brooding in the special circumstances of his own family. Nothing is harder to stand for a child than to live under circumstances that are experienced as being unusual and where the plain truth about these circumstances is withheld from them. Frequently in these letters of children we see an odd peculiarity that almost reminds us of the evolving neurosis. They dwell quite excessively on topics that they have dealt with before. They look at them from all points of view and they come back to them in the letters as if it seems necessary to finish them. To give a typical example, I will cite a passage from one of Beppo's letters. To give a letter to his grandparents he wrote shortly before the sixth of December, the day when Santa Claus is celebrated in the place F. near his institution.

> I don't know if we will celebrate Santa Claus because close to F. hoof and mouth disease has broken out. But they already built the booths. It would be too bad if they didn't celebrate Santa Claus because I really like it. We will go to a cinema. If it only snows soon. Please be so good and send me the sleds. I hope it will snow soon. At least if it would snow we would celebrate Santa Claus . . . That is why I say: we will celebrate Santa Claus. I believe it will snow.
> Best wishes. Beppo

Numerous similar passages of letters show that little Beppo is again and again bothered by questions he can't solve. Without any doubt it is a sexual problem that his soul is dealing with, but also the serious misfortune that has hit his family and that has caused his own and his brother's separation from home is obvious. Also, little Emma, soon after the separation of her parents, showed an insistent clinging to certain topics and a brooding. Everything is confused in his environment and the child is struggling furtively with this. This influences his moods, his words, and his letters. He tries to escape by using expressions that sound precocious and not childlike, but they are nothing other then an instinctual defense against a threatening mystery.

A widower with three children ages 8, 5, and 3 remarried. The eight-year-old Vally wrote to her future mother. The family lives in a town in Bosnia, the bride in Vienna.

> Dear little Mama!
> We are really looking forward to you. Papa is also looking forward. He even might pick you up. Fritzi [the five-year-old sister] is frequently naughty. You will become angry. And Milo [three-year-old brother] frequently pees in his trousers. Please bring something nice from Vienna. Grandmother is also looking forward.
> Many greetings. Your dear children.

Even if little Vally reassures the expected stepmother about the happiness of the family members, we still see in her address "Dear little Mama" an unconscious defence of the child not to acknowledge that this strange woman has the same rights as her biological mother. Her biological mother is to the eight-year-old child, as we know from numerous sayings of children in our psychoanalytic experience, not small at all, even if she is small. Vally wants to establish a barrier in her memory between the mother who died four years ago and the stranger using the word *little*, and at the same time she threatens her with the misdoings of the younger siblings. While quietly expressing happiness, she wants to prevent this woman from coming to S. by saying, "You will be really angry." Only her thought that the new mother will bring something nice from Vienna lets her accept her inevitable fate and the new mother's arrival.

The ending of Vally's letter leads us to a special group of children's letters— "wish" letters. They are the most delightful revelation of the unlimited childish egotism. In their simplest form they are only directed to Santa Claus to tell the parents in hidden words a secret wish. When I classify these letters as a special category, I differentiate them from letters that express a certain desire. For instance, when little Beppo, Max, and Emma talk about their most secret expectations and hopes, we have reason in the fact that wish and desire have a totally different meaning for the child. To have a wish means, especially for a younger child, that he wants to possess something real that he can take into his hands, something he didn't have before. When little Max sent his wish list at Christmas to his sick mother, Arco, he gave long lists of toys and books, but he added nearly superficially: "It is too bad that you can't be here for Christmas." Despite the fact that he is attached passionately to her, he asked his aunt on numerous occasions: "Do you believe that mum is coming to Vienna for Christmas?" Only if a child witnesses daily and every hour the suffering of his sick father or his sick mother, will he try to negotiate with Santa Claus with tragic naivety that reminds us a little bit of the blows and sacrifices of ancient times. An eleven-year-old girl wrote:

> Dear Santa Claus: I would like you to make my mother healthy again. For that I will give my great doll who has all her hair together with all her dresses, to the sick daughter of our janitor so she has something to enjoy. So I don't wish anything for myself, rather than one or two big fairy-tale books, a Christmas tree and lots of Christmas cookies.
> Sincerely yours, Fini B. First hallway, door 7

Beppo in his first year of his stay in V. briefly added to a Christmas letter to his grandparents: "The wish. I am not going to wish many things for myself. I just would like to have a dress and a lanterna magica and the other toys. Nothing else." He asks politely the next year:

> "I am now going to wish for my Christmas presents. I would like to have a military dress, a model train, and a game. I believe that I will get the presents that I wish from Santa Claus. Furthermore, I would like to

have a book so that I can read a little bit. I will give a nice Christmas present to my father.

Finally, he hints at his birthday only indirectly:

> Dear Grandmother!
> How are you doing? I am already looking forward to my birthday and I am curious what I will get. It will be in three days.

Max, whose wishes don't express his modesty at all, writes to his mother shortly before: "I will enjoy everything that St. Nicholas brings to me." And shortly before Christmas: "I asked Santa Claus for a car for mail or moving, and tracks for my model railroad. I am looking forward to Santa Claus and Christmas." He left it to his aunt to write down his numerous other wishes.

Besides the harmless wish letters that express the enjoyment of play and the wish to experience the love of others in most practical terms, there are also other letters even in early childhood that are based on jealousy and envy. A little girl writes to Santa Claus:

> Dear Santa Claus: I would like to ask you for a doll like Elsa's but even bigger. With eyes opening and closing, and at least three dresses. Then, a small room of a doll house like Hansi's but with more furniture, and a Christmas tree, two fairy-tale books and a rubber ball, stickers and other pictures to put in my book, and cookies. Since St. Nicholas I didn't poke my nose anymore. I hope you will keep your word. Your dear Irma.

The motive of jealousy is even more pronounced in the following letter of a nine-year-old girl to the stork:

> Dear Stork: Be so good and bring a little brother to me if it is at all possible. Anna is so conceited since she has got one. [Her girlfriend had been presented with a baby brother a few weeks before.] I will look after my brother when mother is not around. Many greetings. Your dear Martha.

The child is pursuing his wishes so actively that he could not resist using blackmail in the early years. A teacher gave me a letter of a girl in the fourth grade that was written during classes:

> Dear Veit: Please give that big rat candy immediately to me. Otherwise I will report you and Muller that you eat during lessons. The teacher will ask me anyway.
> Your dear friend B.

Later such attempts at blackmail are not rare at all, and they most frequently deal with sexual misdoings.

Even if a child between the eighth and tenth years is pursuing his sexual curiosity somewhat less intensively, the slightest real perception might be enough to initiate a strong interest on the part of the child. The closer the child approaches the beginning of puberty, the more his obvious sexual curiosity is accompanied by sexual envy.

It is only natural that letters of children with this content happen to be found by adults very rarely. They are not normally directed to adults as in the case of those who can't solve the problem of where children come from. On the contrary, these are letters to dear friends and girlfriends. Secretly written and secretly read, they have gotten into the hands of adults just by accident or by mean treachery.

A nine-year-old girl writes to her girlfriend at school:

> Dear Berger! My big sister got it today [i.e., menstruation]. Mayer also says she got it already, but that is not true, she lies. Come along with me at eleven o'clock today, we are going to tell her that she lies. She is mean and can't be our friend anymore. Please get back to me. Yours truly Rosa.

The requested answer:

> Dear Schauer: The teacher is looking in my direction. I can't write. I already told you that Mayer can't be trusted. What did your sister tell you? I really won't get it, will you?
> In a hurry, your Regina.
> We will go there at eleven o'clock together

The hopeless confusion that is caused by half-truths in the little heads is expressed in the following correspondence of two girls, students in third grade:

> Dear Nerver:
> Blau said, our teacher had her P——(you already know what that is, that means she is expecting a child soon). Your true friend.

Answer:

> Dear Mizi!
> I already know that for a long time from my cousin, but if you want to get a child you have to sleep in the same bed with a man for a whole night. Destroy this letter. Your loving friend Eva.

These letters don't need any comment, as do the following of two eleven-year-old girls:

Dearest Berta
Richter's Anna spread out a lot of gossip about you in needlework. She will report to Miss P. [the teacher] what indecent things you are talking about. I don't know what it is, but I assume it is about getting children. But you can really trust me. It is really mean. Both the Richters talk a great deal themselves and nobody is reporting them. Perhaps we simply shouldn't deal with them anymore. Don't be afraid. In true friendship. Your Elsa.

Answer:

Dearest Elsa!
She might go ahead. I will leave school next Monday anyway. And fortunately Miss P. doesn't listen to those reports anyway. I know that you won't say anything. By the way, my father has been already to the school yesterday to give notice. I forgot the book from the library that will get me in trouble.
Kisses. Your only friend Berta.

There are only slight hints to a vivid sexual interest in a letter of a ten-year-old girl to her friend:

Dear Mina!
Can you come and visit me on Sunday? We will be alone at home. [This was emphasized in the original by two to five strong lines.] We will make chocolate for ourselves, then we will go to father's room and pick up the dictionary from his library. After that we will go for the currant bush. Mama will be out of the home anyway. That's great. Kissing you 100000000000000 times, your true friend Karoline.

I only have a single letter from a boy with obvious sexual content:

Dear Kurt! Yesterday Robert showed me something horrible. I tried it the same evening. I got terribly hot and nauseated. Don't tell anybody. He said you know it already. Your true German friend Hans.

The nine-year-old "true German friend" Hans, son of a real German, seems to have learned about masturbation from his teacher, Robert.
At the end I will cite from a seemingly harmless letter of my eight-year-old nephew Max to his girlfriend, one year his senior.

Dear Erna! If you are nice I will come Tuesday. Please prepare
everything for construction, including loam and wood. The tunnel has to
become so wide and deep that it can take us. It has to be quite dark in
the middle. Hopefully the G———s won't show up. Then it is boring.
Then I won't come.
Greetings your Rax-tax.

This letter, together with the previously citated invitation of the ten-
year-old Karoline, gives us a clear picture of the sharply defined psychic
development of the sexes. The girl is tempting her girlfriend by promising
sweets for body and soul, but the boy has some demands and his visit is
dependent on numerous preconditions. Both want to spend their time with
their friend alone, and I believe that "Rax-tax," if he is not interested in the
dictionary yet, has already planned some entertainment which might be
disturbed by observers.

There is a special psychological meaning to those letters in which the writer
either blames others or admits more or less voluntarily his own mishaps. The
former always contain, even if they are written as a joke, something serious.
They express anger about assumed injustice or harsh strictness. My nephew,
for instance, wrote last winter to his mother the following accusation of his
aunt and great-aunt:

Dear Mother! I am not allowed to walk during snow or storm. If I
don't eat my meal I don't get the candies you sent me from Arco.
Because I am frequently naughty, I often get a spanking on my hands.
They force me to drink milk. They won't let me pick my nose. At half
past eight in the evening and seven o'clock in the morning I am not
allowed to speak. When will you come back? Mr. F. visited me last
Sunday and called me a chatterbox, although he talked more to my aunt
than to me. That he calls visiting me! Greetings, your Lumpus.

While writing this letter his anger disappeared and he already enjoyed life
as he brought the letter to the mailbox. Perhaps he hoped with this letter to
influence his mother to come back soon. That is what we might conclude
from the question, "When will you come back?" These accusations against
adults are a natural reaction to uncomfortable pressure, whereas self-accusations often disclose some masochism.

Beppo reported misdoings to his father, not of others but his own; still,
this happened because it was ordered by the director of the institution, who
left it up to the child to choose his own way of reporting:

Dear Papa: How are you? Are you healthy? I have lied many times
already. The day before yesterday I lied again. I told Mr. B., Miss L.,
Mr. F., and Mr. D. (my four teachers) that I have attended school but

this was not true. I realize that I really don't need to lie. That's why I will try to become a good and obedient boy. How are the aunts doing? Are they healthy? Grandmother wrote me and asked why I didn't write a letter to my dad because he now is in Berlin.

Greetings and kisses 100000 times. Your Beppo.

And another time:

Dear Papa: I spoiled my trousers because I was too late to go to the washroom. I stayed where I always used to stay and didn't want to go to the washroom. I am very lazy. I always spoil my trousers because I am too lazy to go to the washroom.

In reality his laziness is not the reason for his mishap; this, according to the father, lies much deeper. At four years of age, at a time when he already had become familiar with the demands of cleanliness and decency, Beppo suddenly lost his mother. His disturbed family life, the missed attention and love that he no longer experienced, had consequences for his confused soul. He started spoiling his clothes to force his environment to pay attention to him. Those mishaps that look quite strange for a four-year-old boy are a result of the opposition against his family members. His father would not give in to Beppo's wish to live at home. He fights against the principle of an institution as a substitute for his father. "I won't do that anymore. That is why Mr. B. told me to write it to you."

This letter is the only one that has no signature. The promise "hopefully not to lie and steal anymore" is given quite cautiously and shows that Beppo's unconscious is not prepared at all to totally give it up soon. He also thinks that lying is not necessary, and this clearly shows the flimsiness of his intentions. It is not so much a matter of principle that lets him freely confess his misdoing. It seems to be more a result of a feeling of security due to the large distance between father and son. There is also a certain stubbornness with which the son emphasizes his mistakes to the father. I conclude that from Beppo's extensive description.

From the first period of learning there is another aspect of children's letters that is psychologically very interesting. We will not be astonished that the child, also in his letters, brings his own person into the focus of the world, his wishes into the foreground, and prefers to speak about his own doings. That is why it seems to be odd to us when Beppo, in his letters to father and grandparents, gives long descriptions of birds and flowers, in which his own lovable personality doesn't play the same role as in the long report about the houses, salad, cabbage, onions, etc., he has planted, about the lottery, St. Nicholas, about bread and sausage that everybody got for the excursion that he really liked. The notes about his newly acquired knowledge in the sciences sounds so instructive that we cannot fail to assume a hidden reason for these reports. It is as if little Beppo wants to say, "Look, father, so many things I have learned without your help, and I will also get to know other things that you do not want to tell me." For example, family affairs, sexual information, etc. This connection seems to be very likely to me because children often boast about their new knowledge before their parents. My nephew, on the other hand, informed by his mother quite early about the burning questions of childhood, doesn't boast that much to his mother, but much more to his friends. The knowledge from school doesn't play as important a role at all for boasting, a fact that I have observed repeatedly in children who have been informed early about material and sexual questions in a rational way. Sexual curiosity and the narcissism of childhood force the young child to become independent quite early and make it known to the grown-ups. In the short finishing sentences of many of his letters, "Greetings Beppo," we see a good deal of striving for independence that is also an expression of infantile self-love. It represents a more sophisticated level of narcissism than in the quiet primitive signature "Your dear Beppo" or "Your beloved friend." In addition, children from rural areas who are not anxiously kept away from family relationships or sexual matters do not know this boasting with school knowledge, even if they know much more than their parents in that respect.

On Child Psychology and Pedagogy (1914)

This paper provided proof that Hug-Hellmuth was regarded as the expert in psychoanalytic child psychology
in the early years of psychoanalysis. "On Child Psychology and Pedagogy," a review article that appeared in
the *Jahrbuch für Psychoanalytisclte und Psychopathologislte
Forschungen* 6:393–404, summarized the development of
psychoanalytic child psychology in the years 1910–1914.
In the original German version, the references were listed
at the beginning of the article. In this manner the publications that were reviewed were outlined in the introduction. Hug-Hellmuth's comments in this article appear to
have reflected a harmony in the field of psychoanalysis
that was not correct. She included references to Adler
and Jung without outlining the sharp differences that had
arisen at the time of the publication of this paper.

The phenomenon that in the etiology of neurosis of adults, sexual experiences, fantasies, and wishes of early childhood have been regularly proven
be important factors, has led to an idea. This idea is that the soul of a healthy
adult, in the broadest sense, reacts also to environmental stimuli in a way
which is strongly individual in style. Further, it seems to be unreasonable
and unexplainable to the environment and the person himself that he is not
free of lasting traces of infantile experiences of the sexual erotic nature.
During the first decade of its development psychoanalytic research restricted
itself to knowledge about the nature of the child's soul through reports of
grown-up patients and from the analyst's own memories. The essence of that
was written down in the "Three Essays" what was to become the basis of all
further work in the area of psychoanalytic child research.

The later investigations could hardly bring something new in terms of
theory. Their value consists much more in a confirmation and the differentiation of Freud's ingenious ideas. After all, the wealth of material available can
only be gathered by careful observation. The fact that numerous authors who
work in this field found in every single case complete agreement of theory and
practice when observing physically and mentally totally differently developed
children who lived under the most heterogeneous circumstances, proves
marvelously the correctness of the theory. However, this reasoning needed
the pioneering work of the creator of psychoanalysis, Freud, with his work
"The Analysis of a Phobia in a Five-Year-Old Boy." This basic paper became
the starting point for others who then worked for the same goal, Jung (20),
Hitschmann (12), Ferenczi (6). The temporary disturbances and the balance

of the infantile soul were traced back to their very roots, with their sexual constitution and sexual traumata.

Freud's work is of importance for not only the fundamentals of therapeutics. From that point on, one tried to free the child from his psychic suffering by clarifying and explaining the reason and the secret intentions of his fears, his shyness, and his great disgust that was inappropriate for his age. This was done by authors such as Friedjung (10) and especially Pfister (22, 23) in his function as a clerical and educational counselor. By using psychoanalytic means, one tried also to understand what it was in the healthy, happy child that explained peculiarities from either mistakes or mishaps that really did not fit into the overall picture of the little child (Freud (9), v. Hug-Hellmuth (16), Jung (21), Spielrein (29)). Thus the double goal of applying the psychoanalytic method to the infantile mental life is characterized as "curing" and "educating"—improving the child's mental life in a therapeutic and educational sense. We attempted to understand the child better than before. With this deeper understanding we wanted to prepare for an era in which the psychoanalytic method executed with knowledge becomes a tool for "education." Psychoanalysis does not share Adler's (Adler et al. (2)) and his followers' point of view that explains psychic functioning with an understanding of the feeling of inferiority or the male protest. The psychosexual development of man which is clearly expressed from earliest childhood on (Wulff (31)) is the field where psychoanalysis digs for the undiscovered treasures of the unconscious in children as well as an adult. In both cases it reveals the most precious material. By careful observation of a child in play and serious activities, during fantasies and dreams, it was possible to prove how even the child's psychic life is dominated by the most powerful of all drives, the sexual drive.

The specific conditions under which psychoanalytic papers on children were written ask for a form of preview that is different from the usual. While with other specialties the new discoveries outline the direction that seems to be most appropriate, in this case it is necessary to organize those investigations according to the main statements of Freud about the mental life of the child. It is necessary to start with the most important and obvious factor of infantile life, love. Psychoanalysis has emphasized the importance of this most powerful feeling in all its positive and negative aspects. This was never done before by educators or child psychologists. Psychoanalysis recognized that the psychic development of the child is mainly dependent on the extent and way of affection that is shown to him from the beginning of his life. Freud (8) tried to explain the specific smiling of all women in the pictures of Leonardo da Vinci from his own indistinguishable memories of childhood. He linked his well-based assumption with very important ideas about the influence of the mother's love during the very first years of the life of the child. The adult asks for the same amount of love that he has received as a child in his first years. The amount of the love received first becomes a measurement for mature years. There is only one point where I would disagree with some authors. When Sadger (27) stated that the only and the favorite child keep up their insatiable longing for love all their life, I have to object. It is my own experience that children become much more demanding in their expectations if they spend their childhood or their puberty with lack of affection. It might be even more important for later life. Much more than spoiled children, they are in danger of experiencing an increased in their narcissism through childhood to adulthood to an extent that can't be tolerated by the environment anymore. They fulfill their own need for affection extensively because nobody else can do enough for them.

The function of auto-eroticism, which dominates the child during that first developmental phase, the child's narcissism, and finally the object love with its ambivalent estimation of the loved person have been described in numerous papers (Hug-Hellmuth (15), Jekels (34), Pfister (23), Rank (25)).

A number of observations make clear that the child's attachment to his father and mother is not free of libidinal aspects. These are soon repressed into the unconscious by cultural barriers (Abraham (34), Freud (7), Hitschmann (12)). This disapproved libido of the child is enforced by the sexual secret between the parents that excludes the child. This causes the heterosexual love, jealousy, and hatred, besides the still existing affection towards the parent of the same sex. "The analysis of the phobia of little Hans" (Freud (7)) for the first time clearly showed the infantile ambivalence of love and hatred toward the father. Similarly, Jung in a paper emphasized how little Anna quite remarkably withdraws from her mother after the birth of her brother (Jung (20)). The ambivalent feelings toward the parents frequently start, as Freud has stated, because of infantile sexual curiosity, with a certain event that is disapproved by the child, that is, the birth of a sibling. If he does not succeed in suppressing his hatred, one has to expect the formation of a neurosis formally expressed as a phobia such as the animal phobia of little Hans (Freud (7)), the phobia of an earthquake in little Anna (Jung (20)), or the fear of streets in a case that was mentioned by Abraham (Abraham (34)). If he succeeds by reaction formation, then hatred is replaced by an overwhelming tenderness toward the glowing competitor. The Oedipus complex can be preserved, sometimes hidden, sometimes quite obvious as in Abraham's case (Abraham (34)). The hateful wishes against the health and life of father and mother, changed by the neurosis into a fear they might experience an accident, stem from the incestuous libido of the child that is directed to these persons respectively or directed to its suppression. As Freud (7) and Jung (20) stated, hateful wishes are forcefully directed against siblings. This occurs not only against the younger ones especially around the time of their arrival, which is fed into by the fear of losing the love of the surroundings; but also the younger child is not connected to his siblings by pure sympathy only (Hug-Hellmuth (15)) and he also envies the special right of the firstborn, even if that fact doesn't guarantee any right to title (Hug-Hellmuth (15)).

The disproportion between what one wishes for and what one receives in love makes man suffer the most during his years of development, when he is a "being " child. Suicide among adolescents can be ascribed to real or assumed lack of love in the most cases; only those give up their lives, who have given up to hope for love, or those who assume that they have to give it up. Most often this is the last act of resentment directed against the authority of the parents and the school. That is, the revenge of young people for the withholding of love they had hoped for. The child feels the conflict between early sexual activity and unresolved problems of sexual life by committing suicide. The mystery of death has been a mixture of horror and lust up to the beginning of puberty. By deliberately dying, he punishes himself for deeds that were considered sins by the prudishness and foolishness of his environment, whose psychic and physical consequences have poisoned his future life.

From observations in the field of infantile sexual activity, thumb sucking is the most primitive form of autoerotic stimulation of other erotogenic zones. Furthermore, infantile sexual activity is expressed by active and passive exhibitionism such as anal and general excretional libido partly exercised genitally, partly in different erotogenic zones and by playing with the growing breasts (Jekels (34), Tausk (30)). On the basis of their analyses, Freud and his disciples have repeatedly stated that real physical dangers are not the worst consequences of infantile masturbation, but rather it is the threats of grown-ups that result in castration anxiety and in self-accusations in later years. This was reasonably described by Ferenczi (Ferenczi (6)). The castration complex also plays an important role in another aspect of life, especially of the boy. He understands the sex difference that he has observed occasionally in his sister or other little girls as a consequence of threats of castration often made to these boys. Thus girls appear to him as inferior beings. Seemingly the child gives up the urge to masturbate and only exercises it secretly with anxiety and self-torture that give an aspect of restraint and shy depression to his character. Here we see in its most important aspect the "influence of sexual role models" on character as mentioned by Freud. A realistic understanding and explanation of the consequences of masturbation is a real mystery in psychoanalytic research. This cannot be fully recognized until infantile masturbation is no longer generally considered vice but rather as a natural satisfaction of drives. Only in its damaging excessive forms does masturbation have to be opposed like any other tendency of premature development.

The early selfishness of the child, caused by dealing with his own sexual organs whose functions he experiences lustfully, is intimately connected with his interest in his own body as well as that of others. This is expressed by his love of exhibitionism as another form of infantile sexual activity. Even if education powerfully opposes both activities, the child still has much more opportunities to watch than to show. He can also use animals if he can not fulfill his voyeurism in his environment (Little Hans (7), Little Hahnemann (6)).

Infantile sexual curiosity represents a third field of psychoanalytic research in children. Freud writes in his "Childhood Memories of Leonardo" (8): "Perhaps most, but certainly the most gifted, children pass through a period of their lives starting with their third year that one could call a phase of infantile sexual curiosity." A sexual interest that is powerfully shown in characteristic questioning at this age does not suddenly disappear only because it is rejected by the adults. There is the everyday observation of children who presented themselves as extraordinarily gifted and precocious in the fifth or sixth years of life, who all of a sudden stop their cognitive development (Hitschmann (12)). This points regularly to a disturbance in the psychic life wherever physical conditions can't be found. There is no other phase of development where man has to do so much hard work of suppression as in childhood. This suppression is so disproportionate to the other lines of development of the young child that quite frequently the original intellectual gifts become suffocated.

The mental processes of the child are much more influenced by his feelings than by his intellect. His sexual interest that is first directed to the question of birth, is later directed to the question of procreation. Finally it is sublimated in general questions like "Why, where, and how" that are dominated by an egocentric disposition. The ancient childhood question about creation really means: How and why were my siblings born? What did my parents have to do with my and their birth? Infantile curiosity is not content for too long with the fairy tale of the stork. He has his own thoughts about the problem of creation and this causes the first doubts as to the honesty of his elders. Storks, a children's pond, etc., acquire another meaning for the child. They become his tool of scorn toward the adults as the child triumphs over them because of the burning questions he has answered himself. As far as birth and procreation are concerned, the fantasy of the child comes to the same results that are expressed in the sagas and needs of all nations. Rank in his beautiful paper has described this agreement (Rank (24)). In children we find fantasies about birth that stem from the excretion complex—the "lumpf"—the theory of little Hans—being probably the most popular in child theory about birth.

The fantasy about the inversion of generations seems already to be a product of suppression (Jones (34), Jung (20)). The identification of delivery and vomiting represents a quite primitive belief. The fantasies about dying and death play an important role in the fantasy that old people turn into angels after their death and again become young humans.

Infantile interest doesn't stop at the solution of the mystery of birth, but is quite early connected with the role of the mother. It soon shifts to the father, without assigning him a specific role. In addition, mythology and children's beliefs take the same themes. Life-creating power is assigned by some of them to eating, kissing, or the intimate pressure of naked bodies, especially the buttocks, and urine and bowel gases (Reitler (26)). Again, for others a sadistic perception of intercourse gives them quite a good explanation for the parents' secret, as it is revealed to the child by some noises during the night (Reitler (26)). These speculations which more or less satisfy a child's curiosity undergo considerable change during the years according to the individual level of experience. They are kept in their original form well into adolescence, especially by the "best-kept" children who for the sake of their parents do not want to know anything because of their "obedience." Therefore, they reject anxiously anything that could reveal the truth. A splendid example that acquires its specific value through autoanalysis is given by Spielrein (29). Later these children quite frequently are deeply terrified by their perception of the maturational processes of their own body which they consider as a divine punishment for some misdoings (Petersen (32/11)).

Whatever the theories invented by the child to orientate himself within the confusion of sexual impressions and imagination, they will influence his later life. This is a fact seen in the psychoanalytic therapy of every neurosis. "This kind of thinking and doubting becomes the model for all later intellectual work. Lack of success in solving problems and the first failure may paralyze for the time following (Freud (9)). In his paper on Leonardo, Freud expresses this idea in the following words: "The impression of failure of the first attempt of intellectual independence seems to be lasting and deeply depressing" (Freud (9)).

To keep sexuality a secret is probably the most serious sin of parents against their children. It is the greatest cause of abrupt breaks between parents and children as soon as they become more mature.

The immense influence of the family on the psychic development of the child is still emphasized within certain limits only. To transgress these limits is prohibited by the parental narcissism of the researchers themselves, or by the internal hesitation to hurt the self-love of others too much by the clarifying of a problem and its deepest connections. They do not admit that most mistakes and misdoings of the child have their roots in their sometimes very fragile relationship with their parents and siblings. Psychoanalysis has succeeded in tracing back those relationships to their roots in some cases (Freud (9), Hug-Hellmuth (16)). Each time it could be shown that childish boasting and lying, even theft and other misdoings of adolescence, stem from the infantile desire to assign greater representation to the parents than could be matched by reality, to complete with them in terms of power and effectiveness, or to get rid of a competitor for the affection of a loved person. The wish to promote the parents into identifying with them probably represents the most important cause for all stubborn misdoings of children. Psychoanalytic research finds also in other misdoings—pigheadedness, disobedience, showing off, and passion for gossiping—secret connections to the parents and their representatives, educators and teachers, as well as siblings. Fantastic sexual lies have led to expulsion from school for many children unless a thoughtful advocate was found. The advocate could have understood the dark connection of everyday life and the reactions of the maturing psyche that are not at all proof for rottenness but for an increased and premature activity of drives (Jung (21)). Caring admonition and enlightenment according to the psychoanalytic talks of Pfister (22, 23) are the best tools for cure.

Psychoanalysis values one area of psychic experience in its importance for the infantile soul—the dream. Children as well as adults reveal hidden wishes, fantasies, and thoughts that are not represented in their consciousness. Because of this disapproved content, only disfigured, condensed, and sublimated material comes to the surface. The work of suppression and sublimation in an awake state is done by the child so much more transparently and with such obvious resistance that it can be seen by an adult. It is also easier to understand children's dreams. Van Raaltes's opinion that "children's dreams generally have to be interpreted according to their manifest content without any symbolic interpretation of their elements" is not acceptable to me with its exaggerated caution (Van Raaltes (34)). We do not have any reason to believe that the unconscious remains silent in children's dreams. The reason is that education specifically asks for intense suppression in childhood and this causes the most colorful forms of fantasy and daydreams. Infantile originality erupts again and again in early years despite education's unintended tendency toward suppression. It is represented by demands that turn the child into the enfant terrible! The dream of the child uses the available quantity of suppressed material as it does in adults. For both, it represents the revelation of those wishes that are inhibited during the day. The child believes in the reality of his dreams for so long and so strongly because their affective roots gratify their daytime disappointments (Hug-Hellmuth (13, 34)). Rational cognition already tells the child that the dream only represents an empty illusion, but his unconscious does not want to give up this manner of lustful satisfaction. This is one reason why it is so hard to awake children from their dreams. During a dream a child re-experiences his love and his hatred unrestrictedly. Beloved people die; they meet misfortune and are rescued by the child. He finds himself in terrible situations, and then experiences increased attention and care with which father and mother free him from his anxieties. This rescue might only be another piece of the child's dreams, or even better, father and mother may really wake the child from his terrifying dreams. The analysis of children's dreams clearly shows that groups of sexual fantasies influence the dreams as much as they dominate the life during the day. Masturbation as a tool for active and passive exhibitionism plays an important role in the child's dream, because its lustful experience is the first that is suppressed during the development (Tausk (30)). Children's dreams reveal the secret facts of education. They truly reflect how the child copes with compulsion internally. Freud's statement that whenever someone reports a dream to someone else, he follows an often unconscious intention, applies to the child accordingly. The older the child, the more complicated his dreams, and he only reveals to adults those details which appear harmless to him. Using this deviation, he more often reveals his secret thoughts and feelings to his peers (Jung (21)). Because of his irresponsibility in the dream, at least when dealing with child censors he is protected from certain accusations that certainly would be made if he would confess a daydream. The child understands quite early that real wishes experienced during the day form the basis of the dream. This understanding is rejected by the adult.

We have learned two things about the educational value of child psychoanalysis. While for a neurotic child, a psychoanalyst with planned treatment is clearly indicated because we deal with obsessional and anxiety symptoms that interfere with the psychic and often physical development, the psychoanalytic influence on the healthy child has to be played by ear according to the observations made by parents and educators who are familiar with "in-depth" psychology. In this case, the often stated tendency to make the child less "harmless" must not be feared. In young children, an admonishing or reprimanding word is often quite sufficient to clarify the unconscious motives of his behaviors and talk. Later he will be more willing to open himself to the influence of such psychic "orthopedics" the more cordially he is connected with the person who tries to advise and support him. The extraordinarily favorable results that were reported by Pfister (22, 23) are proof of the successful application of the psychoanalytic method in education and pastoral care. To both apply what Freud said about education: "It can be considered without hesitation as an initiation to overcome the pleasure principle and replace it with the reality principle."

Even more important than the positive aspect of the pedagogic-analytical approach, is the negative aspect. According to Freud, it consists of a threefold renunciation by the parents. According to numerous observations reported in the references, they have to give up the concealment of sexual fact, the suppression of infantile sexual life by inadequate firmness, and an excess of punishment and threats, for example, the castration complex (Spielrein (29), Petersen (34)). The parents have also to sacrifice the part of their narcissism that lets them envision higher and better beings in their children than would be possible in reality. Finally, parents, especially mothers, have to give up the idea of wanting their children to satisfy their own need for love.

References

1. Abraham, K.: Psychische Nackwirkungen der Beobachtung des elterlichen Geschlechtsverkehrs bei einem neunjährigen Kinde. *Z.I.*, 1913.
2. Adler, A., und Furtmüller, K.: Heilen und Bilden. Ärztlich-pädagog. Arbeiten des Vereines für Individual-psychologie. Verlag E. Reinhard, München, 1914.
3. Andreas-Salomé, Lou: Von frühem Gottesdienst. *Imago* 2, 1913.
4. Beaurain: Über das Symbol und die psychischen Bedingungen für sein Entstehen beim Kinde. *Z.I.*, 1913.
5. Bleuler, E.: Eine kasuistische Mitteilung zur kindlichen Theorie der Sexualvorgänge. *Jahrb.* III, 1912.
6. Ferenzi, S.: Ein kleiner Hahnemann. *Z.I.*, 1913.
7. Freud, S.: Analyse der Phobie eines fünfjährigen Knaben. *Jahrb.* I, 1909.
8. Ders.: Eine Kindenheit Serinnerung des Leonardo da Vinci. *Schr.* VII, 1910.
9. Ders.: Zwei Kinderlügen. *Z.I.*, 1913.
10. Friedjung, K. J.: Über verschiedene Quellen kindlicher Schamhaftigkeit. *Z.I.*, 1913.
11. Ders.: Beobachtungen über kindliche Onanie. *Zeitschr. f. Kinderheilk.*, Bd. IV, H.4.
12. Hitschmann, E.: Gesteigertes Triebleben und Zwangsneurose bei einem Kinde. *Z.I.,*, 1913.
13. Hug-Hellmuth, H.: Analyse eines Traumes eines 5½ jährigen Knaben. *Zbl.* II, 1911.
14. Dieselbe: Vom wahren Wesen der Kinderseele. *Imago* II, 1912. Mir Beiträgen von Lorenz, Reik, v. Hug-Hellmuth, Spielrein, Klette, Harnjk, Nanis.
15. Dieselbe: Aus dem Seelenleben des Kindes. *Schr.* XV, 1913.
16. Dieselbe: Kindervergehen und Unarten. *Z.I.*, 1913.
17. Jones, E.: Die Bedeutung der frühesten Eindrücke für die Bedeutung von Vorliebe und Abneigung. *Z.I.*, 1913.
18. Ders.: Psycho-Analysis and Education. Papers in Psycholanalysis, 1910.
19. Ders.: The Value of Sublimating Processes for Education and Re-education. Papers on Psychoanalysis, 1913.
20. Jung, C. G.: Über Konflikte der-kindlichen Seele. *Jahrb.* II, 1910.
21. Ders: Ein Beitrag zur Psychologie des Gerüchtes. *Zbl.* II, 1910.
22. Pfister, O.: Anwendungen der Psychoanalyse in der Pädagogik und Seelsorge. *Imago* I, 1912.
23. Ders.: Die psychanalytische Methode. I. Band des Pädagogium, 1913.
24. Rank, O.: Völkerpsychologische Parallelen zu den infantilen Sexualtheorien. *Zbl.* II, 1911.
25. Ders.: Ein Beitrag zur infantilen Sexualität; anschlissend v. Hug-Hellmuth: Ein weibliches Gegenstück. *Z.I.*, 1913.
26. Reitler, R.: Eine infantile Sexualtheorie und ihre Beziehung zur Selbstmordsymbolik, *Zbl.* II, 1911.
27. Sadger, T.: Das einzige und das Lieblingskind. *Fortschritte der Medizin*, 1911.
28. Über den Selbstmord, insbesondere den Schülerselbstmord, Diskussionen der Wiener psychoanalytischen Vereinigung. *H.I.*, 1910.

29. Spielrein, S.: Beiträge zur Kenntnis der kindlichen Seele. *Zbl.* III, 1912.
30. Tausk: Zur Psychologie der Kindersexualität. *Z.I.*, 1913.
31. Wulff: Beiträge zur infantilen Sexualität. *Zbl.* II, 1911.

Small Contributions Can Also Be Found In:

32. *Zentralblatt*, I. Band, 1911: von Stekel, S. 236, 614, Witt, S. 235; II. Band, 1912; von Friedjung S. 604, Hárnik, S. 37, v. Hug-Hellmuth S. 227, 603, Maeder, S. 137, Putnam, S. 328, Petersen 473; III. Band, 1913; von Hitschmann S. 37, Stekel S. 444.
33. *Imago*, I. Band: von Reik, S. 298.
34. *Zeitschrift*, I. Band, 1913: von Abraham S. 256, Bleuler S. 556, Ferenczi S. 381/82, Friedjung S. 71, Gineburg S. 79, Hitschmann, S. 476, v. Hug-Hellmuth S. 371, 470, Jekels, S. 375/76, Jones, S. 562, Lorenz S. 70, Oberholzer, S. 69, van Raalte S. 478, Stegmann S. 561.

War Neurosis in
Children (1915)

Hug-Hellmuth published two articles in 1915 dealing
with war neuroses in children and women ("Die Kriegsneurose der Frau" [War neurosis in women], *Geschlecht
und Gesellschaft* 9:504–14, 1915). The reason the following
paper on children was published in the feuilleton of a
Budapest daily (*Pester Lloyd-Morgenblatt*, March 5, 1915,
1–3), could not be elucidated, but it is interesting to note
that Sándor Ferenczi, who lived in Budapest in 1915,
published also about war neuroses one year later ("Über
zwei Typen der Kriegsneurose" [On two types of war
neurosis], *Internationale Zeitschrift für Ärztliche Psychoanalyse* 4:131–45, 1916–17).

The line of argumentation in both of Hug-Hellmuth's
papers on war neurosis is the same: There is no war
neurosis per se, but it can only unfold on the basis of an
underlying neurotic disposition. Therefore, the war is not
responsible for the neurosis manifestation but only serves
as a trigger for its manifestation. This argument is accompanied by a strong nationalistic pathos in both papers.

Events of war that fully affect our society of adults force individuals out of
boring or fascinating lives. Such events encourage sacrifices and great bravery.
They can create a new person often alien to himself. Rarely do such events
of war pass by a child without any influence, even if the child does not fully
understand the importance and impact of the great storms of war. These
forces unite countries and people who remember their ancient strength and
make them hope and despair, triumph and sigh. Even so, the child's cognitive
and emotional life is still touched by the thundering waves of fate. The
influence of the environment on the child is more intense and lasting than
we suspect or admit.

Since war is the greatest terror that threatens man in his culture, his
habits and inclinations, since war afflicts millions and destroys the work of
generations, it means to the child something very important. This meaning
affects the instinctual life of the child and threatens the normal equilibrium
of the child's soul. The events of war initially inflame the young soul in
enthusiastic imitation. They fill the child's play and this is used to cope
with the day's events. However, with sudden wildness it soon changes and
dominates the entirety of psychic life. However, the child's soul has difficulties orienting itself under the new conditions. External impressions impose
their influences and in addition the child still has to cope internally with
instinctual impulses of a new and unusual freedom that has been liberated

during the days of war. The child's soul cannot always deal with this double challenge. The child can fall ill with different symptoms. We can study these because of their relationship in time to the war neuroses of men.

When we use the term *war neurosis* we do not forget that there really is no such thing in the narrow sense of the word, that is, a neurosis caused by war. We know that the roots for this suffering have to have been laid much earlier. The most common forms of war neuroses, such as hysteria, phobias, and obsessive-compulsive neuroses, are caused by sexual distortions in early childhood. War only serves as a fertile ground to bring about the manifestation of illness. The hysterical symptoms, the obsessive thoughts and concerns are closely linked to current events. Laymen get the impression that the war actually is the cause and not its trigger, as for other neuroses and psychoses, including epilepsy, alcoholism, dementia praecox, and progressive paralysis. The public only too quickly links the disease to the incredible affects the soldier is helplessly exposed to in the field, especially if one sees that a returning soldier repeats and suffers in his fantasies the hardships, the horror of thousand deaths, and the terrible and deeply upsetting cruelties of war. In particular, if in addition the soldier shows a total blandness toward his environment or an affective fixation to certain thoughts or feelings, then it will be erroneously assumed that the war created what had been already prepared and ready to appear in the unfortunate's soul.

Similarly, if we talk about the war neurosis of women and children, the conditions are also set and the war is again only the trigger; whereas, in contrast, the loss of a loved person through death or real or imagined adultery, or a tragic fate, can be felt only as a lack of love in times of political quiescence.

We observe that war neuroses in children can be present in three different main forms: (1) The child displays an exclusive choice of games that fully satisfy aggressive impulses, inborn sadism, and natural brutality on the one hand and the lust of compassion and patience on the other hand. (2) We see sudden failures in learning. (3) A pathological eagerness to support the war with little deeds is accompanied by a neglect of individual interests. Apart from these three main manifestations, we observe an increased dream activity in many children using the material of the previous day. This allows for the freedom and activity of the above-mentioned impulses and themes.

If we consider contemporary games, we acknowledge certain characteristics that can't be neglected. It is understandable that boys' games deal exclusively with the war. However, during wartime this differs particularly from war games played prior to the war. The enemy consists of a few weaklings who are not popular with their peers. They will be forced to play this role if the role of the enemy is not missing altogether. The "mock enemy" in such play is in such a strong contrast to national love and the admiration for the emperor, that enemies really only exist somewhere behind a hill or around the corner.

Therefore, the game lacks its realistic touch. The discharge of physical energy in a real physical fight that normally ends the war game is lacking. Victory is only achieved in fantasy or fought against unwanted peers. Their physical inferiority made them easy targets and precluded an honest fight from the start. If repeated daily, this game causes an unconscious dissatisfaction. The unused physical energy is translated into a roughness of action and a meanness of language. This becomes especially apparent where education tries to influence the child differently. The child becomes wild and uncontrollable. Even the games of girls focus around the one issue of war. The inherent drive to help and comfort, to participate in the others' suffering, makes them quickly invent samaritan or "Red Cross" games that open a wide field for activity. However, frequently their fantasies are so exciting that their games continue into their sleep and cause terrifying dreams. This is a reliable indication of nervous overexcitement.

The other symptom of war neurosis in children is a sudden failure in learning. The child always has an affective motivation in learning. The child learns for his parents and for his teacher. As soon as the child recognizes that his parents are more interested in other things rather than him or his activity, he doesn't maintain his effort in learning. That is, his effort to maintain the sympathy of the loved person ends. He fails. However, the increased "nervousness" that during a time of war prevents children from their zest for learning is again only indirectly caused by the war. Primarily, it is caused by the child's neurotic concern not to be the focus of his parents' interest. The events of the external world attract the adults' attention. The infantile obstinacy against this assumed neglect is the real cause for his tiring interest. In the words of an older boy, "How can I learn if all my thoughts are with the war?" His question can be explained as obstinacy against his parents where the war formed the only topic of interest at their home. In accordance with a general rule that males revolt more violently against parental authority than females, boys show more difficulties at school than girls. The small child who is only learning to adapt to family life and to accommodate to the first demands of orderly behavior, expresses his increased nervousness in exaggerated tenderness toward his environment that has neglected him. The young child also can have spells of discomfort and fear. Finally, the young child can sometimes binge eat to enforce the usual amount of attention and love.

Increased instinctual activity and increased nervous tension become quite apparent on one occasion during the child's daily chores, that is, during supplementary war activities such as cotton plucking or cigarette manufacturing. These activities often prompt a pathological eagerness in the older youth that is supported by sibling rivalry in families with many children. All other interests become secondary. This fanaticism is dangerous to their health.

This causes concern especially during this time when there should be a healthy change of activity for everybody, rather than a preoccupation with one idea.

Considering the different symptomatology of war neuroses in children we have already mentioned, their deeper causes lie partly within the child's soul and partly within his environment. At every age we react strongly to the unfamiliar and strange. In later years people often react with strong defenses. Youth are more curious and eager for constant change. However, when everyday life becomes completely changed, this confuses the child. This happens even if the adults wisely control their conversations in the presence of children. Military transports with eager and cheerful soldiers leaving and other transports bringing home wounded fighters to the hospitals confuse the child's mind. Boys become angry. Because of their young age they cannot participate. That seems to be an injustice to them. Girls feel their inferiority as a double burden because they know that they don't even have the comfort of joining the army later. They experience their own sex as inferior and the value of the male sex becomes exaggerated. In both sexes the wish to be older may become pathological. The general admiration of those heroes who despite their young years helped the heroic cause of their countries is not free of envy and of rebellion against the authority of parents who prevent them from joining the forces. In a clinical case we saw a hopeful young lad direct a deadly weapon against himself killing himself because he was excluded from fighting. He was too young to enlist. A feeling of helplessness prevails in almost all letters that children send to the soldiers and dominates powerful and tenderly poetic words that regularly express honest admiration as well as envy. Such letters inevitably close with the hope that the child who is presently wasting his time at school will eventually join the older heroes of our time. These letters are revelations of internal discontent superimposed on an unprepared mind. Children feel most humiliated when they realize the discrepancies between their wishes and their abilities. Their rebellion against their own insufficiency is very bothersome. It makes them incapable of working. Either their intellectual skills or their physical resistance tire. They push themselves only to collapse after a short period of hurrying and coercion to serve the community.

These internal confusions are accompanied by influences of the environment that gain special importance for the child's psychic life. It is quite understandable that adults would be thoroughly fascinated by the events of the present. Their day-to-day life becomes a mere shadow before the background of the bloody world-drama. Almost every family is concerned about the welfare of their loved ones in the war. Even if a family escaped personal involvement, they may suffer even harder from the general fate and the tragedy of the world's misery. Personal pain may fill the heart and other pains remain silent or fuse with this suffering.

Haunted by neurotic fears and lustful horror at the same time, many people cannot refrain from describing the details of the horrors of war to young children. By their brutal boldness they seduce and poison the young souls. Following their own instincts, they describe every bloody detail of the horrible sadism of war. We can't deny that the child suffers more the more eagerly he listens to these reports. Psychoanalytic research has long proven that exaggerated defenses stem from strong affective impulses that have been suppressed by the unconscious. The exaggeration of this horror, with its unlimited potential for growth in fantasy, persecutes the child with terrifying pictures in his dreams and causes anxiety and sleeplessness. This originally stems from the child's suppressed natural brutality.

Besides the crass descriptions of death and suffering in the field, it is the adults' despondency that also shatters the balance of the youth's soul. Those unfortunate pessimists, for whom the future is equally dark whether we will be victorious or if we would be defeated by the tenfold majority of our enemies, make life difficult for themselves and equally difficult for the youth. Although the child as a born optimist will initially ignore the dark words, slowly the concerns and suggestions and the pessimistic attitude will find its way into the child's heart. Occasionally a whole family is haunted by this pessimism. The child copes mainly emotionally and tends towards affective exaggeration. As he still lacks cognitive control, he soon will be dominated by severe anxiety. This anxiety expresses itself in various forms even if it is not supported by ill-advised intimidation or threats against the child for being disobedient. Although undirected at first, it reflects the natural development of neurotic anxiety and it does soon focus on the hostile bombs, hunger, and infectious diseases. This anxiety has all characteristics of neurosis. It is apparently unfounded and exaggerated. Younger children are more prone to fears of bombs and enemy attacks at night that disturb their rest and sleep. Older children seem to be more anxious about infections and this frequently results in fears of physical contact. The environmental model again becomes important. These anxieties are normally unknown to the child. They appear only where the exaggerated anxiety of adults and the accompanying discussions do not take children into account. This stretches their capabilities beyond their limits. This elicits thoughts and feelings that severely hurt their physical and mental health.

These secondary causes of war neuroses are often accompanied by an anxious parsimony of the parents that a sensitive child will interpret as an unjustified deprivation of his demands, that is, a deprivation of love. Overlooking the real impact of the war itself on the war neuroses in children, we have to admit that this influence is very small compared to influences of his immediate environment. To restrict these influences correctly in these dark days is every mother's prime duty. Even if the youngest children have had to suffer under their mother's nervousness, at least the older children can be protected from a pathologically exaggerated emotionality of the adults. Children should understand the seriousness and greatness of our time. They can sympathize with our entire nation wholeheartedly. However, they have to be protected from overwhelming impressions that their tender souls cannot tolerate.

On Early Loving and Hating (1917)

In 1917 Hug-Hellmuth published two contributions in her *Imago* column, the following paper ("Von frühem Lieben und Hassen," *Imago* 5:121–22) and a book review of Meta Schoepp's *Mein Junge und ich* (Concordia-Deutsche Verlagsanstalt, Berlin, 1910) that appeared in the same issue (pp. 129–31). This paper deals with children's normal behavioral expressions of ambivalence within the family.

1

The bitterness of resistance against the unconscious is a measurement of the truth of the unconscious. This helps to explain the persistence of the unaccepting attitude of laymen toward the "Oedipus complex," toward the ambivalent feelings of a child about his parents, toward his erotically based identification with mother and father, and no less toward the parental love for son and daughter that does not always lack conscious eroticism. Therefore, the acceptance of these psychoanalytic findings in everyday events or in the writings of sensitive authors is very valuable. The following pathology will present a number of such proofs.

Something that was directly observed in children will be presented first:

(a) A four-year-old boy who was attached affectionately to his mother experienced his father primarily as a threatening stronger power who had to be loved simply because he was his father. One day the boy said: "Once I'm big I'll buy a cow for myself and my mother that will bite father."

The combination of "myself and mother" brings up the infantile perception of the togetherness of the mother and child. It was especially the father who had punished the boy repeatedly and harshly because of the boy's exhibitionistic and other strong impulses. The frequent perception of children, especially of boys, that the mother equals the nameless part of their own body that is thought to be so important, might be one reason for the size of the animal. He did choose a cow to execute his thoughts of retaliation against the father. The boy had been repeatedly threatened that a dog would bite off his "bad finger." Therefore, we see that what is to be done to the boy by a dog will be done by a larger animal, a cow, to the big father with the big hands.

(b) It has been the greatest pleasure for two boys, five and three years old, to slip into mother's bed in the morning as soon as father has left the parental bedroom. Contacts with her body are noted carefully. Neither allowed the other to intrude into his area—not even with his finger. Each transgression is followed by a bitter fight—on top of mother's body. The attitude toward the father is influenced by the assumed preference of the mother to one of the competitors. The basic affect of both boys toward the father is explicitly hostile and jealous.

One of the boys died in his sixteenth year. The other one remained fixated to the mother all his life, and she revealed her attitude towards him in the typical behavior of a mother-in-law toward her daughter-in-law.

At age thirty this son noticed, while on a walk through town, a woman in front of him, who attracted him so much that he followed her. When he caught her at a corner and was just going to address her, she turned her head around and he recognized her. He was mortified—the woman was his mother.

(c) The odd habit some children have of calling one of the parents by their first name is found to be more common in boys addressing their mothers. Rarely do girls do the same to their fathers. From my knowledge, hardly ever does a child call the parent of the same sex by their first name. We deal here with identification with the parent of the same sex and unconscious heterosexual attraction.

(d) The following case is presented because no one from my knowledge has yet reported his observations about the development of the Oedipus complex in children who have been raised by their mothers after the parent's separation. We do not have to consider the father because of formal reasons: The parents of a boy separated when he was three years old. The child remained with his mother and he loved her passionately. However, he desired strongly his father up to his sixth year of life even though he was criticized by his father harshly and frequently in those early years. With caution and tactfulness the bright boy assumed that the father didn't play a very good role and had simply abandoned his wife and child. So deep hatred found its way into his soul in addition to his love. It is this hatred that sometimes breaks through, despite the affectionate letters that he writes to the father. "When I'm big and my father is old and he comes to me begging, then I will tell him: I will not give you anything, because when I was little you didn't care for me and my mother. Go away." But again a few days later he insisted on visiting his father during a journey with his mother which came close to his father's house. He hoped to see him at the station and he was very excited during the way from the station to the hotel. He seemed to recognize his father in all passers-by. That is how love and hate struggle in the child's soul and make him premature, confused, and tired.

Despite the tender love of his mother, the boy sometimes took his father's side, for instance, when her clothes appear to him too simple and he says: "If we go to X. [the town where the father lives], you have to put on a nice dress so that father will like you when we see him." He often criticizes her makeup or he does not like her appearance when she comes home hot and tired from her job. Once he is grown up he wants to buy her nice clothes and hats and "many bottles of perfume that make you smell nicely."

This case and the very similar fate of another little girl prove that children whose parents separate have a deep, often unconscious love that coexists with an obvious hatred towards the absent parent. This could be in part a guilt reaction within the child, with the love for the father covering the existing hatred, in defence.

On the Technique of Child-Analysis (1920)

This paper was first presented at the Sixth International Psychoanalytic Congress in The Hague, The Netherlands, September 8–12, 1920. The abstract appeared in 1920 ("On the Technique of the Analysis of Children," *International Journal of Psychoanalysis* 2:361–62) and the complete text was published one year later both in German (*Zentralblatt für Psychoanalyse und Psychotherapie* 7:179–97, 1921) and in English (On the technique of child-analysis, trans. R. Gabler and B. Low, *International Journal of Psychoanalysis* 2:287–305, 1921).

As previously described (*Studien zur Kinderpsychoanalyse* (Vienna) 7:9–16, 1987), this paper anticipates the essential structural elements of Anna Freud's famous book on the technique of child-analysis *Einführung in die Technik der Kinderanalyse* (Vienna, 1927), although Anna Freud never recognized this particular source of her work. It is interesting to compare step by step how strikingly similar the approach of these two pioneers was who must have known one another very well from the meetings of the Vienna Psychoanalytic Society and from their work in the Psychoanalytic Ambulatorium.

"The answer to technical problems in psychoanalytic practice is never obvious."

Freud, *Sammlung kleiner Schriften zur Neurosenlehre*, IV. Folge

The analysis both of the child and of the adult has the same end and object, namely, the restoration of the psyche to health and equilibrium which have been endangered through influences known and unknown.

The task of the physician is fulfilled when a cure has been effected, no matter what ethical and social standards the patient pursues; it suffices that the individual becomes once more adapted to life and his vocation, and that he is no longer liable to succumb to the demands and disappointments of life.

The curative and educative work of analysis does not consist only in freeing the young creature from his sufferings, it must also furnish him with moral and aesthetic values. The object of such curative and educative treatment is not the mature man who when freed is able to take responsibility for his own actions: but the child, the adolescent, that is, human beings who are still in the developing stage, who have to be strengthened through the educative guidance of the analyst, in order to become human beings with strong wills and definite aims. He who is both analyst and educator must never forget that the aim of child-analysis is character-analysis—in other words, education.

The peculiarity of the child-psyche, its special relationship to the outside world, necessitates a special technique for its analysis.

There are three considerations of fundamental importance:

1. The child does not come of his own accord to the analyst, as the grown-up does, but owing to the wish of his parents and only then (and herein he resembles the grown-up) when all other means have proved futile.

2. The child is in the midst of the very experiences which are causing his illness. The grown-up suffers from past experiences, the child from present ones; and his ever-changing experiences create a perpetually changing relationship between himself and his surroundings.

3. The child, unlike the adult man (but very often in accordance with the attitude of women patients), has no desire at all to change himself or to give up his present attitude toward his external surroundings. His "naughtiness" creates in him a sense of great self-importance, indeed a feeling of omnipotence, owing to which he tyrannizes over the people who surround him, and his narcissism which rejoices in the continual attention which he wins from his surroundings will not allow him to give up his wickedness. To the child with strong sadistic tendencies as well as to the child with pronounced masochism, constantly recurring outbursts of fury and punishments are essential to his neurotic personality. We must also include those fortunate natures who adapt themselves even as children to every different phase of life, who remember only the pleasure of "making it up" in the continual quarrels of childhood, and who take a temporary exile in a boarding-school as a pleasant change—we mean, in short, those who can adapt themselves to every change in their environment.

For instance, a small boy, a habitual pilferer, whom I had for treatment, took all his experiences in school and at home just as "a lark" and squared his conscience in regard to his complete failure at school with the reflection: "My father did not like learning either, and yet we are doing so well." Another twelve-year-old boy, a little truant, whom I analyzed in the Vienna children's clinic, enjoyed his stay there so much, on account of the nice food he got, that in spite of his often expressed longing for his parents, he had no desire whatever to depart.

Experience has taught me that girls at the age of puberty are more helpless when confronted by conflicts in the home life, and more sensitive to them, than are boys of the same age. The explanation of this lies partly in the fact that the girl has stronger links with her home life on account of her education aiming more at repression, partly in the fact that she has less power to overcome, by way of sublimation, the incestuous impulses which are ready to burst out at this critical period.

In the case of phobia in a five-year-old boy, Freud has shown us the method (and this has become the basis of psycho analytic child-therapy) by which we can throw light on these psychic depths in a small child where the libidinous stirrings change into childish anxiety. At this stage of life an analysis similar to the analytic treatment of the adult is not possible. One can only apply educational methods founded on psychoanalytical knowledge. A full understanding of the child's world of thoughts and feelings will call out its unlimited confidence, and thus a way is discovered to safeguard the child from various errors and injuries. As the training of the young child, both physical and mental, rest especially with women, it becomes essential that we should train understanding and kindhearted women for educational psychoanalytic work.

A proper analysis according to psychoanalytical principles can only be carried out after the seventh or eighth year. But even with children at this early age the analyst must, as I will show later, turn aside from the usual routine, and satisfy himself with partial results, where he thinks that the child might be intimidated by too powerful a stirring-up of his feelings and ideas, or where too high demands upon his powers of assimilation are being made, or where his soul is disturbed instead of freed.

Generally speaking, there are two groups of these child-patients; namely, those who know from the beginning, or soon learn, in what the treatment consists, its aim and object, and those others who owing to their tender age, or to the fact that they do not suffer personally from their symptoms (for example, in the case of marked homosexual tendencies), or owing to individual factors (such as a feeble constitution), cannot be enlightened as to the object of the analytic treatment. Such children can be safely left to the idea that the analyst spends these hours with them in order to communicate some knowledge to them or to wean them from some misbehavior, or to play with them, or from a special interest in them.

For instance, a delicate thirteen-year-old boy did not doubt for a moment that I was, as his mother said, a friend of his father who was in the war, and that I came to wish the youngster many happy returns of the day. As he had an impediment in his speech, he also accepted quite trustingly the further explanation that I would teach him to speak distinctly, and he actually tried himself to speak more clearly.

The mother of an eleven-year-old boy, who loved him completely in his fantasies and dreams, chose, without my sanction, a form of introduction which I thought might have proved harmful. She said that a friend of hers was very much interested in children's dreams and would like him to talk to her about his own. However, the course of the analysis convinced me that no harm had been done, for the somewhat artificial accounts of dreams given in the beginning were after all only reflections of his conscious and unconscious daydreams.

No rule can be laid down for the appropriate moment to tell the patient the aim of these talks; experience and personal tact are the only reliable guides.

In close connection with the above matter is the formulating of the obligations which must be carried out by the adult patient at the beginning as a sine qua non if a cure is to be effected. Right from the beginning one understands that in the case of the second type of psychoanalytic patients one must abandon the demand for absolute openness, and uncensored expression of everything which comes into the mind, and instead put forward this obligation only at some favorable opportunity. In the case of the first-mentioned group, however, those more mature young people who often have already had instruction concerning psychoanalysis from some other member of the family who has already undergone treatment, it is often suitable in the very first hour to demand that they shall be completely frank and shall not talk over the treatment with their comrades, their brothers and sisters, or other members of the family. Of course, in connection with this enjoining of secrecy, we must not overlook that commands and prohibitions are the very means of tempting the young to transgress.

The period of time devoted to the child's analysis is generally conditioned by the attendance at school, which the parents do not want on any account to be shortened. Apart from the few cases where the young patient has special difficulties in preserving the continuity, I have always found that three or four hours a week, if the analysis is carried on long enough, leads to successful results. An exact keeping to time appears to me of the greatest importance. It involves a self-education which the young person must undergo. Sometimes it needs strong self-control to reject some important communication which the child has kept back till the end of the hour, but to concede to such demands would mean that the patient was allowed to get the upper hand.

While the educative analysis of children of more mature age (say, from fourteen to eighteen) resembles more that of the grown-up—for in the very first hours, we can speak of the factors in the treatment, of positive and negative transference, of resistance, and of the significance of the unconscious psychic tendencies in the whole of our experience—the analysis of the younger or backward child proceeds on different lines from the beginning.

I consider it inadvisable to take the young patient to the consultation with the analyst. The child feels himself exposed and humiliated while he waits in another room during the consultation, and often this creates in him excitement, maybe anxiety, resentment, defiance, shame, all of which endangers the subsequent treatment, or at least makes the beginning much more difficult. If one has to break down a resistance before getting an opportunity to build a bridge of mutual understanding, one is, so to speak, confronted with a task similar to that of clearing away a heap of debris which lies at the other side of a yawning chasm.

Just as the first meeting between the analyst and the young patient should take place in the latter's home, so should it be with the treatment itself. The analysis must go on independently of the whims of the patient, who can very cleverly contrive to have a slight indisposition which prevents him coming, or arriving in time, or he may play truant in the analysis hour. The child not only lacks interest in the money problem (which for the grown-up is a continual stimulus to make him continue the treatment uninterruptedly), but in addition he knows that he has an opportunity of causing his parents expense and of satisfying his own defiance and desires for revenge. Of course, every child when at the height of a positive transference tries to transfer the analysis to the home of the analyst; but I have always gained the conviction that even when external circumstances demanded this change of place, such a change proved not to be lasting. However, much of the time and energy of the analyst is burdened by this demand, since he can only see daily half the number of patients as compared with those treated by his medical colleagues, and although an absolutely undisturbed and private talk in the patient's own house is difficult to obtain, nevertheless these evils seem to me trifling compared with the greater one of letting the child decide the external conditions of the analysis. Another consideration is that the parents, in spite of all their devotion, very soon feel that chaperoning of the child to and from the analyst's house becomes impossible and this difficulty is used as a reason for terminating the treatment—a situation well known to every child-analyst.

However favorable may be a temporary absence from home for difficult children, nevertheless I have my doubts as to the value of psychoanalytic treatment for them in any kind of institution, whether they are boarders or day-pupils, for one reason because the child finds the necessity for secrecy in a situation where he feels himself more important than his comrades very difficult to endure, and for another, because he easily becomes a target for their ridicule when he has to have a special "treatment hour," about the aim and object of which the other children cannot obtain information. What the treatment will be like in future happier times when perhaps some of my ideas for the founding of psychoanalytic homes for young children have been realized I cannot foretell, but I believe that it will need quite special tact, great educational skill, and experience to meet successfully the great difficulties which will arise in psychoanalytic treatment owing to collective life. The jealousy among the patients themselves, the making of comparisons not always favorable to one's own analyst, the exchange of confidences between the children about their analysis which cannot be prevented—all these things are difficulties which must not be underrated. Nevertheless, I believe that the creation of psychoanalytic "homes" will either solve the problem of the guidance of the "difficult" child which so many parents and schools fail in, or at least make the problem easier.

An important difference between the analysis of the child and of the grown-up results from what seems a merely external circumstance, namely, whether the patient should lie down or sit up during treatment. For the very juvenile patient, this question is already answered by the limitations which his age imposes. But also in the case of the older child the notion of "lying down" produces in the child an anxiety situation. To lie down awakens in the child the memory of some real or imagined scene of being overpowered: one will be afraid of a beating, another of an operation, and both are overcome by their secret feeling of guilt, a fear of castration. Adolescent patients imagine themselves while lying down to be under hypnosis and exposed to rape. Seduction fantasies of both homosexual and heterosexual nature which are projected on to the analyst play a great part with so-called nervous boys and girls when they have to lie down.

A fifteen-year-old boy who came for my educative treatment on account of a serious phobia of thunderstorms and earthquakes, confessed to me in the course of analysis that he would certainly have resisted the treatment if he had been obliged to lie down on the sofa which, he had heard, a family acquaintance had to do in his analysis, for he was in continual dread of being hypnotized. As a matter of fact, this boy had worked himself into such a serious condition of excitement during a consultation with a nerve specialist at home, who tried to hypnotize him, that he cried out "Police" and finally dashed out of the house in a panic into the street.

I have never noticed that the success of the analysis is in any way imperiled by the fact that the analyst faces the patient.

The first hour in treatment is of the utmost importance; it is the opportunity for establishing a rapport with the young creature, and for "breaking the ice." It causes much strain and stress to the beginner and nearly always opens up even to the experienced analyst new methods of approach and new guiding lines. But no rules and no program can be laid down; the intellectual development, the age, and the temperament of the patient must determine which course to pursue. In the case of more mature patients, often the right course is for the analyst to say as much openly, in order to gain their confidence wholeheartedly.

The mother of a nervous girl of fourteen introduced me to her daughter as a friend whom she had not seen for many years, but the girl was not to be deceived by this; after a little while she inquired: "But who are you really?" My honest explanation, that I was interested in young people who find life very difficult and are unable to grapple with it, and that I should like to help her to get on better with her mother, had the desired effect. The girl became strongly attached to me and came to me for advice about all matters which disturbed her, as to her "second and real mother."

Sometimes, in the case of those patients who obstinately shut themselves up, a ruse is helpful. For example, a nine-year-old boy with suicidal impulses, during the first hour took not the slightest notice of me, but simply laid his head on the table and made no response to any remark. A fly passing close to my face suggested to me the idea of pretending that I had got something in my eye. At once the boy, who always wished to be in the limelight, jumped up, saying: "Please let me see, I will get it out; but you must not rub your eye." Thus, with his proffered help the ice was broken, because he felt himself of use to me. Every time, after this, when a strong resistance made him retire into silence, I had only to ask for his advice or his help, and the analysis once more progressed favorably.

A ruse which, in my opinion, never fails, is to tell a young patient about the misdeeds of other children. As one has already been sufficiently informed by the parents about the misdemeanors and peculiarities of one's little patient, one need not be afraid of inciting the child, by such accounts of others, to similar naughtiness which he has not indulged in up to the present. No child has so far been harmed, in either a sexual or any other way, by a properly conducted analysis. Though a temporary increase in bad behavior may lead the layman to such an idea, the analyst is able to appreciate it as a sign of progress.

The reaction of the child to this kind of beginning may be of three types. Often the patient reacts with a story of similar misdeeds, which at first are described as having been done by another child, and only later on admitted as his own. Or, secondly, he may reply with a fierce denial: "I have never done such things!" From the analysis of the grown-up, we are aware that such emphatic denials are tantamount to admissions. Thirdly, the child may accept the information with absolute indifference. Then we can scarcely be wrong in assuming that the parents have misunderstood something in the behavior of the child, or that behind the known facts something more is hidden.

When dealing with children of seven or eight years of age, the analyst can often pave the way by sharing in the play activities, and thus he can recognize several symptoms, peculiar habits, and character traits; and in the case of these very young patients, very often play will be important throughout the whole treatment.

A seven-year-old boy, who suffered from severe insomnia accompanied with compulsive laughter and tic, which made me suspect he had watched the parental sex-life, manifested during daytime complete apathy: he lay on the carpet for hours without speaking or playing; he ate a great deal but without enjoyment or selection, and apparently had quite suddenly lost his former strongly marked desire for caresses. In the analysis he would allow me to play with his toys for the whole hour, with scarcely any reaction on his part, and seldom gave me an answer, so that it was difficult to decide whether he had taken in at all what I said. In one of the first treatment hours I told him about a little boy who would not go to sleep at night, and made such a noise that his parents could not sleep either. I told also how little Rudi made a noise too in the afternoons when his father wanted to rest; so his father became angry and Rudi was whipped (Little Hans's reaction to this was to run to the sideboard and take down a "Krampus" and to beat me on the arm, saying: "You are naughty!"). I went on to tell how Rudi was then cross with his father, and wished his father were somewhere else (To this the reaction was: "My father is at the war." Actually his father, an officer of high rank, was on active service throughout the war, and had only returned to his family in Vienna on short leave.) Suddenly Hans took his little gun and said: "Puff, puff."

The next day his death wishes toward his father showed themselves more clearly. He was playing with his toy motor car and several times ran over the chauffeur, whom I had made out to be little Rudi's father. I pretended to telephone the news of his father's accident to the little boy. Rudi was supposed to weep bitterly at the news, and then I said that although Rudi had formerly wished his strict father away, now he felt very sad, because in spite of this wish, he really loved his father very much. The reaction of little Hans was very characteristic; he listened to me, lying on the floor, asking me eagerly now and then, "What does little Rudi do next?" Suddenly he jumped up and ran out of the room. On the following day he reacted in the same way when our game was repeated, at his request. In his sudden going out of the room, we can see clearly the working of the unconscious. It also shows us an important difference in the course of psychic functioning in the grown-up and in the child. Whereas in the analysis of the adult, we aim at bringing about full insight into unconscious impulses and feelings, in the case of a child, this kind of avowal expressed, without words, in a symbolic act, is quite sufficient. We learn, indeed, from the analysis of the child that in him the psychic events take place in quite different layers from those of the grown-up, that they may be more closely or more remotely connected with each other and that in the child many impressions leave clearly marked traces in spite of never having reached the threshold of consciousness. Even analysis does not make conscious these fragmentary memories of "primordial scenes." The blending of new impressions with these former takes place, perhaps, in the preconscious, and it is left to later experiences at a higher stage of development to bring them into consciousness. This would supply a further explanation of the fact that the very earliest impressions which are very much alike for all human beings (such as, for example, the methods of upbringing) lay the foundation for neurosis in some while others pass through them unharmed.

It is most rare for the young patient to put out his psychic feelers, or to talk freely during the first treatment hour, since he is full of mistrust towards his analyst, who is the father- or mother-imago, unless it so happens that an extreme bitterness against his parents or brothers and sisters compels the child to break out into complaints and abuse. In such cases, it is necessary to manifest to the young patient the greatest forbearance and a full consideration of his troubles.

The communications or symptomatic actions in the first treatment hour are of the greatest importance, for they demonstrate the nuclear-complex of the infantile neurosis.

A fifteen-year-old boy came to me for analytic treatment on account of severe anxiety conditions, which he himself speedily declared to be "anxiety of anxiety." The first thing he said was: "In our form at school, the two best pupils are Jews, I come next, and again after that, the next best are Jews, and the rest are Gentiles." By this formulation the boy betrayed his ever-gnawing feeling of reproach against the father, who owing to marriage with a gentile, had become a convert from Judaism to Protestantism.

Little Hans, to whom we are indebted for valuable insight into the mechanism of the child's psychic functioning, was aroused from his complete apathy by the following game: I saw in the looking-glass that he poked his finger into his nose, and I said: "Oh dear, whatever is Hans doing? I don't want to see such a sight!" Whereupon he stood in front of the mirror, smiling roguishly, and said, "Don't look!" poking his finger again into his nose. Of course, he expects me to forbid him and untiringly repeats this game, only exchanging his nose poking for putting out his tongue. This game symbolizes to him the oft-experienced strictness of his father, which he tries to evade by keeping secret his little misdeed.

A sixteen-year-old suffered in a marked degree from inferiority feelings, owing to squinting. She spontaneously covered up my spectacles which lay on the table—a symptomatic action which revealed that she was unwilling to be reminded of eyes or their abnormalities. She admitted to me later on that this defect of mine had for a long time disturbed her affectionate relations towards me.

A ten-year-old boy, who was rather a failure at his work owing to his very extreme habit of daydreaming, in the first treatment hour informed me how greatly he disliked the pose of the hero in a performance of *Lohengrin* which he had witnessed. He ostentatiously turned his back toward me, imitating the singer's position, declaring it unsuitable for a performer on the stage, asking me: "Surely, Doctor, an actor should not stand in such a position in front of the public?" After a short course of analysis, my original suspicion was confirmed, namely, that the boy was suffering from a strongly repressed exhibitionism.

The first communication of a fourteen-year-old girl, who was harassed by painful brooding, was a very contemptuous criticism of the geographical teaching which she received at the age of ten or eleven, which consisted of continual repetition about "climate" and even now in the high school it was the same subject all over again: climate, the position of the sun and its shadow—these were pursued with the same persistency. "Whatever is the object of teaching the movements of the sun to an eleven-year-old child who cares nothing about the subject?" and so forth—this complaint filled up the whole hour of treatment with the greatest monotony, and in the subsequent hours she continually returned to this subject, until at last was revealed the connection between this question and what was really the girl's main interest—sexual intercourse between human beings. In a roundabout way (first under the guise of her great liking for horses—she was greatly interested in books on horse-breeding—then of her interest in description of travels and the love relations of foreign peoples), the main preoccupation finally emerged: "For how long a period do the men and women of foreign races have intimate relations with one another (having in mind her own father and mother)?"

The demand for "active therapy" which is made for the analysis of the adult is also of importance in child-analysis. It is certainly advisable for quite a number of patients that during the course of analysis they should be given small tasks to perform. Especially in the case of the patient who suffers from strong inferiority feelings, if a due measure of work be demanded of him, his self-confidence will be strengthened.

The shy, dependent weak boy (of whom I spoke above) who had difficulty with his speech and suffered a great deal from the ridicule of street-boys, surprised his grandfather after a six months' treatment by his manly, self-reliant behavior with his seniors. The boy, who formerly would scarcely go outside the house, improved so much by analysis that he joined in walks, and went along, first for me, then for his mother, to execute little commissions for us—which he carried out very successfully.

More important than making positive requests is the avoidance, as far as possible, of any direct prohibitions, and, again, more valuable than both prohibitions and commissions is talking over things together. This mutual weighing up of the pros and cons of a given situation will influence the self-confidence of the patient repressed by his inferiority feelings.

No more for the child than for the adult can a program for the course of analysis be laid down. Kind and sympathetic attention, encouraging, occasionally joking words at the right moment, a loving interest in all the trifles to the child, indicate the way to gain the full confidence of the young creature. In addition, to forget nothing and to confuse nothing said in previous sittings—this completes the demands made by the child upon the analyst. How far, and when, free association should be made use of, can only be decided as the circumstances arise. So far as my own experience goes, Abraham's remark that older people need more guidance in analysis than the younger ones holds good for both the young child and the adolescent. Perhaps we would add that in the case of these latter, greater care has to be used than with the grown-up. True, it is difficult to disentangle deep-rooted and rigid ideas and feelings, but the greater plasticity of the youthful mind lends itself easily to the danger of unintended suggestion instead of yielding to the patient the clearest possible insight. Over and over again I have been able to prove to myself that children know far more about the things that go on in their surroundings than we grown-ups, owing to our anxious solicitude, wish to admit. Does it not sound almost tragicomic to receive unexpectedly the confession of an eleven-year-old girl (whose repeated questions about the sexual act I have carefully tried to answer step by step) that when she was five her mother enticed her to look through the keyhole and thus spy on her father when having intercourse with a prostitute!

Of course, dreams play their part in child-analysis also, but we need not fear, any more than in the case of adults, that resistance will produce a more intense or imaginary dream-experience. The so-called night-dream signifies only a daydream to which perhaps the child would never otherwise give expression. And here I wish to emphasize the difficulty there is in getting some children to speak out freely all their ideas because they cannot free themselves from the habit fixed by the daily teaching, namely: "not to talk nonsense" and so forth.

Although naturally in child-analysis technical expressions, such as the Oedipus and castration complex, exhibitionism, etc., cannot be made use of; nevertheless, the real facts must be made clear. Even in the case of a very young patient, it is necessary to explain certain phenomena in the course of treatment. He will quite easily understand the meaning of "resistance" if first it is explained to him in connection with "the negative transference," that is, his refusal to speak out of a spirit of defiance; and later in connection with the "positive transference," that is, his feeling of shame at making a confession to the analyst which is humiliating to himself or his family; and in the end he will understand the readily acquired phrase: "Now I have no more to say."

Out of the resistance which expresses itself in the form of unwillingness to humiliate his family, we can find a way of explanation concerning the negative transference, which is generally much more readily accepted than the idea of the positive transference. Discussion about this latter, even when it is quite clearly recognized, demands special caution in formulating it, because at bottom the child is unwilling to exchange his own parents for any stranger, even when there is every good reason for so doing. In spite of this, however, the child's first attitude at the beginning of the treatment is generally a strong positive transference, owing to the fact that the analyst, by sympathetic and dispassionate listening, realizes the child's secret father—or mother—ideal. Of course he makes use of this attitude at once against his own family. This results in those intensely irritating remarks made by the child to his people, such as "Doctor said I need not do this or that," or "I must ask Doctor first about this." The child takes for granted that the analyst, by listening to his complaints in the treatment hour, is in agreement with him, and from this he builds up his fantasies and attributes to them the value of reality. Also the juvenile patient is continually ready to plot against his parents, and in this he relies upon the support of his analyst. The child, just like the grown-up, when at the height of his positive transference, is unwilling to end the treatment.

The negative transference usually appears first in the form of a fear of being deceived. For everything they say, they demand oaths of secrecy, for their mistrust toward the analyst is the product both of unwillingness to lay themselves bare, and of the countless disappointments which even the most favorable home conditions provide for the child from his earliest years. This is also the reason why he anxiously and jealously watches the interviews between the analyst and his parents and tries to overhear them and shorten them.

We know what an important part is played in the child's psychic life by sexuality, and its observation, and by the diverting of this childish interest by the family circle. The child is accustomed to get very unsatisfactory answers from his parents and other grown-up members of the family to the riddle of sex, and therefore he reacts in two ways to the straightforward talk in the analysis about sexual matters. He feels more important, like a grown-up man, and tries hard to reward the analyst's frankness by greater friendship: on the other hand, as soon as stronger resistance sets in, he is at once ready (owing to his earlier repressions) to belittle the analyst because he has talked on tabooed matters. So strong with the child is the parental authority and the first educational influence, that he expects the same claims to be made upon himself, and the same outlook in life, from every grown-up who is interested in him. To him the analyst embodies, but in much stronger form than to the adult, the father- or mother-imago. On that account it takes a long time before he can feel convinced that the analyst does not take the parent's part, and that he can expect from the analyst full freedom and complete understanding for all his utterances. The child's over-estimation of authority, in both a positive and negative sense, makes the analysis difficult, for the patient watches with a keen eye for any defects in the analyst which gives him an excuse for gainsaying his belief in authority. And the young person, especially the child, thinks he finds this wished-for defect in the analyst's frank talk about sexual problems, and therefore in this phase of the treatment the ambivalence of the patient toward his guide and adviser is most apparent. The notable difference between his parents as they are in reality and their image in his phantasy reawakens once more in its original intensity the very earliest child-wish, namely, that his little heart should once more be able to confide in his father and mother and with this all the old feelings of early disappointment are revived. Owing to this unavoidable conflict which has its foundation in the childish memories of the young soul, and in its attitude to the analyst, arise the fundamental demands made upon the latter by the patient. The chief thing in the analysis of children and young people is the analyst's power of intuition in regard to the sufferer. It does not matter so much whether many complexes are made conscious to the young patient, or how much "insight" he gains, the reaction is sufficient at the beginning. Often, much later, some chance word from the child shows that he has preserved and appreciated at its true value the explanation which he had at an earlier stage. But this acceptance does not take place by means of conscious work: a great part of the psychoanalytic process in the child takes place in his unconscious, and contrary to the case of the grown-up, it remains permanently there, and only a change in his behavior proves to the analyst that his trouble has not been in vain. In my experience, it is those children whose seeming compliance might tempt one to satisfaction, who are the most difficult type for treatment: they are the well-drilled kind, who say yes to everything, but in their hearts say no and act accordingly.

Intuition and patience, these are the foundations which must be laid from the first meeting with the young patient, in order that confidence may rest on solid ground.

An important factor in child-analysis is the relationship between the analyst and the young patient's family. One might think that in this respect the analyst-educator would have an advantage over his medical colleagues, since the child comes for treatment owing to the parents' wish, whereas the adult comes of his own accord, very often quite against the wish of his family. Unfortunately, this idea is quite incorrect. In the case of the child as well, psychoanalysis is looked upon as the last resource, and the parents, who have found all other educational measures fail, have a good deal of mistrust even of psychoanalysis. In spite of this, they expect a "miraculous cure" which shall remedy in the course of days the mistakes of years. And the relatives cling to this expectation, in spite of the analyst's quite explicit information that the duration of the treatment cannot be fixed in advance because it is dependent upon the individual character of the child, but that it will certainly stretch over several months. I have proved over and over again that the relatives from the very beginning of the treatment have privately settled in their own minds a time limit, and this they maintain, incapable of sufficient insight to understand that to break off treatment half-way through means waste of time, trouble, and money. Of course, the psychoanalytic treatment itself is held responsible for the consequence of the premature breaking-off, namely, that there is a considerable intensification of the original trouble— and this is produced by the child (in part consciously, in part unconsciously) owing to his revolt against the loss of treatment which though at first compulsory has become indispensable to him. The parents' criticism of the treatment is made more poignant owing to their painful consciousness, mingled with shame, anxiety, and bitterness, of having failed in regard to their children's successful training. In addition, the knowledge that the analysis reveals all the mistakes made in the upbringing of the child in spite of the best intentions, and that the analyst obtains an insight (very undesirable from the parent's point of view) into intimate family affairs creates in most parents distrustful and anxious feelings. This reluctance to lay bare family affairs proves a greater hindrance in the case of child-analysis than in the case of the adult, for the latter is willing to sacrifice, for the sake of his own recovery, the consideration he holds for his family. Another difficulty arises from the over-anxiety of the parents to further and hasten the analysis by their cooperation. The mothers, at all events, nearly always show a desire to make use of "active therapy." It is terribly difficult to convince them that their work lies in quite another direction and that they are really acting as helpers if they show the child during the treatment the greatest possible measure of patience and forbearance. They must develop the understanding that the young mind during the analysis has to go through a process of recrystallization, during which first the old values are destroyed; and this destructive process cannot take place without disturbances, and these shocks have an outlet in an increase of the very difficulties and peculiarities which have to be eliminated. Quite usually after a striking temporary improvement in the symptoms (arousing in the parents premature expectation of cure in a few weeks or even hours in spite of the analyst's emphatic warning as to the duration of the analysis), a marked change for the worse takes place. Some children rebel more violently than ever against the parents' rules and regulations: others who have failed in their work owing to their extreme phantasy-life, will take advantage of the unwanted freedom to express now without check their daydreams, and for the time being, they turn away from their work more completely than before. This apparent deterioration in the outward behavior of the child, which reveals his psychic condition, is regarded quite differently by the parents and by the analyst; the latter sees in it a good sign for the further progress of the analysis.

It is not easy to convince the parents that the renunciation of the desire for the children's success in work during the process of analysis holds out the promise of that very success when the treatment is over. They are very unwilling to allow as much importance to a psychic trouble as to a physical one. Just as no father would think of sending his child to school when suffering from pneumonia, so no demands must be made for study from the child suffering psychically.

The narcissism of the parents explains their extreme jealousy, experienced especially by the mother, when they see their child so ardently attaching himself to the analyst. In this connection an important task devolves upon the analyst who has to explain to the mother that the positive transference is a passing phenomenon but one necessary to the success of the analysis, and in no way deprives her permanently of her child's love.

In spite of the difficulties which prevent the relations between the parents and analyst being so friendly as might be desirable in the interests of the child, this relationship is inevitable. It is a legitimate demand on the part of the parents and furthers the treatment. For the child passes over, instinctively and, unlike the adult, without conscious criticism, everything which has no "feeling-tone" for him and which is settled and done with. Consequently, very often we learn nothing in the analysis of difficulties at home or at school, because the child does not feel the need to revise these scenes, and his interest in them disappears as soon as they have played their part according to his expectations. In addition, we must not forget that the child consciously also keeps secrets. In order to ascertain some special date, or the accuracy of some memory, it is sometimes useful to question the parents; and further it is valuable for obtaining an insight into the earliest stage of the patient's life. It is here that the parents can satisfy their desire for active cooperation in the analysis, by means of written replies to the analyst's series of questions, concerning the physical and psychic development of the child in early infancy, and these communications throw a valuable light upon the surroundings, the outlook on life, and the educational system in which the child has grown up. It is of special importance in the process of analysis to refrain from touching on certain matters, such as infantile masturbation and how it ceased, and to overlook a decided denial in respect to certain matters which we all know (just like the interest in the digestive process, etc.) must be answered in the affirmative by every child. This emphatic denial of all kinds of "nastiness" affords the analyst guiding lines for the treatment of the sexual problem.

I consider it impossible for anyone to analyze properly his own child. This is so not only because the child hardly ever reveals its deepest desires and thoughts, conscious or unconscious, to father and mother, but because in this case the analyst is often driven to reconstruct too freely, and also because the narcissism of the parents would make it almost unbearable to hear from their own child the psychoanalytic revelations.

The relations between the analyst and the patient's brothers and sisters has also a bearing on the course of the treatment. Usually the younger ones are eager to share the patient's confidence, whereas the elder ones, owing to a secret feeling of envy and animosity, and a half-expectation of betrayal of themselves, keep aloof. Both of these attitudes are judged with equal hostility by the patient, who watches with jealous mistrust the relation of his special confidant with his brothers and sisters and is unwilling to give up his phantasy of the analyst's hostile attitude towards the latter.

We may sum up our knowledge obtained from child-analysis in a few sentences. Almost always we find mistakes in education, through which a bad disposition or a harmful experience, instead of decreasing in destructive effects, is fostered. Too much strictness on the one hand, and too much leniency on the other, with nearly always a lack of consistency in the upbringing, bring about these evils, from which both parents and children alike suffer. If the parents themselves were analyzed, in all probability fewer children would be in need of analysis.

New Ways to the Understanding of Youth
The Hug-Hellmuth Lectures, 1924
(A Condensation)

This is probably Hug-Hellmuth's last publication and again an anticipation of a later publication of Anna Freud. *Neue Wege zum Verständnis der Jugend—Psychoanalytische Vorlesungen für Eltern, Lehrer, Erzieher, Schulärzte, Kindergärtnerinnen und Füsorgerinnen*, Leipzig und Wien, 1924 (New ways to the understanding of youth—Psychoanalytic Lectures for parents, teachers, educators, school physicians, kindergarten teachers and social workers, Leipzig and Vienna, 1924) is probably a summary of Hug-Hellmuth's activities at the Psychoanalytic Ambulatorium and attests to the fact that the psychoanalytic movement in Vienna tried to broaden its base and to make professionals dealing with children knowledgeable of the new theory of child psychology. Again it is rewarding to see the similarities between this publication and Anna Freud's later lectures for teachers and parents (*Einführung in die Psychoanalyse für Pädagogen: Vier Vorträge*, Stuttgart 1930 [Introduction to psychoanalysis for teachers: Four lectures, London, 1931]). The wealth of clinical material seems to be well integrated in these lectures and the thematic structure makes it easier to follow and grasp the concept of Hug-Hellmuth's presentation.

Since the book contains about 120 pages, we have decided to provide the English-speaking reader with a synopsis of the text. We will maintain the original organization into a series of twelve lectures: (1) Ways and Goals of Childrearing; Basics of Freudian Theory; Basics of Psychoanalytic Terminology. (2) Early Disappointments; The Child's Emotional Attitude toward the Environment. (3) About the Unconscious. (4) The Sexual Drive. (5) The Child's Sexual Curiosity; About Sexual Education. (6) Educational Difficulties in the Family and in School. (7) The Child's Anxiety. (8) Fantasies of Children and Adolescents. (9) Children's Play. (10) Children's Dreams. (11) Mental Health. (12) Psychoanalytic Educational Counseling.

Lecture 1:
Ways and Goals of Childrearing; Basics of Freudian Theory; Basics of Psychoanalytic Terminology

Ladies and gentlemen! I know from the registration list that you come from different professions that all focus on the child. As teachers, social workers, school physicians and educators, mothers and mothers-to-be, you all want to learn about Professor Freud's ingenious creation, psychoanalysis and its implication for the system of childrearing. Everybody who deals professionally or privately with children will be trying to lead those he is entrusted with to a certain level of development. This level of development is supposed to facilitate the daily struggle of the child. Only a few people realize their early hopes and dreams. The majority lose their ideals within the daily struggle for survival; the dull resignation of old age finally dispenses with early dreams and longings. But at least they want to see better days for their children. They want their children to avoid all the mistakes that they themselves or their leaders ever made. The other extreme is represented by those who self-righteously watch their children mirroring their arrogant selves. They forget about uniqueness, but only break the child as they attempt to press him into rigid forms.

Parents and educators are quite different. Some of them spoil their children. They anxiously protect them. Others train their children in renunciation. Hardening and strict self-discipline form the basis of cognitively oriented childrearing. With both ways we see frequent failures, even in cases of obvious success. Looking closer we can see that there is a deep rift between old and young. Where are the parents who fully understand their children? Adults only know a fraction of their children's experiences. The lack of time is not the only explanation. Adults also too easily forget their own childhood with its specific interests, wishes, and follies. Their critical view of the child's spontaneity leads to tragic mistakes. They apply their own standards. These are the reasons why adults don't fully understand. They lack the most important knowledge of the unconscious.

Eight years ago, when I first talked to a larger audience about the discoveries of psychoanalytic research and its implication for the educational system, I had to assume that my audience didn't know anything about it. Things have changed since then. The psychoanalytic influence on the development of ideas increases every year. Magazines and newspapers cater to Freud and his ingenious work with more or less appropriate articles and reviews. I assume that there is nobody among you who hasn't heard about psychoanalysis. Therefore, I will restrict my overview to those points that are important for the understanding of basic terminology.

Between 1880 and 1882 the Viennese physician Dr. Josef Breuer treated a girl with a serious nervous disease, a severe hysteria. If one of your loved ones showed a similar symptomatology, you might worry about a brain disease. The judgment of a physician is quite different. Such a state in young patients after psychological trauma is not at all desperate. Breuer placed her in hypnotic sleep, and while she was in this "hypnoid state" asked her to reproduce her experiences that were dominating whenever she was unconscious. Her fantasies revealed thoughts and wishes at the time of her father's illness and death. During her treatment, which she called "talking cure," Breuer succeeded in relieving her symptoms by making her remember those emotionally important experiences. Breuer's cathartic method was identical to that of Charcot, Freud's important teacher in Paris between 1885 and 1886. Janet, Charcot's student, elicited the mechanisms of hysteria even further.

Freud applied Breuer's cathartic method to other patients. But soon he dispensed with hypnosis as an unreliable method. Without hypnosis he tried to discover what had been unknown to both patient and physician. By pushing, by reassuring about the right moves, by putting on hands and suggesting, he succeeded in making his patient remember. This method was tiring and time-consuming. The most important result of these trials was the realization that all these memories actually hadn't been forgotten but they were buried. A blocking force enabled the patient to hang on to his symptoms. Freud regularly experienced it when dealing with those patients. He called this process repression. How does this happen and what is the content and the fate of the repressed? Every wish, every longing, every drive asks for satisfaction by reaching its particular aim. Education and culture erect moral, ethical, aesthetic, and social demands that are not necessarily coincidental with the individual drives and their demands. A short fight decides the relative strength of each drive involved. The weaker is repressed from consciousness.

Freud used a good example to explain the dynamic understanding of repression. A person in an audience is disturbing the presentation by audible comments and laughter and is finally physically removed from the room. The disturbance is repressed and the lecturer continues his presentation. To prevent the disturbance from recurring, some members of the audience guard the door and function as "resistance." This description becomes complete when we identify the lecture hall with the conscious and the outer room as the unconscious.

The conflict would be solved if the unwanted idea would be permanently repressed. If we return to Freud's example, we can picture the person rampaging and shouting outside the door. Finally, the organizer's authority succeeded in an agreement that allowed the repressed person to return to the audience with the promise to behave himself. Organizer and disturber have made a compromise that allowed his return in fashion. The repressed drive has not simply disappeared. It assumed another form and returns to consciousness behind a mask. It has become a hysterical symptom.

An example from my own practice might highlight the relationship between the repressed and the hysterical symptom: A twelve-year-old girl came to psychoanalytic treatment because of a fear of needles. This was expressed in eating and swallowing difficulties. She was tortured by the idea that a needle might have fallen into the food and that she, her mother, or her brother might die. Analysis made her remember two misdeeds from early childhood. As a five-year-old girl she had repeatedly stuck a needle into the upholstery for a nanny she disliked, who then in turn hurt herself considerably on one of these occasions. The little girl was successful in maintaining her innocence and directed the blame onto her seven-year-old brother. He was punished with a spanking and banned from the family dinner. The girl had many reasons to forget about both her own hateful attitude toward her nanny as well as the unfair punishment of her brother. When a new cook started work, her shortsightedness caused a justified concern about her ability to work. The now twelve-year-old girl developed the fear that either her mother or her brother would swallow a needle. By developing an eating disorder herself, she assumed the previous role of her brother who had been excluded from the family dinner. Swallowing difficulties had replaced her "swallowed" acknowledgment of guilt. After clarification of these circumstances, as well as those of forbidden games she had played with her brother, her psychological eating disorder and her fear of needles subsided.

Educators might take a special interest in the following example from my own practice: A fourteen-year-old girl, normally developed physically and emotionally and an eager and well-tempered student prior to her illness, suddenly made herself impossible with compulsive laughter that infected her classmates. The teachers saw the general discipline endangered by this disturbing behavior. The principal advised the parents to remove the child from school and have her prepared by a private tutor for the final exam. A physician, a friend of the family, referred them to me. The mother, cognitively quite a limited lady, emphasized in our preliminary meeting that the girl did not make fun of one of the teachers' pregnancy as the teachers suspected! This was because the girl was supposedly quite ignorant about sexual matters that were not addressed at home.

At the beginning of therapy the girl was shy. She liked to scribble, but she destroyed whatever she drew. Other children at school would talk appropriately about rendez-vous and lovers. On one occasion she violently rejected her teacher's suspicion regarding the reason for her laughter. If the other girls hadn't mentioned the pregnancy, she wouldn't have recognized the fact.

During her twelfth session she spontaneously asked: "Doctor, do you always wear small hats or do you wear large hats as well?" She watched me very attentively. I answered: "I always wear small ones since large hats only fit large bodies." She smiled and said: "Doctor, I'll tell you the truth why I always have to laugh at school. Whenever a female teacher stands in front of us [Frau Dr. X, now pregnant, normally sits], I imagine them with a hat that makes them look ridiculous, small women with large hats and tall women with small caps that look like birds' nests. Miss Y always wears a cylinder that makes her long-shaped face reach the lamps. That makes me laugh and it's worse the more I try to suppress it. All other children look at me and of course they start to laugh as well, which causes a uproar."

I won't bother you with the details of the analysis, except for the fact that the girl vehemently rejected a discussion about the origin of children, since "she knew everything already." Her knowledge was quite confused. In summary, her sexual denial served as a powerful defense against her suppressed sexual interest.

Five weeks later, after she had told me "everything" that her parents said she was not supposed to know, she reported an idea that had come to her the night before. "Last night I remembered that once my mother had a little hat and secretly I made fun of her. I went with my mother to sit final exams. When we entered the streetcar to return home, I recognized two boys who looked at my mother and laughed. I look at her myself and I realized that her hat was by far too small. One of the boys bent forwards and I saw his tummy. He pointed at my mother and both of the boys cried with laughter. It was only then that I recognized that my mother was curiously big and I remembered Mary telling me about the birth of her little brother. I was terribly embarrassed. The boys left later and one of them made an indecent gesture. This happened in June. Soon thereafter I was sent to my grandparents for five weeks and when I returned little Edith was at home. She looked disgusting, full of wrinkles, vomited all the time, and wet herself. I never want a baby. Anyway, I'll never marry."

After three months in analysis she had been cured, attended school between May and the end of the term without difficulties, and her academic career and her life during the following years were uncomplicated and happy.

These examples have illustrated a common principle of suppressed material. The suppressed ideas, feelings, and wishes share the character of something embarrassing, intimidating, or forbidden and are removed from consciousness.

Ladies and gentlemen! We repeatedly heard about elements being removed from consciousness while other forgotten elements become conscious again. It's now time to emphasize the basic difference in understanding between psychoanalysis and academic psychology. Academic psychology understands 'psychic' as 'conscious.' Freud goes further: His cases demonstrated for him that psychic processes happen beyond the patient's control but nevertheless continuously influence his ego. This happens in the unconscious. These are mainly the suppressed fantasies, feelings, and wishes we talked about earlier.

Further studies helped Freud to differentiate between conscious, preconscious, and unconscious processes. Psychic phenomena are conscious if we fully control them. Preconscious processes are not present but can be remembered; they might enter consciousness at any moment. They are remainders of impressions without interest or strong accompanying affects and therefore were physiologically forgotten. The unconscious finally remains outside our control although continuously influencing our ego.

Psychoanalytic therapy has found ways to solve psychic conflicts better than suppression does. The patient might become convinced that he can fulfill the previously rejected wish without damage to his personality; he totally or partly accepts a suppressed wish; a young lady who only had homosexual interests was freed by psychoanalysis not to give up her sexual preference but to enjoy her relationships without self-blame and feelings of guilt.

If acceptance of the suppressed wish is unacceptable for the patient, there is still another way. The wish can be directed toward higher, acceptable goals. This is called sublimation. Finally, the conscious, unacceptable wish can be controlled by self-discipline. It replaces the automatic and therefore insufficient mechanism of suppression. Thus psychoanalysis always contains an educational aspect.

Generally, psychoanalysis always aims at making unconscious, ego-disturbing processes conscious. It is a therapeutic-educational method to make sick souls recover and to integrate the patient as a competent member of society. It succeeds if the patient follows the basic psychoanalytic rule: to report all ideas to the analyst, absolutely truthfully, with naive openness, even in moments of embarrassment. It will take endless will power and effort to fight the resistance against the realization of the hidden aspects of the soul.

Lecture 2:
Early Disappointments;
The Child's Emotional Attitude
towards the Environment

Ladies and gentlemen! During our first meeting we have become familiar with the ways and goals of education that are pursued by parents and educators due to their perception of the environment and their ego ideal. We investigated the reasons for failures in the educational system and we acknowledged the lack of understanding of the child's soul as the main reason for those failures. Finally, I attempted to develop the basics of Freud's ideas. However, as we proceed, I will make you familiar with the most important ideas we didn't mention yet. I will now turn to the main topic: early frustrations and the child's need for love.

The fact that man greets the world with a scream lets us assume that birth itself is not a pleasant encounter. Before I accept a case for treatment in my practice, I have the parents fill out a questionnaire. The first question is, "How was the child's birth?" The answer regularly is "difficult" in children who are described as strong-willed, rigid, hard to influence, and uptight. Somatically, these children often present headaches and bowel disturbances. Experienced pediatricians would have to confirm my assumptions before we would be allowed to generalize.

Some habits and tendencies of children document the fact that man brings with him unconscious memories from his intra-uterine life to the noisy outer world. We find traces in the sleep position of children and adults. Like a fetus, they pull their legs up and cross their arms in front of their chests. Others cover themselves even during hot summer because "it is so warm and silent" under the blanket. The retreat of an anxious child into mother's lap and the feeling of security and protection from hostile power when his head rests in her lap, might reflect the longing back to the womb.

The disturbances of his comfortable life brought about by the measures of upbringing determine the infant's first emotional attitude toward his environment. These are rejection, defense, and hatred. The procedure of cleaning remains uncomfortable with the cold temperature, the attack of big hands, the passive turns of the body, and sponges and towels badly adapted to his soft body. He defends himself with screams against these invasions into his quiet existence.

Slowly affection develops as the child realizes that hunger and cold are helped by the environment. Those feelings are directed toward the caretaker, normally the mother. She who gives food is the object of the infant's first love.

I will refer you to a book that provides a close look at female puberty, *A Young Girl's Diary*. I can praise it without hesitation because I didn't write it myself, but I edited the book. Freud called it a gem for adolescent research. In this book the most secret experiences of young people are uncovered. This book should be a must for all parents, educators, and teachers.

Let's return to the pleasures and frustrations of the early days. Having just overcome the horror of birth, the infant faces yet again another trauma when being weaned from the breast. This is the second separation from mother and it is badly tolerated. The mother also suffers from the weaning process. The child's complaints during the weaning period force some replacement for the lost breast in the form of constant care. He becomes the center of the household's attention and defends this position even at a time when conscious memories of the weaning period have long since waned. Each younger child then successfully competes with him for this position. The older can express his jealousy towards the younger quite drastically.

Some years ago I treated a seven-year-old boy because of enuresis, day and night. All local treatments, massage, electric treatment, baths had failed as well as admonishment and punishment. Finally, he came for treatment to me. During his analysis the intelligent boy himself gathered a list of six factors that were responsible for his bad habit. Among them was the identification with his two-year-old brother, who wasn't punished for his mishaps. This happened to be one of the major factors. After treatment for a few weeks his symptom improved only to worsen again during the summer break when he was subjected to the constant nagging of his nanny. The parents attributed the later complete success to his enrollment in a boarding school where he obeyed the rules out of a fear of embarrassment. Well, I think embarrassment would not have helped without analysis.

Generally we call the return to earlier developmental stages regression. In contrast, we call adhering to an infantile stage infantilism—for example, a seven-year-old girl holding on to the bottle. While psychic infantilism is quite frequent among the mentally retarded, regression plays an important role in often well-educated neurotic people.

Suddenly digestion previously considered very important and often attended to by the whole family is declared indecent. Countless lustful experiences of early childhood are turned into taboos that prove the insensibility of the child's environment. Although the child's curiosity compensates for these early damages, they remain contained and feed into any new disappointment. The child has to learn to renounce his exceptional place. Entering school has special significance in this context. The child is only one among others. The remarkable change that takes place in the child during the seventh and eighth years, sometimes later, seems to be influenced by this school "trauma."

Everybody harbors a tender glance and a friendly word for the young child. The older the child grows the less attentive his environment becomes and he has to renounce this preferential treatment. This demotion is met with great disappointment. A four-year-old boy who had been admired all his life for his beauty one day was unrecognized on the streetcar. "Mama," he said, astonished and intimidated, "nobody said 'What a cute boy' today."

There is yet another blow to the child's narcissism to come. He comes to recognize that learning to read doesn't happen overnight. The underlying attitude survives. The child often fails in learning because he can't achieve his goal immediately. The emotional bond children develop with important people leads them to learn for somebody—father, teacher—and only much, much later for themselves.

The strong ties to his parents explain why the child suffers the harshest disappointments with them. Father and mother are idealized figures and the inevitable recognition of their weaknesses and mistakes, their inconsistencies and limited power shakes the child's soul heavily. The conflict of fantasy and reality leaves the young in a lonely position. They are waiting to detect the inconsistencies of their parents' words and behaviors. Two views of the world face one another and so they live in mutual misunderstanding. The child's soul fights numerous aches that are caused by the surroundings. However, can the environment be really blamed, or are the aches partly due to the child himself?

Egotism that we reject in adults, with all its expectations and assumptions, does not spoil the lovely picture of the child. Neediness and demands are his rights. This is caused by the need for care and the helplessness that characterize the early days. However, he resents the measures of education since they disturb his comfortable existence. His first attitude is defense, and thereby, hatred. The child enjoys lustful satisfaction in connection with his body only during the earliest days. Every part of his body is a potential source of pleasure. The child experiences the auto-erotic stage of life. By experiencing pain he recognizes the parts of his body as a comprehensive unit whereas he considered them separate before. He comes to the recognition of his ego and the arrival of personality. The auto-erotic stage is followed by the narcissistic.

Let me introduce a nonscientific but understandable differentiation between egotism and narcissism at this point. The egotist exploits all situations and people he meets for his personal advantage. His attitude is described by the question "What advantage do I have?" The narcissist who is in love with himself more than with anybody else sees only himself even in his beloved partner and he is characterized by the ongoing striving to be admired by others. His eternal question is, "Am I loved, admired, accepted?" These quite different values explain the helpfulness and sacrifices that the narcissist is willing to make as well as the scrupulousness of the egotist. The qualitative difference does not prevent both attitudes from existing in one person. It only results in occasional fights between conflicting drives as we have acknowledged them before between incompatible wishes. The relative strength decides who looses out in a given situation.

The understanding of the narcissist is very important for education. If reason fails, education often appeals to the infantile narcissism. The attempts to lead a child, especially the behaviorally difficult child, the right way with love alone are nothing other than appeals to his high-handedness. The insult to his self-love by punishments, strict prohibitions, and commands is answered by disobedience and stubbornness.

We recognize early a change in the child's emotional attitude toward his environment. He starts to experience attention and care as lustful, since they bring relief to the uncomfortable situations of hunger and cold. He begins to direct parts of his auto-erotic, narcissistic inclination toward his caretaker. Since his mother is normally the earliest caretaker, she also becomes his first love object outside of himself. The emotional bond between mother and child decides his later emotional development. Mothers are the teachers of love. All the tenderness in words and behavior they exchange live eternally in the child's heart. Even if the spoiled child suffers from life's roughness, expecting an abundance of love everywhere, he also has a large emotional stock. He never will be as unhappy as the unloved child who himself lacks the ability to love. He also demands an abundance of love but since he was cut off early he can't pay back even minimally. Nobody told him how to love.

Soon the child involves others in his microscopic emotional world—siblings, grandparents, aunts, servants, and finally toys. I would like to add here that in contrast to the normal psychoanalytic understanding, I regard object finding as occurring earlier in development than object choice. Choice seems to me to be a higher intellectual achievement than finding. If we are allowed to make any assumptions at all about the earliest psychic life then we can assume that the first external object the child finds is his mother's breast that he regards as part of his own body during the auto-erotic phase of his life. Along with the narcissistic comprehension of those body parts as a unit the child also discovers objects separate from himself.

Life tells us that harmony between siblings is not the rule, although adults would like to see this differently. There is indeed no reason to be particularly happy about the arrival of another brother or sister. If the four-to-six-year-old has already learned to hide his feelings and to suppress his forbidden wishes, his rejection of the sibling will not be shown openly anymore. In older children hatred is suppressed in the very beginning and, especially in girls, replaced by admiration and motherly care. The younger child also harbors malice against the older brother or sister. Enviously he tries to seize all their privileges, later bedtimes as well as walks that he is still too small for, or the larger piece of cake.

Both single children as well as children with siblings are at psychological risk. The single child is at risk because of the exclusive contact with adults that endangers his psychological development and adaptation in society. The children with siblings express their difficulties by jealousy, envy, and malicious joy. The "middle" child suffers as well. He is always the "fifth wheel," as one twelve-year-old remarks. The early orphan feels abandoned regardless of being raised in an institution or by relatives. His fate becomes the more difficult the more love his original family and mother gave him. He always feels extraneous from the family and community that have accepted him. Twins also lead a special life in the family. Even if they have shown initial jealousy, especially with regard to their mother, they often cling to one another later, more than other siblings. This might have tragic consequences for both of them. They lose contact with others and stay together without partners until death.

Since we only hesitantly acknowledged the ambivalent nature of sibling relationships, we will find it totally unacceptable that the child's attitude toward his parents is also ambivalent. Even the young child sometimes meets his parents with stubbornness, anger, and meanness. This doesn't exclude a loving attitude as well. A two-year-old boy who intensively loved his mother told her to go away whenever his wishes were denied. A five-year-old surprised her mother after a walk she wasn't allowed to join with the bitter remark: "I don't say 'hello,' I don't know you!" Children understand much better than we can love and hate at the same time.

Early on we observe that the little boy loves his mother in a different way than he loves his father. He protects her, shares his secrets with her, wants to sleep in her bed, and claims her for himself. He admires and envies his father for his stature and power, his omnipotence that also interferes with his intimacy with his mother. Therefore, he appreciates his father's absence from the family. He even wishes his father's removal because he then can claim his mother just for himself. Since he lacks the adequate concept of death, equating distance and death as reversible qualities, he doesn't mind to exaggerate his fantasies to death wishes. A father's death frees mother for the little boy. He can marry her, a wish that is hardly missing in any boy's dreams. Typically he wishes to marry her once he is older. The little boy behaves like his unfortunate brother in Greek mythology. He is a little Oedipus who wants to slaughter his father and to marry his mother. Pressed by educational influences, he suppresses his incestuous wishes and the sensuous qualities are replaced by tenderness.

The relationships between daughters and their parents are similar. Their inclination toward the other sex is rarely as aggressive as that of boys, but more shy, withholding, and passive. In both cases the forbidden incestuous drives are slowly suppressed, but during puberty they sometimes strongly reappear. But by then the incest taboo is unsurmountable and the boy hides his inclinations behind rudeness and the girl behind an irritability that is hard for her to understand. The ambivalent attitude of the boy toward his father is expressed in the resistance against his authority and those who replace him—teacher, educators, authorities, and the state. Both boys and girls in their adolescence live in a kind of no-man's land: hostile resentments against siblings, erotic inclinations toward father and mother—all those unacceptable feelings that have been suppressed by systematic and unsystematic influences break free and throw the adolescent soul into fights and despair, doubt, brooding, and despondency. Those youngsters with a healthy psyche will eventually find their way out of these difficulties. They loosen their attachment to the beloved ones of their early childhood. They look for a new love-object that will satisfy their erotic drives, their libido. However, there are also those who will never have a companion because of their total fixation to parents or siblings.

I don't want to close my presentation today without explaining one phenomenon that appears quite regularly during psychoanalysis and is even one of its prerequisites. Without exception the patient soon behaves toward his analyst as he did toward his parents earlier. He sometimes expresses great sympathy for him, tries to impress him and talks and behaves as if he wants to be absolutely honest and open with regard to his own secrets and those close to him. Hostile and friendly feelings toward the analyst soon appear side by side. This happens to be the same ambivalence that we acknowledged as the child's feelings toward his parents. Therefore, the analyst comes to represent both father ad mother. We call this relationship that is characterized by the coexistence of love and hatred toward the physician, positive and negative transference. There is no psychoanalytic treatment possible without transference, both in children and in adults. As man has to separate from the father and mother figures of childhood to reach his potential, the patient has to reduce the amount of positive and negative transference at the end of treatment to a minimum to lead his own life without influence and guidance.

Lecture 3:
About the Unconscious

Ladies and gentlemen! We now follow what we have said in the first two lectures with regard to those events that later become the sources of serious disappointment because of the child's never-ending hunger for love.

A healthy drive for survival dominates the child's existence under the pleasure principle. According to Freud, education is the teaching of the overcoming the pleasure-principle and acceptance of reality. Its goal is the dominance of the reality-principle. The powerful adult beats the child in this fight. The child's fantasies, wishes, and drives give way in part to demands of shame, disgust, and morality. The unacceptable is repressed, sometimes unsuccessfully. It continues its existence in the unconscious. The eminent importance of the unconscious for individual life and attitudes requires further consideration.

We have to answer three questions:

1. Where does unconscious material come from?
2. How do we know about unconscious activity if it is not recognizable and it is beyond our control?
3. How does the unconscious show itself in everyday life?

Freud discovered that the symptoms of neurotic patients were inevitably rooted in the patients' pasts, in experiences that have been totally forgotten but that may reappear by applying the psychoanalytic method. Today's suffering was prepared by important events in infancy that were mostly sexual in nature. Freud was able to state that neurotics suffer from reminiscences, unconscious remnants of memory. Both for the neurotic patient and for the healthy individual, the personal past becomes an inexhaustible source of unconscious activity.

In psychoanalytic practice three ways lead to the discovery of the hidden processes:

1. The free idea, the indiscriminate association.
2. The observation of parapraxis, symptomatic and accidental actions.
3. The interpretation and explanation of dreams.

Let me give you a few examples, one from my own life and two from the lives of children. In the summer of 1920 the Berlin Psychoanalytic Clinic invited me to give a series of lectures on psychoanalysis and education. Since I was quite depressed by recent personal events, I hesitated. Finally, I only agreed to start the series on August 12 because of Professor Freud's insistence. When I reread my confirmation that I wrote on July 17, I recognized that I had actually written the date as *July* 12. This one slip was not enough. All formalities for my passport were completed when I recognized that my visa remained valid only for July 10 to August 14. I went back to have the error corrected and the officer showed me my visa application. I had written down the wrong dates a second time! That day I returned home slightly embarrassed and not very enthusiastic about my plans.

The fourteen-year-old girl whose compulsive laughter we have already discussed gave a delightful example of a slip in writing. When she was asked to write about the bark beetle, she wrote about the bit beetle. She started laughing when she recognized her mistake. This resulted in her being punished. In her analysis she admitted that she sometimes eats during classes and that she is afraid that she once will have to answer with bits of food in her mouth.

Losing, misplacing, and mishandling things represent another group of slips. A seven-year-old boy had stolen some candies from the birthday-plate of his little brother. He intended to eat them at school in full sight of his envious classmates during the starving days of the war. However, when the little boaster got to school and tried to pull the candies from his pocket, he discovered that he had lost them on his way to school. During his analysis for enuresis the intelligent lad found out by himself that this represented a self-punishment for the stealing and the intent to boast.

Returning to the theoretical aspects, we see how two intentions fight each other: the longing for the unusual pleasures and the shame about one's own wishes and the wish not to break with the rules of upbringing. Both intentions impose their claims without losing out completely. A slip can be so meaningful that it simultaneously serves to hide and to fulfill the wish. Each example carefully analyzed would bring about the same result. Parapraxes are the result of suppressed instinctual impulses. The initial suppression has failed and survives in the unconscious. Parapraxes therefore are compromise formations that represent both success and defeat.

In Freud's illustrative example comparing the impulse with the listener in the audience, he also mentioned an authoritative personality that decided about the expulsion and readmission of the disturber. Similarly, there is a psychic force at the border between conscious and preconscious, and then again between preconscious and unconscious. We call this force a censor that acts like its rigorous sister in the media to make sure that certain facts don't become public.

If we assume that the tendencies are suppressed if they are in contrast to demands of the ego, and of social and cultural requirements, we can also suspect where the roots of those tendencies can be found. The roots are seen in disapproved wishes of a gross, egotistic nature, or in narcissistic, hateful, and sexual fantasies. Impulses of brutality and revenge also reappear in the parapraxes. All of these tendencies are in conflict with the moral, ethical, aesthetical, and social requirements of the ego. The violation often leads to self-punishment of various kinds. The material in Freud's "Psychopathology of Every-Day Life" informs us about their variety.

In summary, we can state the following about parapraxes:

1. For their owner they appear to be unintelligible.
2. They have a meaning that is often recognized by others as an indicator of important psychic events.
3. This meaning remains hidden from the person involved and it is normally vehemently denied.
4. Superficially parapraxes look like momentary disturbances of attention due to physical or psychological causes.

We said that free association is a necessary tool for psychoanalysis in uncovering the unconscious activity of the neurotic patient. If we were accustomed to interpret parapraxes as meaningful expressions of unconscious activity, we could save the child's soul many difficult conflicts. We could support them in their secret and difficult struggle. Their understanding would provide access to secret wishes, expectations, and hidden thoughts of our children.

Lecture 4:
The Sexual Drive

Ladies and gentlemen! It is the goal of eduction to help form the young person's instincts that strive for unfolding in a way that serves both the needs of the child and of mankind in general. Education has to promote some instincts with knowledge and care while permanently suppressing and limiting others. Education must refine them with loving discipline and help to sublimate them to make them useful for the individual and society. In other words, the goal of education is the appropriate use of drive-promotion and drive-suppression.

Textbooks of official psychology identify instincts for food, movement, possession, play, instincts to communicate and socialize, instincts for knowledge and honor and at last, during puberty, the sexual instinct. Cases of early sexual activity, "premature" expressions of sexuality in childhood, are considered pathologic and referred to physicians. An unhealthy sexual life of parents and ancestors as well as seduction are held responsible for those sensations that "hurt body and soul." The authors of such textbooks have to judge this way since they equate the sexual instinct with the instinct for procreation. Official psychology links sexuality to the genitalia, that is, sexual equals genital. This view restricts the understanding of sexuality. It takes into account sexual behaviors that serve as preparation for the intercourse of adults but overlooks and denies the sexual character of identical behavior in children. Active and passive looking, touching, stroking, cuddling, caressing, and kissing are stimulating for children as well.

Analysts find surprising and sometimes strange characteristics in the case histories of their neurotic patients. Their love life regularly plays a dominant role in the etiology of their illness. During therapy the analyst discovers that disturbances in his patients' erotic life are mainly responsible for the symptoms.

The regular and remarkable emphasis on sexuality as the source of pathogenic intentions of neurotic patients led to Freud's distinction of two groups of instincts. The first group consists of the ego-instincts that support and maintain the ego, like the instincts for food, movement, and possession, the educationally important instincts for activity, play, and imitation, the instinct for honor, and the social instincts. The other group consists of the sexual instinct and its components. This distinction helps us to gain some understanding of confusing psychological activities. Freud has reformulated some of these concepts in his recent book *Beyond the Pleasure Principle*. The initial therapeutic goals of psychoanalysis explain why psychoanalysts first studied primarily the sexual instinct while lately they also study the ego-instincts. We still follow those lines. We deal primarily with the importance of sexuality and its development and expression during psychic development. The sexual instinct determines the direction and the goals of our love life and sex life. It has a significant influence on our psychic development since it has one quality that the ego-instincts lack. Hunger can only be satisfied by food after being repressed temporarily; thirst even more so can only be alleviated by a drink. The most brilliant book, the most exiting landscape leaves us unsatisfied if we are hungry and our thirst isn't satisfied by the most beautiful sonata.

This is different from sexuality. We often hear that inventors, explorers, and scholars lead an ascetic life like monks where eroticism and a healthy sexual life have no place: I just mention Newton or Kant. In their intellectuality they succeeded in distracting the sexual instinct from its natural goal and redirecting it to other areas like arts or science in a desexualized way. We call this intellectualization or sublimation. The characteristics of distractibility and sublimation distinguish the sexual instinct from ego-instincts that require an adequate satisfaction.

The psychoanalystic school is accused of tremendous and unjustified exaggeration of the sexual instinct. However, there is no other area of life as hidden as one's own sexuality. Neurotic people are no exception. During psychoanalysis they only very reluctantly uncover their sex life. Quite regularly analysis leads back to adolescence. With its physical and psychological changes, certain impulses, previously suppressed into the unconscious, reappear. Even further back, impressions and experiences of a sexual nature during childhood are recreated and prove to be the sources of present symptoms. This is the real core of Freud's teachings.

People believe that a healthy child is asexual. Freud explained that this reflects a rigid adherence to this belief that should have been proved wrong by simple observation of a remarkable phenomenon: amnesia, the forgetting of the early days of childhood. Adults regularly remember events back to their seventh or sixth year in a coherent fashion. Then we meet the "big, black hole" in our memories. Now and then we remember vague and unintelligible pictures that might have been related to certain events.

It is Freud's merit to have taught us to realize the activities of the child's soul without indignation and false shame. By broadening the meaning of sexuality beyond the limits of procreation, Freud has opened for us new ways to the understanding of the child's soul. Sucking is one of the earliest lustful activities of the child that is sometimes maintained into the seventh or eighth year or even longer. Fingers, toes, and lips, the edge of the blanket or a rubber nipple are sought for satisfaction.

Some people develop a life-long preference for their oral zone. The extraordinary sensitivity of the mucosa of mouth and lips predisposes this area for satisfaction. We call these areas erotogenic zones. We call this phase of self-satisfaction the oral or cannibalistic phase. Pure language has maintained some expressions related to this phase, for example, "He could have eaten her alive."

Similar to these first organs of the digestive tract are the endograms, anus and urethra. They are erotogenic zones rich in muscles and mucosa. The child understands his bowel movements as his first creations. His products are given to a loved person. The adaptation to cleanliness is gradual. The genital area becomes emphasized and another way of auto-erotic satisfaction, onanism, or masturbation is discovered. Freud assumed that almost nobody escapes infantile onanism. We can safely assume that it starts around the tenth or eleventh month, and is practiced against all obstacles only to disappear after the end of the first year. Then a sexual latency period lasts until the third year of life. Up to then the strongest fulfillment of instincts is linked to the oral and anal areas, while the genitals only play an inferior role. We call this period pregenital.

After the first latency period the picture changes. The instinctual drive, the libido, reappears and we observe a wave of sexual desire the satisfaction of which is now linked to the genitals. The child rediscovers his genitals for the second time as a source of pleasure. He experiences the genital phase of his development. Intellectually, this period is characterized by continuous questioning. This is the time of delightful sayings, the time when all children show signs of originality and ingenuity that make narcissistic, ambitious parents look happily into the future of their child.

Terrible threats disturb the lustful activity again and the child suppresses this wave of sexual activity. They become sublimated and partly they are secretly satisfied. The child soon learns to hide the disapproved manipulations from the adults because of the threats and actual experience of punishment. Therefore, the child appears to totally renounce sexual pleasures during this second sexual latency period until puberty or at least prepuberty, i.e., the tenth or eleventh year. The analyses of children tell us that libidinal impulses become less vigorous during this period but never disappear completely. The new sensations of physical and emotional maturation terminate this second latency period.

Masturbation was considered by physicians as severely damaging to body and soul. Recently, a more liberal attitude has become predominant. Now and then a physician gives an enlightening lecture to warn against those pamphlets, mostly written by laymen, that describe the dangers of masturbation in a sensational manner. The physician tries to advise the young how to control their instincts by healthy living, sports, alcohol-free nutrition, and avoidance of sexual excitement. However, younger children don't have the opportunity to hear those lectures. They are left alone with their desires, fear, and self-accusations. Even with their good intentions, their parents and educators themselves are unadvised and make mistakes.

The danger of masturbation, if not practiced excessively, is not physical but psychological. The practice itself is not dangerous for psychological development; rather, it is the threats and the rude attempts to stop it, whether in infancy or in older children. Thoughtless threats to cut off a finger or the penis are taken very seriously by the child. They trigger the boy's fear of castration and elicit the humiliating opinion in girls that they have experienced this horrible punishment already in early infancy. This fear of castration never leaves the child. It becomes the focus of numerous imaginations and fantasies that are effectively linked into the castration complex. A vain fifteen-year-old boy nevertheless ran round with uncut fingernails and his hair covered his forehead. Each intervention led to dramatic scenes. His mother had to bribe him to have him go to have his hair or his nails cut. His analysis showed its first result when he cut his nails himself and a week later he proudly entered his session, asking: "Frau Doctor, don't you recognize something?" His disfiguring mane had disappeared and he had gone voluntarily to the barber. Soon after, he laid down during his session with an embarrassed laughing and smile. The castration complex had been loosened, the fear had started to disappear.

We recognize these fears and fantasies only during analysis. Even there they are uncovered only with greatest resistance, since the child fears that the analyst might disclose his fantasies to his parents.

Girls, besides sexual intimidation and masturbation fantasies, suffer psychologically most from acts of seduction. The general characteristics of the masturbator are constant embarrassment, shyness, insecurity, and an unfree presentation. These are also the characteristics of the seduced child. Seduced children cling rigidly to their first mode of satisfaction. Especially for women this might become a tragic attitude. Psychoanalysis has never advised young people to have premature intercourse. We only want to liberate youth from guilt feelings that kill the joy of life and creativity.

When growing up the child is not content with pride, his own nudity being admired; he also wants to observe others. Lustful showing is joined by watching. He uses every occasion to watch his mother dressing, washing, or taking a bath. "Mother-and-child games" and "doctor games" provide ample opportunities for both watching and showing, passive and active exhibitionism.

These instincts are partly suppressed, partly subliminated, and reappear as interests in the performing arts, theater play, and some sports that also satisfy skin and muscle eroticism. The drive to watch is partly turned into curiosity. This is directed especially toward the natural sciences.

It is one person's pleasure to hurt a loved person; another's is to be tortured by somebody he loves. We call the former sadists and the latter masochists. The cruel person enjoys the sufferer's pain but he lacks an emotional bond with the tortured subject. This is a prerequisite for the sadist's satisfaction. Freud's valuable publication "A Child Is Being Beaten" is a result of intensive studies of this pair of contrasts, sadism and masochism. He assumes that masochism has developed from primary sadism by additional guilt feelings.

A ten-year-old boy, recently brought to me by his mother for analysis, give us a classical example for a pseudo-masochistic disposition. He passionately loved his mother and despite his age he did not renounce the privilege of his earlier years by coming into his mother's bed. However, he would beat and strangle her, causing welts on her body. Her helplessness when he knelt on top of her and her fearful screaming for the help of a nervous neighbor caused a tremendous rage in him. That was followed by intense psychic exhaustion. He would later claim to repent and he would ask his mother and God for punishment. He would start to beat himself. He was a sadist or, better, a masochist, since feelings of guilt and revenge played an important role. We also might assume that narcissistic humiliation played an important role.

Those adults who are over-polite only to strangers but have only bitter and degrading comments for those close to them probably have treated their best companions the worst. The masochist also intellectualizes the tortures of early childhood, the "pleasure of suffering." The concentration on sorrow, the wallowing in real or imagined inferiority, the raging against one's own soul are ways of psychic masochism. The masochist succeeds in being a burden to others.

The exaggerated neediness of the anal instinct during the first years and its repression by education is regularly accompanied by strong sadistic tendencies. They are directed toward persons whose orders and prohibitions are regarded as disturbing the anal libidinal tendencies. The child lives through a sadistic-anal phase. It precedes the wave of genital-sexual activity around the fourth year and forms the pregenital stage together with the already-mentioned oral or cannibalistic phase.

Ladies and gentlemen! I appreciate the attention with which you have followed my discourse. However, I know that you have one important objection. Certainly, all of these observations might exist. Some of them we have observed ourselves. Yet, why are we justified in calling them sexual? We understand what is quite differently. Certainly, we ordinarily call sexual what serves the function of procreation. But Freud has extended the meaning of this word. You will later acknowledge the similarity of infantile sexual goals with those of some adults who have become somehow stuck in their sexual development. As you know there are full-grown people who consider watching the "love" object as the goal of their erotic desire. Others find fulfillment in exposing themselves. We call the former voyeurs and the latter exhibitionists. Others find the greatest pleasure in torturing the loved partner or becoming tortured by him. These are the sadists and the masochists. There are also those who retire into themselves for their sexual satisfaction. Finally, there are those who love exclusively persons of their own sex, the sexually inverted or homosexuals.

The fact that those adults are sick and inhibited in their eroticism shouldn't prevent us from recognizing the similarities in sexually healthy individuals where these aspects play a more or less important role. I am thinking of the importance of visual clues in partner choice, the sensation of the smell of the young female body and her hair for men or the joy of kisses and embraces. While in fully developed, healthy adults the partial instincts work together toward the physical union with the loved partner, the child, according to his immature sexual organization, follows each of his partial sexual instincts—

oral, anal, nasal, exhibitionistic, genital, and psuedo-masochistic—independently. The first object of early infantile libido is the own body. Observations of young children tell us that the areas of the body concerned with food intake and digestion seem to be predisposed to achieve certain satisfactory goals because of their sensitivity. The first phases of pregenital organization seem to be predisposed because of their sensitivity to achieve certain satisfactory goals. During the first phase of pregenital organization the child wants to put everything into his mouth. He wants to incorporate everything in reach. The second sadistic-anal phase is well known to mothers and caretakers because of its problem with defecation. Incorporation and elimination are the characteristic activities. The pregenital organization during the oral and sadistic-anal phase is followed by the genital organization. This is dominated by the castration complex and the Oedipus complex.

During the second sexual latency period, those interests fade under the breakdown of the Oedipus complex and the influence of castration anxiety, only to reappear as early as during prepuberty, during the eleventh or twelfth year. With the lack of sexual interests the intellect unfolds and the ego-instincts develop. This is the time of learning, when the child acquires numerous new skills. He starts to integrate socially.

Before turning toward the characteristic changes of puberty, I want to summarize the characteristics of infantile sexuality according to Freud:

1. Each partial instinct is looking for satisfaction independent from the other partial instincts. The genitals originally don't have a special role in this respect as compared to other parts of the body.

2. The satisfaction of instincts happens in close proximity to certain functions of the body that have been emphasized by the caretaking activities.

3. One's own body becomes the first libidinal object. Object finding and object choice then slowly direct part of the libido toward external objects.

During puberty the infantile sexual organization experiences profound changes. Incestuous inclinations toward the heterosexual parent, libidinal attachment to sister or brother reappear supported by the bodily changes. Moral objections try to suppress them. Masturbation is picked up again with strong guilt feelings. The psyche is unprepared for this experience. Opposition to authority, discontent with the existing, intensive fights that become symptomatic as the typical features of adolescence: opposition to authority, discontent with the existing, intensive searching for new forms, independence versus freedom, and difficult religious struggles lead to internal dissent. Unprepared for their suffering, without leadership or advice, they struggle for a new Weltanschauung. Pacts are made with members of their own sex while maturing functions strive for the other sex. Social demands have a prohibitive function. Therefore, both girls and boys frequently experience a short period of homosexual inclination that only temporally replaces the heterosexual relationship.

Now the liberation from the erotic bonds with mother or father has to take place. The object choice of puberty is a new choice. This choice unconsciously reflects the ideals of the initial love objects of early infancy. With physical maturation completed, psycho-sexual organization has reached its peak:

1. Influenced by the physical changes of puberty, the partial instincts have renounced their individual drive for satisfaction. Orgasm has become a privilege of the genital zone.

2. The aim of the mature sexual organization is another, heterosexual ego.

Many have observed that physical and psychological maturation rarely happen synchronously. Bernfeld was the first to clearly describe this phenomenon. For premature children sexual neediness precedes sexual ability, the result of a long psychologic process. Others again experience a prolonged psychological puberty with physical development preceding their psychological puberty with physical development preceding their psychological maturation. Some lack psychological puberty completely. They become people without any intellectual interests, without much psychological energy, and remain just average.

Fliess stated that man has a bisexual disposition. Adapting to cultural demands, the homosexual tendency gives way to the only practical heterosexual tendency toward the different sex. To me the integration of the father into the girl's emotional life therefore seems to be extremely important: this extension of her object cathexis avoids the certain fixation to her mother and therefore she finds her way to the other sex. Early ambivalence toward the father might serve as a protection against homosexuality in the boy. The remainders of homosexual inclinations together with sublimated exhibitionism and sadism predispose a person to become a leader of a political party.

Without numerous traces of sadism there are no good surgeons, teachers, and educators. Imagine a dentist or surgeon who has completely overcome his early brutal impulses and can't operate because he feels so sorry for his patient!

The sexual organization of the early years forms the basis for gifts, inclinations, and character. Initial ways of pleasant activities represent the frame. Education builds the house that becomes comfortable for its owner and useful for society.

Lecture 5:
The Child's Sexual Curiosity; About Sexual Education

Ladies and gentlemen! We have repeatedly heard that the child experiences a period of intense curiosity. This normally happens between the third and sixth years of life. Their own body and the origin of little babies forms the foci of their interest. One of the functions of constant questioning is the child's attempt to be permanently involved with preferred person. Sexual interest hides behind masks. The first question of the child's sexual curiosity is not the question about the sex difference. For the child this is a matter of clothing. He directs his interest toward the adult females in his surroundings. The less he succeeds, the more his curiosity is inflamed. He recognizes the sex difference, devaluating the female and overestimating his own, male sex. Three-year-old Kurt watching his newborn baby sister on the changing table. Curiously he observed her naked body and turned away with a derogatory smile: "Kurt pipi, Eva nothing!" Devaluation of the female body is connected to another feeling concerning the boy's own body. The recognition of the fact that the girl is missing the body part that is the reason for admonishing, punishment, and the threat of castration creates the suspicion in him that his punishment has already taken place in the girl. The fantasy that the girl has lost her penis because of masturbation and the fear of the same fate create the castration complex.

The girl also discovers the difference of the sexes at some point. She experiences herself as being neglected by nature and as being helplessly inferior. She envies the boy. Therefore she wants to compete with him in all the urethral games that provide opportunities for male exposure. She doesn't want to stand back from the roughness and uncontrolled freedom. Later she competes with him in education. The increased commitment, driven by the unconscious wish for compensation of the physical disadvantage, explains the girl's striving for participation in scientific work. The "masculinity" complex dominates her whole life. There won't be any woman who hasn't at one point experienced her femininity with bitterness and deep humiliation. Only those women who succeed to be happily in love can be at peace. She then owns in the man what she has not been given by nature. Dr. Karen Horney, in her brilliant article on the genesis of the female castration complex, has dealt with its incredible importance for the fate of women.

The sexual curiosity of the child won't stay content for too long with the answer that the stork is delivering the children or that god is sending them through his angels. Soon enough there are doubts as to how the stork is able to find the right house. Since children even today are not told the simple truth and because they can't believe in the tale of the stork, they have to come up with their own explanations. Fairy tales help. Finally, one of his playmates will tell him that mother's tummy is cut open to give birth. This is the sadistic birth theory that is often maintained right into puberty.

Birth, pregnancy, and the child form the center of the girl's sexual interest for years. She is identified with her mother and narcissistically overestimates everything connected with her. She maintains her basic question, "Where does the child come from?" The opportunity to solve the mystery by observing animals is an important reason for the love of animals.

From my observations and my experiences in analysis, I believe that there is a male counterpart to the girl's sexual envy or penis envy. This is his fantasy, that he and all men can have children. Melanie Klein reported about a four-year-old who imagined what he would do once he became a mother. A ten-year-old boy came into analysis with me because his fantasy life prevented him from learning and alienated him from reality. He experienced his fantasy world as being real. He seriously reported about heroic adventures where he had prevented disasters. The first success in treatment was encountered when he called his reports "novels" rather than "experiences." They had been full of unconscious death wishes against the father, libidinal impulses for his little sister, and birth fantasies, prominently about the mother's role.

The primal scenes that are never, even in analysis, remembered, are important. Their cognitive reconstruction during analysis often results in symptomatic improvement and legitimate their artificial recreation. These primal scenes most likely have been experienced and suppressed during the first years.

Interest in death is closely related to the interest in creation. The curiosity as to the nature of the soul, and man's fate after death represent the child's attempt at sublimation.

All the theories that the child developed in close proximity to his observations and the communications of peers and adults are rarely remembered. Most older children even declare firmly during their analysis that everything they know came to them through their own effort.

According to my own experience, children between the ages of eleven and fourteen experience a second question phase in prepuberty. This is rarely recognized since it is often repressed due to the earlier experiences with rejection during the first phase. Sexual interest again forms the focus but is well hidden behind questions of a scientific, social, or artistic nature. Only when the analyst is fully trusted the desire for the truth about sexuality can break free. There are questions that the young person wants answered. His own family life mainly determines the fate of his ideas. His concerns and secret wishes are reflected in his fantasies about the sexual life of adults. *A Young Girl's Diary* documented how the older child is embarrassed by her parents' intimacy. Rita understood why fourteen-year-old Erna separated herself from her pregnant mother. In addition, she commented that "I didn't like her from the start," as her judgment about another pregnant woman.

Older children are often interested, not in anatomy and function only, but also in the diseases of the genitalia. The fear of castration, strong guilt feelings about masturbation, and suppressed incestuous impulses form the basis of such interest. The connection between aging and sexual life is of equal interest.

There is no absolute rule as to the best time and way of sex education. We never know how much the child knows or how the knowledge was acquired. According to Freud, we always educate too late. However, from my experience, sometimes we educate too early. Yet, I can't see any danger as long as one condition is consistently met by adults, that is, to honestly answer according to the child's capability whatever he asks seriously. If the child knows that he can expect the truth, then he won't hide his sexual interests. The most important information has to be provided at puberty and in my experience even as early as prepuberty. If he is equipped with accurate knowledge, his own sexual development and that of others won't become the object of sleazy speculation or prudish rejection. Children have to learn to respect and value the female sex as being equal. They have to overcome the unconscious remainders of their reaction to the perception of the sex difference. This won't happen by suppression but only by open discussion. This only happens where trust and honesty form the basis of the life of adults and youth.

Lecture 6:
Educational Difficulties in the Family and in School

Ladies and gentlemen! The writer who recognized that we often love someone for his weaknesses was quite right. This is particularly true with children. After emotional upsets in a family, the loving bond between parents and children often becomes even closer. This only happens where children don't have to ask for "forgiveness" when they are still tearful and bitter about the injustice done to them. This only happens where wise parents allow time. Reconciliation has a deep meaning. Infantile narcissism triumphs in recapturing the temporarily lost love of the parents. The child feels omnipotent both in triggering and placating the parents' anger. Confessions teach us two things. They demonstrate the way in which the child repeatedly fails and accumulates guilt. In addition, they uncover the parental narcissism. It drives fathers toward harsh punishment and the mothers towards futile complaints. A child was never changed by repeated blame, ridicule, or skepticism about his potential for change. To be degraded in front of siblings or relatives is very humiliating for a child.

People who are wrongly accused of a misdeed might develop in two directions. Some suffer from continuous mistrust and a fear of becoming suspect. They try everything to lead an immaculate life or become criminals. The others try to compensate toward others what they have missed. They develop an exaggerated sense of justice that leads them to either excuse every misdeed or they become the merciless judges that prosecute with the harshest punishments. They all are unable to forget. They can't overcome the injustice that had been done to them by their first loves, their parents.

To orient ourselves I will differentiate the child's misdeeds according to moods, bad habits, and mistakes instead of symptoms of a disturbance in psychic development. All three forms reflect libidinal restraints of education or one of its successes: conscience. According to Freud, conscience is the condensation of everything that is considered good or bad by the child's environment. Therefore, it is a result of education. Connected to religious beliefs and accompanying guilt feelings, it becomes much more powerful than external forces during the time of puberty.

Mistakes represent the most difficult problem for education. We call mistakes those deviations that cause severe concern for the further characterological development.

First, I want to deal with the moods of the child. Pediatricians frequently deal with mothers' complaints that their child, often an only child, won't eat properly. The physical exam is normal. The expert explores the amount of attention and tenderness demanded and provided. He finds that the child recognizes the mother's anxiety around eating. To eat "for mother" or to punish her by refusing to eat is a most powerful method for a two- or three-year-old to make his point.

I learned from analyses of younger children that the wish to stay small plays as an important role as the wish to grow up, when it comes to eating problems. When it was tried to convince the child to eat by telling him that he wouldn't grow up tall otherwise, it had no effect. The child didn't want to give up certain privileges of the smaller child. He saw the potential of food refusal as a tool not to grow and thereby outgrow that phase of being small. One boy declared quite convincingly: "No, no, I don't want to grow up; I want to stay small, very small," and showed the size of his thumb.

Boys often exchange their reluctance to eat in later years for a greediness that is not easily explained by their increased healthy appetite. Its origin from jealousy and the wish to boast can be easily proved in families with a large number of children or in institutions. Indecent talk that spoils others' appetites warrants the sufficient amount of food and at the same time satisfies anal-erotic and sadistic impulses.

Similarly, the child knows how to keep the household on their toes with excretion problems. Dr. Helene Deutsch reported in her observation of "Lover's Grief in a Two-and-a-Half-Year-Old Boy" about the boy's difficulties with eating and excretion after his nanny had been sent away. Many children show severe constipation as soon as a familiar person is not available to help. All experienced caretakers know about the bad timing of many children with their defecation that invariably makes them the center of the family's attention.

This way the child dominates the early situation and the habit becomes a mood due to the affective involvement. Some moods assume the character of a habit due to their steadiness. We see the same phenomenon in older children. The play moods of younger children resemble the later inconsistencies in serious activities, leisure time, and friendship. Hereby, I don't mean the friendship that is dictated by family traditions but a friendship between children that starts as a free decision, and the influences that solidify and endanger it. The *Diary* presents valuable material on this topic.

Even if adults suspect or know about the reasons for the child's behavior, the child's moods or habits, they still assume the cause to be environmental. The adults rarely try to find out about true sources and motives. Examples can explain children's naughtiness from their wish to be punished. The child forces the acknowledgment and satisfaction of his narcissistic desire to be the center of attention of parents, siblings, and the class at school.

We call gross deviations from the socially accepted norms where the child satisfies his impulses to watch, show, smell, or listen, mistakes. The indecent gestures of older children are remainders of these infantile activities.

Bedwetting and soiling of clothes are considered to be unsettling manners. During my analysis of a seven-year-old boy, he maintained this habit. I discovered a number of different psychogenic roots: the regression towards the behavior of a smaller child, an identification with the two-year-old brother who was much envied for his special role in the household, and an identification with his mother, who, during a severe illness, had to use the bedpan. Furthermore, his father and grandparents had promised an award whenever he stayed dry for one week. In order not to lose these privileges, he had to relapse again and again. Finally he confessed that he liked the feeling of warm dampness. Stubbornness and revenge against a nanny who repeatedly woke him up at night contributed to his behavior. This intelligent boy discovered all these implications himself and his behavior gradually improved. However, the nanny happened to destroy the success with constant nagging. When he finally stopped, the parents therefore attributed his improvements to his stay in an institution and his feelings of honor in the community. This is in contrast to our experience that bedwetters of both sexes who live in boarding schools can't free themselves from their habit despite their terrible suffering from the ridicule of their peers. Parents and educators should also understand that bedwetting might be a replacement for masturbation. There are other replacements as well, like nose picking, scratching, moving of clothes, or playing with the budding breasts.

The observation of stubbornness and obstinacy teach us about the overlap between moods, bad habits, and mistakes. They have their roots in anal eroticism and can become persistent characteristics after single episodes of occurrence. Sulkiness and obstinacy, the stubborn crying and kicking of babies, later transform into open opposition or resistance.

During my analysis of a ten-year-old boy I was able to prove the sources of his behavior toward strangers and family members. His nine-year-old sister was always demonstrated to him as a model child. "Of course, 'girly' is always well dressed, white dress and white shoes with a huge ribbon and then she shows off, bows and chirps: 'Hi, how are you?' and the other ladies also chirp, 'What a nice girl, what a pleasant girl.' I stand on the side for a long time already without anybody noticing me and suddenly mother asks me, 'Well, Fritz, greet the ladies. Can't you greet them?' I couldn't speak a word and therefore I don't greet at all anymore." He also knew other ways to express his dislike for greeting people. Sometimes he shook somebody's hand, greeting the person in dialect and accompanying this with grotesque bows. He used the dialect to ridicule his distinguished upbringing and to intimidate his mother.

Grimacing shares similar roots. Hurt narcissism, obstinacy, and revenge impulses cause grimacing. The embarrassment that the adult recognizes in these grimaces and gestures is the expression of guilt feelings because of forbidden sexual thoughts, wishes, and behavior. One of my analytic patients didn't miss a single session without grimacing, affected speech, and threatening gestures in front of the mirror. All expressed his temporary anger towards me and also his parents who are always symbolized by the analyst. The child rarely finds understanding educators when he uses foul language. The teacher rarely recognizes the suffering of a soul that is confused by sexual half-knowledge.

Mixing up words and clowning has a deeper meaning. It helps to hide immodest wishes, to share sexual knowledge without fear of punishment, and to abuse somebody without consequences. Similar motives cause the secret codes and secret groups of older children. This also expresses the desire to claim secrets that are really nonexistent and to have secrets like father and mother, who communicate in incomprehensible languages and by unintelligible suggestions.

The deeper understanding of the many behavioral difficulties at school would frequently reveal them to be caused early and to be still asymptomatic neuroses. The uncontrollable roughness of some boys, their unnatural desire for fighting or boxing, give us a hint as to their amassed libido. Likewise some girls, chatterboxes during school hours who disclose their secret sexual knowledge and yet try to alleviate the tension by displacing it to more innocent topics. We see the dreamer who never knows what the teacher was just talking about to be suffering from unintelligible sexual-erotic feelings. The child who is always moving seems to indicate a later compulsive activity. Corporal punishment doesn't help, nor does the reprimand of the little chatterbox. They need educational-medical supervision and kind and understanding acknowledgement of their emotional suffering.

I don't have to emphasize the roots of exaggerated narcissism and sexual prematurity in cases of misbehavior and naughtiness. This is often admired by peers as "bravery." In one of his smaller papers Freud discussed the habit of some children to throw objects out of the window. Freud assumed that there is a deeper meaning to this game. He thought that the child wished to remove his younger siblings. He doesn't wish to throw away inanimate objects but to throw out the living objects who have disturbed his comfortable position.

I would like to mention another bad behavior of younger and older children that is also one of the most frequent: vandalism. Adults fight it with useless tools because of their own ignorance. I have never seen that a child gave up his destruction because of corporal punishment. Vandalism can be seen in children as young as two years of age and it often continues into the tenth and twelfth years. The child wants to discover the interior of things and the interest of his own body is displaced onto things that are easily accessible. Sexual curiosity is eventually the source of all interest to explore the inner aspects of objects. All destruction is the activation of sadistic impulses and sexual curiosity.

The third part of our considerations deals with the child's mistakes and their exaggeration or under-appreciation. A number of mistakes could be avoided if educators knew more about their causes and development. The inability to adapt to reality is an important factor. Lying is the most widespread mistake in infantile and adult years. Since people don't refrain from lying as adults and as educators, their fight against lies in children is even harder.

One generally assumes that a child under the age of four doesn't lie. If he deviates from the truth the reason lies normally with a lack of understanding, language development, or an error in memory. We might be closer to a solution if we differentiated between subjective and objectives lies. I call subjective lies those that help to emphasize or prevent oneself from punishment or rejection. Subjective and objective lies have the same sources, infantile narcissism and the emotional attitude toward parents, siblings, peers, teachers, family, and other people. Furthermore, the attempt at self-protection is important for white lies and lies because of fear of punishment.

We realize again and again that for the child the verbal lie seems to be more important than a lie in behavior. This is because for the child the spoken word has more implications than past action. This seems to be related to the intimidating power of verbal prohibitions but also to the power of the kind and loving voice of the mother. The greater severity of verbal lies also explains why children tend to shake their heads rather than saying "no." The habitual liar belongs to those children who are most difficult to raise. He combines in himself all different kinds of lies. The simulation of illness frequently has the same reason, namely, to be the center of the parents' attention. There is nobody who hasn't been a liar or thief in childhood. This seems to be common knowledge in a number of proverbs. Education tries to convince the child of the principle of "my" and "your." He learns to respect the possessions of others easier than those of family members. This experience should alert us. Every child steals at home. Initially the little thief doesn't acknowledge that he is doing something wrong, since morality is alien to him. He only hides because of fear of punishment. A child steals what in reality or in fantasy he is deprived of. This deficiency is a lack of love. To steal from his parents means to him to steal love from them. At the same time he identifies with their possessions, their wealth and power, and he takes revenge.

An eleven-year-old boy came into analytic treatment with me because of continuous stealing at home. Once he came to a session with the confession that he had secretly eaten sixteen of his mother's pralines. Although there was enough room in their apartment, the boy didn't have his own room but slept in the salon. Whenever there were guests he had to sleep in his mother's room. This had been the occasion of his theft. We were also interested in the number of pralines that equaled the number of guests that night. He had eaten the guests that had displaced him from his bedroom! He took revenge.

Analytic material shows some interesting consistencies of choice. Boys preferably steal from female members of the family. Many steal from women since they despise females. From my own experience I want to emphasize that by far the most thefts are done by boys, well explained by their despising of the female sex. Analyses of adult females regularly show the fantasy to steal father's masculinity. However, this is something I couldn't reproduce in my analyses of younger females.

I repeatedly make one observation during my analytic work that gives rise to the following theoretical consideration. This is the close link between stealing and a desire for sweets. The first thefts almost exclusively deal with sweets and food, even if there is no shortage. The child later steals money. The trials of adults prove repeatedly that the oral drive plays an important role. I assume that the particular sensitivity of the oral zone is responsible for this particular deviation.

I do not want to finish my considerations without mentioning other misbehaviors, such as running away and truancy. There is always something unachievable that pulls these children away from home. Runaways and truants lack love.

One of the greatest difficulties parents and teachers have to face is the child's failure at school. The more the parents have invested themselves in their child's education and success, the more vulnerable and helpless they are when met by this disappointment. They blame their child and the school, since they don't know the real cause. The forced renunciation of immediate gratification of libidinal needs during the early and adolescent question periods causes a failure of the ability for sublimation.

Lecture 7:
The Child's Anxiety

Ladies and gentlemen! Any talk about educational difficulties has to include one phenomenon that has the potential of severe disturbance of family life, the anxiety of the child. It is often underestimated, but in its importance it is sometimes also nurtured and supported by exaggeration.

To give the right impression, we will first deal with the general appearance of anxiety and its modes of expression. The multiple dangers of everyday life warrant everybody being familiar with the feelings of anxiety. "Anxiety is the biological adaptation to danger," according to Freud. The preparation for anxiety, triggered by external dangers that result from instinctual conflicts, advises us to flee if we are not strong enough to meet the challenge, e.g., the attack by a wild animal. Or it advises us to fight back, to defend ourselves if we feel strong enough, or even to risk an attack that doesn't leave enough time for our enemy to attack.

Dangerous situations cause terror if we meet them unprepared. "Anxiety prevents man from terror," states Freud. Anxiety is an affect and characterized as a psychic phenomenon of innervation and accompanied by physical and psychological sensations, like flushing or pallor, tachycardia, dyspnea, tremor, weakness, and helplessness. As with all affects, we lack consideration and ego control when we are afraid.

The exemplary American child psychologist and researcher Stanley Hall, who enthusiastically received and applied Freud's teachings at the age of seventy, lists in his investigation of anxiety a number of objects and situations that might trigger this particular affect. For example, darkness, open air, open places, closed rooms, crowding, solitude, cliffs, bridges, tunnels, trains, ships, wild animals, cats, mice, frogs, spider, caterpillars, butterflies, snakes, thunderstorms, sharp edges, and blood.

In an overview Freud acknowledges those triggers that have a role in eliciting real anxiety. Recognizing these stimuli, man reacts with real anxiety. His reaction is linked to an attempt to escape in an impulsive expression of self-preservation.

This also applies to situations that have some inherent danger, like a serious thunderstorm, train and boat trips, horrors of revolution, solitude, life-threatening crowding, epidemics, serious operations for ourselves or our loved ones, meeting crazy or drunken people, burglars or thieves. But there are also numerous people who are afraid of things that we recognize as being quite innocent. Their fear appears to be quite unsubstantiated and therefore ridiculous. Mice, butterflies, worms, frogs and toads, heavy traffic, the silence of the alps trigger intense anxiety and sometimes especially with animals disgust. It seems funny if a big and strong man can only cross an open place when accompanied by a six-year-old, or if a woman has to return to her front door three times after leaving the house to reassure herself that she has really locked it. Children's anxiety at night time, *pavor nocturnus*, also appears to be inappropriate and futile. All these people fear things that are normally not able to trigger real anxiety, and they suffer from neurotic anxiety. It differs from real anxiety by the disproportion between the trigger and the anxious response.

Early observation teaches us that the first expressions of infantile anxiety are directed at strangers, while situations or objects themselves rarely trigger an anxious response. In contrast, children touch everything within reach and take it to their mouth. They do not know about any inherent danger of objects. We can also not assume that mistrust causes this response since this requires an intellectual capacity far beyond this age group. The infantile anxiety is explained by disappointment in life. It also represents the first anxious situation. For Freud the Latin root of anxiety, *angustiae* for "narrowing," seems to indicate the time of man's first anxiety when he had to pass the narrowing of the maternal vagina that impeded breathing. All later anxiety states therefore would represent a repetition of the anxiety at birth.

The infant's longing for familiar faces and his disappointment with the unfamiliar are transformed into anxiety. We now understand why the child reacts fearfully to loneliness and darkness and why it is often sufficient to take a child's hand in the darkness and talk to him to alleviate the anxiety. "Aunt, talk to me until it becomes light!" This wish of a little boy explained to Freud the causes of infantile anxiety. The child doesn't fear darkness but loneliness. He misses the loved person. His need for love is unsatisfied. Anxiety therefore stems from unusable libido. The longing in the dark becomes the anxiety of darkness. Solitude and darkness trigger the first situational phobias in childhood.

Some reasonable educational measures might trigger anxiety. We have to warn of the dangers of traffic, of falling out of the window, the danger of dogs and horses, sharp edges, scissors, needles, fire, and water. Swallowing of poisonous substances, stones, buttons, and belladonna are dangerous, as is the company of strangers.

We are alerted if children seem to express exaggerated fears, almost in a pathological way. One child who had been warned wanted to keep his company away from a "dangerous" street, another child insists on being tied to the bed at night after his little brother died from a fall out of the window. Other children suffer from a sudden fear of dogs and horses that prevents them from going outside. A child fears a needle and anticipates the death of a loved person from swallowing one of them. Children bluntly refuse to greet a stranger or run away from a drunk or anxiously avoid him. These anxieties are not related to normal real anxiety but are very similar to the neurotic anxiety of the adult. There is not much of an inborn tendency towards real anxiety in children. Normally, the child underestimates the inherent dangers because of his narcissistic overestimation. He thinks that he can do everything and better and that he knows everything better than others. He doesn't doubt for a second that he can tame a wild horse or carry loads that are too heavy even for an adult man.

Single children or favorite children assume dangers where there are really none because of their exaggerated libidinal neediness and constitutional disposition. These children tend to become neurotic. Guilt feelings from the Oedipal and castration complex and disappointments push them toward phobias, the most frequent neuroses in childhood. It is model and prerequisite for the anxiety hysteria. Phobic people hide themselves against the external danger that has now replaced the internal libidinal threat. Freud was able to prove the anxiety mechanism during the analysis of a five-year-old boy with an animal phobia. Hostile feelings toward the father, stemming from jealousy of the tenderly loved mother, were transferred to horses that are quite suitable for a symbolic father-replacement due to their size and strength. Anxiety becomes phobia once it becomes fixated in one complex, as in this case. The patient even loses his anxiety but he achieves this at the price of restraints and restrictions. He invents a ceremony.

Among other hysterical symptoms, a seventeen-year-old girl suffered from a phobia of burglars. When she was left alone by her sister for a week during the summer holidays, she couldn't sleep at night because of her fear that a thief or murderer would hide under her bed. Finally she was even afraid to use a flashlight to shine under her bed. But she invented some protection. She put her potty and two pair of shoes around her bed and connected them with the laces. The analysis of this ceremony led far back to her early childhood and revealed erotic fantasies and wishes past and present.

A fifteen-year-old boy, in treatment for severe anxiety attacks, was only able to sleep by strictly maintaining a certain ceremony. At night he put an open knife, a hammer, three sharp nails, and a snack on the table and a rope and a book under his pillow. Knife, hammer, and nails were thought to help with attack and defense against a burglar and the rope was meant to bind him. The snack was supposed to serve after the fight and the book as a distraction from terrifying memories in the early morning. Loud talking or singing is also a kind of self-defense against the fear in the dark room. By pretending the presence of a second person, the child escapes his anxiety.

The relative frequency of infantile phobias make it advisable that pediatricians, educators, and teachers be familiar with their etiology, to advise the parents as to the right means of intervention.

I mentioned earlier the phobia of the seven-year-old boy of falling out of his bed who wanted to be tied to his bedside. This might give us an idea of the etiology and history of this affect. As you remember, this was the child whose two-and-a-half-year-old brother had fallen out of a second floor window when he was unattended for a moment. He died three days later from the severe head injury. The older brother didn't show any particular signs of sadness. Shortly thereafter the family went for holidays and returned to Vienna by the end of September. The child had brought a belt back from the holidays and suddenly demanded to be tied to his bed every night. Nothing would change his mind. The thorough thrashing that his grandfather recommended also wouldn't have helped the course. The child was sick. He suffered from severe and unconscious guilt feelings toward his brother. The well-known sibling rivalry that he had frequently expressed in pushing and shoving was at the core of his delusion that he had actually killed his brother. This delusion dominated all his play and his attitude toward his environment. He repeatedly destroyed the towers and bridges we had built during his sessions, horses with cars had terrible accidents on steep hills; and he didn't like a loved person to stand close to the balustrade of a balcony. His unconscious only expressed these expectations and concerns in a well-masked manner. People around him didn't recognize his fears during the day. During an arduous analysis over several months he became consciously aware of his death wishes against his brother and this cured his phobia. Today he is a well-groomed twelve-year-old who accompanies his father for mountaineering, on ski and slide tours without any signs of nausea or other forms of anxiety.

There are justified warnings in the educational process but there is also an inappropriate amount of castration threats and sexual intimidation with regard to anal interests, exhibitionism, and sexual curiosity. Many educational measures result in infantile anxiety. One of Freud's students and former followers, Dr. Alfred Adler, the founder of the school of Individual Psychology, assumed feelings of inferiority, weakness and helplessness to be etiological. In one form this type of anxiety seems to be correct to me. That is the masked anxiety of the Jewish child who presents himself as boisterous and bold because of his racial complex. Early experience teaches him to expect hostility and hatred toward himself and his family. He finds hatred instead of love. However, as soon as the child realizes that anxiety is unsuitable for self-determination, he hides himself in arrogance. Understanding this matter, the school should deal appropriately with the racial complex of the Jewish child.

We don't have the time to deal with all forms of infantile anxiety in detail. Most common is the fear of loneliness and darkness. We observe animal phobias influenced by the Oedipal complex. Small animals regularly indicate an unsuccessful suppression of strong anal eroticism. These tiny animals often represent similarly sized particles of the feces. A most common anxiety is pavor nocturnus. Here the child satisfies his need for love by anxious screaming, tossing, and turning. Normally, he achieves his goal to sleep in his mother's bed. Fear of washing is quite understandable. As adults we can't imagine how helpless the child feels when a huge hand brushing over eyes, ears, nose, and mouth with a wet sponge.

Older children suffer from fears about school, punishment, and examinations. They are anxious to be on time for school. We can't deny that the child experiences the school as a place of punishment. The motive lies deep. From analyses of those cases, we know that the child suffers at school from unconscious thoughts of hatred and revenge that can climax in death wishes against the own mother. The teacher plays an important role as a paternal symbol. Analyses of adults taught us that the fear to be late is often accompanied by urinary urges and sexual arousal. Examination fears frequently transform to fears of public embarrassment in adolescents.

Laymen as well as physicians blame frightful experiences for the phenomenon of stuttering. Although appearing later in life, its origin can be traced back to early years. Although I don't have too much experience in my own practice, I always found a generally anxious disposition and a phenomenon that had been described by Freud, that is, the stutterer initially doesn't transgress the prohibited terminology of early anal, urethral interests. He initially only stutters around these words and much later extends the stuttering to other vocabulary. Therefore, regression to an earlier stage of development seems to play an important role in stuttering.

A typical female fear is that of falling. It becomes particularly unbearable with males present and disappears during solitude and darkness. This is often explained by a pervasive modesty. The erotic wishes that hide behind the symptom explain that this fear to fall is based on moral weakness and the unconscious desire to "fall." The confusions of adolescence, unconscious guilt feelings, and reappearing disappointments often trigger religious or social fears in adolescents. This can be expressed as fear of divine punishment or as a social phobia and desire to be alone. The fear of blushing is typical for this age. Suppressed exhibitionism, guilt feelings around masturbation regularly play an important etiological role. Fears of seduction express prohibited sexual desires.

Caretakers have to learn to understand the mild symptoms that indicate the potential for later severe pathology. Their understanding will help them to teach self-confidence and self-discipline. Teaching then becomes a tool of enlightenment and caution rather than intimidation.

Lecture 8:
Fantasies of Children
and Adolescents

Ladies and gentlemen! I want to deal with the little run-away. His tragic fate is determined by his fantasies that promise what reality withholds from him.

The child's tender-sensuous wishes to secure the exclusive possession of father or mother is accompanied by hostile feelings against the interfering parent. The Oedipal complex can become so powerful that the child's psyche collapses under its dynamics. He escapes this danger by using fantasies that promise fulfillment of his dreams. He develops the fantasy that his real parents were distinguished rich people who had given him to foster parents that were never really able to love him. He looks for these idealized parents far away. This is the fate of the unwanted child, either being late in a family of many children or arriving at a time where marital strife makes a welcome unlikely.

Children don't make the same differentiation between fantasy and reality as adults do. This doesn't exclude a well-developed sense of reality in the child. His wishes that originate in an instinctual life, contradictory to the necessities of every-day life, are so powerful that compromise formation becomes more difficult. The child doesn't lack the ability but the will to control reality. He is more flexible and suggestible and this blurs the border between fantasy and reality. His own wishes always seem realistic. If they remain unfulfilled, he blames his environment, experiencing internally what has been withheld from him.

Fantasies are replacements for pleasures. Since life is characterized by an endless series of renunciations imposed universally by education and culture, we find the same common fantasies everywhere. These are typical, caused by wishes like being big. They reflect the ambiguous attitude toward father and mother, brother and sister. The Oedipal complex finds its sublimation in rescue fantasies toward the mother or women in general or caretaker fantasies toward the father.

The frequent flagellation and punishment fantasies of childhood have been the subject of one of Freud's detailed investigations. He won important insight into the pseudo-masochistic disposition of the child, about the primary character of sadism, and the development of masochism from sadism with the addition of guilt feelings. These fantasies in children stem from their guilt feeling because of their incestuous attitude toward their parents and their masturbation.

Paradoxically, wishful fantasies are also the reason for the boy's frequent castration fantasies. To lose his penis appears to him as a justified punishment and relief from temptation. We clearly see the transformation of unsatisfied libido into anxiety. Operations frequently form the core of painful-lustful fantasies that represent castration in boys while they symbolize, sometimes quite openly, the girl's wish for pregnancy.

An eleven-month-old girl watch fascinated when two flies landed during their love-play on her blanket. When the same blanket was spread over her bed three days later, she pointed at it with a clear "Sssss." At the age of three and a half years she was affected by a severe fly-phobia. Shortly before she had been prohibited to continue with a lustful doctor game that she played with a boy her age. Within a few days I was able to clarify the primal scene for her, using beetles that she was not afraid of. We found the connection to the doctor game: The flies noisily touch one another at body parts under taboo as she did with this boy. The flies are "naughty animals" since they want to continue their games on her, therefore she would be punished, since "you can't punish flies." Since she knew that she had been inside her mother's womb before birth, we didn't have any difficulties to explain the creation of animals. We also found again that the child accepts certain explanations as being correct for the animal without consciously drawing conclusions as to how this applies to man. Her anxiety of flies was replaced by a tender curiosity. The child's sexual curiosity is at the basis of the love for animals.

Thunderstorms, earthquakes, and train collisions were the most potent of nine phobias that a fifteen-year-old boy was suffering from. He was most concerned about himself and his mother whom he virtually tied to the house by his fears. When I talked to the mother, she mentioned that the boy had been born during a three-day hurricane. The storm delayed the arrival of the midwife. Therefore, the child was born during the chaos of a natural disaster. He certainly didn't have any conscious memories and even the repeated talk in the family didn't make it a personal experience for him. During his analysis, he developed intense fantasies about the impact of such a storm on mother and child, resembling his own intense fear. For external reasons the analysis had to be terminated after nine weeks. According to friends the boy had changed completely. The clumsy and shy boy who anxiously avoided any contact had become cheerful and open and looked actively for company, but his fears that tyrannized his mother and sister were essentially the same. By the next winter I unexpectedly received a letter from his mother, who told me that the boy would go alone to the theater and for skating during a storm. Mother and sister then could live a normal life again.

These primal scenes are not remembered during analysis. They can be only reconstructed, but this reconstruction brings the patient forward in his healing process, and this result justifies the means. Analyzing neurotic patients, we often find fantasies about returning into the mother's womb. We call these daydreams, womb fantasies. We don't mistake their real meaning even if they are obscured behind death wishes, etc. To rest in the tomb from all the suffering and hurry on earth, to return to dust that man once was made from, returning to mother earth for an eternal life—all these fantasies basically mean to return to the paradise that was lost at birth. Common sense has a much better grasp on this than the civilized man alienated by science and sophistication, as shown in this remark of a simple farmer's wife about the behavior of her five-year-old son after the birth of his younger brother: "I don't know what's wrong with him. He doesn't move from my side; it's as if he wanted to crawl back into me." The unconscious memory about intra-uterine life was reactivated by the birth of the younger brother, yet without becoming fully conscious.

Freud rightly interprets fantasies as replacements for denied satisfaction. They allow for freedom from internal or external pressure. Ethical and moral conflicts find an escape. They combine individual and social demands in a way that could never be achieved in reality. During prepuberty and puberty, erotic fantasies often dominate the imaginative and emotional spheres. They turn out to be the only means of discharge of libido at the time of strongest demands and also the most forceful restraints.

A sixteen-year-old neurotic girl, who was restricted to her home because of her severe phobia of people, reported in her analysis how she had developed fantasies early on that allowed her to join her family on walks in the country. There she was always accompanied by the fantasy of an unknown loved man, with whom she had a silent conversation during these walks, who led her over rough ground and shared snacks and drinks. She resented any contact with her real company and was not to be disturbed in her "secret world." She was seen as being grumpy and unsociable while she was enjoying her enchanting intimacy in fantasy.

Children's fantasies and daydreams disclose their carefully protected wishes. For the expert the child's dreaminess, his suggestions and talks are telling, even if they are at times misjudged as lies. Another way that is normally not considered for exploration are the fever fantasies of children. If the environment was not preoccupied with the child's health at this particular moment, they would see their secret imaginations. I don't have any material in this area. Guilt feelings regularly play an important role in daydreams with younger children more than older ones. The illness itself and the prescriptions represent punishment and expiation. These fantasies typically include thoughts about dying, funerals, the parental pain, as well as the embarrassing idea how the siblings share in the remaining toys, books, etc. During puberty, erotic fantasies dominate. By their high intensity they cause a prolongation of illness, since the patients don't want to give up their patients' role, just as younger children who don't want to lose their family's attention. The hysterical patient flees into his illness to avoid the disappointments of normal life. The young patient experiences his illness fantasies as a satisfaction of his erotic desires and what has remained unsatisfied during childhood.

A sixteen-year-old girl in analytic treatment for her strong inferiority feelings because of her squinting disclosed fantasies that she had held at the age of twelve during her appendicitis. In her dreams she loved her physician as groom and husband. She would bear him a child and was close to death because of him. He took care of her and brought her to the Riveria where she spent, again as bride and wife, wonderful days. This now formed the core of her masturbatory fantasies. Appendicitis and pelvic diseases are well suited for pregnancy fantasies, as we know for the analyses of adults. I don't consider it an accident that this girl fell sick from a fatal flu during her analysis and prolonged her dying until her family doctor and professor was in attendance.

Fairy tales and sagas, songs and sounds should become a precious heritage for the child's soul. They speak simply but powerfully about the old days with simple experiences and primitive feelings at a time when the child is still susceptible and inclined. We know that the child's waiting desires, imaginations, feelings, and impulses will jump like wild animals onto the corresponding literature, and that's why we don't recommend reading frightening stories at bedtime and why we recommend to parents to keep their bookcase locked from their children.

A strong bond of educated parents in the fields of literature and arts often elicits an early interest in serious literature, for lively art. Identified with father, mother, or an admired teacher, the maturing child seriously deals with the poets' works and their biographies. Love therefore encourages the child's interest in education if the role models have ethical and aesthetic value.

Daydreaming, as we have got to know it, is the most important product of fantasy. If fulfills ambitious presumptuous and erotic dreams that have no place in every-day life. It realizes hateful and deadly wishes that otherwise have to hide in the dark. All these impulses wear disapproved, offending, and therefore secret characteristics. Their owner is very reluctant to disclose them. Unconscious daydreams are the source of nightly dreams and poetic production. According to Freud and Rank, art provides the way back from fantasy to reality. Theatrical works of adults as well as children, their drawings, tales, and poetry have to be appreciated in this way. Present attempts to reform schools and education try to realize these considerations.

Lecture 9:
Children's Play

Ladies and gentlemen! We have looked in depth at those sources that cast dark shadows on family life, the bad behavior of children, which we now better understand as symptoms of psychological disturbances, fears, and fantasies that carry them away from the values of reality. Today we want to turn to a friendly aspect of a child's life, the most charming and important one—his play.

In free and unrestrained play, the child's soul disclosed spontaneity and originality. Only his play is spontaneous, all other activities are forced by education
and models. And the child provides himself some relief by approaching the
serious chores with a playful attitude. Already at the early stage where he is still
quite passive he understands to turn the bothersome procedure of washing,
bathing, and dressing into entertainment and fun. Riding and swinging on the
pillows sweeten the getting up in the morning, each piece of clothing is used
for peek-a-boo, he escapes the washcloth a hundred times only to be caught
again as a wild animal that waits to attack from under the table or bed, tooth
brushing becomes the imitation of a fountain, and he doesn't become tired
even if the dressing lasts for hours. Later we will hear how far the upset of those
who care for the child is justified in these situations. At the table he wants to be
accompanied by a kitten or bird and likes to imagine that on his plate are silver
or golden fish that he has to eat. These little games make it easier for the poor
feeder and normally only fail if the child has an organic illness. But older children also like fantasies during their chores that mother has assigned to them for
her own relief or educational purposes. The boy who carries wood and coal from
the basement can't take on enough of a burden to imitate the big and strong
"coal man" whom he envies for his noisy shovel and his dirty black hands, or
the little girl who can't find enough dirt when she is handling broom and brush
to thoroughly clean the floor. A thirteen-year-old girls, always studying her
books, had the chores to set the table at mealtimes, to attend father's flower
bank, and to wipe dust, and she made them more pleasant by imagining that
she was preparing the home for her loved husband. Narcissistic and erotic
wishes are therefore fulfilled in play and make the demands of reality more
acceptable.

The source of all play is the child's wish to be big. Therefore, nearly all
games contain an element of imitation of adults or older children. Jumping
as far as the older brother, throwing the ring as versatilely as father, caring
for and yelling at the doll as mother does—adult behavior always serves as
the model for the play. We will deal with the child's motives later.

The French infant-researcher Compayre wrote in his book *L'Enfant des
trois ans:* "A good history of child play would allow us to follow the progressing
development of all skills from day to day." And it would do even more: It
would show how all drives are activated in play, since play is the only place
to set free all different drives. This is why we can't understand play in a
strictly teleologic or operational sense, since this would not recognize the
importance and satisfaction of drives and impulses. Freud says that they "try
to guess the child's motives, but they don't appreciate the economic aspect,
the pleasure principle." The Hungarian psychoanalyst Sigmund Pfeiffer has
fully appreciated this aspect. Analyzing a number of infantile games, he
proves the similarity between them and other products of the unconscious
like fantasies and dreams, which we will deal with later, and lapses that we

already spoke about. Suppression, displacement, condensation, symbolization, identification, and rationalization all contribute to the eventual form of the play.

All play starts out from situations in reality, lustful or uncomfortable, as long as there is some affective quality to it. Everybody knowledgeable knows how illnesses, physical examinations, and small operations that the child had to undergo are quickly transformed into games. He repeats with peers or his doll voluntarily what has been a major project with some necessary bribery from the parents: immunizations, the visit of smaller and bigger children to the dentist, etc. Some hatred and narcissistic ambition finds its discharge that way. One of my little patients, a five-year-old boy, went, accompanied by his mother, to the dentist. Next day he transformed our session into a session at the dentist. He was the dentist and I played patient and mother: "You are not to cry since I can't work that way. Open your mouth wider," he commanded and was quite disappointed that I willingly follows his instructions. "You have to cry, otherwise it is no game." The mother hadn't been very good, he commented disrespectfully, and the dentist had to scold at her. He ridiculed his mother in this game and a strong hatred that he rarely expressed directly otherwise found a welcome discharge. On another occasion he had to see the doctor because of heavy earache. After a long struggle the doctor examined him with the otoscope. The boy again transformed this into a play, this time with a little girl: the mother had difficulties in preventing him from seriously hurting the girl, who had to suffer from his revenge that was meant to hurt the "bad doctor." Children with strict upbringing also tend to be very strict when playing "mother and child" or "school." He takes revenge at the innocent and helpless replacement of the original tormenter. He changes his passive role in reality into an active play in his play and discharges part of his undirectable affect. This explains that despite the reign of the pleasure principle, unpleasant experiences are also playfully repeated; play helps the child to cope with them.

Freud observed the play of a one-and-a-half-year-old boy. The little boy was prematurely developed in his cognition but he didn't resist any educational measures and particularly never cried whenever his mother, whom he tenderly loved, left him for hours. "This good child had the sometimes disturbing habit to throw away whatever small objects he could get hold of. . . . He accompanied this with a long 'o-o-o-o' with all the signs of interest and satisfaction, and his mother translated the 'o' into 'away.' Freud assumed this to be a game and that the boy used the toys to play 'away' with them. Later another observation proved him right. He used a long thread with a spool and threw it behind his bed with a long 'o-o-o' and greeted its reappearance when pulling it back with an excited 'Da!' " He could play this game of disappearing and reappearing for hours, especially the first part, although Freud emphasized that the second part obviously was more pleasant for him.

His interpretation was again confirmed by a later observation. "When one day the mother returned after a couple of hours she was greeted with a 'Bebi o-o-o' that at first remained unintelligible. But the mother soon found out that the boy had found a way during these long hours to make himself disappear. He had discovered his own image in the mirror that almost came down to the floor. He crouched down so that his own image disappeared." Freud assumed that "this game was connected to his great cultural achievement, his renunciation of satisfaction, gratifying himself by making those objects disappear and reappear that were within his power." And he correctly concluded "that the disappearance of his mother couldn't have been by any means a pleasant or even neutral experience. His game satisfied a normally suppressed impulse for revenge. The throwing of the object had the obstinate meaning: "Well, go, I don't need you, I send you away myself." The report of the mother, quite unfamiliar with psychoanalytic thinking, confirms this very well. She talks about her one-and-a-half-year-old daughter who followed her all the way down the hallway and spat at her when she was about to leave against the girl's will. The mother very well understood the feelings of this girl who otherwise was a very loving and tender child. It would be interesting to know if this child renounced the rationalization of her impulses in a play since she had expressed them openly before.

Let me give you another example that shows quite nicely how an unpleasant event can become the topic of a play if the child is allowed to realize his hateful impulses. A four-and-a-half-year-old girl loses her privileged position with the arrival of a little brother, especially since this child is ill, cranky, and doesn't sleep well. She repeats everything with a doll that the brother does to her. And the little doll cries so loudly that the adults have to intervene. With an obvious and hateful pomposity she puts herself and her doll Gerti— her brother's name is Gerhard—into the center of the adults' attention. Two months later the mother noticed a long trace of sawdust in the girl's room. The dolls are examined and, as if turns out, the baby doll as a gaping wound between her legs: The girl castrated her. She realized in her play what she wanted to do to her brother, whose anatomy she had recognized with jealous astonishment. All the accumulated envy and jealousy was discharged in her play; at the same time she identified with her mother and therefore became her father's wife.

In this play the child expresses all the secret imaginations, wishes, and striving that education tries to suppress. Fighting and catching games represent the early developing possessive drive; all kinds of competition, being physical or mental, are nurtured by the narcissistic drive for honor. They are avoided where the balance of powers makes a success unlikely. There we often meet the killjoy who ends every game by fighting or blaming his partner to avoid the inevitable defeat. He avenges his hurt narcissism with perfidious obstacles; he disturbs intellectual games where he doesn't have a chance with clowning, or he uses the same prohibited means that he blames his partner for, and he is full of helpless rage when caught. He hates cooperative games since he is dominated by his feelings of inferiority. But he still comes back since his narcissism can't stand the lasting superiority of others. He suffers from over- and underestimation of his ego-values.

The violence and persistence that the sexual drive uses to resist the influences of education let us assume that we will discover their influences in the child's play again. And true, there is almost no game where the sexual drive is not emphasized in its direct or sublimated expression.

Exhibitionism and the drive to observe dominate all theater games. Costumes, processions, and funerals, theater-show gymnastics, and other sports have their origin in the lustful watching and self-exposure. These games lose their attraction with their audience. A five-year-old boy who liked to climb and jump gave up as soon as he recognized that the attention of his audience turned toward somebody else. "But you don't look," he blamed his mother when she dared to return to her book after having repeatedly praised him.

We frequently find that the child's play provides an excellent opportunity to satisfy the anal- and urethral-erotic impulses. The smallest are uninhibited by disgust to play with their excrements when unsupervised, to soil clothes, hairs, face, and hands. Memories of coprophilia live on as intentional soiling of public places and school washrooms by older children, some adolescents' phrases on walls and public lavatories. Urethral competitions on the street and elsewhere satisfy the exhibitionistic as well as curious impulses and the male ambitiousness at the same time. Even if these activities vanish later, water and soil remain for similar pleasant activities. The attraction of play often lays with the eventual outcome as much as with the creations, throwing little pieces at one another. Children who lack the artistic gift will emphasize this aspect of the game most. Girls' preference for cleaning the dollhouse and the doll's clothes have the same origin.

The fascination of fire also is the reason for the child's play with it. Common sense connects play with fire with other bad habits of the child that are quite familiar to the analyst. Fire and water, the incompatible elements united in the child's instinctual life! The little bedwetter we heard about before reported that he regularly felt a strong urge to urinate when he was playing with fire and that he was playing with fire and that he suppressed this by pressing his thighs together, which made him feel very hot, and suddenly he would feel the moisture. "Like the fire expires in the oven and created cold and grey ash, the most heat becomes cold and wet"—that's how the little natural philosopher summarized his experience. Every parent knows from own memory about the anal-erotic satisfaction of "doctor game" and "mother-and-child game." And the success of a doll that can eat as well as defecate proves that both the uncle who brought it from Paris and the producer successfully used the unconscious memories. Bjoernstijerne Bjoernson describes in his psychologically interesting novel *Es flaggen Stadt und Hafen* the marvelous dollhouse that even seduced a sixteen-year-old to seemingly forgotten play—the room with beds and cupboards where nothing was missing that "makes a real bedroom." And little Scupin really starts to love his play-parrot after having drilled a little hole in his back that allows him to retrieve the paper pieces that he has fed by mouth before.

Sadism and masochism, the contrast pair of tormenting love, is more or less present in all fighting or competitive games, the rough and tumble play of the boys, teasing and scolding games, and in school games. The little sadist wants to play teacher or, if forced to be the student, she will give way to all the bad behavior and malice that reality normally doesn't allow.

The strong erotegenicity of muscle activity makes the child prefer movement to stagnation. Wrestling, boxing, climbing, gymnastics, and swinging frequently lead to boys' first erections that frighten and please at the same time. These premature sexual stimulations also explain the favorite hobby or riding horse, toys that should be banned from a hygienically blameless chamber anyway. In his autobiographical memories Fontane praises the wonderful walking on stilts. Like other children who enjoy their position on father's shoulders watching people, they normally don't match in size, from above the little man on stilts walks gracefully in self-determination and arrogance above the crowd. Once when stilts were fashionable I heard two boys of seven and eight years who shouted at an envious other lad: "Up here the air is clear!" All games where a child can excel are sources of narcissistic pleasure. The "as well" or "even better" makes them try very hard and to take a risk when he is almost sure about the outcome. The smaller child never doubts the power of his own ego that even influences the chance. Most preferences of games can be explained on the basis of narcissistic satisfaction and narcissistic insult. They also reflect the child's affective ambivalence for his environment.

The recognition of drives as important demands a close observation of the playing child. He will intuitively resent observation since he feels discovered in his hidden thoughts, wishes and desires. In his instructive "Das Kinderspiel als Frühsymptom krankhafter Veranlagung," that is, "Children's Games as Early Symptoms of Pathologic Disposition," the Swiss analyst and pastor Pfister demonstrated by an analysis of a twenty-five-year-old man how his symptoms had been prepared by a pathological relationship with his mother and peers that was expressed in peculiar games. His increased fantasy activity, the creation of his own distant fantasy world, the urge for exhibition, the compulsive classifying and systematizing, dominated his play as well as his neurotic symptoms later.

Physical and psychological constitution determine the child's play behavior. They influence choices and preferences as well as the way games are played. The excessively orderly and pedantic anal-erotic doesn't succeed in playing since he is spending his time arranging his toys, which often becomes the game itself. Construction set and sewing kit provide the opportunity to put stones, buttons, spools, needles, pearls in order according to size or color, in rows or ornaments; he likes to contain his possession in little boxes that he carefully labels and this itself becomes his favorite game. His pleasure in classification and system will prompt him as an adult to plan his schedule systematically and to carefully stick to it. If he is a merchant or civil servant, he can't create enough tables, statistics, catalogues, etc. The behavior of a little collector whose pockets are full of all possible junk, who finally doesn't know what to collect, becomes suddenly understandable if we draw the connection to his infantile constipation. The collector is the born anal-erotic. The child that starts a hundred games without finishing one of them, who takes everything out of his toy box without tidying up afterwards, shows an inconsistency that lets us assume difficulties in concentration that will become calamitous in later life. It discloses a resistance to association that prevents him from professional consistency or steadiness in his Weltanschauung.

Important as it is, play observation needs to be done cautiously. To interpret correctly, the child has to be observed when he feels alone and unobserved.

The sex preferences in toys reflect the long process the child needs to recognize the sex differences, beginning with complete ignorance and progressing to recognition of differences in clothing and later to facts that in concert with educational prohibitions give rise to the male castration complex and the female male-complex that are closely related. The undifferentiated toys progress to horse and car for boys and doll-house and doll for girls, differences that are initiated by adults and only later accepted by the children themselves. Four- and five-year-old boys like to play with dolls if the pleasure in them hasn't been spoiled and girls enjoy mail- and beer-trucks, cars and trains that are supposed to be boys' toys. The fact that little boys enjoy the uninfluenced play with dolls as much as girls let us assume that it is not so much the maternal instinct that makes this play attractive but the opportunity to boost one's own omnipotence by identifying with the mother.

Playing with dolls provides an opportunity for strong identification with the mother and therefore also with the desired position toward the father; to have a child with him is the clear message of little girls as well as boys as long as their attitude toward him is feminine. A five-year-old girl will carefully distinguish between dolls given to her by her father or her mother. The "daddy" dolls are preferred in clothing, care, and treatment, and for a long time they go to bed with her; the "mummy" dolls played only Cinderella, although they were as beautifully dressed and equipped. Dealing with dolls also allows the feeling of unrestrained revenge against the mother and other members of the household whom the child has to obey. Here we meet again unpleasant experiences that form the core of a later transformation into play. It will be interesting to investigate if some girls' rejection of dolls has some correlation with what Groddeck called the hatred of children with wet mothers. This would be the proof that hatred represents the strongest infantile affect, probably because of being the earliest, as well for the fact that not maternal instinct but the bond with mother and father are the reasons for an acceptance or rejection of dolls.

The doll then leads the way to the animal. There boys behave differently from girls. While girls are more interested in the aspect of ornaments, the boys are interested in training; they expect obedience and training. Their attitude is a model for their later position in the family.

Under the continuous influence of adults and because of his own male overestimation, the boy soon gives up the girls' games, his aggressive drive leads him to the rough games of his male peers, and secretly he only sometimes participates in the girls' games. And he feels embarrassed if he is caught by another boy and quickly finishes the game with an expression of his possessive impulses. The girl values her participation in the boys' games quite differently. She feels very much honored, outdoing her female peers if she is accepted by the boys. The sexual over-estimation of the man, the male complex of the female dominate the character of common games.

The parents' concern with a single child lets them look for a companion that compensates for the lack of a sibling. But they rarely meet his expectations since he doesn't want to lose his privileged position among his friends—he wants to be everybody's pet and tyrant at the same time. Therefore, he often feels lonely even among his peers and he has difficulties participating in their games. His soul doesn't provide any space for the creation of a communal sense. He lives in his own world full of beautiful fantasies, that are alien to the social child. The drives of children who grow up with siblings and friends find their objects of satisfaction in these children, while the single child chooses the adults of his environment or himself. He becomes a peculiar loner who doesn't have any means for a social life. And if he finally finds somebody to play with he overwhelms him with the energies of his unsatisfied instinctual life. Insatiable in his lonely fantasies, he becomes similarly demanding with his friends. He lacks, as the Viennese pedagogue Aichhorn calls it, the "Ruhepunkt," that is, "the soul's resting point," that everybody, adult and child, needs in order not to become ill and miserable. He will only find it if seriousness and playfulness in his existence are filled with the right amount of fulfillment; the successful mixture then is expressed in the child's play.

Lecture 10:
Children's Dreams

Ladies and gentlemen! Today we will turn toward one of the most interesting problems of psychoanalytic research, the study of dreams. Everywhere and at all times dreams have been attributed a deep meaning. And the further back we go in man's history the higher we find dreams and their respective interpreters. Wealth and honor were promised to those who predicted victory from an emperor's dream; but they often also lost life and freedom if they predicted a worrisome future. The prophetic power that was attributed to dreams explains not only its extraordinary value with educated laymen and commonfolk through the ages, but also the objections science always had to seriously deal with them. Therefore, we find that dreams are described in textbooks of psychology in the appendix and as something not worth paying attention to. It therefore shares the same fate as the phenomena that Freud called unconscious that are not denied in their existence by modern psychologist but interpreted as more or less distorted expressions of consciousness, the subconscious.

Similar to his discovery of the unconscious, Freud also was the first to realize the meaning and importance of dreams. Although he did not interpret dreams as prophetic experiences, he learned to understand them as important expressions of present and past psychic experiences. The words of the Greek scholar of the fifth century B.C. Artabonos that "dreams mostly contain what people think in their waking state" only requires the addition "and feel and wish" and we have reached psychoanalytic territory. In his work *The Interpretation of Dreams*, he demonstrates, by using his own dreams and those of neurotic patients, how dreams, just like lapses, express suppressed present and past wishes that were denied their fulfillment. Every dream contains a fulfillment of a wish.

Before we demonstrate the wishful character of dreams that sometimes is rather difficult to recognize and therefore serves as a major argument against the interpretation of dreams, we will describe other characteristics that differentiate dreams from wakeful states, mostly aspects that make their understanding more difficult. If a child or adult returns from a walk and reports an exciting event on the street, then they won't fail to claim their credibility by naming other witnesses or they can even show a reliable object to prove their report. The objective experience therefore can be proved by people or objects. Different in dreams. We lack any possibility to convince our audience that in our dreams we were able to spend billions or that we walked on the water, anxiously but safely. We have to accept their doubts as to the credibility of our reports; we can't prove dreams, they are without evidence.

Dreams are also timeless in terms of both their content and their duration. We don't know how long they last. We can only tell that, since we looked at our watch at midnight and woke up fifteen minutes later, it can't have lasted longer than a quarter of an hour. We know when we woke up but we don't know when it started, and it might have lasted only seconds. But also with regard to its content, time is not relevant. In our dream we might have talked to a colleague, when all of a sudden he is replaced by our dead father as we see him cutting roses during our childhood. But this is not really the garden that we used to play in as kids, it is the secret place where we exchanged our first loving kisses. Immediate and remote past pass by at a fast pace; people we met yesterday give way to those that we haven't met for years or that we have lost by death forever.

The lack of evidence and timelessness are just two of three characteristics that confuse us when we are studying dreams. The content is often unclear, confused, and not precise; it appears, when superficially reported or remembered senseless even stupid, like lapses. We happen to be in impossible situations in our dreams. We and others talk "nonsense." People we never met behave like old friends or enemies. Dreams show an uncertain picture to our wakeful ego. We vainly look for explanations. It requires an interpretation to explain its content. The uncertainty requires and facilitates the interpretation. We will understand more once we have described the first aspect of the wishful nature of the dream.

In children's dreams wishes are fulfilled clearly and directly. A four-year-old boy saw the first Christmas trees at the market one week before Christmas. In the morning after having a dream, he demanded to have back that wonderful Christmas tree that "stood in the corner of the room, with all the candles and good stuff and a great bright star on top." He couldn't be convinced that he had "only dreamt." Another child, a six-year-old, who after a stomach upset had been forbidden to eat fruits, reported the next morning that in a dream he had eaten a basket full of strawberries sent by grandmother. We realize in this dream the unsatisfied wish so clearly that we wouldn't object to Freud's statement "Every dream is a fulfillment of a wish." We accept this when we deal with the so-called good dreams of adults that fulfill the dreamer's ambitious plans, bring wealth, let him join absent loved ones, and even have him reunite with those who have already died.

We meet a lot of resistance when somebody remembers a terrifying dream that woke him up sweating and with pounding heart. He never wished to be disturbed at night by burglars and thieves or to fail an exam; nobody could claim that a dream in which living relatives are all of a sudden dead would represent the fulfillment of one of the dreamer's wishes. And everybody knows from his own experience how absurd the statement is that every dream contains a fulfillment of a wish. That's how it looks superficially. But if we proceed to the depths of psychic activity, we soon realize that we have to take back our quick judgment. We remember how the study of parapraxes taught us to accept them as remnants of disapproved instinctual drives that, banned from consciousness, live on unconsciously only to reappear at a convenient occasion in more or less disguised form. We saw how the fantasies of children and adults realize wishes, expectations, and hopes that reality has no place for. As in those daydreams, the unfulfilled wishes, past and present, reappear in our nightly dreams. Infantile desires that became victims of disgust, shame, or conscience, narcissistic and erotic wishes we didn't want to give up despite their hopelessness, will be satisfied in our dreams.

But these tendencies don't appear immediately; they are linked to events of the immediate past, happenings during the last days. These day-residues link the dream with the experience during the waking state. Whatever the dreamer remembers the next morning we call the manifest dream; quite frequently this is fantastical, unstructured, even without any sense. We don't know what to do about it as long as we don't understand the hidden "latent" content using sometimes difficult interpretation. It then proves its internal coherence, disclosing past and present secret wishes of the dreamer, that careful analysis demonstrates to be of a mostly sexual-erotic nature.

When we studied the parapraxes we heard about a power that decides if a psychic content has access to our conscious. It tells us whether an internal or external perception about our internal life or our environment has to be suppressed into the unconscious. Freud calls this power the censor. We meet it again in dreams. It makes sure that wishes that are incompatible with cultural demands of our own ego or society at large don't show in their offending nudity but use some disguise in expression and form; the censor is most important around sexual-erotic issues, which inflame the strongest desires. Freud realized by analyzing his own dreams and those of neurotic patients that some symbols are common property of mankind; they are not invented in the dreams but we find them in the people's language and jokes, their sayings, in tales and sagas; you will best understand this from Kleinpaul's interesting book *Das Leben der Sprache* (The life of language). Emperor and empress mostly stand for our parents, prince or princess normally for our siblings or the dreamer himself. Death is symbolized by a departure. Often the dream uses a figurative description that we call reversal into the opposite; unknown persons replace familiar ones, high-necked clothes stay for far-reaching exhibition. Large masses often hide a secret. All objects of significant length like sticks, trees, drills, knives, bottles, snakes, worms, etc., symbolize the male genital; weapons like spears, arrows, revolvers are quite suitable as its substitutes because of their aggressive character. Objects with a cavity like boxes, baskets, bags, and round fruits are used to designate femininity. A threat by a wild animal can be translated into a sexual attack. Microscopically small animals often represent children and, analyzing children's dreams, I repeatedly found them to be anal-erotic symbols. Stekel, who has reported his rich experience with dream interpretation in his valuable book *Die Sprache des Traums* (The language of dreams), understands the use of *right* and *left* as the designation of the moral judgment of human behavior as right or wrong, good or bad. The expression *Frauenzimmer* (for woman) explains the symbolism of "room" (*Zimmer*). Dreams about endless waters normally symbolize birth fantasies; falling into the water regularly means being pulled out of the water, i.e., being born. The dream about stays in dark tunnels or caves indicates womb fantasies. It belongs to a group of frequent dreams that we therefore call "typical." There is rarely a single person who hasn't been in an embarrassing outfit in his dreams, anywhere between a missing tie and complete nakedness. This typical, embarrassing dream unknown to the small child often appears during puberty and accompanies us throughout our life; suppressed infantile exhibitionist impulses are looking for rationalization. The five-year-old boy who discloses his curiosity by telling us, "I'm not looking," was dreaming during this time of increased interest for nudity that he had been in Wörishofen and all "the ladies didn't wear anything, even Aunt Bertha [who recently had reported about her stay in Wörishofen] didn't wear anything." The dream provides for the sexual curiosity what reality has to deny. A sixteen-year-old high school girl dreams a few days before her final exam that she enters the examination room with bare feet and when she tries to cover them with her bag she realizes that she has forgotten her blouse at home. A professor, an older man, provides her with his jacket and she is embarrassed that he has to spend the time of the examination just in his shirt. Embarrassing dreams regularly are exhibitionistic dreams.

Dreams of laziness are often linked to physical sensations and are often used by children as an excuse for certain shortcomings. The bedwetter excuses himself that in his dream he has already made all the necessary preparations, he explains his lateness with the fact that in his dream the clock just struck six o'clock and therefore he had another hour to sleep or that he had dressed himself in his dream while, when awakened, he realized that he had not done anything.

Dreams about flying and stairs disclose the adult's desire for intercourse. However, they also can be found in children, and therefore there is yet another explanation. I would like to mention at this point that dreams are over-determined. The dreams mentioned that normally end with an abrupt awakening might reflect the forbidden pleasures of climbing for children. The desire for lustful muscular contraction and the narcissistic satisfaction of being admired certainly play an important role. The dream of being "rolled over" is also normally determined by the direct observation of intimate scenes.

Educators should pay special attention to a frequent dream that deals with numbers. Analyzing young thieves, I found that numbers and monetary values play a prominent role in their dreams. The eleven-year-old boy who removed the sixteen guests by eating the same number of pralines reported the following dream: "I am going to the Prater with three friends. We take the 118 streetcar and I wonder if that is correct. There is a kind of fair and one of my friends says that we will put our fathers into the booths. We run away as fast as we can and I recognize that I lose my purse and think: Lucky I am that I left my thousand bill at home. Suddenly I realize that the

Schoenbrunner Pepi [an elephant] is invited for the afternoon and I won't be home. I want to say to my friend, 'lend me 300 kronen so I can take the steamship home,' but he had disappeared. Therefore I run home as fast as I can, but I wasn't at the Prater anymore but in Goisern and mother came towards me and said: 'But Egon I beg your pardon, it's already the thirty-fourth of July and you are still not home. Hurry, daddy is coming at six, you should be in earlier.' "

The ideas that the boy had associated with the numbers disclosed some intentionally hidden and some forgotten events. Regarding the number 34, he had stolen four times 30 kronen from his mother to buy some sweets for himself. At the same time he was expecting unsatisfactory grades ("fours") in three subjects, that is, three times four. The number 1000 discloses the following wishes: the cook gets a monthly salary of 2000 kronen. If he would steal 100 out of her purse without her recognition to make her believe that she actually lost it, he wouldn't have to steal anything for about a month, which would calm his guilt about his "criminal" morality, a saying of his father's. The number 1000 was also determined by anal-erotic jokes of the father. Six o'clock was the time of father's coming home, which was feared by the boy as the hour of punishment for his numerous misdeeds. Shortly before his dream he asked me the following question: "How many members are there to my family?" I answered: "Five, your parents and three children." "Wrong guess. We are six, since 2 times 3 equals 6. The parents have multiplied themselves three times, i.e., 2 times 3 equals 6." Similarly sense-less number games had of course their origin in sexual fantasies. When I once pointed out their senselessness to him, he responded: "I can't do it any better. Once I can do the other thing [i.e., intercourse], I will make better jokes."

The analysis of this dream took a number of sessions and clarified among other things a number of thefts that he had already committed at the age of five and six years, identifying himself with his mother by stealing things from her; in his thefts he lived his strongly ambivalent attitude toward his mother: "Everything my mother owns is my possession as well; mother is my posses-sion. Therefore, I take from her what father gave her." In his sharp contempt for all females, his main critique was that of the woman as a "luxury article who only asks for money and then spends it for her make-up."

A large group of dreams that seemingly contradicts Freud's theory about the wish-fulfilling character of dreams are the anxiety dreams which are quite frequent in children. Most frequent are those about thieves and burglars that we well understand, since the uncomfortable tossing and turning normally calls the mother to the bedside; calming words, caressing, probably a treat or a sweet drink, try to calm the child and frequently he finds a safe place in mother's bed after these dreams. His desire for love is active also at night and he uses the bad dream as a potent tool to achieve what was normally denied. Dreams about ghosts and spooks that like to pick up on horrible stories at nighttime have the same intention: the ghost in the white dress replaces the mother who comes to the child's bedside in her white nightgown to remind him of his toilet needs. The fact that these dreams persist into adulthood is proof that one never forgets the earliest period in life when one was cared for at day and night.

During another typical anxiety dream, the child sees his parents who just were going beside him in a distance, quickly moving away from him. He wants to reach them, he starts running but his legs and voice fail. Father and mother disappear and the child is alone. The often energetic refusal of the child to hold the parent's hand on the street, some hide-and-seek game of the adults and the temporary wish that the parents may disappear to allow for some forbidden activity all cross in this dream. They come quite close to dreams about the loss of a loved person. The infantile perception of death as a temporary absence makes it understandable why these dreams are less frightening for younger children but become bothersome for adolescents and adults. An eight-year-old boy told his mother innocently, "Last night I dreamed you had died and were lying in a white dress in the coffin [Snow White!] and I opened the lid, called and kissed you; and all of a sudden you opened your eyes and said: 'My dear, don't cry, I don't leave you.' " This death dream discloses itself to us as a wishful dream that is double-determined; the mother may die but always stay with the child: at the same time we see the narcissistic belief in the own infantile omnipotence that overcomes death. If as adults we are tormented by dreams where a loved person dies or is suffering from illness or an accident, we only have to remember our hateful, quickly suppressed impulses of the past.

Adolescents experience the odd dream with warnings or restraints and also about occupations, the former representing a conflict between feelings and voluntary control; occupational dreams of young girls reflect in their endless activity their attitude toward life. Jealousy of the older sister makes her engage in household activities; she even excels her sister who always kept time free for her own entertainment. Therefore, she, the dreamer, was the better housewife who would have made her brother-in-law happier.

Let me finish my examples with a number of school dreams that sometimes accompany our whole life. In the embarrassing dream about being late, the fear is often accompanied by sexual sensations. However, the narcissism that makes some adults arrive late at the theater, concerts, and conventions in order to get the appropriate attention, celebrates its triumphs in these dreams. Feelings of revenge are felt if others are to blame for the late-coming. A fourteen-year-old girl had been institutionalized because of a severe conflict with her mother. She dreamt repeatedly during her stay that she would be late for dinner or for school because her mother had lost the key to her cabinet or because she had forgotten to set the alarm-clock. In her dreams she blamed her mother for her own lateness.

Overwhelming demands at school, the general nervousness of life in the city are blamed for the bad dreams where the child comes to school without his homework, gets lost in a chat and fears punishment or fails exams or the presentation of a poem. Again, we don't consider wish-fulfillment in this case. Such dreams repeat themselves in adults as typical dreams of punishment or as examination dreams. The former represents a dream of punishment that is the result of not-so-innocent behavior of the dreamer during wakeful states. It is analogous to the situation where the little boy doesn't behave himself at the table and finally when fleeing the room to escape punishment throws a whole pile of plates to the floor. Rightly he now fears the mother's punishing hand and hits himself: "Don't mother, I'll hit myself." In some cases I found that adolescents in their punishment dreams actually belittle their "judges," as in those dreams of children and adults where the punishing person himself does something wrong and violates moral standards or intimidates the dreamer.

According to Stekel, examination dreams are always connected to examinations that have been successfully passed in reality and they represent unfounded fears of impotency. Sadger explained examination dreams from a consideration of castration anxiety. He explained such dreams as an unconsciously feared paternal question about the son's incestuous desire for his mother, a question for which he will always lack an answer.

In five cases of examination dreams of children and two cases in adults, I have found a slightly different constellation. The adults repeated actual failures and the sexual-erotic relationship between man and woman dominated. "If the examiner had been younger, he wouldn't have made it that difficult for me." "If I would have been as beautiful as X, I would have passed the exam." The female sexual envy always plays a dominant role in her examination dream. In children and adolescents, I found regularly that their failure in reality as well as in dreams was related to their feelings of inferiority and their obstinacy against the father. For example, one example was encountered as "If father had prepared me better [that is, with better sexual information], I would have passed." Another example was seen in "You are forcing me to hide my sexual knowledge and therefore I will fail the exam."

To relate the manifest content of dreams to the internal experience of the dreamer seems sometimes artificial and not legitimate; but the accusation is unfounded, since the analyst doesn't interpret the material arbitrarily but the patient provides with his free associations the material for the interpretation. We see also that the dream has to do some work that is caused by the power of the censor. The true, unconscious content is distorted. The manifest content often is quite sparse, but during the analysis other elements and relationships are added that make it understandable; the dream has condensed the content. Analysis also shows that dreams often set different priorities that would be appropriate. Affects are displaced, main elements appear to be secondary, and secondary issues dominate the picture: this we call the displacement of dream-work. The already mentioned symbolism allows for expression of impulses in a hidden form that will pass the censor. Finally, the elements of the dream are reorganized to guarantee that the dream doesn't appear too confused and sensual. Freud calls this the secondary processing of the dream.

The educator should be interested in the time when the first dreams occur. Observations of expressive movements of sleeping children seem to indicate that this happens during the second part of the first year of life. An almost-one-year-old boy who had been punished physically the day before made a noise during his afternoon nap, "Ht, Ht," that perfectly imitated the earlier sound of the whip. A child will remember his dream for a long time. Experience is real. Only the terrifying dreams teach him to accept the irrationality of dreams.

The educator could learn from the dreams of the child about his suppressed imaginations, feelings, and wishes; unsatisfied sexual curiosity, disapproved exhibitionism, ambivalent attitudes, secret masturbation, and their consequent guilt feelings speak a clear language in his dreams. If these feelings are overwhelming, we hear the dreamer speaking words that should be a clear warning to us. Some deviations that cause internal conflicts will become apparent during these talks. They are a cry for help from a soul that is frightening by its wrongdoing. It will disclose itself, not out of defiance but because of a need for self-protection, for relief from tormenting guilt feelings. The adult doesn't listen to them or to his reports about his dreams at the breakfast table, since he doesn't know that the communication of dreams makes sense and is intended by the unconscious. Those who talk about their dreams often unconsciously intend to have somebody else look into them. They want to disclose thoughts, expectations, and impulses that the dream hides and communicates at the same time.

Lecture 11:
Mental Health

Ladies and gentlemen! The discussion of dreams closed our considerations of single phenomena. Although I tried to meet your expectations during these lectures and to provide some educational advice, I can't close this series without summarizing how to help the mentally healthy to succeed in finding the right balance between impulse satisfaction and restraint, or, in other words, to meet educational expectations and renounce the pleasure principle for the reality principle.

We heard about the many disappointments that interfere with the infantile desire for lustful existence and how education uses disgust, shame, and conscience to restrain uncontrolled impulses.

We can't spare our children these disappointments for two reasons. Cultural demands of our society require that children are familiar with shame, compassion, justice, and aesthetic principles. They must learn to judge themselves and others on ethical grounds and ensure that commonsense and a work ethic develop that allow them to become useful members of society.

The parents present the second disappointment to their children. The ideal figures of early infancy become people with weaknesses and mistakes. The child realizes the limits of their power and witnesses some disharmony at home. Living together with gods makes gods quite worldly. The child responds to this natural developmental with mistrust and withdraws into himself.

Educational boundaries become apparent as bothersome limitations already during the first year of life. This happens especially since children are treated too roughly during this period. Instead of following the child's lead, intimidation rapes the child with threats and punishments. It doesn't allow for adaptation. Intimidation is the most effective tool to inappropriately interfere with instinctual development. The child's instinctual life reaches its peak between three and six years of age; that is, education demands the most difficult tasks of adaptation and self-control during this period. During the first five years of life, all potential lines of development are fixed through his earliest experiences and the intentional and unintentional influences of his environment. The direction of internal evolution is outlined; later influences can only facilitate or hamper them. Man becomes what he will become during the first five years of his life. This finding justifies and should explain to you why I direct your attention again and again onto this short period, though physicians probably expected that I would focus on the schoolchild. However, the development of gifts, character, individual traits, and mistakes of the schoolchild comes from the foundations that have been laid during this early period. Whatever love he received or missed during this first phase, whatever model was intentionally or unintentionally given to him, will forever continue to work and will give content and form to his soul. The independent processing of external input dampens the optimistic expectation that one could arbitrarily predict and influence from outside. We have to assume that our influence has a minimal impact on how the child will eventually develop. The only thing we can provide within narrow limits is that the child does not suffer from an excess or lack of impressions that form his imaginative and affective world.

How man in his adult years uses his psychic energy, how much he invests his libido in objects or withdraws into himself, how much distraction and sublimation of his sexuality he achieves—this is prepared by the impressions during the first five years of life. During this time he slowly develops the ideal image of his own ego. Freud relates the development of ego-ideal and super-ego to the child's earliest relationships with his parents. During this time he identifies with both parents. The mother loses her capability for full identification during the time of infantile sexual curiosity when the child judges her natural anatomy as inferior. Therefore, the father remains as the ideal model in the Oedipal conflict. The influence of the admired and feared father imago facilitates the development of the super-ego and, at the same time, the critical authority that permanently criticizes the real ego: the conscience.

Knowing that these first five years are decisive for the psychic development, the educator is to meet one main challenge: The child's education starts with the education of the adult and his self-discipline.

In this sense especially, the parents have to succeed in a threefold renunciation. They have to refrain from lies, small or big, from the family lie that accompanies man from his first cry to his death. Some build their existence on the attempt to pretend more than they can meet and to suggest internal and external values that they don't possess. This "superior" lie is disguised as family honor, social position, and boasting, and exaggerates the child's over-estimation of his parents to a delusion. He believes that simply his name, his assumed wealth will open every door for him where he only finds closed doors. Hurt and intimidated in his arrogance, he is in disagreement with himself and society. Others are characterized by the anxious attempt to minimize their family; they almost indulge their real or imagined poverty; they are ashamed of their upbringing and their education and admire everybody else rather than themselves. According to their model, their children develop into shy, pressed, and devout people who always apologize for their mere existence. This "inferior" lie elicits feelings of inferiority that prevent external success and internal satisfaction.

The parents also have to learn to refrain from conventional lies that find their most critical judge in the 'enfant-terrible.' The cover-up and excuse of infantile misbehavior or embarrassing events in the household from father by the mother, from parents by all-too-weak grandparents and aunts or nannies that fear for their position, causes a fatal dependency from the child: When guilty, he feels like dominating the situations, and on the other hand, he always is afraid to disclose himself or be disclosed by the one who shares his secret. Instead of gaining insight into his mistake, he tries to assure silence by obedience or sweet-talk. If someone else is wrong, he will attempt blackmail.

The nice lies, those that carry promises that are never fulfilled, are poison for the young soul. A fifteen-year-old boy who tyrannized his whole family with his fears couldn't overcome the fact that his mother had promised something to him at the age of four that never materialized. She had promised a trip on the first weekend in spring when the weather was good. Somehow she couldn't make it, and the nanny replaced her. For the boy the whole day was spoiled, and he carried his secret anger and resentment for years.

A seventeen-year-old girl wouldn't stop during her analysis to list all her mother's unfulfilled promises until we finally came to her earliest disappointment—one made by her father, a passionate mountaineer who had promised her a trip to the mountains if she would tolerate her immunization. They were empty promises. On his next trip her mother accompanied him. All feelings of jealousy and mistrust against father and mother focused around this event, their deepest cause, of course, being the tragedy of the Oedipal complex.

The great damage that is done by the sexual lie demands the second great renunciation from the parents. The inappropriate secrecy, the exaggerated rigidity towards the infantile sexual curiosity that uses systematic threats to intimidate the little boy, has to disappear. It only destroys the most promising aspects of the psychic development. It destroys the healthy eroticism of the older boy and adolescent by the threat of physical and psychic deterioration following masturbation. The instinctual life of girls is limited prematurely by the constant admonition that "one doesn't do that," in adolescent girls by overemphasizing the value of virginity that leads only to lasciviousness but never to cleanliness. Distinguished shame is replaced by pretentious prudishness that hides the secret desire for erotic experiences.

These are the influences that work during adolescence. Some lead a wild life after having outgrown their parents' authority, and waste their energies. Sublimation for artificial, scientific, or social challenges becomes impossible. Others ascetically despise the healthy rights and demands of a lively and cheerful nature. Lies and threats during their early days cast their shadows on all pleasures. Both raise a serious accusation against those who withheld truth and understanding sympathy from these adolescents.

Thirdly, parents have to renounce their parental narcissism. The parents' self-love that expresses itself in the adoration of their children is the most dangerous threat to youth. The greenhouse of exaggerated time prevents normal growth. Some hope for a genius, while others want to keep their "child" as long as possible. One attitude leads to disproportionate overestimation and to a break-down of artificially supported skills, while the other causes a lack of confidence and will power. The mother especially has to learn to restrict her tenderness during the first five years of life to a modest degree and to let the child decide the distance. She has to restrain herself from the first day when kissing or caressing, from carrying him around or from the bad habit of taking children to the parents' bed. She has to remind herself with schoolchildren not to accompany them on their way to school, not to spoil them during the little chores at home or superfluously support them during homework. The child has to learn to stand with his own person for his actions instead of calling on the parents on every occasion or clinging to mother's skirt whenever his responsibility is requested.

The threefold renunciation of lies, intimidation, and spoiling is the parents' most difficult challenge for education. This not only a negative description but also a complete prescription of positive advice for the educational work.

To develop an understanding for the ups and downs of the young soul by remembering one's own youth is a great art that facilitates the challenges for parents and educators, teachers, and physicians. Jean Paul's saying "Only youthful people, even when seventy years old, can talk to the youth" has to become our motto. To provide opportunities and values as an older, experienced friend is only possible for those who have maintained the experiences of their own childhood. In retrospect, we understand that things that appear unimportant and small to us have an incredible importance and impact for our children. The memories of ambivalence facilitate our understanding for the child's moods as an expression of his internal conflicts. We watch him fight his internal battles that we have overcome ourselves and we learn to understand and respect the child as a person in his own right at every phase of his psychic development instead of perceiving him as a toy. This attitude allows for the most appropriate educational measures. We don't have to and don't want to stop to suppress where adaptation to reality demands the removal of wild branches, but we will let the child have time to perform this adaptation. Part of the useless libido has to be neutralized by distraction, by providing the child with ample opportunity for playing, limiting him only where necessary. In older and more mature children we will use literature, theater, and movies as an appropriate distraction from uncontrolled discharge in actions and fantasies. Gymnastics, sports, and outdoor work provide opportunities for discharge in a suitable way. Education has to use the same routes that the analyst uses to make instinctual conflicts variable for his neurotic patient to allow the young person to adapt his ego demands and sexual wishes to the demands of family, school, and society, to allow him to participate actively and passively in the cultural values of our time. He has to learn to satisfy part of his drives without internal conflict, to redirect other instinctual demands onto more suitable objects and to spend his energy in intellectual, socially responsible activities.

The psychoanalytic finding that children's mistakes, despite their individual organic and psychosexual disposition, are mainly attributable to restraints of instinctual life and affective bonds helps the educator to treat or prevent infantile misbehavior. The appreciation of positive and negative transference between the child and the authoritative personality of the educator will demonstrate why the child seeks close contact or aggressively rejects him. How far he is able to assume a fatherly or motherly role will determine the child's attitude toward him. Here he has to meet the challenge of individualization. The use of positive transference will clearly enhance the possibility of facilitating the child's attitudes toward his peers. The early family constellation helps us to better evaluate certain types of children—for example, the accusing, tyrannizing, enduring.

The long development from the helpless infant to full responsibility is only possible without deviation if there is a mutual trust between those who lead and the young soul. This is based on three factors: the consequence of applying educational measures, truth, and harmony in the family and each individual. The friendly consistency of the adult prevents over-excitement and a congestion of infantile libido. A lack of confidence in the educator, who laughs about whom he punished yesterday, will disturb a child as much as a disharmony at home. The pre-existing ambivalence toward father and mother becomes unbearable when he witnesses splits between them. He helplessly swings from one to the other or turns away from one of them with obvious hostility only to overwhelm the other with all his love. He doesn't mind the parental disharmony since he hopes for the fulfillment of his unconscious incestuous impulses. These traumas destroy the child's soul, and Fontane is right to say, "Merciless, the children will judge their parents."

Education can't save the children from the fights between their egotistic, narcissistic ego-impulses and their libidinal objects, but a friendly and sympathetic attitude can alleviate the conflicts. Then children and their parents and educators will become good companions and advisers who are always reliable and can tolerate silence, which has its place between people who understand one another. With their deeper understanding, teachers and physicians will also support the parents, make them aware of changes and their causes, and therefore prevent some mishaps and deviations.

If eduction is supported by strong responsibility and self-discipline, then we will see the ideal image of a new healthy generation that will realize Nietzsche's admonition: "You shouldn't procreate but up-create!"

Lecture 12:
Psychoanalytic Educational Counseling

Ladies and gentlemen! I welcome your interest in the psychoanalytic counseling service that represents the "new way to the understanding of youth" itself since its foundation in 1923. It is meant for parents who don't have the means to deal with problems of education other than when they have these problems themselves. They want to help their child and themselves, but they are helpless. In their helplessness, they try rigidity when mildness doesn't work. This doesn't help because they lack the understanding basic to their child's behavior.

The purpose of educational counseling is to decrease the tension between child and parents that is caused by opposing and contradictory expectations that again prevent a solution. In mutual excitement they perceive as bad-willed or cold whatever the other party does. To lead them to a gradual understanding of the connection between their open and hidden conflicts is one of our main goals. This is the leading idea for this institution.

Before I report more about it, you will ask which cases come for counseling. These are the same as in a private practice. Mother and father complain that their child is disobedient and obstinate, that he has constant fights with his siblings, not allowing the parents to leave them alone at home. Others are desperate about a failure at school, about lying or thefts that turn the family life into hell. Little bedwetters are presented as well as those "nervous" children who fill their waking time with daydreams. We see poor feeders who leave their mothers helpless.

During the parents' report the children between two and one-half and fifteen years of age are normally present. Their careful observation during the report gives me the first valuable hints as to the functioning of this family. During the second part I will hear the child. To allow for an uninhibited report, the parents normally leave at this point. Like with the analysis of adults, this first contact is of utmost importance. This first discussion is always an accusation against parents and school. With appropriate intelligence it is sometimes possible to establish a connection, during this first meeting, between his mistakes and his jealousy of his siblings or his desire to be as big as his parents. Frequently, the child will talk about sexual experiences if he feels understood. Embarrassed, he will admit to masturbation and his fantasies reveal disapproved erotic wishes. All this is accompanied by strong affect. There is of course the anxiety to have disclosed everything with terrible consequences as soon as the parents reenter the room. But the further procedure reassures the child. Advice might be given with both child and parents present or individually, depending on the case. To facilitate compromise is futile; only explanation of the interdependencies and positive advice helps.

Some cases require psychoanalytic treatment, others require only one counseling session for parents and child per week.

What makes this institution different from other similar ones is the absolute exclusion of the public. This is a consequence of our consideration that both parents and children are not willing to reveal their intimate experiences before an audience. The appreciation of sexual aspects by the psychoanalytic school further emphasizes this aspect. To restrict oneself to superficial advice that might meet the expectations of an audience doesn't do justice to the complexity of an individual case.

There is a second difference in that not only parents but also adolescents come alone for our service for counseling. Lately, we not only see referrals from physicians, institutions, and clubs for social work, but we also see people who have been sent by those who have asked us for help before. This we see as evidence of first success and we have the expectation that this institution might receive the public recognition and support that will make it a provider of social care.

Ladies and gentlemen, I have reached the end of my lectures. Their content was based on Freud's ingenious discovery of infantile sexuality and the unconscious. The insight into the psychic development of the child is his merit. And if I succeed in presenting his findings as a solid base for education with a new orientation, then I have paid back a little of my great debt to the master.

Selected Works Dealing with
Women and the Family

On Female Masturbation (1913)

Hug-Hellmuth's initial papers were about children. Later, she concentrated exclusively on the psychology of women. Finally, she turned toward an examination of family dynamics or, as she termed it, "the libidinal structure of the family." This paper was Hug-Hellmuth's first on a topic relating to women and it was her initial contribution to the psychology of women. It appeared early in her published works in 1913 as "Zur weiblichen Masturbation." It was published only once, in the *Zentralblatt für Psychoanalyse und Psychotherapie.*

An unreserved openness toward the physician is the essential prerequisite and condition of psychoanalytic treatment. Yet, we find repeatedly in the writings of psychoanalysts and in the reproach of gynecologists the expressed complaint that women are rarely honest as far as their sexual life is concerned. Because of embarrassment and despite the fact of this sine qua non of openness that is explained to any patient at the beginning, we are not surprised that we know hardly anything about the sexual erotic life of the healthy or seemingly healthy woman if some events are already concealed and extenuated. As you could assume, this is in part an initial questionable result of today's girls' education, which emphasizes great bashfulness and often results in prudishness and hypocrisy. It is a result also of the fear of derogatory criticism that a woman has to expect from men as well as from other women, whenever she talks realistically and dispassionately about things that have to be active in women as well as in men because of the underlying drive.

Naturally, the most delicate topic is that of masturbation. Even family physicians, for instance, from whom these symptoms are not hidden in children, hardly risk advising the parents to observe and control their child in that respect. Further, they never seem to try to ask an adult questions about masturbation. It is sometimes ridiculous to see what effort is invested in avoiding this embarrassing topic. They ask unrelated questions as to the reasons and symptoms of the so-called nervousness. The same men would step back terrified if a woman would have the guts to speak spontaneously about the deepest and true reasons of her "nervous" complaints. We would assume that female physicians dealing with their female patients would possibly do so without any timidity. But even they restrict themselves only too often to some poor paraphrase. By doing so they prevent an open discussion from the very beginning, even in those cases where it would not only be possible, but even desired. Sometimes some sort of "confession" happens only among women. That is what they call these reports about their own instinctual life or that of their children. This happens among people who feel the deepest sympathy for one another. Even then it happens quite often that these confessions are later withdrawn or at least weakened by all sorts of later objections. I do not believe that my following opinion is wrong. True reports are only to be expected from those women who have been spared the feeling of self-abasement about masturbation. I will describe later the reasons why they have been spared. These are women that have struggled for and saved the full freedom of their soul and their body. However, because of the demands of our culture these circumstances for the life of a woman are rarely given today. We cannot be astonished about the rarity of the material of this topic. Even these women, free of adequate conventional timidity, often talk about their so-called sins with the strongest affect. Because some publications report the "sins of youth, vice of self-pollution," and things like that, even these women lack knowledge. Masturbation is primarily organically caused and has its roots in the development of drives that are not always normally discharged in women.

In his *Three Essays on the Theory of Sexuality*, Freud identified the care of the infant as being the first source of masturbation, especially those procedures for the cleaning of the small infant. This is correct primarily for boys. In girls the cleaning rarely happens so clumsily that it results in an organic stimulation. This is because of the hidden site of their genitalia. Sometimes a strong rubbing is considered to be more stimulating than a slight touching of the skin. This is quite variable in different individuals depending on the sensitivity of their dermal nerves. Consider, for instance, the lustful experience of the gentle stroking of arms, neck, and back. Furthermore, not less likely than the above-mentioned cleaning procedures, I consider inadequate clothing of the infant to initiate masturbatory acts. An event during my seventh year of life might explain this. At that time I often had the opportunity to be present when the daughter of a family friend, who was a few months old, was washed. I watched as the girl blushed and expressed curious sounds whenever the mother or the nursed fixed a so-called linen "pull-through" between the legs. Even more characteristic was my own reaction at that occasion. I pressed my skirt, shifting my glance from the genitals of the child. When my behavior was recognized and forbidden, I restricted myself to pressing myself against a chair or I escaped into the garden where nobody would watch me. Had there not been any dim traces of memory of lust, related to the same procedure in my own infancy, the observation of this procedure would not have initiated my own reaction. A young mother reported a very similar case to me about her oldest daughter. Whenever her four-years-younger sister was protected against getting bed sores in the same way, the older girl pulled a handkerchief, a doll's dress, or whatever she could get, firmly between her thighs.

It's well known that even during the first years of life masturbation is practiced more often by boys than by girls, and the reason for this lies in the physical state. The reports of mothers correspond with those of kindergarten teachers. Boys have been observed much more intensively than girls in that respect. Too much fearfulness and firmness with the usual preferred threats are perhaps the reason why the psychic sequelae of masturbation are much worse for the male than for the female.

Masturbatory activity in girls sometimes completely ceases in the preschool age. It is reactivated eventually during the school age by external stimuli such as probably seduction or unintended mechanical stimulation. Seduction is different, but it seems important to me. It is important not only because of the masturbation, but also because of the psychic sequelae that may influence later development. Masturbation, "the lonely love," is practiced by a woman in exactly the same way and frequency that is in keeping with her conscious or unconscious memories of her first infantile sexual pleasure. This happens until the woman experiences more pleasure in that respect than is concordant with her memories of the first infantile sexual pleasure. To legally protect themselves, adults who abuse children normally restrict themselves to touching and stimulating the external genitalia. Therefore, girls also restrict themselves to these practices until adulthood. This is quite different from girls who are introduced into sexual activity by other children, especially boys. All of a sudden feathers, pencils, and other long objects become important. This is true specially if the boy stimulated her internal genitalia, not knowing what he did. This manner of infantile masturbation, or rather the way in which it was initiated, often influences the infantile imagination about procreation and birth.

As far as the psychological importance of the abusing person is concerned, I think I can say the following. Little girls are seduced by female adults only very rarely. Usually elderly men try to approach them physically. The child feels protected from disclosure because of the age and often because of the social position of the man.

The child trusts instinctively in the caution of the man responsible. Yet finally the male abuser is likely to be discovered and questions asked in the case of a female abuser.

Infantile masturbation can be reactivated by accidental external stimulation of the erotogenic zones, for example, racking, climbing, shading while driving, or washing of urine against the clitoris. However, it seems to me to occur not as often as it is normally considered to occur. We can't neglect that such experiences might have some influence. If they have experienced their first sexual pleasure from rocking and driving, children might especially preserve a certain disposition to similar actions later. However, in general I assume that these reports are not truly honest. There are two possibilities. It is possible that infantile events are suppressed from memory so totally that the nonprofessional will not be able to discover them anymore. It is also possible that a certain dishonesty about sex that is inherent in the female character tries to displace any responsibility for sexual feeling by directing the responsibility to purely physical events or external coincidence. Such mechanical stimulation is rather looked for and will be accepted, whereas the sexual desire was aroused previously by activity with another person. If, for instance, an otherwise obedient child, while in gym, refuses to come down from a climbing pole that perfectly enhances sexual pleasure, then the climbing itself is the "cause" of the masturbatory act only momentarily. The primary cause is the wish of the child to initiate and reexperience the feelings that were previously aroused by the sexual activity of somebody else. It is only normal that the girl uses every opportunity that promises similar pleasure. However, rocking and climbing themselves are not the primary triggering events. This is evident when observing children during these activities. How differently does the "knowledgeable" girl press herself against the climbing pole or the rocking board in contrast to the truly innocent? The innocent girls holds herself forcefully with her small hands, the "knowledgeable" presses her thighs will all power or sits with her legs widely spread and bends her chest. She gives you the impression of the unconscious expression of the coital position. Once these girls are adults, they often have the desire to bend their head back as far as possible during intercourse. This is an unconscious technique to bring their genitals into the most pleasurable position. Similarly the vibration of the clitoris during urination will be intentionally initiated only if the child has experienced titillation of that kind as sexual pleasure. The itching of the genitalia appears, most probably, following masturbation that has been already experienced, and the innocent motive is stressed secondarily.

Without any significant results, physicians and psychologists have written often about the frequency of female masturbation. One group overemphasizes female masturbation because they are making a judgment from position of their own sex. The other group takes the absence of this activity as a special immaculateness. They do not want women to be less than immaculate. This is especially true if they themselves have sisters, a wife, or daughters. According to a poll of teachers of girls from low social classes, and according to mothers without prejudices, masturbatory acts of girls seem not to be as obvious as they are in boys, but still they are rather common. However, masturbation is done less often manually and not restricted to the genital zone, for example, moving about in one place, inadequate spreading of the legs forwards and sideways, or stemming of the legs. Besides the well-known gestures of girls after urinating, these activities are daily observations of primary school teachers who are only too often not able to lead the activity of the child in the right direction. While young teachers simply overload these expressions of human drives with well-pretended innocence, the older teachers do not miss any opportunity to punish the child. The teacher can punish at least by her glances which will be full of disgust and loathing.

These girls are often stigmatized by the indiscrete remarks of a teacher in the eyes of the other teachers and even in the eyes of the other students.

While we consider masturbation as a pure autoerotic activity in infants as well as in children up to the ages of five and six, in later years the school-age child experiences certain fantasies that are similar to fantasies during play. They are formed according to the milieu in which the child is raised. They change by using all events in their own household as well as in the families of friends. In that respect, daydreams that make some children believe that masturbatory acts are a punishment for believed misdeeds or are consequence of a doctor's order, are very interesting. In the first case this is a punishment that was obviously intended by the father and the punishment is the forbidden act. In the second case the fantasy is merely permission for the forbidden pleasure. It might also be that while the other activities of the muscles try to stimulate the clitoris during masturbation, the vagina seems to be an erotogenic zone already. In these cases sexual pleasure is experienced by spreading the legs sideways. According to Freud these rare cases are most likely after an education by peers. Imitation can play a role. For example, imitation of father or mother who, while being ill, had to undergo uncomfortable procedures. Direct fantasies about intercourse can be expected to emerge in children who share a bedroom with their parents. Some proof of this assumption might be seen in the position in which a woman I know surprised her two children while playing "papa and mama." Even as an adult, one of the girls still prefers a heavy pressure on her body by covering herself with a heavy quilt. Without it she is unable to go to sleep. Neither her parents nor she know that she still has not overcome the phase of infantile play in her sexual life. I believe in general that in cases of mutual masturbation of children, the sexual character of the activity will be realized earlier than in solitary masturbatory activity. I remember that despite intensive reading in a dictionary, even in my seventeenth and eighteenth years I was unable to have a clear idea about masturbation. I would have had enough memories of my own childhood, but instead I thought desperately about the nature of the so-called "sins of the youth." Something similar was reported by the woman just mentioned who masturbated several times daily when she was seven years old. She had the fantasy of being a woman who had just married. This was presumably her cousin who was twelve years her senior and who had just married. This was because of delicate remarks of her father about the honeymoon of her young niece. Despite a remark about the sexual nature of her activity, even as an adult she looked for something mysterious behind the word *masturbation*. She even started masturbation again, apparently in compensation for a lost relationship. She did this without feeling to be a "masturbator."

As fantasies change with age and experience, so do the fantasies that accompany and direct the masturbatory act. We have already stressed some of these fantasies in children. A frequent occurring fantasy in young girls while masturbating is that of being ill. They fantasize the necessity of a gynecologic examination and treatment, with hesitation of the girl, and encouragement by the physician. Finally, in her fantasy he starts touching her while in reality the girl masturbates. The excessive, great hesitation of adult patients towards gynecologic examinations by a physician might result from this play, but the root of this aversion has become totally unconscious. Such fantasies often stem from reports about illnesses in families. Even more often, servants don't miss a chance to tell the young daughters about such experiences in lascivious words.

When a woman masturbates after experiencing intercourse, a totally different picture is shown in the fantasies. In this case the external genitalia are not only stimulated by pressure of the thighs, but all the knowledge about intercourse with a man is integrated into the repertoire of the fantasy. Naturally, the masturbation is enjoyed as a stimulus from the beloved or often from a rather diffuse idealized person. Freud's assumption that fantasies are most important for a joyful masturbation seems to be quite correct for women. These fantasies can be so intensive that they trigger sensations without any physical activity. In any event, I believe that psychic masturbation plays an important role in women, because it can lead to a full orgasm without the reproach of any accompanying self-criticism. This probably explains the report of a women who experienced every evening the most peculiar involuntary thoughts and suffered from terrible dreams that she refused to talk about.

The temporary or complete cessation of masturbation in women is still a rather unexplained process. If a woman experiences full physical and psychic satisfaction with a man, it is easy to understand and it is well known that this happens. However, some very reliable people have told me about cases in which masturbation was totally interrupted even during puberty, when as a rule it is excessively practiced. I doubt that in such cases moral scruples are the cause. I know about at least one case in which the adult woman started masturbation again because of unsuccessful stimulation by her husband. Should this mature women have had less energy to defend herself from already known pleasant feeling than a young girl? I know about two girls who up to their fourteenth year tried to achieve their pleasure very openly with every chair and every edge of a table. They stopped their activities at 14, presumably at the time of their first menstruation. It is still possible that their sense of shame led them to restrict themselves to the secrecy of the evening and morning. However, I believe that in such cases of intensive obsession, as it was observed with these girls before, one could expect them to masturbate when they believed they were unobserved. According to the *Three Essays on Sexuality* this activity, caused by the exclusive excitability of the clitoris, is suppressed during the time of fundamental changes in the female body.

Parts of the role specific for a woman during normal intercourse have not occurred yet: The girls finds herself in a transitional state from child to woman. This state's psychic aspect is frequently recognized even by laymen, because of shy, clumsy behavior, over-sensitivity, and an unexpected change from excited happiness to deepest annoyance. This "wave of repression in puberty" favors, and often causes, the lasting cessation of infantile masturbation in girls. This corresponds to a frequent observation in girls' schools that the strongest masturbatory activity appears between the ages of ten and thirteen and becomes considerably rarer in the last year of school. We have the least reliable material about masturbation in the latter years. Even with those women who confess their infantile masturbation without any hesitation as well as their return to self-stimulation because of missing potency or failing understanding of their husbands, nearly no one can remember to have actively masturbated during these years. This is the time of the strongest expectations from a normal loving experience, which fills dreams during night and day with an infinite continuum, from an expressive handshake to a vague imagination of a physical uniting. The fear of a young girl, on the other hand, whose forbidden thoughts can be read from her face, is as dominant as the tormenting thought of not remaining innocent for her future husband.

Especially in our days, many girls find a way of avoiding instinctual activity by sublimating their unconscious sexual desire through intellectual activity. Therefore, it might be possible that a good deal of female youth does not masturbate during this age. But certainly the following case is also not unique. A woman, who has been independent since age eighteen, and lives according to her motto "La donna é mobile," has told me that every relationship comes to an inevitable end whenever she feels forced by nature to return to masturbation. This constant change between normal and lonely sexual activity seems to be exclusively desirable for her. She is able to complete the studies she is doing only after strenuous days of work and by engaging in this type of sexual activity. Only in this way does she feel physically and psychologically comfortable. Even the most liberal people can't regard this case very sympathetically. The border of normal psychic life seems to be crossed. Staying with this case, I will talk about the influence of masturbation on the psychic life of women in general. It is different in girls than it is in women who already have exerted their normal sexual functions. As mentioned earlier, the feelings of fear, shame, and disgust towards masturbation are frequently found in growing girls. I doubt that they always have their roots in the suppression of infantile incestuous thoughts. The educational influences and measures by which a child is discouraged from masturbatory activity must not be underestimated. The inquisitory glances and questions of parents, educators, and teachers as to why the child is looking so bad, why she has rings under her eyes and why her mood seems to be suppressed, do not remain without effect. This occurs even though a girl naturally lacks the fear of castration. Such a system of education created a type of person who goes around with shy glances and with a seemingly unmotivated flushing and terror. She considers every minor discomfort to be of consequence and punishment for her forbidden lust. She feels insecure in a crowd and feels observed by other people, for example, by her parents. In addition, the admonition that a man judges the psychic purity of a woman by her physical integrity, is often repeated to the girl.

In a woman who feels disappointed in her sexual expectations, or who has given herself to an unloved man because of external circumstances, masturbation is often the rebellion against the sexual pleasure withheld from her. She considers her activity as a justified and defiant defense against the inadequate satisfaction by her husband. For example, I know a woman who accused her family harshly of having driven her into masturbatory activity, or more correctly, toward a reactivation of her infantile habit by marrying her to an indifferent man.

Girls and women feel much more freedom if their childhood did not impose on them memories of harsh reactions to masturbation. It is only natural that parents and persons caring for children work with great effort against masturbation of the child. However, it happens less often using politeness and love, which alone are suitable to achieve the desired effect. The child has to be protected against the bad sequelae of excessive masturbation, but she should not become even more handicapped by added psychic damages. In this respect girls might be less at risk than boys. Activities of a sexual nature with boys are much more obvious and better known. According to reports of females, however, a moderate education is rarely found. In these children obsessive masturbation probably ceases earlier than in others, because curiosity and rebelliousness, two important sources of children's masturbatory activity, are not that important in an atmosphere of affectionate explanation. An interruption during the time of development happens quite often anyway, and sometimes masturbation stops completely in some cases. If this does not happen, or if it is reactivated later during maturity because of external circumstances, the woman normally has already achieved inner freedom to the extent that she doesn't consider masturbation to degrade or hurt her. She is already conscious of her right to her body and soul, so that she is spared self-accusations. In contrast to self-torturing characters who deeply regret any masturbation, it happens also that freer women allow themselves this pleasure only if their daily work went quite smoothly, or after professional or social successes. They simply satisfy their libido only when they are in a good mood. They do not know that they confine themselves to an infantile role by compensating themselves for the day's work, or that they reward themselves as their fathers and mothers did previously when they were awarded affectionately for good marks at school. The self-torturing type, in contrast, looks to masturbation for an escape out of her chaos of depressing thoughts and feelings, and she is likely to find a hell. Similarly, she only takes up the forbidden pleasure when forced to do so by depression, and accordingly, her activity appears to her to be a sin and a disgrace which puts a characterizing stamp on her face.

There is an intermediate stage between masturbation, in the narrowest sense, and psychic masturbation than often runs parallel with one or the other. These are the auto-erotic activities that displace more or less obviously the genital zone for another, less indecent erotogenic zone. Biting nails or picking the nose wouldn't always be characterized as being "disgusting" to children if the unconscious of the adults would not recognize their sexual expressions. The mother who tells her daughter, "You are picking your nose so that you will forget the world around you," does not realize how exactly she describes the child's affect. The perceptions of the surrounding reality disappear only during the most intensive sexual experience. The obsessive play of young girls with the hair of their forehead and neck is only badly disguised caress of their pubic hair. It seems similarly obvious that the habit of the woman who longed for constant change in her instinctual life had a similar meaning when she pressed her thumbs and finger rhythmically in her armpit while studying. She would play with her own breasts, up to the point of falling back exhausted and experiencing a genital sensation. This happens primarily in growing girls who had the frequent opportunity to watch breast feeding, and this does not deny the masturbatory character. Clenching one's fists also appears to me as a leftover of earliest infantile masturbation. Because I myself played this game up to the time of puberty, I know that the fading of consciousness, the stiffness and stretching of the body, happens in quite the same way as it does with genital stimulation. The perception, that the clenched hand seems to become bigger and bigger, might be explained by the occasional perception of an erected penis under the clothing of a man. Less obvious is the connection of this "growing" with the parallel perception, that the hand becomes lifeless. Is this the symbolic infantile expression for fainting? This peculiarity is analogous to the report of a woman who felt carried up in the air with her bed whenever she was masturbating. These experiences might be one root of the dreams about flying. Many young girls and women believe that they have to faint during intercourse. They consider it as a measurement of their own loving as well as that of the man. The intensive stimulation of the palate with the tongue has to be considered as a masturbatory act as it can lead up to the point of cramp-shaking of the body or to a fit of laughter. The eroticism of muscular activity and of the mucous membranes in general opens a wide field for masturbatory activity. It is rarely criticized and is considered an acceptable peculiarity because it is directed toward areas that seem to be decent.

War Neurosis in
Women (1915)

This paper was published later in 1915, at the height of
World War I, the same year that Hug-Hellmuth had
published "War Neurosis in Children." Although it was
published in a respectable journal, the *Geschlecht und Gesellschaft* 9:505–14, the tenor of this paper was identical
to that of her earlier feuilleton on war neurosis in children.
The two papers had a shrill, patriotic tone.

The restraint of drives, with their refinement and utilization for the whole
of mankind, is the outstanding cultural achievement that nature has im-
planted into man's soul. The taming of their original direction and their
change toward qualities that we admire in heroes, artists, and scientists
provide a general level for a whole nation as well as a cultural basis for its
individuals. Progress in culture is probably nothing else than the optimal
suppression of drives. This serves the community without forcing the individual into an ascetic existence that would fit poorly with the freedom of human
will. We consider the suppression of drives successful only if the wild
branches have been cut that prevent us from reaching our highest goal of
serving mankind. However, the drives do not turn into dead relics either
within a race or within an individual. Neither are they supposed to become
such dead relics from an ancient time when drives alone determined human
behavior. In their original as well as in their cultivated form, they are what
their name says, the driving force within us. Further, it is the force that gives
birth to the best in human existence.

We begin to value this cultural achievement only if incredible events might
threaten the fate of everybody. This exaggerates instinctual life to such a
degree that the soul eventually collapses. No other horror afflicts and forms
man or makes him look at himself differently. Wars impose themselves on
man with such unequaled destructive power. Millions are its victims, dead
or destroyed in their previous existence. The work of centuries falls into
shambles. Driven forward by its whip, suffering from the inevitable companions of war, terror, and atrocities, the soul makes desperate attempts to
defend itself from the storm. It attempts to maintain its power and spirit.
However, not all succeed. Only too many succumb to this powerful attack of
fate.

The term *war neurosis* was created for this psychic collapse that coincides
with the unbearable weight of physical and psychic rigors of war. This term
is correct only if we are prepared to differentiate between the causes of illness
and the reason for its symptomatic expression in the present. There is no war
neurosis where the war itself is the immediate cause. The cause lies where

we find the roots of all neuroses and psychoses, in a specific constitution and in the actual dangers of sexual activity, of sexual dreams, thoughts, and fantasies of early childhood. Stresses of all kind, death and destruction, accompany soldiers daily in the war and sometimes cause a frightening lethargy. In others, long after their return, their lives are intruded upon by compulsive thoughts or by anxiety states in their sleep. A third reaction is seen where the ex-soldier is thrown into fits and epileptic convulsions. In addition, chronic alcoholism may become manifest that had not been recognized before. In other soldiers we see the development of dementia praecox or progressive paralysis. Laymen witnessing these sudden changes deny vehemently that such cases of progressive paralysis or chronic alcoholism had a long history before the appearance of the actual symptom. It is only understandable that they consider war as the immediate cause of these neuroses and psychoses. Normally, these laymen remain inaccessible to any kind of reasoning, resenting the idea that the war only accelerated what was to become symptomatic sooner or later.

When using the term *war neurosis* or *war psychosis*, we must remember that war serves only as a trigger rather than a cause. We can apply this to all conditions closely related in time to the war that manifest themselves in typical neurotic or psychotic symptoms.

Initially, we expected to find these conditions only in men. Women are rarely exposed to the horrible experiences of the front. However, this does not uniformly apply. We see more and more cases where women show neurotic symptoms that are closely related to the war. Since the coincidence of war with the neuroses in women and men shows this same relationship in time, we may also call these conditions war neuroses. Most frequently, we see hysterical and obsessive-compulsive symptoms, sometimes also typical phobias. Dementia praecox prevails among the psychoses. Alcoholism and progressive paralysis are much rarer. According to a psychiatric report from the state mental hospital, a number of girls between the ages of fourteen and nineteen were admitted who had cut off their pigtails. Psychoanalytic research can explain this self-mutilation. Certainly, cutting off long hair has been practiced by women throughout history in order to allow them an opportunity to participate in the fight disguised as men. However, psychoanalytic understanding reveals symbolic castration and wishes of prostitution. Whatever meaning this voluntary sacrifice of a most beautiful female attraction has, it certainly symbolizes a wish for devotion to men as well. It represents an identification with men and a renunciation of her own sex that, in a double sense, has become futile during war. The eternal irritation of many women that their sex is held to be inferior has been supported by thousands of years of indoctrination. This bears considerable consequences for our social life, for individuals in times of war and as well as during days of peace and calm. A falsely understood liberation from old prejudices may allow the appearance of equal rights and of an equal evaluation with men, but it only continues to hurt women. A nagging discontent becomes apparent during wartime that has its roots in the little girl's sexual envy of the favored boy. This is supported by the higher demands of adaptation to social norms in women and easily leads them into directions that will remain forever alien to them. The true assumption of female inferiority becomes apparent when she realizes that men forcefully master their own lives and fate in such difficult times. In comparison, she may only watch men from a passive position. She is grasped by a nervous over-enthusiasm. She wants to help and participate in the great work. The healthy capable woman proves herself as the worthy helper of the man. At the right place and at the right time, she appropriately accomplishes to calm, to give comfort, and to help. However, a great number of women are not prepared to face the misery of war. They become victims of their well-restrained impulses. Well-protected young girls now care for wounded men. Their constant contact with them, along with the inevitable physical contact, awaken fantasies and wishes. They might want to suppress these fantasies and wishes, but they might not be successful in controlling them. They will recognize that their compassion elicits sexual responses. They will suffer from the conflict between morality and drive the stricter their moral demands are. These women will fail in their caretaking role since they collapse under this conflict. Their more or less conscious libido lets them forget about moral limits and they allow themselves to keep appreciative prisoners of war company. This is aggravated by the sensation of the strangeness to which both men and women are susceptible. Ignorance about a foreign language only seems to heighten this conflict. This perhaps reflects an unconscious memory of early infancy when we don't understand the meaning but only the tone of tender words. Further, there might be yet another early motive that unconsciously influences the behavior of these "undignified" women. From early on girls appreciate their own sex as something inferior. They soon develop the belief that they have to renounce more than the boys, since that is the way they understand moral demands. If there is no profound change during adolescence, the women lives with the feeling of being oppressed and inhibited even if her appearance doesn't suggest anything like that. Now these women cheer the enemy as a symbol of their own sex, by providing to them something they have never experienced themselves. In their pathological striving for the justice they have been denied, they only provide to the enemy what they have been deprived of themselves. Even in this mild form we can't approve of this behavior, and we have to call it neurotic. The pathological identification with the male is illustrated by the following case example. An officer returned from the front with severe rheumatic disease involving his heart and also with a left-sided paralysis. His wife then sacrificed herself and cared for him until his death weeks later.

Immediately thereafter she fell ill with paralytic symptoms that made her as much in need of care as her husband had been before.

In addition to these serious psychic illnesses that we might call war neuroses, we also recognize a number of neurotic characteristics in women who had been healthy and free of such symptoms before. During the last couple of months the sight of women using crutches has become a familiar picture in our streets. This occurred after the first wounded soldiers were released from hospital. It is unreasonable to assume that all of a sudden so many women have become ill with foot problems. In the majority of cases we again see a conscious or unconscious identification with the male. It is probably an unconscious identification, since these women appear to walk just like the soldiers do with their crutches, leaning heavily on them and limping with stiff legs. To laymen these symptoms might appear offensive or at best ridiculous. However, we cannot ignore their neurotic character since it might indicate the beginning of a serious psychogenic impairment of walking. We might also mention that even female fashion meets the women's neurotic need for identification with the male. Rather masculine appearing "war-blouses" and other clothing with the stamp of war have become popular.

Fear is never more prevalent than during a war. It dominates the mind by calling on its most powerful ally, fantasy. As long as it stays within the bounds of reality, this is a natural and a well-understood reaction. However, it becomes neurotic if it is totally unfounded or if it transgresses every reasonable limit. At first the fear is generalized and undirected. But it looks for a suitable object on which it will fixate itself inseparably. It does so as soon as it has found an object within oneself or a loved person. We will assume that a strongly developed narcissism might be mainly concerned with the own person. In contrast, the unfounded and exaggerated concern for another life reflects motives of hatred. Hatred is never missing even in the most tender love. If psychoanalytic findings prove this assumption correct, then we understand why one neurotic woman will suffer from a terrible fear of contagious diseases, whereas another will be plagued by an obsessive fear of a famine. Another cannot help from suffering from her exaggerated concerns about her groom, her husband, or a family member. Looking at women with fear of contagious diseases, we acknowledge two important roots. One root has its origins back in adolescence, while the other has its origins in extended courtships. In general, sexual education of girls is ineffective, insufficient, and more likely to confuse than to inform. Because of this failure in her education, the young girl may understand normal intercourse to be an infection by the male. Soon she is terrified even by a handshake or a kiss. This idea unconsciously survives even if the woman knows better. This might become active in its previous form or as an exaggerated fear of infection. For the second root we can assume that extended courtship causes severe sexual damage. It does so through forced abstinence or frustrated excitement. Similarly, the same results are seen in the neurotic pregnancy fears of newly wed women, if they have decided not to have children. This also can turn into fear of infection. As with any similar modern neurosis we can safely assume a strong component of hatred, wherever we see exaggerated concerns about a husband or parent who is actually in enemy territory. This happens similarly under the surface of sweetest affection. For example, a young woman could not be stopped from wearing black clothing soon after her husband had been called to the front. She was convinced that she would never see him again. To the knowledgeable this reveals more about her inner state than she might want to reveal. Her unconscious recognizes her ambivalence and she suffers from it.

In other cases, the first symptoms of melancholy are indicated by a total hopelessness, the refusal to eat, a rejection of any physical or intellectual activity, and a bland lethargy. As with other symptoms, this had been long prepared and becomes active now because of the actual events of the war.

Other nervous symptoms should be carefully observed, although laymen might still consider them as oddities that belong to the category of "psychopathology of everyday life." Examples of such symptoms are obsessive-compulsive thoughts and behavior. These differ only quantitatively from similar symptoms in men. The returned soldier who is constantly looking for his backpack, or another who is forever cleaning his hands of blood and mud, are well known to physicians, nurses, and many families. Many other soldiers are seen to be insensitive to their environment over the day. Yet they are sleepless at night as the memories of terror have profoundly shaken their souls and taken away all their energy.

In women we also see numerous cases where obsessive-compulsive thoughts and behavior have been triggered by the events of the war in the last few months. Some of the symptoms seem too mild to cause serious concern. For example, there was the case of a young woman who promised herself that she would only go for a walk on days when she received a note from her husband. Even laymen attribute more severity to obsessive thoughts that cause sleeplessness or completely changed behavior toward the next of kin. They acknowledge the existence of a mysterious disease if a soldier's mother never falls asleep. She is tormented by the idea she would not hear the ringing of the courier announcing the death of her son. Similarly, laymen will see illness in a case where a newly wed woman whose husband died at the front is unable to care for her dearly loved two-year-old son and does not even want to see him. In another case a woman firmly expected her husband to return home blind. Such compulsive thoughts are often accompanied by specific fantasies about the way the soldier will die in the war. In these cases we find certain links that are rooted in seemingly long forgotten impressions of childhood and adolescence. They are rooted in developmental stages that are decisive and basic for the adult's mental life.

Two particular forms of neurotic thinking and feeling in women deserve specific mention. One of these forms is found mainly in mothers. This is where even with official confirmation and eyewitnesses accounts, they do not believe in the actual death of their heroic sons. They cannot cope with their loss. This idea itself is so horrible that they keep it away from their consciousness with all available means of self-deceit. They flee into some kind of lethargic state where they remember the happy past when their helpless child belonged to them. At the same time they will not give up the idea that their son will eventually return to prove all officials and eyewitnesses wrong. Nobody will deny that this represents a serious psychic disturbance, the horror of war being the triggering event.

Seemingly less severe, the other form of neurotic behavior is a compulsive description of war atrocities. Women are much more prone to this behavior because of their passive role in the war. Whoever has really seen the ugly face of war is overwhelmed by its naked brutality. His soul is too deeply shaken to form words. However, a woman becomes excited by what she has heard indirectly or read about. These are nameless horrors and atrocities that her fantasy cannot grasp. The images that others could describe are painted by her with flashier colors than reality would ever use. She suffers from compulsive fantasies of misery, but at the same time she cannot defend herself from the lustful horror.

All these symptoms of mental imbalance can develop into severe neuroses if help is not provided in time. The internal help is efficient only where laymen recognize the disturbance as a nervous exaggeration rather than a disease. Its tool is the declared will to handle and overcome the desperate mood of the soul. Where this energy is missing only the knowledgeable physician can effect a rescue one way or the other. Women must be mentally healthy especially during these times. In times of war she is the only resource for her children. The strength of future generations relies on the power and health of women.

A Case of Female Foot Fetishism, or Rather, Shoe Fetishism (1916)

We found this clinical paper to be interesting for two reasons. It picks up the interest that Sigmund Freud showed in foot fetishism in his writing, although his book *Fetischismus* did not appear until 1927. (It appears in vol. 21 of the *Standard Edition*.) Also, Hug-Hellmuth refers back to some of her own childhood experiences that she described in her article on color hearing ("Über Farbenhören," *Imago* 3:253, 1912). This paper was first published in German in the *Zentralblatt für Psychoanalyse und Psychotherapie* 3/5:462-76. It has never appeared in English.

The fact that all cases of fetishism described in the literature are related to men has led me to report the case of a female boot fetishist even though the case has not been analyzed. Although this case happened nearly twelve years ago, it is fixed in my memory because at that time we talked often about it among friends. However, we were not aware of the true meaning of this peculiarity.

The patient was about thirty years old, a woman whose husband, a general, had shot himself after two or three years of marriage. Gossip said that he did so because of his disappointment and dissatisfaction with the marriage. The woman came from a highly acknowledged military family. She was the youngest of three daughters and from early on she was the declared favorite of her father. She loved him passionately. She would walk with him along the streets of the garrison with pride, first when he was a colonel and then when he became the highest and most distinguished general. From early on she had a special love for her father's high leather boots. Her greatest desire was to wear similar boots, which was fulfilled on her tenth birthday. Also, this wish could be met at least in the wintertime. Later she became very interested in military exercises. She was better informed about the military language used than some of the officers. The officers of the garrison courted this favored girl with admiration and compliments, to which she responded with coquetry and without real feelings. She liked only the parades of the cavalry, because "only a man on a horse with high boots is a real man." She rejected numerous proposals before she became engaged when she was twenty years old to an older colonel, thirty years her senior. She would always reply to the objections of her family that this man might be too old for her: "Yes, yes, if he had not these exciting feet," referring to his high boots. The groom, who had recognized the zealotry of his bride, gave her an onyx paperweight with a pair of little boots. Because of his strong sadistic nature, he did not forget to put a tiny silver riding whip in front. This really infuriated the patient. Against the resistance of her family, she succeeded in having her marriage annulled. Fortunately, the colonel died before this could happen. To remember him, she kept the paperweight and a pair of gloves. She said it would have been too embarrassing to ask his mother for his boots.

After many dates with other cavalry officers, she met another colonel at the age of twenty-seven who had come to the town where she lived with her parents. Her father in the meantime had retired from his post as general. The first appearance of this new colonel riding on a horse with high boots was decisive. Despite his remarkable ugliness, which was increased by his sparse beard, he was the ultimate of what this girl idolized. "I fell deeply in love with the most exciting boots I have ever seen," she reported enthusiastically to her friend. Afterwards she admitted that she really didn't know what the horseman had looked like, as she only had seen his feet. "A man is his foot, and a man who has beautiful feet is reliable." This was her motto as far as love is concerned. She often told her friend, "Imagine only a civilian with his low, worn shoes. Is that a real man? Boots make you tremble and again you must love them."

The wedding took place three months after their first meeting. The marriage was unhappy. It resulted in two boys. However, the woman resisted intercourse and experienced it as "disgusting and disgraceful." She was only able to enjoy it while fantasizing of sparkling boots. She advised her friend: "Don't marry! A man with big feet is a monster!" As a little girl she had expressed disgust whenever she was teased by her family for a passion for beautiful male feet. She always replied, "Yes, but only with shoes, a naked male foot is disgusting. I shake if I even imagine the big toe. The nails are always crippled and the small toe can never grow. That is a terrible sight."

When she was thirty years old, suddenly she gave the brush-off to the young officer whom she loved because of his beautiful feet when she saw that he moved his toes in the shoes when he sat beside her. She rejected the courtship of another man because he had wrinkled toes. In a third case she made the decision to terminate a relationship with an officer who was rejected by her father, when she heard that this young officer would appear in high boots or low civil shoes. We have to note finally that the same woman at the age of seventeen or eighteen had a strong platonic crush on her father's assistant and at another time on a cavalry officer. When she was criticized strongly by her sister's girlfriend, she defended herself with the words: "What do you think? I don't care for the men: what I love are their feet. This should be allowed, shouldn't it?" When the cavalry officer misunderstood her admiration and approached her physically, she rejected him with indignation: "That fool! He really believes that I love him instead of his divine feet. Such stupidity is unbelievable!"

The boots had to be shiny. The tops could not be wrinkled, and the toes must not be seen through the leather. No long raincoats were allowed. High boots were preferred also because of their smell.

In addition, she took good care of her own shoes, but without being affectionately attached to her own beautiful feet or her shoes. The one exception to this was her attachment to the pair of high boots that she had received for her tenth birthday. For herself she didn't particularly like Oxfords but preferred high-legged boots—"because of their tight appearance and the comfortable feeling from being laced." All low shoes and sports shoes she rejected fully because "the form of the feet becomes indecently prominent." High boots she called "exciting decent."

If we compare this case with other numerous cases of male fetishism, we see some remarkable coincidences in form and content that point to a similar etiology of fetishism in both women and men. But these coincidences also differentiate this reported case from the frequent female preference for food and clothing, which always has a narcissistic source. The fact that the general's daughter asked for high boots at age ten and admired herself wearing them is an unresolved identification with a beloved father. It is also a strong wish to be a boy rather than narcissism, since the symbolic meaning of the foot equals the penis. Self-love started at that point and the child considered herself as being closer to her father by owning the high boots. For the adult the boots are not only a condition for sexual arousal, but sexual symbols like the shoes or heels in Gerda's heel phobia. The become the object of erotic feelings. I do not know if one characteristic of fetishism, the sexual manipulation of a fetishistic object, is missing in this case. The strong repression of sexual drives in women, especially when perversely activated, might censor the report. I well remembered the explicitly erotic arousal, the "excitement" she experienced. It points toward a characteristic of a true fetishism that her total and only interest in men was her interest in their footwear. The man himself was only the unavoidable ticket for the fetishistic object. Not only does she refrain from normal sexual intercourse, she makes her marital duties bearable only through her fetishistic fantasies.

Her behavior toward the naked foot before and after her marriage seems to be of special importance. What does happen is always preceded by a special love, and afterwards the foot replaces and becomes a symbol for the penis. We realize the connection. At one point the attention of the child must have been directed toward her father and his genitals. Later this is repressed because of the threat of criticism and displaced to a less embarrassing part of the body, the foot. In its role as penis substitute, it has to be covered, and this again has to meet certain expectations because of the idealization of the object. Sparkling or newness, for example, might equal innocence. Considering these connections, we also understand why the girl called high-boots "excitingly decent." Because of this repression we understand why the girl reacts with disgust to the movement of the toes. I do not dare to hold that in her disgust toward wrinkled toes and nails she associated fantasies of castration. Strangely enough, she didn't show any disgust for the smell of feet. This was important in this case, in contrast to other cases, except perhaps for her preference for the smell of the leather.

The masochistic aspect of this case of shoe fetishism is clearly expressed: "Boots make you shake and you have to love them at the same time." This girl tightens her high boots to the extent that welts remain. When this happens it is not without the unconscious association to the high boots that enclose the shank tightly.

Finally, I would like to mention an over-determined factor in this fetishism. Her father was an explicit hand fetishist. Her statements of the character of a man being dependent on his feet go clearly back to expressions of the general, her father, about the connections between character and the form of the hands.

The Middle Child (1921)

This paper was Hug-Hellmuth's last contribution to her section on child psychology in *Imago*. It was published in *Imago* 7:179-97 as "Vom 'mittleren' Kinde." Compared to her other publication of that year, the previous paper on the technique of child analysis, the writing is awkwardly flat. It appeared to be a great step backward to a style that she used at the very beginning of her career. In a manner similar to her first papers, she provided a short introduction and a few psychoanalytic considerations. Then she used an abundance of clinical examples to illustrate a variation on a common theme.

We are used to hearing that the special position of the "only" child in a family leads to a very specific development that is not at all favorable, and that this form of development is not intended or expected by the parents. The love that spoils him and that makes him the center of the attention of the house, causes the "only child" to look everywhere for the same amount of devotion. This trying for attention everywhere and his inability to accommodate to other children cause him to become different. This increases the discrepancy between the love-spoiling atmosphere at home and the cold world outside. The prematurity that is developed by the siblingless child by his continuous dealing with only adults is normally appreciated by the parents as a sign of being unusually gifted and a reassurance of future importance in life. The disappointment is great when the "only" one goes to school and this apparent originality disappears. In his new school environment where he is only one among others, he misses for the first time the usual overestimation of his self. He feels set back. Quite often, he then tries to force the attention by intrusiveness. If this doesn't work, he becomes sensitive, resents his teachers, and becomes arrogant and unbearable for his schoolmates. He presents with a picture of the little asocial man he will become later. Often he fails early in his academic performance since he "already knows everything" because of his exclusive interaction with adults. In short, the spoiled only child changes into a hardly educatable "nervous" child that will fail badly sooner or later in his social skills.

The fate of the "favorite" child develops quite similarly. Perhaps his orientation in life is even more difficult because his happiness in childhood was based on the setback of his siblings. He then feels that it is necessary for his own satisfaction to be preferred over his peers. He experiences his own exceptional position as a double burden because of a constant fight and envy of his siblings and his looking for the same constellation through out his life.

Psychoanalytic research has pointed out repeatedly that even if siblings live together under the most favorable circumstances, we do not normally observe a paradise-like life of happiness or of happiness and of joy that laymen like to assign to the child's psyche. We know from the example of the "only" child that he is infuriated by strong jealousy once a sibling questions his powerful position in the house. We observe him watch the little sibling with threatening looks. Some hateful words and gestures may express his attitude toward the unwanted new member of the family. This attitude is not loving at all. In addition, we know about quite ambivalent feelings of the younger children toward the older children. Therefore, we do not expect a truly loving atmosphere in a home. On the contrary, we have accepted the fact that the child's feelings toward siblings are strongly ambivalent.

Professor Freud once said that it seems that one discusses the sexual instruction of the first-born, while adults don't seem to be concerned about the later siblings. Further, he said that perhaps one is doing right in leaving the decision with the children to answer these questions. This led my attention to investigate the important factors for the psychic development of other siblings, especially the "middle" child. I did not find any remarks about the fate of the middle child in the literature. Until now no one has paid special attention to the middle child. His fate in life to simply get along with the other children seems also to be his fate in child psychology. It seems important enough to me that the middle child deserves some special attention. It clarifies for us the peculiar biography of many women and men, people that have wasted their whole life striving for love, praise, and wealth, but always ended up sitting on the earth between two chairs.

Unfortunately, it is not very easy to collect a great number of observations of middle children because of the one- and two-child families of our days. Nevertheless, my research was spread over a couple of years and I managed to collect a considerable number of cases out of which I would like to highlight the most interesting ones. For the lesser part they stem from psychoanalytic practice because there we see more only children and oldest children that outnumber the middle children by far. This fact is easily understood because of the exceptional position of oldest children and the only child in the family.

I have to mention that by the middle child we understand the second of three children, or in a broader sense, a child that is separated from his other siblings by considerable differences in age on both sides.

The middle of three sisters (fifteen, twelve and ten years of age) complained, "It is a disaster to be in the middle. Emmy [the oldest] believes that she is a big shot already and she is hardly fifteen years old, and Mary, that little brat of ten years, thinks she is the same as me. Sometimes they say: 'You are the big one, you should be more reasonable, and you shouldn't be silly,' or 'Give in to the smaller one because you are already quite reasonable.' On another occasion: 'Leave Emmy alone, she has to work. Go and play with Mary; or the two little ones.' It has always been like that. When I was seven years old I went into second grade at the G. Institute. I was very proud that now I was to go to school as well, and because Emmy left normally for her 8:00 gym or French class quite early, I was even allowed to go on my own on several occasions. Then all of a sudden a kindergarten opened on the first of December and mother enrolled Mary because she didn't like her to be at home alone the whole morning. Now we have to go together with Mary led by the governess and I had to go with them. I was furious and either I left them behind or followed them at a distance of one block. This got me into trouble sometimes. Even now it is always like that! Whenever I accompany Mary, I am the big one and have to watch her, especially since she was hit by a carriage last year without being hurt. However, whenever I go with Emmy, then I'm the little one, and I am supposed to follow her obediently.

"It is a similar situation about our clothes. First, Emmy and I have the same clothes, and all of a sudden she gets special ones and Mary and myself wear the same clothes. Sometimes they consider us even to be twins. It is the same story with eating, going to bed, and going everywhere. Two years from now I am supposed to go to a dancing class together with Mary, and I think I will give up dancing entirely because she reports what I am doing, who I am looking at, and to whom I'm talking. I always have two spies. If we had only two children, then I would only have one spy. However, now I have two—sometimes Emmy reports on me, sometimes Mary, depending on whom I am with.

"When children are invited to our place, normally Emmy has her afternoon and I am allowed to invite one or two girls as well. Although only little children come to visit Mary, only Greta comes to visit me. Greta is the sister of Kurt and Edith. I never have a company of children all for myself. Only on one occasion was I allowed to invite a bunch of kids for my tenth birthday. Mary caught colds and then Emmy caught one, and the whole party was canceled. I never caught a cold. It is odd anyway. From the very beginning Emmy and Mary suffer from all diseases—e.g., measles, scarlet fever, diphtheria—and they always have them together. Then, much later when I got sick, I had to lie down in my bed all by myself; when they are sick, I am not allowed to go to school as well, and again I am alone. Sometimes they seem to tease me with that. However, the worst of all is if we have a big excursion or get tickets for the theatre. At first I was too small to go there, but now all of a sudden Mary is big enough. It is always like that—with books, pieces we play on the piano, etc. I really would prefer if I myself or one of them wouldn't be at home. Then there would only be two and everything would be different."

Next, I will report and quote from the analysis of a bright thirteen-year-old boy who was somewhat retarded in his body development, who had brothers fourteen and nine years of age:

"It is a real misery. All children in a family should be of the same age or they should form two groups when there are more children, e.g., six or eight. Then there wouldn't be such injustices, e.g., when Robert gave us some clothes. Fritz was given a suit made of Robert's best clothes and I had to take Fritz's clothes, and Karlie got entirely new ones. For heaven's sake, even our grandparents brought Karlie brand-new clothes.

"It is the same thing at meal times. They say either: 'Fritz is the oldest, that's why he gets the most,' or 'Don't fight Karlie because he doesn't understand that well.' Consequently, Fritz always gets the best and biggest piece of meat. Mother admonishes me, but I can see and I always judge with my eyes what is given to whom. The thing that most infuriates me is the following: When we were still smaller, with Fritz eight years and myself seven, Fritz was always allowed to eat the rest of the sweetdough out of the pot because he was the oldest, and now of course Karlie gets it because he is the smallest. I never get anything and such injustice infuriates me. Then I run wild and make a big fuss! It is just the same with the books in the shelf; Fritz simply takes them since he is going to school. He takes whatever he wants. However, whenever I try to take a book, I am told, 'The bookshelf is not your business.' I have frequently thought that three children in one family appears to me like head, body, and feet. The middle part is always tightened by the clothes, e.g., by the belt, but head and legs are free. They are allowed to do whatever they want. The head can turn around and look with its eyes wherever it wants, and think and talk whenever it wants. The feet can stand or walk or run, but the body in the middle can't do anything on its own. You all know the story of Menenius Agrippa about the stomach and the other parts of the body. This story showed that all parts of the body have the same value. This is supposed to be the same with children in the family. However, father always has a favorite and mother too. Consequently, there should be only two children in the family. In other regards, if there are only two children, it is much better. Each of them as his own privileges, one being the older, the other the younger. One allows the other his privileges because he himself also enjoys some. There are no fights or discussions. However, the middle brother is always at a disadvantage. He has no privileges and no rights. He has to share either with the older or with the younger brother. He is never independent but he is always an addendum or simply in the middle between head and feet. That is the same within a community. On the one hand are the nobility and the rich who own everything; on the other side, workmen and poor who at least have the right to apply for charities. In the middle are the civil servants, the middle class that don't own anything and do not even get anything from the charity because they are too embarrassed to ask for it. That is exactly what happened to my Aunt Louise. They don't have anything but they also can't ask for anything. The only good thing is that they only have one child, but again it is only a girl. It would be perhaps best if a family had two children. One of the children could die as soon as the third child arrives so that there are only two in the end. That would be good for both of them."

A nine-year-old girl describes her life in the family with her eleven-year-old sister, Marietta, and their five-year-old twins Hänsel and Gretel as follows:

"Marietta is the declared favorite of father and Hänsel of mother. There is nobody for me. Not even my Aunt Rosa because Gretel is her favorite. They all tell me that I would be the favorite of my grandmother, but this is simply not true. Her favorite is Fredy, Uncle Walter's son, and in our family she doesn't have a favorite at all. Perhaps Grandmother likes to some extent Marietta or even more Hänsel, but nobody particularly likes me, at least not so much that anybody recognizes. Yet, they complain about me and say that I am naughty and rebellious. It seems a matter of everyone else being preferred but myself. I am always expected to give in to the two little ones, but Marietta is given the idea never to give in to me, 'because she is the big one' and therefore I have to follow. Really, I have better ideas! Whenever there is a big children's party, I never know where to go. Marietta and her friends stop talking as soon as we—that means myself and my friends—enter the room, and then they talk in some sort of secret code while we are playing lottery. Staying with the little ones is simply too boring for us. I'm not going to play around on the floor or play in the sandbox or jump around, even if I do it now and then. Further, I am told that I am not supposed to be so rough, and I have to watch that nobody gets hurt, an that includes not allowing clothes to get dirty or torn.

"In the evening I have to watch the little ones because Marietta has to study, according to Mama, because Marietta goes to secondary school. I don't have to do anything for school, and so I have to watch the little children. Other people have a governor or a nanny, but in our family we have to do it all ourselves. When Anna [the servant] was ill, I had to do the dishes and clean the shoes because Marietta, of course, doesn't have any time for that, and the twins were simply too small. I am really the 'Cinderella' in our family. Hopefully, later, there will come a real prince who will rescue me. . . The worst point is my clothing. Since the war I basically have only had one new dress, and Marietta's clothes that she has grown out of are changed for me into 'new clothes.' When mother wanted to change my winter coat to a new one for Gretel, Aunt Rosa immediately intervened and said: 'It's really not worth it anymore—the coat is too shabby. I will buy one for Gretel.' Now I really care for my green dress that I got from Marietta, but I really want to see what will happen later, if it will be given to Gretel."

A nineteen-year-old girl who grew up with a three-year-old and a sister three years her junior, expresses her opinion about the family life with siblings as follows: "There should be only two siblings, a brother and a sister. When I get married and have my own family, I want only two children—absolutely—first a boy and the next year a girl and that's it! Watching Rejene, I see how bad it is if a child is alone, how he is spoiled and even then not content. Little Linda always wants a brother or sister for herself, but Uncle and Aunt, especially Aunt, do not want to hear about it. However, if you have three children, as it was in our family, one is always too many. It was really luck for me that Liddy got married early when she was seventeen and a half years old. The time of her engagement was terrible for me. Before Liddy and myself spent a lot of time together, and Margit always was considered to be the small one; but this changed dramatically with Liddy's engagement. All of a sudden I was thrown in together with Margit. A bride is of course grown up, even if she is hardly seventeen years old. This dramatic change often infuriated me so much that sometimes I did the most horrible things. I believe this was the main reason why I went to a boarding school in Germany for two years. When I came back, Margit and myself were at least alone. I had seen so much more of the world by that time and this really impressed her. One really has to suffer a lot as the middle child because the older one is always set up as an example to you, even if you remember very well that she hasn't been an angel at all, and you yourself have to be always a good example for the little ones."

It is interesting to learn how other family members see the fate of the middle child. In his analysis, a highly intelligent fourteen-year-old boy, the oldest of three, described the relationship with his middle, twelve-year-old brother, Ado, and his ten-and-a-half-year-old sister Ella, approximately as follows: "Ado is well off. At times he can do what would be really appropriate for me as the oldest. Then again, if it suits him, he can behave like me. If it suits him even better, he joins Ella. He is really a bum. Basically, one can't blame him because he is neither the oldest nor the youngest. Anyway, I tease him whenever I can. For instance, at mealtimes I always turn the plate so that the smallest piece faces him. He doesn't care too much about the meat, but becomes angry when it happens with a good dessert. I do this especially if we have guests, so that he can't fight back. Frequently I hide some of Ella's things and then blame Ado. When playing theater I'm of course always the director and I give him the worst roles. That bothers him. Of course, he complains to mother, as he is her favorite. Mother always says I would be her explicit favorite as Ado was three years ago, but he has remained mother's favorite. Starting on the day, which I have almost called his death day, when the doctors had given up, he clearly became our mother's favorite. I remember one scene very well. When I was ten years old and Ado was about seven, he got a toy box to practice magic for Christmas. Of course, Ado, the dummy, didn't achieve anything in magic technique, whereas I could do everything. He became so infuriated that he hit the magic egg on a hat, so that the handle broke without his recognizing it, and then he complained that I had broken the handle. However, Ella had witnessed it. From then on he was always teased because of his 'magic' with a handle, and the angrier he became, the more we teased him. I remember something very delightful. Ado, the blockhead, knew about certain indecent things that I already told you about, before I knew about them. He had told me, 'Isn't that ridiculous?' At age six to seven, he already knew everything because I was between eight and nine when he told me. Shortly after that he explained it also to Ella, which really caused a tremendous scandal. It is not right that the younger brother comes to tell the older everything. He has lost my respect and he has caused my hostility. He declares himself as being somewhat more important and I certainly cannot stand that. I was supposed to know everything before him, and then to tell him. That would be correct. Things being as they were, I really suffered. It is also natural that when learning, he wouldn't let me tell him anything. I agree with him. Father also should realize that. I often have the feeling that he will know more eventually than I do, although I can ask you [Dr. Hug-Hellmuth] for everything and can really talk to you about everything. The stupid guy didn't even know at age seven what three plus five is, and so Ella had to tell him. In general, Ado's first grade was a comedy. He didn't grasp math and so he was awarded with cookies and sweets if he was successful. However, he cried if he didn't get the sweets as long as he didn't solve the problems. Finally, our little sister Ella came along and gave the answer and got the sweets. And Ado's anger—that was really something! Sometimes I even felt sorry for him when he was told: 'Look at Ella, she doesn't even go to school and knows it already,' or 'Your report card won't look like Kurt's. He always has had A's.' Now in the meantime that has changed. In primary school he had only A's, and then in the first class in high school, it was really a smash . . . Sometimes I really believe that intentionally he plays the role of a blockhead, but why does he become so angry whenever Ella or myself are given as examples to him? Really, I wouldn't like to be in his place; I want to be either the oldest or the youngest. The middle one is at a disadvantage. He is teased a lot. For instance, in the Renner family, Frieda is teased by George as well as by Mizzi. Ado often says that he is at a disadvantage because the oldest are elegant and cheeky and Ella, the youngest, one couldn't count on anyway. She is the youngest and she is always complaining and she is a girl. That is why the middle child has really no siblings but only enemies. We are three children in the family, enemies that observe, betray and hate. Well, he is not totally wrong and I don't envy him. Really, I am glad that I am not in his place."

Finally, I will report a mother's judgment about the psychic development of the middle of her little girls (five, eight and nine years of age):

"During the first three years of life, Lotta was a happy and socializing child who got along with the one-year-older Magda very well. Shortly after the birth of little Paula, Lotta fell down from a swing and broke a rib. She was confined to bed for a long time, and initially the doctor was afraid of a possible scoliosis, but that fortunately didn't happen. From that time on Lotta changed her attitude toward Magda. She became a tyrant, moody, rough, ever-hateful toward her older sister. However, she enjoyed passionately and closely little Paula, who could do anything to her. That is how it is even today. She mothers the little one, does her any favor, and takes over responsibility for all of Paula's wrongs. Because of that she was punished frequently and unjustifiably. Sometimes Magda becomes jealous towards the little one who is spoiled by everybody, especially by her father, but Lotta finds it all right that everything is focused on Paula. But whenever somebody deals with Magda, Lotta can hardly hide her anger, which sometimes becomes a bitter fury. Initially we blamed the illness for the sudden change in the child's behavior toward Magda, but also the birth of the youngest might possibly play its role. It is odd that she always feels put at a disadvantage and set back by Magda, but doesn't complain when Paula is preferred."

Little Lotta once talked about her situation as follows: "It really makes you feel very uneasy if you have an older sister. Paula is to have it better someday. Magda spies. She complains about me to father, whose favorite is Paula. That is why I have to look after her and watch whatever she does. When Magda went to Holland, I was happy. I didn't ask for a trip myself because I rather wanted her to go to Holland again or to Switzerland. Mother always says that I'm quarrelsome, but when Magda was away, there was not a single fight. She wants to be in charge all the time when we play and she is only one year older than I am! I really like to do Paula a favor because she is so little and cute. Magda never does me a favor although she is the older. On the contrary, I am to follow her and I have to agree with whatever she wants. We fight for every toy, especially the dolls and the dishes. Why am I supposed to give in? It is also quite unfair that I am supposed to go to bed at seven thirty, shortly after Paula whereas Magda is allowed to stay up until half past eight. Everywhere she is considered to be the 'big' one, but actually we are nearly the same height. I can't play with Magda on the piano for four hands. It fails all the time because she intentionally plays too fast, so that I am left with a bar at the end. Then the teacher or mother tells me that I have made a mistake! Sisters should never be forced to play compositions for four hands. I really have a crush on Paula. She is so cute and little that you can hardly get angry at her, although she sometimes happily scratches and pinches, but she is only five years old. That is why I can't understand mother telling me, 'See, Lotta, you get along so well with Paula and take everything from her, but you are so unfriendly to Magda, just as if Magda were only five years old as well. At least mother should understand, even if father does not.' "

I only can report one middle child who was raised among numerous siblings. She is an eleven-year-old girl whose oldest siblings are a sixteen-year-old sister, followed by twelve-and-a-half-year-old twins, a boy and a girl, who lead a life that is totally independent from the other children. The second last child is a nine-year-old somewhat retarded boy, and the youngest is a four-year-old girl. The middle eleven-year-old is totally isolated by the special groupings and peculiarities of her siblings. She most often plays alone, or she disturbs the games of the other children because of her noncompliance, her sensitivity, and her unlovable, precocious attitude. She suffers from the isolation within that group of children. However, she resists all advice. She uses books or toys of the other siblings, but she literally goes out of her mind if one of her siblings even dares to touch one of her things. A simple touch is enough for her to give up this thing, permanently. At mealtime she ensures anxiously that none of the others get more than she does. She always has to differ from her sisters in her dress, and she even tries to reject the others in the community by changing the spelling of her second name. When questioned she explains: 'That's quite natural. If I do everything as the others do, I will get lost among so many kids. Rene [the 16-year-old] is always recognized because she is the oldest and has a special name; then there are the twins, and a big fuss is always made about them, as if it would be something special to be a twin. Everybody feels sorry for Fred, and that is why everybody tries to comfort him and Julchen is the youngest and terribly spoiled. So I am left! In addition, I have a horrible name. I like it best when nobody asks me for my name so that I don't have to answer: Toni. In general, nobody cares for me because there are enough other children, and I just hang on. I become most angry whenever Uncle Emil says: 'Oh well, then we have Toni coming late with a face as long as a towel.' Am I really useless, why do I live in this world at all? And why do we have so many children? I am always terribly embarrassed whenever somebody asks me how many siblings I have. When I answer, 'Unfortunately another five' then people laugh and I am even more embarrassed. That is why I prefer to go by myself. If I could have been at least either the oldest or the youngest, I would be content."

Despite its diversity, the presented material shows some common features in the psychic development of the middle child. Intensive observation destroys the illusion that happiness and satisfaction are increased by having a great number of siblings. On the contrary, we see that the middle child is as much exposed to special sufferings as is the only child. In the presented as well as in other cases known to me, the current feeling of doubt of the ego seems to be almost typical, the uncertainty as to which direction the child should orientate himself to. According to his own needs, the adult sometimes considers him to be the big one among the siblings and sometimes the little one. This triggers an ever-changing desire and longing for an already passed or not yet reached phase of life. The wish to be "big" like the older brother or the older sister is shared with every second child by the "middle" child. However, no other child follows the privileges given to him by the older one, and they remain through all the years of childhood and adolescence as an undoubted possession. The "middle" one has bad luck. He has hardly begun to enjoy his privileges when they are questioned by his successor without being replaced by other privileges. He doesn't become "mother's big boy" or "big girl," but remains somewhere between big and small in some sort of "no-mans-land." He is not spoiled anymore because the little one is. The position of the big one is given away, and there he swings back and forth insecurely between his siblings. He poorly accommodates to his double role, copying the weaknesses of the older one on some occasions, and becoming an example for the younger child on others.

The adult's labile estimation of the middle child causes anger in those who are considered to be responsible for his indecisive state. He is full of hostility, sometimes against the older, sometimes against the younger sibling, and his wish to be freed of one of them is openly or covertly expressed. As he becomes educated, certain early infantile wishes are strongly suppressed. Thus an eleven-year-old child will not comment on the birth of a later arrival in the family by saying, "The stork has to take it away again," but instead we hear what he thinks about the right number of children in the family and give the eternal wish the following form: "I would really prefer if I myself or one of us wouldn't be here. Then there would be only two of us and everything would be different." From the lapse of a fourteen-year-old boy: "Now I nearly said 'death-day.' " Of course, we understand the same attitude of the oldest for the second child.

The constant feeling of being set back that frequently causes an almost unconscious irritation in dealing with the other sibling increases with the years. Especially during prepuberty, when sexual knowledge overwhelms and confuses the child, the relationship between the middle child and the other siblings often becomes more and more unfriendly. His position in between does not let him get close to the older brother or the older sister, who are envied because of their advanced sexual knowledge and their greater physical maturity. Also he feels superior to his younger sibling and consequently he ends up standing isolated between those who are not siblings, but enemies that observe, betray, and hate. The older children understand this unfortunate position only too well because of their own misdoings toward the younger one, and they feel sorry for or despise the child that stands in the middle.

The child's wish to be alone with only a brother or a sister is enforced by his desire to see the relationship of the parents repeated in the relationship among the children. Following the example of the father, they should not have more than two children and this ideal is to be realized by many young people in their future marriage. They simply fantasize the ancient children's game of "father and mother". This game is most liked and most common amongst children who have grown up with only one other sibling; because the "child" in the play ideally is a doll that keeps quiet about what it sees or hears.

The primary erotic relationships of a child with his parents, and in a broader sense with the adult family members, again and again feed into the early dissatisfaction of the middle child who is discontent with his fate. He suffers from the thought that father and mother chose one or the other of the children as their favorite, and that he, the middle child, has hardly anything. Grandparents and aunts frequently concentrate their special attention on the oldest or the youngest as well. He attributes all the small duties in the household that are given to him as proof of his role as a Cinderella. The real or imagined loss of love makes him moody, suspicious, noncompliant, and thoughtful. Not infrequently he fails in school as soon as the youngest also attends. The parents' interest in the first developmental steps of the oldest one is considerably weaker for the second. This child actually recognizes this loss only when their attention is then shifted on to the successes of the youngest. The "hanging back" in learning soon incapacitates his effort because the reward doesn't fit the amount of work. Because of the identification of the little girl with the mother, we understand that she still lives the younger child, although this child provides her an occasion for jealousy and envy. She mothers this child and withstands tyranny but becomes hostile and rejecting toward the older sister.

The middle of three children of the same sex and of similar age experiences the most painful vagueness in his position at home. Sometimes unconscious remainders of infantile discontent become especially dangerous for the middle of three sisters. If not only the older sister but also the younger one happen to make happy marriage choices of partners before her, the idea of marriage of the middle is frequently given up.

The fate of a girl between two brothers develops much more favorably. Because she recognizes quite early the physical and mental superiority of her older brother, she develops quite early her true femininity through living with him. He is cared for by her with jealousy. Because of the influence of the older brother the "child-woman" is born, where the younger one develops a strong motherly attitude. Consequently, she quite fortunately integrates those qualities in a woman which always attract a man. She escapes the fate of those girls who only have older brothers with whom they compete in their cognitive development.

The dark side of the life of the middle child is spared probably most likely for a boy between two sisters. If he is quite close in age to the older one he soon acquires first place among the siblings, while the two girls naturally get close to one another.

Normally the natural cheerfulness of a healthy child covers the conflicts of his young soul. His individuality darkens and obscures what is considered typical. Thus quite frequently we see that the middle child also harmlessly and happily enjoys his being. However, the careful observer does not miss those characteristic features that are typical for his middle position, even if they are sometimes very weak.

Fairy tales miraculously reflect everyday life and they can tell us about the fate of the middle child. Nearly all this follows from the known traces of the birth order. The middle of the "three sisters with the glass heart" did not have to suffer as hard as the oldest sister. However, her heart is damaged and with a crack in her glass heart she has to be content to participate only in the happiness of the youngest one as an observer. In this example, the youngest one is regularly the happiest. If it is a boy who acts like a hero, he marries a princess. If it is a girl, a prince comes to marry her. Only the youngest of the "four capable brothers" shares the fate of the oldest. The two middle brothers, by gaining excellence in one particular area, lack the opportunity to learn the art of life, and consequently all four spend their life unmarried, without extraordinary joy or suffering, within a life of quiet contemplation. Only one of the fairy tales talks about the middle of three sisters as the most fortunate, while the oldest and the youngest become beggars that have to beg from their formerly hated middle sister, Two Eye, who is hated by One Eye and Three Eye. They are proud to be different from all other human beings, but they hate Two Eye because she has two eyes like all the other humans. Further, she is rewarded with wealth, love, and happiness. The oldest and the youngest are separated from other human beings by their abnormalities. The middle one is rewarded because she is like the other human beings. Two Eye seems to me to be the symbol for a middle child who, because of her less privileged position, has to learn early to accommodate and to support. Later this attitude helps to fill adequately his place in life. It makes good sense that the fairy tale talks about three sisters, because women especially need the capacity for adaptation. Without this gift the woman remains like One Eye and Three Eye, a beggar in her loving relationships despite all real or fantasized advantages of body or mind.

Psychoanalytic Findings About Women (1921)

The psychology of women in the early days of the Vienna
Psychoanalytic Society was clearly a male issue. Except
for a few unusual women—for example Lou Andréas-
Salome ("Zum Typus Weib," *Imago* 3/1-14, 1913)—contributions by women authors were confirmations of the
male vision. This remained true even in the later years,
as shown in Helene Deutsch's "The Psychology of
Women" in 1944. The following paper has been published only once before, in German in 1921, as "Psychoanalytische Erkentnisse über die Frau," in the *Archiv für
Frauenkunde und Eugenetik* 7/2:130-38. In it Hug-Hellmuth presents a more balanced view of female psychology.

In his outline for "Nora," Ibsen writes: "There are two kinds of mental laws, one for men and a totally different one for women. They don't under-stand one another, and women are judged in everyday life according to the laws of men, as if women shouldn't be women, but rather men."

This difference between men and women can be looked at from three different points of view: social, biological, and psychological. Some aspects deal with the difference between men and women as it is observed in individ-uals and applied to everyday life. Biology emphasizes the difference between male and female seen from the perspective of sexual function. Psychology finally judges male and female to be active and passive. This point of view is the most important when applied to psychoanalysis.

As far as love is concerned, the man normally plays an active role and the woman a passive role. However, women experience a phase of infantile feeling where they consider themselves as being thoroughly active, that is, male. During the auto-erotic phase, there is no other source of lust other than her own body and the nurturing breast of the mother. Besides other auto-erotic activities, this is the time of infantile masturbation that is practiced more or less intensively by probably all children. This purely male period of the female child, which sometimes is extended into the third or fourth year of life, declines dramatically in later years, to be terminated within the normal development by the powerful repressive forces of adolescence. The girl gives up male activity in favor of the man whose aggression is more attractive than the passivity of women and which she values highly.

A sociological view of men and women demonstrates in a great number of individuals, either in a biological or in a psychological sense, that pure masculinity or femininity is rarely found. Yet, a mixture of both is found in

248

every individual. It is a human disposition to be bisexual! According to the individual's psychophysical constitution and the influence of one's environment, sooner or later the development of the homosexual aspect is suppressed. It is suppressed in favor of the heterosexual aspect which is directed toward the other sex. The heterosexual aspect is the only one that is useful for modern society. Female development is dominated by two influences that have immense importance for the fate of women and their role as a partner. This was discovered by psychoanalysis. The first is the early infantile discovery of the anatomical differences of the sex which causes the "masculinity complex" of women. The other is the female's close attachment to her father that stems from early childhood. No woman can withdraw from these influences. How a woman copes with them or is defeated by them is a complicated matter. The strength of these influences, their mutual promotion or inhibition, how they are favored by education and environment and the psychophysical disposition, determines the final result.

Using his extremely rich material, Freud writes in his paper "Some Character Types Met within Psychoanalytic Work": "As we learn from psychoanalytic work, women regard themselves as having been damaged in infancy, as having been unreservedly cut short of something and unfairly treated, and the embitterment of so many daughters against their mothers derives, ultimately, from their reproach against her of having brought them into the world as women instead of men."

For the little child, the differences of the sex are emphasized by clothing. Clothing is estimated highly, especially by boys. The first pair of trousers means a social promotion to them. Even if we recognize that little girls become aware of sex differences later than boys, we assume erroneously that these observation occur in late childhood or even in adolescence. The recognition comes particularly early for little girls who are raised among bothers of similar age. Such girls normally react with feelings of discrimination and humiliation. The normal reaction is a tomboyish acting-out and imitation of boys, physically and mentally.

It is quite appropriate, considering the strong reaction of the girl's soul toward the real or assumed injustice, to add envy to the feeling of disadvantage, since she feels that boys were favored by nature. The envy of women toward men disappears or more correctly, is strongly suppressed whenever and as long as a woman is happily in love. The beloved man provides her with the masculinity she was deprived of during her childhood years. However, this envy does return again and takes the form of anger towards individual men. It also takes the form of grotesque hatred that includes all men whenever love temporarily or permanently cools off. In addition, we see the disgusting spectacle when women oppose their own femininity that they experience as being inferior. If these women are well read and are able to write a little bit, books and pamphlets are born that bitterly criticize men and condemn all masculinity. However, they are really written because of disappointment with only one man. They are written by women who are defeated by their "masculinity complex."

Hostility between sexes is normal and the source that feeds into it is not unknown to us. The overestimation of masculinity by men and women exists. The man expresses it by his "need" to protect and care for those he loves and by his contempt and degradation of the hated woman. The man cares and supports women and children in general who are the most needy members of society. According to the same overestimation, the woman experiences a naive admiration of her lover but also a sexual envy that so often appears as an envious completion. The cry of women for equal rights in the social field can't be totally explained by their economic needs. Unconscious envy at least feeds into this battle against men. Higher education of women has its roots partly in the revival of the unconscious sexual envy of the little girl toward the boy. The reason for this mutual hostility is the same. It is the sexual difference between men and women and the everlasting alienation and mystery between the sexes that can't be overcome by the most intimate exchange. It is a tragic fact that the sexes do not understand one another because they do not know about one another, their needs, their conflicts, or their expectations.

We switch now from psychology to sociology. However, I am not going to talk about these problems right now because they are far from our topic. We will restrict ourselves to the acknowledgment of the facts and acknowledge the truth in the curse of God that applies to all generations of mankind: "I will set hostility between you and women." We understand now why the ability to hate as well as the ability to love will never disappear between men and women, It will not disappear as a pattern of repetition. It will not disappear as individuals experience and suffer from the whole spectrum between exclamatory happiness and bitter anger. We look for its roots neither in the cognitive life, nor in social conditions, but in sexual matters, as discovered by psychoanalysis. The second aspect that becomes important for the development of women is the girls' attachment to their fathers. During the first period of life, men are psychologically self-sufficient. They are their own sole love object. They derive all love from their own egos, and they live through a primary stage of affect, a period of auto-eroticism. Probably this is the happiest phase because it is independent of the environment. However, men are also needy and helpless at the same time. The environment is well aware of their neediness and it has the tools and the wish to fulfil them to raise the child. The young child reacts to that with love as soon as the first basis of intellect helps to overcome the basic hostility toward every external influence that is compulsively rejected in the beginning.

The first external love object of the child is his caretaker, normally the mother. This integration of the external world into his sphere of feeling and the finding of an object is the first cultural task of the child. With increasing mental activity the child chooses his objects independently according to the environmental impressions. First, the father is chosen. He is soon followed by the other family members, inanimate objects, and finally by animals and foreign beings. Object finding and object choice are done by the child by giving up his exclusive, self-sufficient existence. He integrates himself into society. From that point on he is sexually determined.

Soon the boy acquires a protective role toward his mother. However, he constantly realizes the existence of his father with his size, power, and his older historical rights. Because this is felt indignantly, the boy's feelings also acquire a dubious ambivalent character. The little son does not only love his father, he is also hostile toward the feared competitor for the mother. He is full of jealousy. At the same time he also tries to imitate and to identify with him because he is impressed by his size, his strength, and power. Thus the boy does not only resist giving up his first love object, the mother, for the sake of the father, but he tries to be like his father. He places himself into the role of father's substitute. Innumerable words of children prove these desires. The behavior of the little girl is analogous with regards to the mother.

However, the development of the girl's feelings toward her parents tend to be different from the boy's. First, her affection remains and is directed toward the mother, or another female caretaker. However, the integration of the father into the emotional life of the girl is the stronger factor. It works positively for the development of the cultural obligations of the woman. She turns away from her own sex to the other and thus executes in her earliest childhood the step from homosexuality to heterosexuality that becomes important for her mature sexual life.

In boys, development is not that easy. At this point I would like to emphasize that the analysis of the male psyche is generally much more complicated and more interesting than that of the female. The analyzed male provides richer and deeper material and more variability connecting egocentric and social interests. This enables us to conclude that the internal life of women is exceptionally suppressed. This is perhaps because suppression it is much more strongly and exclusively focused around sexual interests. Men have more opportunities to satisfy their sexual desires. The special passivity of women in their sexual activity, which also forms the attraction of femininity, enables us to understand that fact.

The behavior of the little girl toward her father shows the typical attitude of the passive and thus seductive woman. Weakness and neediness are the adequate tools that open the field for her father and his later successors to activate their "male" qualities. The woman keeps this attitude toward the other sex consciously or unconsciously for her whole life. She seduces almost by her "intellectual inferiority" and when she loves, she lets him teach even where she might truly know more than he does.

However, even in situations where the woman considers herself to be an equal partner for her husband, she repeats a similar constellation from her childhood. By going back to the memories of early life, we repeatedly find a passionate desire of the little girl to be a boy and to identify herself with the father. In their object choice, these women are looking for a duplicate of what they once tried to be themselves and what they still carry in their conscious as an ideal equivalent: the youthful father who integrates lover, friend, and father in one person.

This sort of attachment to the father does not only explain the numerous cases where young girls tend toward elder men. In addition, it explains the woman who prefers a "feared" tyrannical man to a more tolerant one. This points to the phase of her life where the little girl, despite all love, experienced the father as a threatening power.

Certain physical and psychological characters, disadvantages, and peculiarities are looked for or avoided during the object choice of later years simply by identifying the lover with the father according to the appraisal of certain qualities experienced during childhood. That is why some women consider a man inadequate if he smokes or wears a beard, whereas others consider a beard or smoking to be a prerequisite for their love. The same applies to the like or dislike of the father's profession, his attitude toward sports, or his musical talents. The positive aspect of these prerequisites leads to the mysterious déjà vu of love, and we understand it as unconscious affective memories of childhood. However, the unhappy choices that often break the faith of women normally happen also because of the strong bond, the attachment to the father.

In addition to the incredible importance of the attachment to the father, we are not to overlook the influence of the brother, especially the older brother. The brother often represents a duplicate of the fatherly figure for the girl, and often becomes the only idol that leads the choice of a love object of the young woman toward peers or even younger men.

Whatever image influences the erotic feeling of women, they can acquire a happy development of their ego only if they manage to separate in time from the first male love object of childhood. This second important step of erotic development that prevents women from aberrations of their mature psyche normally happens during puberty.

The girl's father complex does not contradict the temporary identification of the daughter with her mother that we observe quite frequently during the first years, and then again during adolescence. The daughter plays the role of the youthful mother who appears quite lovable. However, she turns at the same time to mother as a confidante, as a friend, because the strange, unknown, male element is felt as being hostile. This occurs especially during adolescence when the girl inevitably has to realize the differences of sex. We know that Freud has understood the bitterness of some daughters toward their mothers as being due to the basic grievance that they were born as women instead of men. During later years, when the girl assigns the voluntary determination of the sex of a child to the father because of his active role in love, she turns her anger against him for having created her as a woman instead of a man.

These factors that influence the fate of women partly explain a phenomenon that causes the most troublesome experiences for women in intimate relationships with men—sexual anaesthesia or frigidity. I am not speaking about the frigidity that is caused by organic abnormalities but about the frigidity that is psychological. Psychological frigidity is most likely much more frequent. Indeed, the psychoanalysts of frigid women have regularly discovered causes of a mental nature. First, we have seen the influence of childhood masturbation in determining sexual expectations of the mature years. Besides the fact that psychological development causes other conditions of lustful experience for the adult woman than for a child, normal love life asks that the woman give up the active role she had acquired during the time of infantile auto-eroticism. This is aggravated by her own education, which prohibits everything that is connected with an erotic, sexual life and sex in general. The woman brings into her marriage her personal mystery, which is characterized by a mixture of lust and terror. For more than one woman, sexual enjoyment stays connected with an aura of the prohibited. Often, these are women who have to break their marriage compulsively. It is their habit to commit adultery in fantasy or reality. Men rightly judge them to be identical.

The tendency to experience lust and sexual love only by breaking the law is caused by wrong educational styles and is accompanied by something new and unexpected: the feeling of disappointment. Not only does the woman expect much more enjoyment, it is impossible for her to experience it at the beginning of her marriage for anatomical reasons. She also does not understand the aim of the male desire. She is embarrassed, offended, and outraged. All the words from childhood that were unforgotten and had suppressed her infantile interest in the sexual matters of men and animals, returned in full force and turned a formerly lustful sensation into a disgusting experience.

This is the vantage point from which we begin to understand the estimation and importance of virginity. The woman sees in the man the destroyer of her virginity, the "gift" of nature that she has learned to estimate as her most valuable possession. Virginity is considered by her as an equivalent substitute for masculinity. She wants to "give" herself to a man, while at the same time she feels robbed by him. This conflictual relationship between giving and taking revives the old hostility. She considers the man as being a brutal force she can't escape. Even when healthy sexuality and strong attachment prevent these hostile impulses from becoming conscious, they are never lost. They are always waiting for an occasion to justify an outbreak of anger.

It is a sign of true wisdom that according to the religious laws of some primitive tribes, the defloration of the wife is not the duty of the young husband but it is exercised by an old woman—that is, a mother substitute—and in other tribes a priest performs the rite—that is, a substitute of the first authority figure, the father.

A marriage suffers from these unconscious hatreds and by the eruptions of a continuous oversensitivity that is much more characteristic for women than for men. It is very real during those horrible waking hours of the night when one can grasp the silence. The degradation of the husband in front of children and servants represents the most disgusting expression of this hostility. The scenes do not only exist in the insane brain of Strindberg or the neurotic feeling of Gerjestein. They have turned thousands of real marriages into hell.

Psychoanalytic knowledge teaches us to understand why this terrible alienation between spouses normally starts with the woman. It is an expression of the reaction of women to their role in sexual life that was given by birth.

Once our sexual customs will have changed in the way that sexuality for the child will become considered as something natural and beautiful, and once we will have replaced suppression of sex by a graceful cultural acceptance of sex, men and women will go into marriage with more knowledge, cleanliness, and enjoyment. A way of life that will appreciate the sexual instinct will make Nietzsche's words less obvious: "The unresolved difficulties in relationship of character and mentality of parents are continued in the character of the child and cause his internal story of suffering."

In this little paper we did not discuss the psychoanalytic discoveries concerning "the pure female type" who considers relationships with a man as an ideal. Nor did we discuss "the mother type" who considers the child as the highest level of development in a relationship. Nor did we deal with the psychoanalytic experience and the special deviations in love and marriage that are experienced by well-educated, academic, and professionally independent women. These difficult topics require separate consideration.

The Importance of the Family for the Fate of the Individual (1923)

In the last two years of her life, Hug-Hellmuth published two lengthy papers concerned with psychoanalytic thinking about the functioning of families. Initially, she was concerned about how families exerted their influence on the individual. This paper, the first of the two, was published in the *Zeitschrift für Sexualwissenschaft* 9:321-34, as "Die Bedeutung der Familie für das Schicksal des Einzelnen."

Even if we had observed and understood life correctly, within the soul of the infant, with all of its complexities, something would have been lacking. Even if we had understood the infantile soul with its intellectual, affective, and characterological aspects of its development, it would not have been enough. It was not until the advent of psychoanalytic research that the complex phenomena of the development of infantile life was understood. It was only then that phenomena of infantile life could be traced back to depths of mental functioning that had never been reached before. The hostile psychologist rejected the clarifications of Freud and his followers, because of their own emotional bias. However, psychoanalysts took the opportunity offered by the highly critical arguments and sharpened their observations of psychic life. Their observation of the phenomena of psychic life deep under the surface was improved. It is because of the association with the in-depth work of psychoanalysis that during the last decade general psychology and youth research have begun to pay attention to infantile sexuality. Research on questions that had been simply ignored previously, or strongly denied, or silently passed by, are now dealt with intensively in many papers as if these topics have been a long-standing and acceptable interest. At this time, only the time of onset of infantile sexuality and the manner of its expression cause some anxiety and caution about psychologists. Psychologists do not like to assume that masturbation is exercised by nearly all children at some point in their life. They seem no longer to object to the existence of early erotic feelings in children. However, one still feels that they tend to view these perceptions as a symptom of precocity. Therefore, in doing so, they reject the central point of Freud's theory. The acknowledgment of the very important consequences of this normal phenomenon for the fate of the individual is avoided. The erotic feelings of the child taunt his parents with their strong ambivalence expressed in love and hate. Love and hate are shared in the appreciation of father and mother. This is recognized in boys and girls in their earliest years. It is limited by the immediate influence of education. Further, it is limited secondarily by hope. It is later directed differently when it seems to become totally forgotten like other phenomena of early childhood that are not thought to be important for later stages of development. However, because the small child is an affective being, an emotional person, these primitive feelings do not just disappear without trace. They remain to form the basis for the later development of affect and character. Psychoanalysis succeeded in proving this connection from early infantile affect to later adult affect and character. The connection between affect as an infant and affect in character as an adult has always had an instinctive expression in the sayings of one culture through the generations, the words used in our language, in fairy tales, and in our myths.

The spoiled "single child," the youngest and the favorite child only feel comfortable in the lap of the family because only here do they find the incredible overestimation of their ego. That is reflected in the external world by sometimes calling them *nesthäkchen*, (that is, "hooked up to the nest"), and, indeed, those children are so much anchored in the narrow environment of their home that they can hardly acquire an adequate attitude toward their environment at large. Extreme in their demands for love, they always feel set back in school, and their narcissistic overestimation of their ego makes it impossible for them to adapt to their peers. They are longing for friendships but because they claim their friend exclusively for themselves and want to be the center of attention at any time, their desire for a faithful companion remains unsatisfied. Those children and adolescents often acquire the friend that reality denies only in daydreams and fantasies. They withdraw into a world of fantasy that leads other people to the premature conclusion that they are pathologic liars, since these people lack the key for understanding their particular world, As adults, these people who are alienated from reality still look for the recreation of their original home where they had been the unquestioned center of attention and finally become isolated and awkward since they are disappointed by reality. A similar type, appropriately described as *Muttersoehnchen*, that is, "mother's little son," is represented by the child that hangs on to mother's skirt for all his life and has grown up in an unfree and dependent position, always needing the motherly caring woman, who spoils him, protects him from every rough experience, and even provides for him with her own work. Hebbel's life was formed from such immortal memories of childhood, and they also explain why others die without getting married and again others go restlessly from one woman to another. They all are caught in a futile search for the mother model in every woman. Ongoing attachment of the boy to his mother can also lead the man with a corresponding constitution into homosexuality. Sadger was able to prove in a great number of analyses of homosexuals that those men in their desire for young lovers are looking for the mother figure they had as little children, equipped with the male genital. Thus the homosexual is not desiring a man but the manly dreamed woman of his childhood. The fact that such boys are called *muttre* has its good reason in the obvious erotic attitude and relationship between mother and son. On both sides the feelings are not free of unconsciously libidinal characteristics, which are lacking in the relationship between mother and daughter of normal sexual disposition, but are similarly found in the relationship between father and daughter.

The typical attitude of the little child toward his parent is approximately the following: after a short, extremely happy period in which the child experiences auto-erotic self-sufficiency, independent from the external world, he gives up his initial rejection of the environment as a disturbing factor of his happy existence and turns initially toward the care person who helpfully meets his needs and helplessness. The love that originally was exclusively directed to the own ego has to accept the split. Giving up the self as the only object of love in favor of another object is the first cultural accomplishment of the young human being. Once he has successfully found his object, he soon takes a further step. The person's first love is regularly the caretaker of the child, normally the mother. She herself teaches the child to accept and integrate another human being, the father, into his affective life. He finally is followed by the other members of the household, toys, animals, and finally also strangers, if they meet the child with love. The obviously narcissistic quality of the infantile feelings for others later determines the choice of objects during puberty and adult life. Those who never overcome the early infantile stage of purely narcissistic feelings do not know how to spend their wealth of love and tenderness, they cannot answer the love of others and are never free to simply give.

At an early age we can observe that the little boy in his feelings for father and mother differs significantly from the little girl. Already the three- and four-year-old attempts to protect and rescue the mother whom he tenderly and jealously loves. He claims her for himself and tries repeatedly to surprise her while dressing and during other intimate acts. He does not like to see his father's intimacy with her. He tries to interfere as best he can and from time to time enjoys a longer absence of his father, whom he really admires and envies because of his size and power. At those times he wants to sleep in father's bed at his mother's side and in his fantasies is looking forward to a time when father will be dead and he is able to marry his mother. Those daydreams that are rarely lacking in the early experiences of little boys are later suppressed by moral pressures and quite frequently reappear during puberty as spells of violent rebellion against the fatherly and every other authority, as well as in a romantic crush on a mature woman. But also quite frequently the longing for the mother, unconsciously assumed to be prohibited, is suppressed and turned into rude behavior toward her and the female sex in general. The sexual arrogance of the growing male despises women because of the assumed inferiority of the anatomical difference. This remains the only way to cope with the incest taboo during this time of growing desire.

The psychic life of the girl develops accordingly but in opposite directions. She cannot help but have a certain hostility toward the mother whom she also loves at the same time, and she needs the adored father with deeply felt love. This bond to the father, and the "male complex" of the woman that is based on the early infantile disappointment about the recognized sex difference, determine the fate of the girl. The bonds to the father explain why young girls frequently choose older men as love objects and why the eroticism of women is so often quite formal and rigid. Because of the fixation to the father, we also understand why popular girls finally live unmarried or choose quite late a partner in a more rational decision, when they cannot cope with their sexual drive any longer. This is similar to their childhood dream to replace mother after her death as father's partner; a dream, that was later suppressed from conscious recognition. Later the way into a legitimate marriage is blocked by the same attitude. The unconscious incestuous attachment of the child to her father is so strong that she loves in any partner only her father, to whom our moral codes prohibit. The only choice for those girls is between the total renunciation of fulfillment and a crossing of social barriers that ends in eternal self-accusation. As for the former, the woman can never break out of her obedience to the father who himself prohibited the unconscious libidinal striving of his blossoming daughter; as for the later, the woman finds the strong bond which was formed by her childhood experiences with the father without being able to free herself. Furthermore, the woman who crosses the social barrier finds herself displaced when she becomes a mother and also exposes a new human being to contempt because a merciless and stupid moral code will later ostracize both the mother and the child who was born out of wedlock.

Innumerable individual fates can be explained because of the attitude of the family. Because of an excess of motherly or fatherly love that the child reacts to in a truly narcissistic manner, both the son as well as the daughter develop differently in their affect and later often lack to take part in the experience and enjoyment of a healthy erotic life. Finally, they grow old in isolation because they always looked for the inaccessible father or mother in all their love objects. We find numerous examples in the psychoanalytic literature; I will only name Jung's "The Importance of the Father for the Fate of the Individual," Friedjung's numerous publications on the "nervous" child, Sadger's "On the Psychology of the Only and Favorite Child," and my own publication "Psychoanalytic Findings about Women."

In this paper I am not going to talk about the importance of an excess of love on the fate of the child, but would like to have a look at those cases that lack affectionate love during their early youth and maturation. These are the frequent and unwanted later children in families who already have a number of siblings; those who stem from unhappy marriages and who are born because the sexual union of the parents has become a pure duty; stepchildren and orphans for whom the dead parent was replaced by a strange person through remarriage, or those who now spend their days in an orphanage or with relatives after a short period of a more or less happy family life; children from split marriages who have been transferred into a strange household by a remarriage; adopted children and children found on the street; and finally, the child born out of wedlock and fatherless, who has to bear the worst burden in our society.

It is not correct to say that all those children spend their early days without being loved; but they all have in common that at some point a disappointment of their love overcomes them like a catastrophe because of the real or imagined loss of father or mother. Those who previously have experienced the support of tender care suffer most from the recognition that they are irreversibly thrown out of the heaven of their early years. Daily observation shows us that they develop differently because of the tragic fate of their mother. Not because of a lack of love, just the contrary; because the mother, especially if abandoned by her own partner, focuses all her love that previously was split between her partner and the child, on the child. Such a child now experiences an excess of love that is especially hurtful for the boy. For the superficial observer, this child resembles strongly a single child, with whom he quite often shares certain characteristics like prematurity, demandingness, and a straightforward and power-conscious attitude. But normally his development takes quite a different direction, because he lacks the quiet atmosphere of a secure, self-sufficient family life, and because sooner or later learns the isolated position that society has defined for him and his mother. He lacks his father's name which he eventually recognizes when he goes to school and he cannot rely on his father in his fights with others, a father who knows and can do everything. His insisting questions that the mother feels to be cautious make her use excuses and lies. And the child, especially a son, will never forgive her later for her dishonesty. It becomes the reason, when he has to be told the truth, for him to call her a whore. We know from analysis of children and adults how brutal sexual enlightenment by peers and servants, or the early observation of sexual scenes, often demean the parents for the child because he cannot bring this unfaithfully acquired and secret knowledge into concordance with the sacred figures of father and mother. For the child who was born out of wedlock, this knowledge has almost tragic consequences, since the mother cannot even legitimize herself because of the sanctions of church and society. Quite frequently this new knowledge of the truth injures the whole personality of the child. Even if he already up to this point hasn't been easy to handle because of the maternal adoration, he suddenly becomes hard to educate and resents any educational influence, fails academically, and develops a concerning tendency toward totally immoral behavior. It looks like he wants to take revenge at a society that always make him feel his isolation by putting himself outside its norms. In addition, the boy now turns his hostility that is normally paired with infantile love for the father vehemently towards the environment. Those tendencies especially occur during the puberty of fatherless boys, and they ask for a strong and at the same time endlessly patient hand to prevent those who are alienated from themselves and society from deviation and suicide. Even under normal circumstances the boy during puberty tends toward rebellion against any authority—i.e., basically against the father—and has to fight serious struggles around moral and religious questions and for an independent view of the world. A growing number of adolescents ask, with stubborn negativism toward life, "Why was I born by my parents into this world? I did not ask them to do it." This will be unconsciously turned by those children against the mother, even if they consciously make the father responsible for their unwanted existence. Similarly, the accusation that, according to Freud, every girl sometimes makes toward her mother, "Why did she give me birth as a girl?" will regularly turn later, according to my own observation, against the father, who because of confusing knowledge about sexuality in adolescence, is thought to be the only one who is sexually active and thus can determine the sex. But the accusations of the illegitimate child are not always primarily directed against the mother, but they are reflected in his attitude toward the female sex in general in boys, and to the male sex in girls. The young person either avoids men in general or meets them with a cautious cynicism. Every girl is available to him, he despises the woman, at the same time feels a strong desire for her but secretly only dreams about a legitimate relationship with a single woman. In contrast to his father who abandoned his mother, he intends to lead an orderly family life. His hatred is consciously directed from the mother to the father to be able to adore something in her, especially after she has died. This attitude can later be found quite frequently in girls because of their identification with their mother, while the same attitude in boys seems to be the result of a strong sublimation. His still existing hatred is then often directed against female relatives. The relationship of the illegitimately born girl with the mother, with the father, and the male sex in general is characterized by simultaneous defense and desire to suffer a similar fate as her mother. She feels sorry for her mother as soon as she has suppressed her feeling of contempt that she shares with society, she sees in her the innocent victim of a rapist, and she meets every man with lecherous shyness or flirtatious boredom. In both cases she behaves according to the formula "I know the game, keep your distance." Later, the hesitation of many men is proven right to marry a girl of illegitimate descendants and make her the mother of their children. Not because the mother did something wrong during the education of her daughter, but the daughter, because of unconscious identification with the mother, follows her in a similar way.

We do not know anything about the psychic life of man in the prenatal intra-uterine state, but I think one can call it a disposition for hesitation, when children, who were conceived unwillingly have been born reluctantly after a pregnancy that was conceived as an unwelcome burden, present themselves quite frequently with a weak, sickly constitution and senile appearance, and express remarkable irritability early in their first weeks of life, with an accompanying lack of normal infantile vitality. Those unwanted children, regularly born late into an already existing family, who disturb the family habits by their unanticipated appearance, instinctively feel their ambivalent acceptance even if they are most carefully looked after. At least they tend from an early age to withdraw whenever they are defeated in their struggle for omnipotence, and they early develop a sullen, closed personality at a time that is normally characterized by uninhibited joy, happiness, and the prevailing expectation of receiving love wherever they are. A number of them later feel the irresistible urge to run away. Quite different from other runaways who flee an educational institution or foster home only to return to the lap of the family, these children are searching elsewhere for the love that they were refused at home. Those unsatisfied quite frequently follow the idea that they have to look for their true parents who previously had given them up for adoption, and this fantasy feeds into their urge to repeatedly run away from home. They are the incorrigible tramps who never settle down as adults, never keep a job or a profession, and quite a number of them later suffer a miserable death. Abandoned children and foster children who lack the love of early days also belong to this group. The latter often expect that when they are accepted into a well-situated family, the tenderness and enthusiasm with which they were greeted will last eternally and will grant them a special position. The disappointment that is caused by the quiet run of everyday life makes them often long painfully for their earlier family. If their biological parents are still alive, they accuse them of an unloving attitude; that is, this really means that they hoped to find better parents in the new home, namely, those parents in their fantasies of early childhood. The dependent child, finally, has never experienced the tender love of his mother that is so important for the development of human beings, and his acceptance by strange people is normally executed quite soberly. He grows up as a really unloved and unwanted intruder and he never knows who his parents were. He belongs to nobody and seriously suffers the lack of a home. Like nearly everybody who was unloved in his youth, he later fails to establish a loving relationship himself. He cannot evoke love in others since he himself as a child was never loved and never taught to love himself. Only one thing has remained from his deficient time, the excessive longing for real love. This excessive desire does not allow him to reach the average. What I said about the catastrophic disappointment of the development of a young soul also applies to early orphans. Even if the orphan is transferred from a less than ideal home by the death of one or even both parents into a much more favorable environment, the disturbed and confused soul does not easily acquire a new balance within this totally different environment. Even the most efficient care in an orphan home or an educational institution does not recreate the atmosphere of tenderness that characterizes even the most sober home with its unconscious eroticism. He can only feel really happy, that is, fulfilled in his libidinal needs, if a lucky fate gives him a father or mother who herself really experiences in this child a satisfaction of their own infantile ideal. This ongoing search for tenderness by this lonely infantile soul is the main reason for the romantic attachment of an orphan to educators or teachers of both sexes. If a child, after the death of passionately loved parents whose favorite he was, is raised by a relative, even the greatest affection proves to be unsatisfactory for the needy soul of the orphan. Here two circumstances have the utmost importance. A serious illness of father or mother, which normally results in a certain neglect of the child's soul, makes care for the child most important. After a short or long period of painful loneliness, he subtly sees himself as the center of attention and he hopes to defend this position that is most welcome for his narcissism. But he soon experiences that the people who provided him with a home don't want to be disturbed by him in their own interests, that they accepted him in their circle but don't want to make him its center. This disappointment is sufficient to let the child try to obtain by force and bad behavior what he could not get by a more pleasant attitude. Some bad roots that would have been suppressed in a normal home by the routine of everyday life are not developed because of the everlasting feeling of rejection and lack of love. Since his predominant features tend to lead into a concerning characterological development, this young lonely person tries to obtain by force a degree of attention and concern from his environment that represents only a weak compensation for the loss of the love of his parents. It is not ingratitude that turns him into an unwelcome companion who is difficult to cope with, but it is the result of an unconscious longing for father or mother.

The abandoned child, the early orphan, the illegitimate child, they all lack what Aichhorn saw in every dissocial child, "the quiet point." They all suffer from a disturbance within their limited environment while they are children, a disturbance of society when body and soul start to mature. This sociability always is the result of a lack and an excessive desire for love; during their restless search for a familial soul, they finally lose their ability to love themselves, the worst fate that can happen to man.

I have described the children of conflicts and split marriages as another group for which the psychic development is dominated by the restricting influence of the family constellation. Those are the cases which are the most hopeless for psychoanalysis. Among them the worst again are those following the type "my child, your child, our child." Both parents have a child from a previous marriage and now have together a third one. The well-known hostility of the older child toward a small intruder will cause worse intimidation of siblings in these families because of the instinctive and therefore unchangeable dislike for the "strange" parent. After separation of his parents, especially, the single child expects that from now on the love of the parent of the other sex will focus on him without any split, and he is disappointed and embittered when he observes his parent's remarriage. Repeatedly I have made the observation that hatred is more strongly directed toward the "new" mother than the "new" father, although one would have expected that if the woman already had a son and the man a daughter that they bring into their second marriage, the hatred of the girl would be directed toward the new mother and that of the boy toward the new father. In reality, the accusations are almost always directed toward the woman in the household, regardless of whether she is the biological mother or the stepmother who is only resentfully accepted as an aunt, especially by the girls. Nearly all of the children of split marriages have a common feature: a nearly pathologic longing for the lost parent. This parent becomes hopelessly overestimated, is perceived as a victim and made an idol, which rarely reflects the true personality. This exaggerated longing for the far, unreachable father or mother figure also represents an accusation against the other parent who is still around. This becomes especially clear in children who lost father or mother by death and who have now to live with a stepmother or a stepfather. If the remaining parent stays unmarried, the memories of the dead parent disappear, sometimes surprisingly fast. They are immediately reactivated whenever real or only fantasized marriage plans of the father or mother evoke the fear of losing the loved person to a stranger. The addition of step-siblings increases the difficulty of adapting to the new family. The child takes revenge on the new siblings for the assumed lack of love or unfaithfulness of the father or the mother toward the dead partner with whom the orphan identifies himself. Sibling rivalry in this situation is clearly a secondary phenomenon that is evoked by the disappointment by father or mother.

The particular pressure that is put on a child by a dysfunctional marriage explains even for nonprofessionals that those young souls lose a good deal of their characteristic cheerfulness and naivety. One regularly assumes that the child suffers from the more or less obvious disagreements and the increasing split between the parents when he has to take sides. One of them then acquires an overtly hostile attitude toward the other. This behavior is normally understood as being caused by the passion and directness of the child's soul and by his intellect being one sort of agent-provocateur. Because the erotic bond of the child to father and mother is less well known and recognized, his behavior is only partly understood. The child does not suffer from the disagreement of his parents because he needs a harmonious living together, but because the marriage still remains preserved despite failure since the loving parents don't leave the marriage and live solely for and with the child. The child cannot cope with the undecided struggle, not among his peers where fists make the decision, and not among those adults to whom he belongs. Taking sides means for him, as for adults, to try to help win the struggle, actively or by supportive words. He always intends a definite split of the fighting parties. When a child witnesses day by day the maternal disagreement, the real danger lies in the fact that this perception of marital differences feeds into his fantasy of possessing one parent exclusively for himself by alienation of the other partner. The child withdraws into fantasies, consciously thinking about ways to preserve the cohesiveness and harmony of the family, but unconsciously striving to fulfill the unconscious incestuous wishes. Because at the time of those experiences the incest taboo has already erected a solid barrier between permission and inhibition, the young soul is tortured by a nagging feeling of guilt because of his strong passion for the one and the hatred that might culminate in deadly wishes for the other parent. This guilt feeling is also located in the unconscious, but it sends messages to the surface and makes the child shy, anxious, and pigheaded and spoils the entire later life. And if father and mother accuse the other partner rightly or wrongly of unfaithfulness, the young person will perceive every affectionate love as something prohibited or will identify only secret experience with an assumed happiness, siding with the accused parent. Thus the child does not suffer under dysfunctional marriage because he doesn't succeed in preserving a harmonious life of his first love object, but because the ongoing disagreement destroys the last bond of their common life, the daily routine. Every child, after he has overcome the first surprise about the differences, would probably try to feed into them to gain the indisputable and sole possession of the unconsciously, sexually desired parent. The analyses of children who grew up under such circumstances prove the described mechanisms with utmost clarity.

It is impossible to acknowledge the importance of the parents for the psychic development of the child without paying attention to the influences of the siblings or the lack of siblings. The observation teaches us that for a single child to grow up without siblings results in certain characteristics. This has frequently been described and one is concerned if, because of the exclusive experience with adults, the child is lacking part of the naive happiness that can only be found in exchange with other children. An astute observer can soon prove that life among siblings does not proceed in a unanimously harmonious fashion as the adults would wish and expect, but that hostilities and intimidations among siblings are the rule. They start out with the unwanted arrival of another brother or sister who questions the omnipotence of the older child. The competition for the love of father and mother soon becomes a mutual one. The younger child envies the older because of his privileges and he himself is suspiciously observed in his role as the small one. During this time of envious observation of real or imagined preferences, characteristic traits form that do not fit with the personality profile of the adult—that is, we see highly educated and distinguished people express shortsighted envy for a more favorable person, and this might disturb our picture of this personality if we did not know about its infantile sources. This person is still stuck with his childhood. He regresses unconsciously back to the time when he could hardly cope with the preference of his brother or sister by his father, mother, or another loved person. Adulthood is also positively influenced by the ambivalent relationship between siblings. It happens quite frequently that brother and sister who were attached during childhood with exaggerated tenderness—the older sister becoming a second mother of the brother several years her junior, or the older brother presenting a younger and therefore much closer imitation of the father—miss the point when they should leave the idol of their childhood for somebody else. Bound to the loved companions of their early years, they can never decide on a marriage, a fate, frequently and movingly described by Ernst Zahn in his novels. Most often twins are the victims of such unbreakable bonds of affection. As children they lived a life that could not be intruded upon by anyone, and this becomes an example for their whole life.

One would assume that in a family with a number of children the lives of the children would be more simple and less endangered and that especially the middle child would escape the hurtful experiences of the first child as well as the younger child. Reality opposes such optimistic expectations. The middle child has also his specific sufferings. Sometimes being big, sometimes small, according to the moods of the adults, he lacks firm ground. He does not have the privileges of either the oldest or the youngest child, and he just runs along. The position of the child whose siblings are of the same sex and not much different in age seems to be most serious, while a girl between two brothers often matures quite favorably, by developing both her female qualities toward the domination of the older brother, as well as her motherly qualities toward the younger. A boy between two sisters does not suffer severely from the fate of the middle child because the greater privileges characteristic of his sex help him soon to overcome even his older sister in her rights.

"To compare the existence and the results of childhood, one has to add some relationship with an aunt or grandaunt," Goltz writes in his *Buch der Kinderheit,* or *Book of Childhood.* We also would like to remember how Selma Lagerlöf complained about the death of her grandmother as the turning point in her infantile existence, when together with her grandmother's coffin the fairy tales were carried away from her home. She had been the tireless narrator to whom the children always listened with attention. The group of people who impress the child's soul irreversibly has to be enlarged by grandparents and aunts. The influence of the latter is lasting, if she lives in the family. This type of family used to be more common. In those families the aunt was the good soul of the home. Such a real aunt was a second mother; full of love, tenderness, always calming and balancing, she gives all the unused treasure of her heart to the children of her sister or her brother. Frequently, her favorite prefers her—and she always has a favorite—for his own mother. Since affectionate feelings for her, unlike the deep-rooted feelings for the parent, are less ambivalent, she protects the child unconsciously from disastrous attachment to the parents. The grandparents incorporate for the child the disappeared good old days they always consider in high spirits. There is always a Christmas atmosphere around them. There is no better place for the infantile narcissism to be admired and spoiled than in the grandparents' quiet home. And they experience in their grandchildren—they again each have a favorite—only the bright side of giving and receiving love because the shadows of education and responsibility are past them. Children acknowledge their grandfather and grandmother as the moderate negotiators in situations when they fear their parents. They represent the advocates whom the child often needs in his drive-dominated activities. And since the mother also acquires normally a soothing and compromising role, it seems to be easy to understand that grandparents are seen by the children as some sort of mother substitute. Psychoanalysis teaches us that a similar inferiority complex against the female sex, which is conscious in boys and unconscious in girls, also characterizes the relationship with the grandparents despite all affection and love. This results from the recognition of physical or mental inadequacies because of their age and because of the rarely conscious idea that the sexual secret that is the focus of infantile thoughts and feelings has lost its attraction for those aged people. For a child, it is incompatible with the role of a grandfather to remain after the death of the grandmother or even to have a child in this new marriage. It is more natural for the infantile soul to identify aging with death rather than with new life. The dying of the grandfather and grandmother confronts them for the first time with the secret of dying, and accordingly the familiar figure of those loved ones becomes the symbol of death for the child, as God often has grandfather's features in the child's fantasy. The children's faith and the first metaphysical concepts are connected to those figures who are separate from the child by two generations but are still felt to be very close because of the presence of their view of the world. The family exists in which the child grows, and the experience of those early years will leave its traces and the young soul of the individual is formed under these influences.

The Libidinal Structure of Family Life (1924)

"Die libidinöse Struktur des Familienlebens" was Hug-Hellmuth's second and last paper in the last two years of her life on the functioning of the family from a psychoanalytic viewpoint. Compared to "The Importance of the Family for the Fate of the Individual," it suggests that she was less concerned about the influence of the family on the individual, realizing how interdependent the forces of family dynamics were. These two papers marked an important step in Hug-Hellmuth's theoretical thinking. In effect, she opened a completely different perspective for the psychoanalytic understanding of the family.

The fact that man begins his extra-uterine life with a cry and then basically just sleeps except for some interactions for feeding, can be seen psychologically as a rejection of his new surroundings only. Obviously the child prefers the stable and moist warmth, the quiet darkness and rhythmical movements of the womb—to which he had been accustomed to for so many months—to the bright, noisy, and rough outside with its dry and every-changing atmosphere. If we are entitled to say anything about the feelings of the newborn, then he would fight against his environment. The infant is fully happy only when he is asleep or when he is feeding. Anything else in his surroundings is just an irritation to him during his early life. The drive for survival of every normal being tries to avoid a state of ongoing discomfort. His healthy instinct leads him toward a satisfaction of his drives that were given to him by nature as a valuable gift. Proper rearing satisfies his longing for food, the most important ego drive during this phase of life. The mother's breast offers milk, the hand which caresses and cleans the child unconsciously offers sexual gratification to a partial degree. Without intention, the caregiver shows the places that are able to evoke primarily sexual feelings because of their high sensitivity. Through nursing the infant learns to suck: cleaning procedures result in a feeling of tickling of certain parts of the body where mucous membranes joins the mouth, the genitals, and the anus. He discovers that parts of his body are the source of sexual pleasure. He experiences the auto-erotic period as one of happiest self-sufficiency. During this time of animal-like well-being, the infant does not yet know the difference between his small body and the world. Only through pain does he experience his body as a comprehensive whole, as his own self. His first laugh is now focused toward this self. Thus the auto-erotic stage is followed by a stage of narcissism or self-love.

The helplessness and need of the infant, which are met by the kindness of the nurse, quickly modify his perception of the world. He recognizes that his discomfort is taken care of and changed into relief by a particular person. This person becomes the first recipient of his love, which was directly only toward his own self before. The first outside love object for the child is his nurse, generally his mother. Discovering his mother as his first love object is the first cultural deed of mankind by which he learns to relate affectionately to his own kind. This first choice is clearly narcissistic-egoistic, according to the rule "He who loves me and gives me pleasure, I will love in return." This is a self-love that is projected to the outside. These emotional ties between mother and child determine the child's later erotic feelings. The mother is the child's first teacher in the subject of love. Here, destiny is formed for the "only," as well as the "undesired" child. According to these first experiences, both are insatiable for love. However, the only child can perhaps draw from his own resources, while the undesired child can respond to the desired overwhelming amount of love only with his own modest and average feelings. In this surplus of love and lack of love lie the explanations for the various ways to reach and select their love objects.

Soon the infant will include a second person, his father, in his small repertoire of loved ones. In a normal family the mother will play the role of mediator. Quickly the other members will follow, such as family, toys, and animals, and last are the strangers and friends who meet the child with affection and resemble known and trusted family members. According to Freud, the child's first positive affection is accompanied by an identification with a loved object. This theory fits well into the assumed estimation of foreign objects in the auto-erotic stage. Certainly the differences between himself and the outer world were not known to the infant in the beginning. The mother's breast and his little fingers and toes were equally accessible sources of delight. With sucking motions he tried to incorporate one as well as the other. This tendency will be repeated in the process of identification. What the infant enjoys he will incorporate into himself, and because reality forces him to relinquish this desire, he has to go the opposite way by trying to become part of the loved person instead, as if the other were his second self. The process of identification with a love object plays an important role in the life of older children especially during adolescence. There would be no friendships or youth organizations such as Scouts or Girl Guides without it.

The sexual tendencies of the child dictate the manner by which feelings are fulfilled—exhibitionism, sadism, masochism, the desire to touch, etc. The direct influences of upbringing and the indirect influences of cultural demands restrain the libidinal movements—especially toward parents, sisters, and brothers—as undesirable in our society. Yet the undestroyable traces of the early homosexual, neurotic feelings for the father and mother are the foundation for development of character and temperament. Analytical research done on the mental life of homosexual men has convincingly shown that, if there was a constant tie between the boy and the mother, this later became instrumental on the basis of a constitutional disposition. Such men desire very young male sexual partners, namely, a mother figure that was given masculine genitals by the fantasy of the little child. The homosexual does not desire a man, but the "phallic woman" of his early childhood. Thus a close relationship to the father in infancy protects the child from staying linked too closely to the mother. Integrating the father figure in his psychic life is the second cultural task that becomes very important to the girl for her major role in life as a wife.

Once social and ethical values, such as feelings toward others, pity, and gratitude, have been established and recognized, the narcissistic connotation of feelings, inherent in all children, is somewhat reduced. However, unconsciously it is still influential in choosing a partner, a love object during puberty as well as during maturity.

Uncompromised observation of the affective relationship between child and parents reveal qualities that are not freely admitted. The relationships between mother and son, father and daughter have clear erotic connotations. These are even found in the normal relationship between mother and daughter and father and son. The sweet tenderness between the small boy and the mother is unconsciously well understood by her. The boy feels he is her knight in shining armor, her protector and lover, her "little man." Although he admires his father for his size and strength, he sees him as a dangerous rival. His feelings for him are ambivalent, two-faced in love and hatred. At times he would love to be free of him. He would have his mother all to himself; he could sleep in her bed; he could even marry her, if the father were only dead and he could take the father's place in the house. Therefore it is understandable that he enjoys his absence, at times even wishes his father to be dead, not having mature notions of death yet. The small boy behaves like the unhappy man in the legend of Oedipus Rex who killed his father and married his mother. His innocent happiness in his fantasies is short-lived. Through education, he soon is filled with guilt about his primitive incestuous desires. These incestuous feelings for his mother and the hatred for his father form the content of the Oedipus complex. The Oedipus complex and the castration complex are both experienced between the ages of three and six. Here, the father again acquires the role of the avenger because of the child's sexual involvement in masturbation and exhibitionism.

He feels that his mother is not accessible anymore, even rejecting. He notices the special secret between mother and father in their bedroom that he often shares with them. Furthermore, any erotic scenes he may witness may drive him to the idea of wanting different parents, because his own parents now frequently challenge his feelings of grandiosity. He would love to have a mother who would fulfill his secret desires and a father who would not be in his way when he achieves his desires. His fantasies will provide him with "true" parents, who are richer, nicer, and more elegant than those two people he calls "father" and "mother." In the fantasized family story that has been invoked by his incestuous desires and his guilt feelings, he sees himself as the "estranged" boy. He sees himself as searching later for his true parents under difficult circumstances and he sees them as rescuing him from his existing imprisonment. In addition, the girl takes revenge for the disappointments by putting the mystifying father into an erotic position where her mother can only jealously watch them.

Sooner or later, the infantile love and incestuous desire for the parenting figure of the other sex will become unconscious through education and change into fondness—only to be awakened once more at puberty with its dramatic changes of body and affect. However, the incest taboos are strongly established and not easily ignored. Yet behind all masked behaviors, that is, unrealistic affections or extreme rudeness against everything feminine, behind the opposition against any authority, especially that of father, or behind oversensitivity among some girls, lie these hidden feelings. The healthy soul finds an escape from these internal fights. It loosens the ties to its first love objects, its parents. They will now serve as role models during puberty when the choice comes for new love objects of the opposite sex. In the case of adolescents who could not fully part from their father or mother, the young man will look for an older woman and the young girl will prefer an older man. Where the individual could not free himself of his infantile love objects at all, he stays indecisive in his choice, and all his erotic feelings will drain away. They have become victims of a fixation to their childhood idols.

Children who experience a normal and warm family life that is free of an unhealthy spoiling atmosphere, will emerge undamaged from their childhood dreams and fantasy world. Life will become tragic for those who grow up in a family with serious ongoing conflicts. The illegitimate child soon feels his special position into a cruel society has cast him and his mother. At last when school begins he realizes what it means not to know his father's name when the other children assure him of the humiliating truth that his embarrassed mother could not tell him. The boy's reaction is to unconsciously detest his mother and to secretly see her as a prostitute. Later, in his eyes all other women are prostitutes too. Because of his hatred for women, he will become a "lady killer" for whom all women are available, or he will simply hate women. The illegitimate girl, as soon as she has overcome conventional discriminations, sees in her mother a martyr of love, abandoned by her husband. Such girls identify with their mothers and would like to take revenge by hurting men, or they are afraid of men, carefully avoiding them as the root of evil. These illegitimate boys and girls lack the early attachment to their fathers because it was destroyed by premature rejection. The rough reality of their parents' sexual life is always difficult for children to bear, although it may be sanctioned by society and the church. It is far more difficult for illegitimate children to understand, and the awareness hurts as frost does in a spring night. Their strength is broken even before they become aware. Therefore, it is understandable that the illegitimate child is less able to resist normal temptations compared to a child growing up in the security of a family. His delinquency is an unconscious protest against the unfairness and unkindness of society. The "fatherless" child places himself outside the normal circle, exactly where society has placed his mother. A stepchild suffers similarly, as he feels that he has lost his remaining parent when the new marriage takes place. If this happens to a boy who has lost his mother, he often acquires "feminine" feelings for his father. He identifies with his mother out of love for his father. The little boy behaves like a wife. His fantasies develop like those of a little girl with unconscious desires. He would like to be his father's wife and to have a child with him. With the help of these feminine feelings he tries to remove his stepmother from her role as a lover. In his identification with his dead mother, he wants to rejoin her with his father.

Children, procreated without love, unwanted to be born, lacking the quiet atmosphere of a harmonic marriage of their parents, suffering in the middle of a fight after the parents' separation, being an early orphan, whose relatives can't accommodate him, or being abandoned, living in an institution or with children, are never loved or are longing for tenderness. They tend to live in a world of fantasy with their family story at its core.

We also have to consider the child's affective relationships with the other members of the family to understand their importance for the development of the child's soul. It makes a difference whether a child grows up as an "only" child or as one of many siblings. The differences in years or sex as well as advantages or disadvantages and the number of children have a great influence on children's relationship toward one another. Often the child suffers more from his siblings' advantages than from his own disadvantages. The relationship of siblings is not always correct or right at all. Often they show the unfriendly behaviors of the firstborn towards the new arrival, and as Freud stated, "Every child feels like the firstborn toward the next arrival." He rightly considers the newborn as a threat to his present power. All the affection he shows toward the younger one is mainly the product of childish imitation and of the influence of the family that tries to convince him of the advantages of having a younger sibling. The unfriendly behavior is often also the product of the surroundings, as if a kind of living toy had been provided which he could oppress. The reality is rather disappointing, as the adults carefully watch his approach and eventually defend the newborn. Furthermore, he has to share their love and finds himself removed from the center of attention. This is shown by hatred in speech and behaviors. The older the child, the better he can hide his true feelings. Sometimes he succeeds in totally suppressing his hostile attitude. Especially girls often show a kind of motherly love toward the newborn. The original jealousy breaks out infrequently in the form of harsh punishments imposed on the younger sibling, especially around the issue of toilet training or other behaviors.

The younger child has mixed feelings toward the older siblings. The younger child is jealous simply because of the real or assumed rights coming with the seniority of the older sibling. In spite of this jealousy, brothers and sisters who are only slightly different in age are the preferred comrades for all allowed or prohibited games. Especially the latter cause a strong feeling of cohesiveness. There is a great bond between the siblings that are only a few years apart. A sister who is only a few years older is like a mother to the younger sibling because she has more understanding toward certain pleasures than the mother. At the time of engagement or marriage of the older sister, the younger will identify with her sister's choice and fall in love with the same person, or in contrast detest the choice of her sister with hateful criticism. An engagement or marriage in the house is always very stimulating for the fantasy of the "little" one.

The "big brother" in a family, despite of all the hostility that occurs, is a role model for all the personality characteristics the younger sibling still lacks. When the older one has difficulties with his father, this brings him closer to the younger brother. To the younger sister he can become an image for her erotic feelings toward her father. Unconsciously she will hold on to these feelings, even when she is grown up. Her choice for a love object will then most often be a younger man. If the ties between siblings are too strong, they will eventually prevent any further relationship. This often happens to twins. After a period of strong infantile jealousy, they get very close, with deep affection for one another. They will live like a couple apart from their peers. If one falls in love, the other will choose the same person as a love object and as a result they will both give up the relationship, or one of them becomes the platonic partner in his twin sibling's marriage, who has succeeded in becoming independent.

The assumption that the middle child can escape all these dangers must be doubted. Because this child has predecessors and successors, this double misfortune causes sufferings. The parents will consider him sometimes as a grown-up like the oldest child and at times as a baby like the youngest, according to their own comfort. The middle child seems to be just part of the crowd. He has lost the position of the newborn and everything that is excitingly "special." In the heart of a parent, an aunt, a grandfather or grandmother, he will survive easily any hatred and jealousy from the other siblings. The importance of erotic behaviors should not be underestimated. A special relationship with the grandparents sometimes evokes a strange tendency to lose oneself in the past and in memories. Such people often feel isolated from the present and only the past seems to be meaningful.

The ambivalence of feelings and the incestuous desires towards fathers and mothers are repressed into the unconscious, and the resulting feelings of guilt influence not only their capacity for erotic experiences. The development of the ego ideal happens within the attachment to the parents, and similarly the human being is formed following the demands of his ego. According to Freud, the first positive attitude of the child is accompanied by the identification with a love object. This understanding is complimented by the understanding of the auto-erotic value of the infantile body, the environment, and also the breast of the mother. The child identifies first with the mother and since he can't incorporate the mother, he has to become part of her. The identification with the father that probably follows soon is perhaps created by a dark feeling to ensure the possession of the mother by taking father's place. On the other hand, he identifies with the father by loving what mother loves. The sayings of the three- to six-year-old venture some assumptions about the unconscious activity of the young soul. The ego-ideal or "super-ego" of the child comes from this infantile identification with the parents, and his greatest desire is to be or to become what father and mother appear to be. However, the mother won't remain the desired model for long, because soon her sex will be considered as inferior. The dislike of women by the boys, the sex-envy ("penis envy") of girls, dethrones the mother as an ideal and only the father remains an idol. Because of the feelings toward his father during the earliest year, and because of later, strongly ambivalent feelings during puberty, the father ideal is not only that of a glowing, desirable model, but one of a power that must be feared and obeyed. From these feelings the critical part of the self, the conscience, is developed, constantly facing the real self versus the super-ego. So the owner of the super-ego learns how far he still is from optimal development.

The sensual aspect of the ties children have with their parents appears in a new light once they become fathers and mothers themselves. In their love for their child, the unconscious sexual undertones cannot be overlooked. If one has lost the mature partner through death or fate, the child frequently becomes a kind of erotic toy to the remaining parent. But even in happy marriages a father feels that the tenderness a mother shows toward her son cuts into his own right. The mother is equally jealous about her daughter receiving any generosity from her father, which in puberty is marked by into jealous overprotection. Although the mother often sees a competitor in her maturing daughter, it is the father who will cause difficulties when it comes to marriage. Because of his unconscious libidinal aspirations, he will restrain her from marriage by making her "independent" through education. The mother often frustrates any plans of marriage the son may have, especially if he is the "only" or the "special" one. Chained too closely to her, he sees the years of a potentially happy marriage go by and disappear. These children who are loved too much, are made too dependent on their parents, become lonely when they are old. They do not dream up a family story, they experience it in all its strength. This can be caused only by the narcissistic-egoistic love of others.

The correct assessment of erotic aspects and ambivalence within the relationship between child and parents can go wrong. Siblings and other family members help in understanding a number of mistakes and educational difficulties of childhood. Some examples may be given here. Eating disorders, bowel disorders, and disturbances of sleep (*pavor nocturnus*) can in many children be traced back to an insatiable demand for love. Poor grades, among other reasons, often derive from a stubbornness against the parents, or the need to be the center of attention. The grandiose expectations of parents lead to boastful lies, while being too strict with the child forces him to use white lies. Disobedience in the small child as well as in the school child and the characteristic rebellion in teenagers have the same roots: rejection or disappointment of their love, first experienced with father and mother, and reappearing in later life with other loved persons.

Epilogue

In this book we have presented everything we could find about Hug-Hellmuth. We have described her early life, her family and her work. Because much of her work remained untranslated and was not well known, we selected examples from her published papers, for translation and inclusion here. We have commented on some important points about Hug-Hellmuth as we discussed her and her work; and now we want to summarize our conclusions, and emphasize and clarify what in our view is most important.

What were Hug-Hellmuth's contributions to child psychoanalysis? This can be best answered by comparing her work with that of her apparent contemporaries, Anna Freud and Melanie Klein. In doing so, however, we shall find that their work really came later than Hug-Hellmuth's.

Hug-Hellmuth started to publish her psychoanalytic material in 1912, when Anna Freud was seventeen years of age and a high school student. She was several years away from her first tentative analytic work. Anna Freud probably first used analysis in 1923.[1,2] In 1912 Melanie Klein did not yet know of psychoanalysis. It was two years before she read any of Freud's works and possibly entered into psychoanalysis with Ferenczi.[3] So we can place Hug-Hellmuth's introduction to psychoanalysis at least seven years before Melanie Klein's. It is harder to place Anna Freud's introduction, as in a sense it was always around her.

It was not until 1927 that Anna Freud and Melanie Klein published their first important papers.[4] Anna Freud's first publication on the technique of child analysis did not appear until 1927 in German (1928 in English).

Anna Freud began to attend the meetings of the Vienna Psychoanalytic Society in 1919 as a guest; she was twenty-four years old and a nursery school teacher. Hug-Hellmuth was already on the scene, forty-seven years old, a published author, well known, and a respected member of the society. We do not really know Hug-Hellmuth's views or feelings about Anna Freud. However, we suspect that she was jealous of her younger, more favored colleague. Anna Freud, remarkably, said little about Hug-Hellmuth over the many years remaining in her own life.

Hug-Hellmuth's paper "On the Technique of Child-Analysis" was published in 1921. It represented a revised edition of the presentation she gave to the Sixth Congress of the International Psychoanalytic Association in The Hague the previous year. This seminal paper was also published in German as "Zur Technik der Kinderanalyse." We must emphasize that the presentation at The Hague congress in 1920 and the papers of 1921 were the very first works on the topic of the technique of child analysis. Furthermore, what Hug-Hellmuth said was not idiosyncratic; she presented the central concepts and techniques of Viennese child analysis. She became, at about the same time, director of the ambulatorium or clinic of the Vienna society, a position to which Anna Freud succeeded her after 1924.[5]

During the years 1922 to 1935 Anna Freud published only a small amount (the equivalent of less than 200 pages in English translation).[6,7] This thirteen-year publication record falls considerably short of Hug-Hellmuth's twelve-year record both in quantity and in originality. The situation changed only in 1936, when Anna Freud published *The Ego and the Mechanisms of Defense* and entered an entirely new phase of her lengthy and successful career in psychoanalysis.[8]

Melanie Klein also published her first works in the early twenties, after she came to Berlin from Budapest. Nearly all of her papers between 1921 and 1927 dealt with child psychology and development. In a 1927 paper she summarized the technical aspects of her work for presentation at a symposium on child analysis held by the British Psychoanalytic Society. Her paper included a response to Anna Freud's recently published book.[10] Klein's conclusions gave a good overview of her earlier thinking and clearly delineated the differences between herself and Anna Freud. Initially these were differences in the dynamic understanding of child development, and these led to differences in technical approach.

Anna Freud referred to Hug-Hellmuth only rarely in her writing over the many years of her psychoanalytic work, a total of four times,[11] and all her comments were very brief. In comparison, Melanie Klein was almost verbose. We can assume that Anna Freud knew of Hug-Hellmuth and was well acquainted with her work. This would follow from their both being part of the small psychoanalytic community in Vienna. They met at the Vienna Psychoanalytic Society meetings. In 1927 Anna Freud said about Hug-Hellmuth's work, "Hug-Hellmuth tried to replace the knowledge that is normally gathered by free association of the adult by playing with the child, seeing him in his own home, and trying to become familiar with all his intimate daily circumstances." Years later, in 1947, Anna Freud linked Hug-Hellmuth closely with Melanie Klein when she stated, "Connected with the names of Hug-Hellmuth in Vienna and Melanie Klein in Berlin is the development of the so-called play therapy, where the spontaneous actions of the child with small toys replace the free associations of the adults and are interpreted as symbolic expressions of the unconscious."[12] Anna Freud did not mention the other characteristics of Hug-Hellmuth's work.

Melanie Klein referred frequently to Hug-Hellmuth as the first practicing child analyst. She emphasized three aspects of her work: (1) Hug-Hellmuth considered only children over the age of six suitable candidates for analysis; (2) Hug-Hellmuth had a pessimistic view about the therapeutic efficacy of child analysis; and (3) Hug-Hellmuth viewed it as necessity for the therapist to have an educational influence on the child.

In 1927 Melanie Klein wrote about Hug-Hellmuth: "In her paper 'On the Technique of Child Analysis' . . . written after four years of work in this field, which gives us the clearest idea of her principles and her techniques, she made it very clear that she deprecated the idea of analyzing very young children, that she considered it necessary to content oneself with 'partial success' and not to penetrate too deeply in analysis with children, for fear of stirring up too powerfully the repressed tendencies and impulses or of making demands which their powers of assimilation are unable to meet. . . . From this paper, as well as from her other writings, we know that she shrank from penetrating at all deeply into the Oedipus complex. Another assumption to which she held in her work was that in the case of children not only analytic treatment but also a definite educative influence is required of the analyst."[13]

Did Klein really wish to criticize Hug-Hellmuth or was she attacking Anna Freud indirectly? We can see why she might want to criticize Anna Freud through the readily available conduit of Hug-Hellmuth. But from another perspective, the distinction is irrelevant, the main point being that Klein gave proper attribution to the concepts she was discussing.

Klein's description of Hug-Hellmuth's approach is important as it touches on all areas of the heated controversy between herself and Anna Freud. They would later become the two most prominent pioneers in child analysis. Klein treated very young children. Hug-Hellmuth and then Anna Freud insisted on the fulfillment of certain developmental requirements. These would be in psychosexual development, and mainly the establishing of a secure superego. Klein was also quite optimistic about the efficacy of analytic treatment. Hug-Hellmuth and then Anna Freud highlighted specific obstacles to the analysis of a child, obstacles represented by the child's level of development and dependency. Klein developed Hug-Hellmuth's use of play into a play therapy, which served as a therapeutic vehicle to replace free association. She could then make interpretations in detail of the symbolic expressions of the unconscious.

We see that Klein, and to a lesser degree Anna Freud, identified Hug-Hellmuth's approach at least partially with the specific technique of her opponent. This makes the actual content of Hug-Hellmuth's paper on the technique of child analysis even more interesting. In this paper, she described the goals of child analysis, the differences between child and adult analysis, and the technical problems of child analysis in detail. She emphasized that the goal of child analysis was not only the cure of symptoms. Analysis should try to achieve educational effects and to implement moral, aesthetic, and social values. Finally, she added that a goal of analysis was the formation of a strong personality. Therefore, with such broad and deep goals she did not speak of "child analysis" but of a "therapeutic-educational analysis" of the child. The analyst met the child as a real person, as a teacher, and as someone who provided the child with ample opportunity for new identification.

It is instructive to compare the acknowledgment that Hug-Hellmuth's work received from her two famous successors, Anna Freud and Melanie Klein. Anna Freud mentioned only a few differences between her technique and Hug-Hellmuth's. One was play therapy. Although, she never did describe how she differed from Hug-Hellmuth, she emphasized how she differed from Klein. Play therapy at that time was not part of Anna Freud's own therapeutic inventory. It had been described before at length by Klein. There is no indication in Hug-Hellmuth's work that she had developed a specific technique involving play, and the term *play therapy* does not appear anywhere in her writings. But indirectly, because of the emphasis in Hug-Hellmuth's writings on play as such, we can draw some limited conclusions. From her description of therapeutic situations we know that she used toys, and that she had the child play with them. Hug-Hellmuth did not put forward the crucial point in Klein's understanding of play therapy—that play is the direct expression of unconscious material. Anna Freud's 1927 linking of Hug-Hellmuth with Klein thus cannot be defended.

Comparing Hug-Hellmuth's descriptions of technical aspects of child analysis with Anna Freud's later publication in 1927, we find striking similarities: the emphasis on the therapist's role as an educator; direct involvement in the patient's life; the hesitation to analyze too deeply; the exclusion of children before latency; and the "warming-up phase" needed to establish a strong alliance with the patient. They are all features that Hug-Hellmuth had discussed in detail, now described by Anna Freud as "my methods," without reference to Hug-Hellmuth. It remains unclear why Anna Freud referred to Hug-Hellmuth so rarely, and always in very vague and general terms, and her few comments could lead to the conclusion that Hug-Hellmuth's approach was more similar to Klein's than to her own.

Klein, on the other hand, was more specific when she mentioned Hug-Hellmuth's contributions. She criticized the mingling of educational and therapeutic efforts, this being also one of her main objections against Anna Freud's technique. She also did not agree with the implementation of a particular "warming-up phase." She objected to the idea that child analysis had to exclude preschoolers because of their cognitive and psychosexual development during the pre-Oedipal stages.

The translation of Hug-Hellmuth's 1924 lectures makes it difficult to deny that she was the first child psychoanalyst. A comparison of Anna Freud's 1927 book, derived from a lecture series, with Hug-Hellmuth's more detailed and expert text, should make the latter's primacy clear. Hug-Hellmuth's text describes a technique that Anna Freud described later.

Were analysts of the time aware of Hug-Hellmuth's last published work, *New Ways to the Understanding of Youth?* Maybe not. We have to note her last will and testament, where she demanded that nothing should be written about her work. Further, by 1924 Anna Freud was firmly in place as heir to her father. Perhaps duty demanded and loyalty ensured Anna Freud's position immediately.

Hug-Hellmuth's work has remained largely unrecognized. We can suggest at least six causes for this: First, the tragic circumstances of her murder upset and embarrassed the Viennese psychoanalytic community. This may have led to a disregard of the value of Hug-Hellmuth's work as long as it was attached to her person. Its value could be readily accepted if it was attributed to someone else, such as Anna Freud. Secondly, Hug-Hellmuth condensed her contributions to the technical aspects of child analysis. They were presented only in the paper she gave at The Hague in 1920, the two papers of 1921, and the little-known book of 1924, her lectures. In these years child analysis had not yet become an established area of special interest within the psychoanalytic movement. Thirdly, her work remained largely untranslated into English until recently. Fourthly, Hug-Hellmuth was not given proper credit for her work by Anna Freud who took credit for this work for herself. Fifthly, Hug-Hellmuth was closely identified with education, and this has been used to deny her status as a psychoanalyst. The sixth and most important reason for the neglect was Hug-Hellmuth's problematic personality.

In trying to understand Hug-Hellmuth's contributions, a full knowledge of her publications is necessary. The almost complete absence of reference to the Hug-Hellmuth lectures of 1924, and the difficulty today of even finding a copy of the book, is important. Up to now no one has been in a position to make an informed judgment.

The defense of the myth of Anna Freud's primacy seems to occur along several lines. One is an emphasis on the scandal of the diary. In this scandal Hug-Hellmuth was accused of fraudulently producing a diary. Whatever the truth is about the diary, if one places too much emphasis on the assumed scandal, the scandal becomes all there is. Similarly, there is a concentration on the fact of Hug-Hellmuth's murder, with the emphasis on yet another scandal. When the scandals are emphasized, Hug-Hellmuth's importance is passed over and ignored. Hug-Hellmuth is referred to in a dismissive manner, for example, as an "educator orientated toward psychoanalysis." This is to ignore the evidence of her work as a child analyst, although every concept outlined by Hug-Hellmuth in 1920, 1921, and 1924 is later described as a basic element of the child psychoanalytic technique of Anna Freud.

Hug-Hellmuth's key role in what has been described as the "search for a psychoanalytic pedagogy" deserves some elaboration. This movement took place in Europe in the early years of the century, 1905 to 1938.[14] Many other important figures such as Berta Bornstein, Anna Freud, Alice Balint, Steff Berstein, Siegfried Bernfeld, Willie Hoffer, and August Aichhorn later became active in the movement.

There are two main points to be made about this early phase of Hug-Hellmuth's involvement with education and psychoanalysis. The first is that Hug-Hellmuth saw an educational role as being necessary in the analysis of a child. The educational approach was directed at both the individual child as a patient and the parents. This was to become part of the approach she described in her later work.

Second, she saw that psychoanalysis could make an important contribution to the field of education. It provided teachers with an understanding of the unconscious and of human emotions, and could make possible the education of some children who could not be educated before. Hug-Hellmuth in effect, considered child psychoanalysis as a form of special education.

Later, both of these points would be used against her or forgotten. It would be forgotten that she was the first to emphasize the role of a preliminary educational approach to child psychoanalysis. It would not be forgotten that she emphasized the importance of psychoanalysis to education, but this emphasis would be distorted to make it seem as if she saw child psychoanalysis merely as a form of education and not as a therapy in its own right.[15]

There were many connections between education and psychoanalysis in the early history of psychoanalysis, and Hug-Hellmuth was in the center of the two fields in the earliest years. It was in Vienna that the most significant effort at collaboration took place.

Psychoanalytic commentators have tended to focus on one side of Hug-Hellmuth's attempt at collaboration. They describe her as an advocate of a psychoanalytically influenced philosophy of education. In these descriptions, she is not portrayed as a true child psychoanalyst, but as a pedagogue intent on being the first to establish child psychoanalysis as an approach to education. They neglect her actual work as a psychoanalyst and disregard her attempt to establish psychoanalysis as a branch of special education. She is sometimes portrayed as one who merely used psychoanalytic methodology and a psychoanalytic observational stance in teaching and educational theory.

We can clearly see in her writing an attempt to create a field of education enlightened by psychoanalysis. But, she also saw psychoanalysis as a form of special education, a treatment that would make the education of some children possible. In recent times, it is much more common to find other types of psychological intervention into the classroom—psychometrics or a variety of techniques based on behavioral psychology. Psychoanalysis has entered the classroom only on rare occasions.

It is important to the history of the technique of child psychoanalysis to stress that Hug-Hellmuth advocated an educative approach to the actual psychoanalysis of children. She was the first to describe how a psychoanalytic technique was needed which prepared the child by teaching him or her about psychoanalysis. In her technique this was the first part or introduction to psychoanalysis.

Hug-Hellmuth has confounded biographers and historians by having two major interests. Willie Hoffer, a younger contemporary psychoanalyst, observed the following about her: "Her primary aim was to harmonize psychoanalytic aims with those of the family, school, and society. Hug-Hellmuth's first step was to practice child analysis in the child's home or in a children's ward. . . . She spent most of her time finding out secrets that the child had intentionally withheld from educators—and thus she opened the door to the child's fantasy life. As she did so, the child tended more and more to act out his conflicts, to the great bewilderment of his parents. This of course often endangered the continuation of the treatment. However, where it did continue, improvement often followed. . . . her attempts were mainly characterized by the treatment of children of latency and prepuberty and were aimed at a better adaptation of these children to the environment by alleviating superego demands and by encouraging sublimation of instinctual drives."[16]

Hug-Hellmuth abetted her neglect by others by neglecting herself. Because of her early traumas, she may not have been able to do otherwise. She was unable to relate to other people in an intimate manner, and she did not have friends, except perhaps for Sadger (who was an odd person himself). She was distant from her half-sister. The only other relationship that she had was with Rolf, and from what we can discover she was not close to him. We know only that she watched him and wrote about him. When forced by Antoine's death into a closer relationship with Rolf, there is no evidence that she entered into a loving relationship with him. On the contrary, her attitude toward him appears to have been distant, hostile, even mean. She kept away from all others. Lacking friends, she did not create any nucleus of a following of colleagues or students.

We think we need to be reminded of Hug-Hellmuth. Since her death, knowledge even of her existence has practically disappeared. There is a great deal of vagueness about her and her contributions to the origins of child psychoanalysis. We felt it was necessary to investigate her and her work, for to postpone such a project any longer would virtually ensure her complete anonymity. Most people who would have known her personally are dead. In the years since her death only two reviews of her and her work have sketched elements of her life. Wolfgang Huber published a paper about her in German in 1980, and Martin Drell published a similar paper in English in 1983. Angela Graf-Nold's recently published book about Hug-Hellmuth in German suffers from a lack of significant archival material, and more seriously, she depends too much on questionable theorizing when she uses only the autobiographical hints Hug-Hellmuth provides in her published scientific work.

Hug-Hellmuth made too many contributions to the field of psychoanalysis and child development to allow continued neglect. We hope that this book will be helpful in establishing her true importance for the psychoanalytic movement. Sigmund Freud respected her. In a letter to Karl Abraham, referring to his grandson Ernst, the son of Sophie Freud and Max Halberstadt, he said, "A strict upbringing by an intelligent mother enlightened by Dr. Hermine Hug-Hellmuth has done Ernst a great deal of good."[17] We hope that this book will revive interest in Hug-Hellmuth and that others will discover more about her and her contributions to the development of child psychoanalysis.

Chronology

1830	Birth of Knight Hugo Hug von Hugenstein, Hermine Hug-Hellmuth's father.
1848	Knight Hugo joins the Austrian Army.
1864	Knight Hugo fathers Antonia Farmer out of wedlock.
1866	Knight Hugo's application to legitimate Antonia denied. Injured in battle, he resigns from the military.
1867	Knight Hugo hired by the military as a civilian.
1869	Knight Hugo marries and the illegitimate Antonia comes with him.
1870	A baby born to Ludovika, Knight Hugo's wife, dies within two weeks.
1871	On August 31, Hermine Wilhelmine Ludovika, later to become Hermine Hug-Hellmuth, is born.
1873	Knight Hugo loses all his money on the stock market.
1874	Another baby, Emilie, born to Ludovika and Knight Hugo, on May 21; dies on June 27.
1875	Ludovika, Hermine's mother, develops a pulmonary disease.
1879	Antonia (Antoine) receives an educational grant, and Knight Hugo is reported as having two daughters.
1883	Ludovika dies on May 18.
1887	Hermine enters the University of Vienna as a special student, the first year women are allowed to do so.
1898	Knight Hugo dies on January 31.
1900	Hermine leaves the University of Vienna.
1904	Hermine is graduated from a Gymnasium in Prague. Antonia obtains her Ph.D. from the University of Vienna. Hermine enters the University of Vienna as a regular student.

1906   Rudolph Otto Hug born to Antonia in Graz on May 17.

1907   Hermine meets Dr. Isidor Sadger.

1909   Hermine Hug von Hugenstein obtains her Ph.D.

1910   Hug-Hellmuth works as a teacher.

1911   Freud mentions Hug-Hellmuth in a letter to Jung.

1912   Hug-Hellmuth begins to publish in psychoanalytic publications.

1913   Antoine (Antonia) becomes ill and stops work.

1915   Antoine dies. Rolf is nine years of age.

1918   Victor Tausk becomes Rolf's guardian.

1919   Tausk commits suicide and Sadger becomes Rolf's guardian. *The Diary* is published.

1920   Hug-Hellmuth presents the world's first paper on the technique of child analysis at the International Congress at The Hague.

1921   Hug-Hellmuth lectures in Berlin.

1922   Rolf attempts suicide.

1924   Hug-Hellmuth publishes her last monograph, a book of lectures titled *New Ways to the Understanding of Youth*. Hug-Hellmuth is murdered on September 9 by Rolf Hug.

1925   Rolf is found guilty of the murder and sentenced to twelve years in prison.

Notes

References, sources, and quotations in the body of the text are identified by number. If the text referred to was short, no page numbers have been given. For certain references the following abbreviations have been used:

FREUD–JUNG: Sigmund Freud, C. G. Jung. Briefwechsel. Ed. William McGuire and Wolfgang Sauerländer (1974). English version: The Freud/Jung Letters: The Correspondence between Sigmund Freud and C. G. Jung. Ed. William McGuire. Trans. Ralph Manheim and R. F. C. Hall (1974).

KA: Kriegsarchiv, Vienna.

Lehmann: Directory of Residences in Vienna. Allgemeiner Wohnungsanzeiger nebst Handels- und Gewerbe Adressbuch fuer die k.k. Reichshaupt- und Residenzstadt Wien und Umgebung. Adolf Lehmann (1859).

LG: Protocol of the trial of Rolf Hug, Landgericht Wien, LGi 1924, Zl, 6013/24.

Pesendorfer: Testimony by Mrs. Pesendorfer for the trial of Rolf Hug. December 12, 1924, LG.

PR: Psychiatric Report on Rolf Hug, Drs. Grosz and Stelzer. VR XXXII. 6013/24.

Sadger: Testimony of Isidor Sadger in police investigation. September 10, 1924.

SE: *The Standard Edition of the Complete Psychological Works of Sigmund Freud.* Vols. 1–24. Edited and translated by James Strachey et al. London: Hogarth Press and Institute of Psychoanalysis, 1953–74.

UA: University of Vienna Archives.

Preface

1. The two papers were MacLean (1986a), " 'Analysis of a Dream of a Five-and-One-Half-Year-Old Boy' by Hermine Hug-Hellmuth: An introduction and Translation," and MacLean (1986b), "A Brief Story about Hermine Hug-Hellmuth."

2. This resulted in a preliminary study presented by the authors as "Hug-Hellmuth: The First Child Psychoanalyst" at the 1986 Ottawa Congress of the Canadian Psychoanalytic Society.

Prologue

1. Numerous authors have mentioned Hug-Hellmuth briefly. Anthony (1986a), p. 9, stated that she was "the first to undertake the systematic analysis of children." He qualified this by stating that she proposed a very limited treatment and "very soon . . . faded into the background." Brody (1974), in *Contributions to Child Analysis*, p. 13, stated, "Play as a therapeutic medium for analysis was introduced in 1920 by Hermine Hug-Hellmuth, and perhaps because play has traditionally promoted education, Hug-Hellmuth regarded child analysis to be an educational treatment which needed to be carried out in the home." Dyer (1983), p. 16, pp. 37–40, briefly mentioned Hug-Hellmuth in a short essay that described her failure to develop a technique—not her successes. He described her as someone interested in education and play and who was a mere interlude between "Little Hans" and the real work of Anna Freud and Melanie Klein. Peters (1979) pp. 57–60 offered more detail, but in his summary he stated, "Now we remember her only as an educator enthusiastically orientated towards psychoanalysis, who was deeply interested in children." Ellenberger (1970) mentioned only the later scandal of the diary. However, most inaccurate and unfair was Young-Bruehl (1988). On p. 64 she dealt with Hug-Hellmuth in two sentences. The first stated, "Hug-Hellmuth was a teacher and an associate of the Vienna Society [she was a retired teacher and a full member of the society], whose first publication on 'play therapy' came out in 1913" (this is an error as well).

   What is common in all these references is that they have either relegated Hug-Hellmuth to the status of an educator only, or seen her as someone interested in play therapy. It appears that writers having a Kleinian orientation have called Hug-Hellmuth an educator, while those dedicated to Anna Freud have called her a play therapist. All avoid calling her a psychoanalyst, a status they withhold for their favorite, either Klein or Anna Freud.

2. A long list of people were contacted; few responded. Those who did answer were, with a few exceptions, unhelpful. The two most interesting responses were from Anny Katan and Anna Freud. Anny Katan described Hug-Hellmuth as analyzing children and being jealous of Anna Freud's appearance on the psychoanalytic scene. Anna Freud suggested that nothing should be written about Hug-Hellmuth, even though she acknowledged that Hug-Hellmuth was already a very respected member of the Vienna society when Anna Freud entered. Further, Anna Freud stated that her contacts with Hug-Hellmuth were slight and rather distant. She wrote no more than this.

3. A few pages of unsigned handwritten Gothic German notes were included in the process notes of the trial of Rudolf Hug, Hug-Hellmuth's nephew. They appear to be notes taken from letters written by Hug-Hellmuth to Isidor Sadger. No other biographical material of such closeness to Hug-Hellmuth could be found; no diaries or letters.

4. Hug-Hellmuth's will is discussed in the text. In response to a wish that she expressed in this will that nothing should be written about her or her work, Anna Freud stated in one brief letter to us in 1980 that Hug-Hellmuth's wishes should be respected, even after such a considerable time. Obviously, the authors of this book did not agree.

Chapter 1.

1. KA-Anall.K.1174.

2. KA-KM/1861, 16A10-66/1.

3. KA-KM/1892, 19-9/3.

4. Robert Kann's *History of the Hapsburg Empire, 1526–1981* confirmed the details of Knight Hugo's military records. Kann 1974, pp. 162, 273.

5. KA-KM/1866, 2/218/3.
6. Lehmann 1904.
7. KA-Quall.K.1174.
8. KA-KM 1879.
9. KA-KM/1883, C21-162.
10. KA-Quall. K.1174.
11. UA.
12. KA-Quall. K.1174.
13. UA.
14. Lehmann 1904.
15. Sadger.
16. PA.
17. Sadger.
18. Jones (1959) in *Free Associations*, p. 169.
19. Roazen (1984) in *Freud and his Followers*, pp. 171, 351.
20. This appeared in one newspaper, Die Stunde, on September 10, 1924.
21. Roazen (1984), p. 536.
22. Freud-Jung, 289F, J292, 293F.
23. The first presentation on the technique of child psychoanalysis was given by Hug-Hellmuth at The Hague Congress in 1920.
24. This is most clear in Hug-Hellmuth's last paper, *New Paths to the Understanding of Youth*, 1924, which is referred to in the text of this book.
25. LG.
26. Hug-Hellmuth (1912a), "The Analysis of a Dream of a five and one-half year old Boy."
27. Young-Bruehl (1988), pp. 103–09, 114–15, 122–25, and Grosskurth (1986), pp. 95–99.

Chapter 2.

1. Nunberg and Federn (1974), p. 280.
2. *SE*, vol. 4, pp. 136–39; vol. 15, pp. 131, 142–44.
3. MacLean (1986a).
4. *SE*, vol. 4, pp. 136–39; vol. 15, pp. 142–44; Deutsch 1944, vol. II, pp. 468–89.
5. Bettelheim (1973), *The Use of Enchantment*.
6. From the text of the monograph; the entire concept of "lines of development" is interesting reading in light of the later history of this concept in relationship to Anna Freud, pp. 62–92, "The Concept of Developmental Lines," from *The Assessment of Normality in Childhood: Normality and Pathology in Childhood Assessments of Development* (1965), *The Writings of Anna Freud*, volume 6. As usual, there is no reference to Hug-Hellmuth.
7. From the text of a letter from Anny Katan, July 9, 1985.
8. See Carotenuto (1984). An excellent review of this book was written by Bruno Bettelheim in the *New York Review of Books*, June 30, 1983, pp. 39–44.

Chapter 3.

1. Nunberg and Federn (1967), p. 477, and Nunberg and Federn (1974), p. 280.

2. Nunberg and Federn (1974), p. 302; Nunberg and Federn (1975), pp. 307–10; and Carotenuto (1984), pp. xx and 159.

3. Nunberg and Federn (1967), p. xv.

4. See Carotenuto (1984), pp. 207–12, and 214 for a discussion of Spielrein's influence on Jung's work.

5. Nunberg and Federn (1975), pp. 208–10.

6. LG.

7. LG, PR.

8. Pesendorfer.

9. Sadger.

10. PR and Pesendorfer.

11. Hug-Hellmuth (1920a), A. Freud (1927). We compare these two works in the text.

12. Pesendorfer.

13. Sadger.

14. Nunberg and Federn (1975). This volume covers the important years 1912–1918.

15. Nunberg and Federn (1975), pp. 309–10.

16. PG.

17. LG.

18. The details about Tausk and his unfortunate life are made particularly interesting by reading the conflicting views of Eissler (1983) and Roazen (1969).

19. Sadger.

20. PR.

21. Sadger.

22. This monograph is the most widely available of Hug-Hellmuth's books. This is testimony either to the book's intrinsic interest or to the debate it caused, or more probably to both factors.

23. Bühler (1922), in its entirety, is a good example of this interest. Bühler played an important part in the controversy surrounding the diary, as well.

24. Burt (1921), pp. 353–57, a review of *A Young Girls' Diary* in volume 1 of the *British Journal of Psychology* (Medical Section) 1920–1921.

25. Burt (1921), p. 257, volume 2, of the *British Medical Journal of Psychology*.

26. This introduction was translated by U.R. but not included in this selection.

27. Bühler (1922). The text of this book had importance at that time.

28. Krug (1926), pp. 370–81 in the German text of this reference.

29. Fuchs (1928), pp. 117–20.

30. Huber (1980), p. 130. Hug-Hellmuth held a course on child psychoanalysis in the institute's psychoanalytic out-patient clinic.

31. This was first revealed in Quinn (1987), p. 199. However, in subsequent conversations with Susan Quinn and with Karen Horney's daughter, Marianne Horney Echardt, we could obtain no further details.

32. Anny Katan, letter to G.M., July 9, 1985.

33. Roazen (1985), p. 177.

34. Young-Bruehl (1988), p. 143.

35. We have included the English version in this book as it appeared in the *International Journal of Psychoanalysis* in 1921, "On the Technique of Child-Analysis." The German version, "Zur Technik der Kinderanalyse," was published the same year.

36. Anna Freud, (1927), pp. 3–49.

37. Katan, letter to G.M., July 9, 1985.

38. Hug-Hellmuth (1913c). In the monograph "The Mental Life of the Child," Hug-Hellmuth was clear about the importance of play in child development. Perhaps this is why Young-Bruehl (1988, p. 64) referred to Hug-Hellmuth as developing a form of play therapy—that is, not child analysis.

39. Huber (1980), p. 131. In an unusual and admirable paper, Huber collected many facts about Hug-Hellmuth. The paper has never been published in English; we translated it for our work on this book.

40. Huber (1980), p. 131, and Lobner (1978), p. 16.

41. LG.

42. PR.

43. Horney (1925). Horney was clear in her view of Hug-Hellmuth, as in the same text she stated, "Frau Dr. Hug-Hellmuth was the first to explore in practice the field of child psychoanalysis" (p. 228).

44. The book is hard to find. We eventually obtained a photocopy from the library of the University of Leipzig.

45. Anna Freud, (1930), pp. 73–131. Volume I, of *The Writings of Anna Freud*.

Chapter 4.

1. PR.

2. We wanted to present as much detail as was available about Hug-Hellmuth's murder, not in an attempt at sensationalism, but because the detail afforded us some information about her and her life. In addition to the references already identified, or that will be identified individually, we have summarized the various newspaper reports of her murder. Specifically, the newspapers we used were: (1) *Illustriertes Wiener Extrablatt*, Sept. 10, 11, 1924 (IW); (2) *Reichspost*, Sept. 10, 11, 1924 (RP); (3) *Neuigkeits-Welt-Blatt*, Sept. 10, 11, 13, 1924 (NW): (4) *Neue Freie Presse*, Sept. 9, 10, 11, 13, 1924 (NF); (5) *Wiener Zeitung*, Sept. 10, 1924 (WZ); (6) *Der Abend (Wiener Stimmen)*, Sept. 9, 10, 11, 1924 (DA); (7) *Arbeiter-Zeitung*, Sept. 10, 11, 1924 (AZ); (8) *Der Tag*, Sept. 10, 11, 13, 1924 (DT); (9) *Die Stunde*, Sept. 10, 11, 1924 (DS); (10) *Neues Wiener Tagblatt*, Sept. 10, 12, 13, 1924 (WT); (11) *Deutsch-Österreichische Tageszeitung*, Sept. 10, 11, 1924 (DO); and (12) *Neues Wiener Abendblatt*, Sept. 10, 1924 (WA). Unless a specific citation appears important, newspaper accounts will be covered by the general reference NP.

3. NP.

4. NP.

5. Sadger.

6. NP.

7. Testimony during the police investigation, Hermine Wojta. LG.

8. Sadger.

9. LG.

10. Bernfeld (1925), p. 106.

11. Hans Aufreiter, October 7, 1981, in a letter to G.M.

12. Freidjung (1924), pp. 337–338.

13. Deutsch (1973), p. 136. Roazen (1985), p. 442, referred to Hug-Hellmuth as "unelegant."

14. Deutsch (1973), p. 137.

Selected Works on Child Analysis: Introduction

1. Beitelheim (1982).

2. Gay (1988).

Epilogue

1. *SE,* vol. 10.

2. Young-Bruehl (1988), pp. 130, 132, 140, 1655. Dyer (1983), p. 54. Peters (1985), p. 49.

3. Grosskurth (1986), pp. 69–72.

4. Freud, Anna (1927), "Einführung in die Technik der Kinderanalyse," or (1928) "Introduction to the Technique of Child Analysis; Klein (1927), contribution to "Symposium on Child Analysis," *International Journal of Psychoanalysis* 8/1.

5. Nunberg and Federn (1975), that is, volume 4 of the minutes of the Vienna Psychoanalytic Society that cover the important years of 1912–1918, Peters (1979), p. 59. In this well-written book, "Anna Freud: A Life Dedicated to Children," and Lobner (1980), see p. 16.

6. *SE,* vol. 15, pp. 136–38.

7. Freud, Anna (1927); see p. xvii from the "Publishing History of 'Four Lectures in Child Analysis.' " Vol. 1 of *The Writings of Anna Freud,* 1922–1927. International Universities Press, 1974.

8. Freud, Anna (1936), "The Ego and the Mechanisms of Defense." Vol. 2 of *The Writings of Anna Freud.* IUP, 1966.

9. Klein (1927), contribution to Symposium on Child Analysis, *International Journal of Psychoanalysis* 8/1.

10. Freud, Anna (1927), "Einführung in die Technik der Kinderanalyse."

11. These are: (1) Freud, Anna (1927), p. 35 of "Lecture Two: The Methods of Child Analysis;" (1945), p. 7 in "Indications for Child Analysis," *The Writings of Anna Freud,* volume 4. In a pithy, diversionary reference, Anna Freud stated, "Certain child analysts (Hug-Hellmuth in Vienna, Melanie Klein in Berlin and later in London) developed the so-called play technique of child analysis . . ." (2) Freud, Anna (1966), p. 49 in "A Short History of Child Analysis." Here Anna Freud made two succinct, singular references to

Hug-Hellmuth: (a) "child analysis occupied no more than a section [of the widening scope of psychoanalysis] represented almost simultaneously by Hug-Hellmuth and after her by me in Vienna." This is a highly inaccurate statement. It compresses the time of Hug-Hellmuth's career as an analyst to that to fit with Anna Freud's then much briefer existence on the scene. (b) "Hug-Hellmuth and Ada Mueller-Braunschweig were in a teacher-pupil relationship . . ." No proof of this relationship could be found. Yet, the stress of this quotation seems to be a denial that Anna Freud was a pupil of Hug-Hellmuth's. In the same paragraph Anna Freud stated, "Ideas [about child analysis] as well as techniques developed individually and independently." This is demonstrated to be untrue. (3) Freud, Anna (1970), see p. 209 of "Child Analysis as a Subspeciality in Psychoanalysis," from "Problems of Psychoanalytic Training, Diagnosis and the Technique of Therapy, 1966–1970." In this paper, Anna Freud stated in reference to Hug-Hellmuth, "Hug-Hellmuth, Melanie Klein, myself and the Borsteins for children . . ." [that is, developed child analysis.] Certainly the order of the names is correct. However, the variable of time has undergone such a compression that you would think that they all did it almost exactly at the same time. Which is a neat way to describe the history in an inaccurate manner.

12. Freud, Anna (1927), p. 35 of the 1966 revision of her writings.

13. Klein (1927), contribution to Symposium on Child Analysis, *International Journal of Psychoanalysis* 8/1.

14. Cohen (1979), pp. 190, 192–94, 213.

15. The two main authors who write in this fashion are both biographers of Anna Freud: Dyer (1983) pp. 16, 37–39, and Peters (1979), pp. 57–60. At least they showed some evidence of considering Hug-Hellmuth. The most inaccurate, brief, and demeaning account of Hug-Hellmuth was written by another biographer of Anna Freud's, Young-Bruehl (1988).

16. Hoffer (1945), pp. 296–97, volume 1 of *The Psychoanalytic Study of the Child*.

17. Abraham and Freud (1965), p. 197.

Works of Hermine Hug-Hellmuth

1912a. Analyse eines Traumes eines Fünfeinhalbjährigen (The analysis of a dream of a 5-½-year-old boy). *Zentralblatt für Psychoanalyse und Psychotherapie* 2/3:122–27. Trans. George MacLean, in *Psychiat. J. Univ. Ottawa.* 11/1 (1986): pp. 1–5.

1912b. Beiträge zum Kapital "Verschreiben" und "Verlesen" (Contributions to the subject "Lapses in writing and reading"). *Zentralblatt für Psychoanalyse und Psychotherapie* 2/5:227–80.

1912c. "Versprechen" eines kleinen Schuljungen (A "lapse of speech" in a small schoolboy). *Zentralblatt für Psychoanalyse und Psychotherapie* 2/10–11:603–04.

1912d. Das Kind und seine Vorstellung vom Tode (The child's concept of death). *Imago* 1/3:286–98. Trans. Anton Kris in *Psychoanalytic Quarterly* 34 (1965): 499–516.

1912e. Über Farbenhören: Ein Versuch das Phänomen auf Grund der psycho-analytischen Methode zu erklären. (On color hearing: An attempt to clarify the phenomenon on the basis of the psychoanalytical method). *Imago* 1/3:228–64.

1913a. Über erste Kindheitserinnerungen (On first memories of childhood). *Imago* 2/1:78–88.

1913b. Vom Wesen der Kinderseele. (The true nature of the child's soul). *Sexualprobleme* 9:433–43.

1913c. Aus dem Seelenleben des Kindes. Eine psychoanalytische Studie (The mental life of the child: A psychoanalytic study). Ed. S. Freud. Leipzig and Vienna: F. Deuticke Trans. James Putnam and Mabel Stevens as A Study of the Mental Life of the Child. Washington, D.C.: Nervous and Mental Disease Publishing Co., 1919. Reprint. New York: Johnson Reprint Corporation, 1970. Also published, trans. James Putnam and Mabel Stevens in *Psychoanalytic Quarterly*, 5/1 (1918):53–92; 5/2:193–227; 5/3:291–322; 5/4:398–427; (1919) 6/1:65–68.

1913d. Kinderträume (Children's dreams). *Internationale Zeitschrift für ärtzliche Psychoanalyse* 1:470–75.

1913e. Zur weiblichen Masturbation (On female masturbation). *Zentralblatt für Psychoanalyse und Psychotherapie* 3/1:17–25.

1913f. Claire Henrika Weber: "Liddy." *Imago* 2:521–23.

1913g. Mutterliebe (Mother love). *Imago* 2: 523–24.

1913h. Ein weilbliches Gegenstück (zu Rank: Ein Beitrag zur infantilen Sexualität). (A female counterpart to Rank's "a contribution to infantile sexuality"). *Zentralblatt für Psychoanalyse und Psychotherapie* 3:371–72.

1913i. Kindervergehen und-Unarten (Child misdemeanors and naughtiness) *Zentralblatt für Psychoanalyse und Psychotherapie* 3:372–75.

1914a. Kinderbriefe (Children's letters). *Imago* 3/5:462–76.

1914b. Kinderpsychologie, Pädagogik (On Child psychology and pedagogy). *Jahrbuch für psychoanalytische und psychopathologische Forschungen* 6:393–404.

1915a. Ein Traum der sich selbst deutet (A dream in which one appears as oneself). *Internationale Zeitschrift für Ärztliche Psychoanalyse* 3:33–35.

1915b. Die Kriegneurose des Kindes (War neurosis in children). *Pester Loyd* 62/65: (March 6, 1915).

1915c. Die Kriegneurose der Frau (War neurosis in women). *Geschlecht und Gesellschaft* 9:505–14.

1915d. Einige Beziehungen zwischen Erotik und Mathematik (Some relations between eroticism and mathematics). *Imago* 4/2:52–68.

1915e. Ein Fall von weiblichem Fuss, Richtiger Stiefel-fetischismus (A case of female foot fetishism, or rather, shoe fetishism). *Zentralblatt für Psychoanalyse und Pyschotherapie* 5:462–76.

1917a. Von frühem Lieben und Hassen (On early loving and hating). *Imago* 5/2:121–22.

1917b. Mutter-Sohn, Vater-Tochter (Mother-son, father-daughter). *Imago* 5/2:129–31.

1919. Tagebuch eines halbwüchsigen Mädchens. Leipzig and Vienna: *Internationaler psychoanalytischer Verlag*, 1919. Trans. Eden and Ceder Paul as "A Young Girl's Diary." London: George Allen & Unwin, 1921. 2d ed. New York: Thomas Seltzer 1921.

1920a. On the technique of the analysis of children (a report). International Psychoanalytic Congress, Sept. 8–11, 1920. *Int. J. Psychoanal.* 1:361–62.

1920b. Child psychology and education. Trans. Barbara Low. *Int. J. Psychoanal.* 1:316–23.

1921b. Kinderpsychologie und Pädagogik (Child psychology and pedagogy) *Bericht über die Fortschritte der Psychoanalyse in den Jahren 1914–1919*. *(Beihefte der Internationalen Zeitschrift für Psychoanalyse* 3:224–57). Ed. S. Freud. Leipzig, Vienna, and Zürizh: Internationaler Psychoanalytischer Verlag.

1921a. On the technique of child analysis. *Int. J. Psychoanal.* 2:287–305.

1921b. Zur Technik der Kinderanalyse (On the technique of child analysis) *Zentralblatt für Psychoanalyse und Psychotherapie* 7:179–97.

1921c. Vom "mittleren" Kinde (The middle child). *Imago* 7/1:179–97.

1921d. Psychoanalytische Erkenntnisse über die Frau (Psychoanalytic findings about women). *Archiv für Frauenkunde und Eugenik* 7/2:130–38.

1921e. Correspondence between reviewer of this book [*A Young Girl's Diary*] and H. Hug-Hellmuth. *British Medical Journal of Psychology* 2:257–58.

1923. Die Bedeutung der Familie für das Schicksal des Einzelnen (The importance of the family for the fate of the individual). *Zeitschrift für Sexualwissenschaft* 9:321–34.

1924a. Die libidinose Struktur des Familienlebens (The libidinal structure of family life). *Zeitschrift für Sexualwissenschaft* 11:169–77.

1924b. Neue Wege zum Verständnis der Jugend. Psychoanalytische Vorlesungen für Eltern, Lehrer, Erzieher, Schulärzte, Kindergärtnerinnen und Fürsorgerinnen (New ways to the understanding of youth: Psychoanalytic lectures for parents, teachers, educators, school doctors, kindergarten teachers, and social workers). Leipzig and Vienna: Franz Deuticke.

Bibliography

Abraham, H. C., and Freud, E. L. eds. (1965) A psychoanalytic dialogue: The letters of Sigmund Freud and Karl Abraham, 1907–1926. London: The Hogarth Press.

Anthony, E. James. (1986) A brief history of child psychoanalysis. *J. Amer. Acad. Child Psychiat.* 25/1:8–11.

Bernfeld, S. (1931) Kinderheim Baumgarten: Bericht über einen ernsthaften Versuch mit neuer Erziehung. Berlin.

———. (1925) Notice: Dr. Hermine Hug-Hellmuth. *Int. J. Psychoanal.* 6:106.

Bettelheim, B. (1973) The use of enchantment. New York: Basic Books.

———. (1982) Freud and man's soul. New York: Knopf.

———. (1983) Scandal in the family. *New York Review of Books*, July 30, 1983, pp. 39–44.

Brody, S. (1974) Contributions to child psychoanalysis. In R. Eissler et al., eds., *The Psychoanalytic Study of the Child*. Vol. 29. New York: International Universities Press.

Bühler, C. (1922) Das Seelenleben des Jugenlichen. Versuch einer Analyse und Theorie der psychischen Pubertät. Jena.

Burt, C. (1921) Review of *A Young Girl's Diary*. Prefaced with a letter by Sigmund Freud. Translated from the German by Eden and Ceder Paul. London: George Allen and Unwin. *British Journal of Psychology*, Medical Section, 1:353–57.

Carotenuto, Aldo. (1984) A secret symmetry: Sabrina Spielrein between Jung and Freud: The untold story of the woman who changed the early history of psychoanalysis. New York: Pantheon.

Cohen, S. (1979) In the name of the prevention of neurosis: The search for psychoanalytic pedagogy in Europe, 1905–1938. In B. Finkelstein, ed., Regulated Children/Liberated Children. Educational perspectives.

Deutsch, H. (1944) Psychology of women. Vol. 1. New York: Grune and Stratton.

———. (1945) Psychology of women: A psychoanalytic interpretation. Vol. 2. New York: Grune and Stratton.

———. (1973) Confrontations with myself: An epilogue. New York: Norton.

Drell, M. (1982) Hermine Hug-Hellmuth: A pioneer in child analysis. *Bulletin of the Menninger Clinic* 46/2:139–50.

Dyer, R. (1983) Her father's daughter: The work of Anna Freud. New York: Jason Aronson.

Eissler, K. R. (1983) Victor Tausk's suicide. New York: International Universities Press.

Ellenberger, H. (1970) The discovery of the unconscious: The history and development of dynamic psychiatry. New York: Basic Books.

Fine, R. (1970) A history of psychoanalysis. New York: Columbia University Press.

Friedjung, J. (1924) The psychoanalytic movement: Dr. Hug-Hellmuth. Translated by J. Aufreiter and H. Warnes. *Zentralblatt für Psychoanalyse und Psychotherapie* 10:337–38.

Freud, A. (1927) The methods of child analysis. In vol. 1 of The writings of Anna Freud, *Introduction to Psychoanalysis*. 1922–35. New York: International Universities Press.

———. (1966) A short history of child psychoanalysis. R. Eissler et al., eds., *The Psychoanalytic Study of the child*. New York: International Universities Press.

———. (1981) Psychoanalytic psychology of normal development, 1970–1980. Vol. 2 of The writings of Anna Freud. New York: International Universities Press.

Freud, S. (1900) The interpretation of dreams. *SE*, vol. 4.

———. (1909) Analysis of a phobia in a five-year-old boy. *SE*, vol. 10.

———. (1919) Introductory lectures on psychoanalysis. *SE*, vol. 15.

———. (1911) The handling of dream interpretation in psycho-analysis. *SE*, vol. 12.

———. (1912a). The dynamics of transference. *SE*, vol. 12.

———. (1912b). Recommendations to physicians practicing psycho-analysis. *SE*, vol. 12.

———. (1913) On beginning the treatment. *SE*, vol. 12.

———. (1914) Remembering, repeating and working through. *SE*, vol. 12.

———. (1915) Observations on transference-love. *SE*, vol. 12

———. (1916–17) Letter to Dr. Hermine von Hug-Hellmuth. *SE*, vol. 14.

———. (1919) A child is being beaten. *SE*, vol. 17.

Fuchs, H. (1928) Die Sprache des Jugendlichen im Tagebuch. *Zeitschrift für angewandte Psychologie* 29:74–121.

Gay, Peter. (1988) Freud: A life for our time. New York: Norton.

Grosskurth, P. (1986) Melanie Klein: Her world and her work. New York: Knopf.

Hoffer, W. (1945) Psychoanalytic education. *The Psychoanalytic Study of the Child*. Vol. 1. New York: International Universities Press.

Horney, K. (1925) Book review: Neue Wege zum Verständnis der Jugend. By Dr. Hermine Hug-Hellmuth. *Int. J. Psychoanal.* 4:228–29.

Huber, W. (1980) Die erste Kinderanalytkerin. In H. Castager et al., eds., Psychoanalyse als Herausforderung: Festschrift Caruso. Vienna: Verlag Verb.d. Wissenschftl. Ges. Österreichs.

Jones, E. (1955) The life and works of Sigmund Freud. Vol. 2. New York: Basic Books.

———. (1957) The life and work of Sigmund Freud. Vol. 3. New York: Basic Books.

———. (1959) Free associations: Memories of a psycho-analyst. New York: Basic Books.

Kann, R. A. (1973) A history of the Hapsburg Empire: 1526–1918. Berkeley: University of California Press.

Klein, M. (1975a) The psychoanalytic play technique: Its history and significance (1955). Envy and gratitude and other works, 1946–1963. New York: Delacorte.

———. (1975b) Symposium on child-analysis (1927). Love guilt and reparation and other works, 1921–1945. New York: Delacorte.

Krug, J. (1926) Kritische Bemerkungen zum Tagebuch eines halbwüchsigen Mädchens. *Zeitschrift für angewandte Psychologie* 27:370–81.

Lobner, H. (1978) Discussions on therapeutic technique in the Vienna Psychoanalytic Society. *Sigmund Freud House Bulletin* 2:15–33.

MacLean, G. (1986a) Analysis of a dream of a five-and-one-half-year-old boy by Hermine Hug-Hellmuth Ph.D. *Psychiat. J. Univ. Ottawa* 11/1:1–5.

———. (1986b) A brief story about Dr. Hermine Hug-Hellmuth. *Can. J. Psychiatry* 31:586–89.

———. (1986c) Hermine Hug-Hellmuth: A neglected pioneer in child psychoanalysis. *J. Amer. Acad. Child Psychiat.* 25/4:579–80.

McGuire, W., ed. (1974). The Freud-Jung letters: The correspondence between Sigmund Freud and C. G. Jung: Princeton: Princeton University Press.

Nunberg, H., and Federn, E. (1967) Minutes of the Vienna Psychoanalytic Society, 1908–1910. Vol. 1. New York: International Universities Press.

———. (1974) Minutes of the Vienna Psychoanalytic Society, 1910–1911. Vol. 2. New York: International Universities Press.

———. (1975) Minutes of the Vienna Psychoanalytic Society, 1912–1918. Vol. 3. New York: International Universities Press.

Peters, U. (1979) Anna Freud: Ein Leben für des Kind. Munich: Kindler. In English as Anna Freud: A Life Dedicated to Children. London: Weidenfeld and Nicolson, 1985.

Pick, E., and Segal, H. (1978) Melanie Klein's contribution to child analysis: Theory and technique. In J. Glenn, ed., Child Analysis and Therapy. New York: Aribsen.

Quinn, Susan. (1987) A mind of her own: The life of Karen Horney. New York: Summit Books.

Rappen, Ulrich. (1987) Frühe Beiträge zur Technik des Kinderanalyse. Vienna, *Studien zur Kinderpsychoanalyse* 7:9–16.

Roazen, Paul. (1969) Brother animal: The story of Freud and Tausk. New York: Knopf.

———. (1984) Freud and his followers. New York University Press.

———. (1985) Helene Deutsch: A psychoanalyst's life. Garden City, N.Y.: Anchor Press/Doubleday.

Smirnoff, V. (1971) The scope of child analysis. New York: International Universities Press.

Young-Bruehl, E. (1988) Anna Freud: A biography. New York: Summit Books.

Index